THE
GREAT TOWNS
OF
NORTHERN
CALIFORNIA

The Guide to the Best Getaways
for a Vacation or a Lifetime

DAVID VOKAC

Library of Congress Cataloging-in-Publication Data

Vokac, David, 1940-
    The great towns of northern California: the guide to the
best getaways for a vacation or a lifetime/David Vokac.–1st ed.
    p.cm.
Includes index.
    ISBN 0-930743-08-3
    1. California, Northern–Guidebooks. 2. Cities and
towns–California, Northern–Guidebooks. 3. California,
Northern–History, Local. I. Title

F867.5.V65   2003
917.94'10454–dc21   2003050185

Copyright © 2003 by David Vokac
All rights reserved. No part of this book may be reproduced in
any form without permission in writing from the publisher.
Inquiries should be addressed to:
West Press
P.O. Box 99717
San Diego, CA 92169
www.greattowns.com

First Edition
1 2 3 4 5 6 7 8 9 10
Manufactured in the United States of America

Preface

Is it possible to leave the city without leaving its amenities behind? To be as close as a stroll to natural grandeur, while enjoying the comforts of civilization like cultural experiences, gourmet cuisine, and romantic lodgings? In the great towns featured in this guidebook, the answer is emphatically *yes*!

Here are Northern California's getaway towns most favored by nature and civilization. All are proud of their unique locales and heritage–and generous in sharing their bounty. Collectively, they celebrate the diversity and delights of a renowned region.

This guidebook expands on material originally presented in the premier sourcebook *The Great Towns of America*. For the eleven Northern California towns that were featured among the nation's top 100, information has been expanded and updated. Seven additional communities that were prime contenders are now also featured. While sharing proximity to exciting regional attractions and amenities, each of these eighteen special places beckons as a scenic, civilized destination beyond the hustle and bustle of Northern California's cities.

Whether you're seeking a distinctive vacation or a new lifestyle, *The Great Towns of Northern California* is intended to serve as the ultimate guide to the foremost recreation and leisure getaways in this remarkable region. All of the best restaurants, attractions and lodgings are systematically described and rated for each locality. Weather, crime, and other key livability features are quantified and ranked. As a new highlight, in addition to ranking towns by Quality of Life and by Housing Cost, the Vokac Index of Livability and Affordability© presents a unique ratio revealing the relationship between Quality of Life and Housing Cost...with surprising results!

In one year of full-time, independent effort, I personally visited each feature in every great town. No payments were accepted. Thus, every listing is described and rated on merit alone. As a result, I believe that this guide is honest and accurate, with consistent, detailed information about the foremost getaways throughout Northern California.

For everyone who wonders what special places and pleasures await beyond Northern California's cities, *The Great Towns of Northern California* has answers. All the information you need to create a memorable visit...or to explore relocation...tailored to your time, finances, and desires is in this guidebook.

To Joan
whose inspiration and expert help made it possible.

The Great Towns of
Northern California

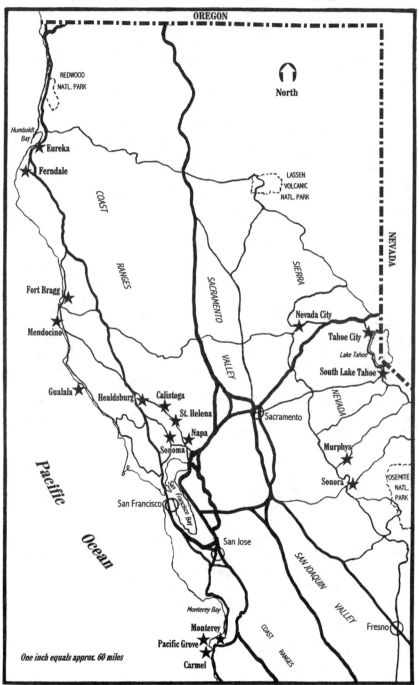

OREGON

REDWOOD
NATL. PARK

North

Humboldt
Bay

★ Eureka

★ Ferndale

LASSEN
VOLCANIC
NATL. PARK

COAST

RANGES

SACRAMENTO

SIERRA

NEVADA

Fort Bragg ★

Nevada City

Mendocino ★

Tahoe City ★

VALLEY

Lake Tahoe

South Lake Tahoe ★

Gualala ★

Healdsburg ★

Calistoga ★

NEVADA

St. Helena ★

Napa ★

Sacramento

Sonoma ★

Murphys ★

Sonora ★

YOSEMITE
NATL.
PARK

Pacific

San Francisco

San Francisco Bay

Ocean

San Jose

SAN JOAQUIN

VALLEY

Monterey Bay

Monterey ★

COAST

Fresno

Pacific Grove ★

RANGES

Carmel

One inch equals approx. 60 miles

4

Contents

Introduction

Picture sandy ocean beaches; a rockbound sheltered harbor; lush vineyards; redwood forests; or majestic mountains. Now, imagine human-scaled towns, with style and pleasures normally found only in cities, in the midst of these idyllic settings. Welcome to *the Great Towns of Northern California.*

This is the only detailed guidebook focused on all of Northern California's towns most favored with both urban charms and picturesque surroundings. It was written to help you discover famous and little-known places that make the region remarkable, and enjoy them to the fullest. The book updates and expands material in the premier guide, *The Great Towns of America.*

A wealth of new information is presented in several ways that set this guidebook apart. (1) All of the best attractions, restaurants, and lodgings (instead of random features) in every locale are identified, described and rated. (2) Attention is focused on recreation and leisure pursuits of interest to adventurous adults and couples. (3) Intimate details are presented for more than one thousand romantically oriented bedrooms in exceptional lodgings. (4) The likelihood of good weather is rated for each month in every locale, and supporting data are provided. (5) Websites are included where available. (6) Visitors and dreamers inspired to consider relocating to a great town will relish exclusive quality of life and affordability data and ratings for each town.

The contents and format are designed to quickly provide all of the information you want to get the most from these exciting destinations within your time, finances, and interest.

Great Towns

Notions vary widely about exactly where Northern California is. For this guidebook, it is California north of Big Sur. Here, a "great town" is defined as a locality apart from major cities with both scenic appeal and memorable leisure-time features.

Size, location, natural setting, and leisure appeal were used in a sequential process of elimination. All communities under 100,000 in population were considered. Places with no clear separation from major cities (hence no independent identity) were eliminated. So were towns lacking major cultural attractions, restaurants and lodgings, or more than a few miles from usable water bodies, dramatic landforms, and/or luxuriant vegetation.

Eighteen exceptional locales were found along the rugged coast, in lush valleys, high in the mountains, by crystal-clear lakes, and among productive vineyards. Collectively, they are Northern California's prime sources of getaway excitement. Individually, each has highlights that make it a worthy destination for a delightful weekend or a lengthy vacation. A full chapter devoted to each locality addresses all natural and cultural

Introduction

attractions; restaurants; and lodgings. The "quality of life" chapter, comparing key livability and affordability factors, may tempt you to stay even longer.

Weather Profiles–the "Vokac Weather Rating"
Weather plays a crucial role in recreation and leisure, and in successful vacations. Because of this, detailed weather information is presented for great towns throughout Northern California. The copyrighted weather profiles for each of the eighteen locales are the most complete in any travel guidebook.

The "Vokac Weather Rating" © (VWR) measures every town's probability of "pleasant weather"–i.e., warm, dry conditions suitable for outdoor recreation by anyone dressed in light sportswear. Average high and low temperatures, rainfall, and snowfall for each month (plus the frequency of precipitation) are correlated. Typical weather that can be expected each month is then rated on a scale from "0" to "10." A "0" signifies adverse weather with almost no chance that shirt-sleeves and shorts will be comfortable. Every increment of one on the VWR scale represents a 10% greater chance of pleasant weather. For example, a "5" is used where there is a 50% chance that any given day in the month will be pleasant. A "10" pinpoints "great" weather, with warm, dry days almost 100% assured. An easy-to-follow line graph is used to display the month-to-month VWR. Generally, ratings of "7" or above indicate a high probability of desirable conditions for outdoor activity. Ratings of "4" or less suggest increasing likelihood that the weather will restrict some outdoor ventures and/or require special clothing.

As an added convenience, each month of the weather graph has been subdivided into four segments roughly corresponding to weeks. Readers interested in "fine-tuning" the VWR will find the smaller segments helpful. For example, if the ratings for September and October are "10" and "6," the position of the connecting line during the last week of September indicates an "8" rating. The implication is that weather during that week will normally still be "very good" but no longer "great."

Attractions
A hallmark of all great towns is that each has a favored natural setting. Every distinctive attraction in and around each locality is described. Included are leisure-time destinations of special interest to adults–like wineries, remote beaches and hot springs–as well as family-oriented places. All kinds of outdoor recreation–bicycling, ballooning, horseback riding, fishing charters, etc.–are also described, and key sources for equipment rentals and guides are named. As an added convenience, popular

7

categories of attractions are listed alphabetically under general headings such as "boat rentals," "warm water features" or "winter sports."

Restaurants

Sampling various styles of fresh regional foods is one of the joys of travel. While ubiquitous chains dominate most cities, almost all great towns embrace instead their celebrated and aspiring restauranteurs and chefs who contribute unique talents to the community's cultural milieu in one-of-a-kind dining places.

In this book, food and atmosphere (including scenic views) are uniformly described for the most noteworthy restaurants from mom-and-pop cafes to temples of haute cuisine. Service is not discussed, because it can vary so much even on a given day.

For each restaurant, the price range is summarized. Meals served *(B=breakfast, L=lunch, D=dinner)* are identified. Days closed are noted but may vary seasonally.

Lodgings

Many of Northern California's most luxurious resorts, significant historical inns, and gracious bed-and-breakfasts are found in great towns where lodgings often have a long and glorious past. This guidebook's emphasis is placed on unique, significant, or homey accommodations instead of omnipresent chain motels and humdrum hotels clustered near freeway offramps. Clean, comfortable budget lodgings are also included for cost-conscious travelers. As an additional trip planning aid, each locality is summarized in terms of its: overall number and quality of lodgings; busiest season (prime time); and average percentage by which rates are reduced off-season.

All leisure-oriented amenities available at each lodging are described, whether natural (like a location on a beach or in a forest) or manmade (i.e., outdoor pool, tennis courts, restaurants, etc.). Where available, toll-free phone numbers and website information are provided.

The overall quality of an average bedroom in every lodging is rated according to the author's six-level hierarchy. The following descriptive terms are consistently used: humble (frayed or no-frills); plain (or simply furnished); comfortable (or nicely furnished); attractive (or well-furnished); beautiful; and luxurious. All major room features–fireplace, balcony, etc.–are also identified. The cost of rooms is summarized.

As a unique bonus, nearly one thousand bedrooms with special views and/or features are highlighted. Exceptional rooms or suites (starting with the best) in the foremost resorts, inns, etc. in each town are identified by room number (or name) and described.

Introduction

Location

Because great towns are inevitably compact, street maps are seldom necessary. To help you locate any listing without a map, all addresses are referenced according to a street number plus distance (to the nearest mile) and direction from downtown. The term "downtown" covers all features within roughly one-quarter mile of the busiest portion of a town's main business district.

Ratings

Features listed in *The Great Towns of Northern California* collectively represent the highlights that contribute most to each town's appeal. All features are rated. Three levels of quality are reflected in the ratings. (1) A star preceding an entry indicates an especially worthwhile source of a product or service worth going out of the way for. (2) An entry is included, but not starred, if it is a notable (but not exceptional) source of a product or service. (3) Many features and activities were evaluated, but not included, if they were judged to be of only average or lower quality or readily available in numerous other places.

Each feature was personally evaluated by the author. No payments were accepted. As a result, each listing is described on merit alone, and solely reflects the author's judgment.

Rating information is somewhat perishable in any guidebook. However, the single-star rating system can help simplify your selection of attractions, restaurants, and lodgings. In addition to the star, the author's opinion regarding each feature's relative importance is further indicated by the length of its description.

Prices

Comparable information is provided about the relative cost of every restaurant and lodging. Because prices change with the economy, it is impossible to know how long specific rates will be in effect. However, relative price levels usually remain constant. For example, a "low-priced" motel (with rooms costing less than $60 in 2003) can be expected to remain a relative bargain in later years when compared to other lodgings–even though the actual price of a room increases–because the other lodgings in that area will typically increase their prices by about the same percentage as the bargain motel. Similarly, a restaurant will usually continue in its relative price category as years go by.

Restaurants: A basic price code was designed to provide a comparable summary of the cost of an average meal at each restaurant. The code is used for all listed restaurants in all locales. Four categories are used to define the cost per person for a "normal" dinner (with soup or salad, average-priced entree, and beverage) not including tip, tax, or wine for the meal. The categories and related prices are: *Low:* under $12; *Moderate:* $12 - $19; *Expensive:* $20-29; and *Very Expensive:* $30+.

Lodgings: A comparable summary of the cost of a room at each lodging in every town is also presented. Cost is summarized in a category that reflects prevailing rates during "high season" (summer on the coast and inland valleys, and winter in the mountains). Where two categories of rates are noted, rooms in the lodging are available in both price ranges. Nowadays, travelers should feel free to negotiate the price of a room since most lodgings offer discounts from "regular (rack) rates" to members of auto clubs, business travelers, government employees, military personnel, retirees, and others. The categories of comparable "rack rates" are as follows: *Low:* under $60; *Moderate:* $60-100; *Expensive:* $100-200; and *Very Expensive:* over $200.

Livability of Great Towns

For those who are enchanted by the charms of a particular great town, the final chapter provides key data for each community. Comparable indicators are presented for *weather, crime, overall livability,* and *housing cost,* plus *basic facilities* and *downtown vitality.* Tables rank livability of each great town compared with the others, and with San Francisco. As a bonus, the unique ***Vokac Index of Livability and Affordability©*** is presented, revealing where you can get the most Quality of Life for the housing cost.

Some Final Comments

All information has been carefully checked, and is believed to be current and accurate. To assure that the reader can continue to get current information, the internet website for each facility (where available) is identified. No malice is intended or implied by the judgments expressed, nor by the omission of any facility or service.

Because this guidebook celebrates the most memorable great towns and their best features throughout Northern California, it will be challenged about some places that were included and others that were left out. Regardless, the author hopes that *The Great Towns of Northern California* will encourage you to discover and experience their special pleasures.

We welcome your comments and questions.

David Vokac
c/o West Press
P. O. Box 99717
San Diego, CA 92169
www.greattowns.com

Calistoga

Calistoga is the only town in America esteemed for both wine and water. Sheltered by oak-covered foothills of Mt. St. Helena at the northern end of world famous Napa Valley, it is surrounded by lush vineyards and renowned wineries. The village also hosts a remarkable cluster of small hot springs resorts, and a bottling plant that ships mineral water worldwide.

Calistoga was founded in 1859 by Sam Brannan, a San Francisco newspaper publisher who became California's first millionaire dreamspinner. Recognizing the potential of the area's warm springs, hot-water geysers, and semi-tropical climate, he developed what was intended to become the "Saratoga of California," rivaling the famous New York resort. He and others also cultivated grapevines. Thanks to Brannan's foresight, Calistoga has quietly prospered ever since as the benefits of natural hot springs and the quality of wines improved.

Today, the classic main street retains a delightful turn-of-the-twentieth-century feeling thanks to skillful renovations and compatible new buildings. Most major spas and lodgings, art galleries, specialty shops, and a coterie of excellent restaurants and bars are located on or near this handsome thoroughfare. Surrounding hills and the picturesque valley feature landmark wineries, a natural geyser, and a petrified forest. Still, Calistoga's unique claim to fame remains the celebration of wine and water with peaceful pleasures—like wine tasting in memorable locales, or soaking in hot mineral water whirlpools, taking ash baths, and enjoying massages in salubrious surroundings.

WEATHER PROFILE

V.W.R. *		Jan.	Feb.	Mar.	Apr.	May	June	July	Aug.	Sep.	Oct.	Nov.	Dec.
Great	10												
Fine	9												
Very Good	8												
Good	7												
Moderate	6												
	5												
	4												
	3												
	2												
	1												
	0												

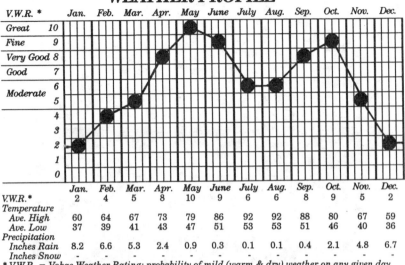

	Jan.	Feb.	Mar.	Apr.	May	June	July	Aug.	Sep.	Oct.	Nov.	Dec.
V.W.R.*	2	4	5	8	10	9	6	6	8	9	5	2
Temperature												
Ave. High	60	64	67	73	79	86	92	92	88	80	67	59
Ave. Low	37	39	41	43	47	51	53	53	51	46	40	36
Precipitation												
Inches Rain	8.2	6.6	5.3	2.4	0.9	0.3	0.1	0.1	0.4	2.1	4.8	6.7
Inches Snow	-	-	-	-	-	-	-	-	-	-	-	-

* V.W.R. = Vokac Weather Rating: probability of mild (warm & dry) weather on any given day

BASIC INFORMATION

Population: 5,190
Elevation: 365 feet
Location: 74 miles North of San Francisco
Airport (regularly scheduled flights): San Francisco - 85 miles

Calistoga Chamber of Commerce   (707)942-6333
   downtown in Old Depot Building, 1458 Lincoln Av. #9 - 94515
   calistogafun.com
Napa Valley Conference & Visitors Bureau   (707)226-7459
   notable link: napavalley.com/calistoga

ATTRACTIONS

★ *Bicycling*
Bicycle riding is very popular on scenic wine-country byways throughout the relatively flat Napa Valley. Bicycles can be rented by the hour, half day or day with related equipment, information, and maps included.
   Getaway Adventures   *(707)942-0332 (800)499-2453*
   downtown at 1117 Lincoln Av.
   getawayadventures.com (closed Tues.-Wed. in winter)
   Palisades Mountain Sport   *(707)942-9687*
   downtown at 1330B Gerard St.
   palisadesmountainsport.com
★ **Ca'Toga**   *(707)942-3900*
   downtown at 1206 Cedar St.
   catoga.com
A handsome building in the style of a Venetian villa has been spectacularly outfitted with the art and artifacts of Carlo Marchiori. The internationally known artist opens his home, one mile north of town, for personalized tours by appointment. The home tour includes the artist's wonderfully fanciful murals, some twenty feet high, throughout his estate. The "Cat and the Canary Cage" room is unforgettable. The grounds include the artist's assemblage of Italian antiquities and further demonstrations of his whimsical flamboyance in a unique abalone-shell grotto, and much more. His urbane galleria downtown showcases his artistic statements: sculptures; masks; stone-relief plaques; porcelain ceramics; wall hangings; and other art objects that reflect the Venetian's unbridled talent for conveying the extravagance and grandeur of ancient Italy. Open 11-6 except closed Tues.-Wed.
Flying
   Crazy Creek Soaring   *(707)987-9112*
   crazycreekgliders.com
   18 mi. N at 18896 Grange Rd. - Middletown
You can have the unique thrill of soaring behind a glider pilot on flights that originate and land in nearby Middletown. Ideal soaring conditions prevail much of the year in one of America's major centers for the sport.
Food Specialties
★   **Palisades Market**   *(707)942-9549*
   downtown at 1506 Lincoln Av.
Palisades Market is the best gourmet to-go destination in Calistoga. Display cases full of regional cheese, pates, sausages, and deli items, plus a wealth of fresh breads and distinctive desserts, are just right for idyllic picnics with local wines. Soups and sandwiches, specialty produce and fresh seasonal groceries

further distinguish the little market. Open 7:30 a.m.-7 p.m.

Old Faithful Geyser of California   *(707)942-6463*
 2 mi. N at 1299 Tubbs Lane
 oldfaithfulgeyser.com
One of the few regularly erupting geysers in the world is located in a private park next to Calistoga. Super-heated water erupts to a height of sixty feet or more approximately every forty minutes, more often when there's a lot of groundwater. The park is open daily with a self-guided tour, a geothermal exhibit hall, gift shop, snack bar, and picnic area.

Petrified Forest   *(707)942-6667*
 5 mi. W at 4100 Petrified Forest Rd.
 petrifiedforest.org
This private park contains well-preserved fossil redwood logs including one eight feet in diameter and more than sixty feet long. Giant trees were buried eons ago when ash covered a forest uprooted by the concussion of a volcanic eruption of nearby Mt. St. Helena. Walking trails, a museum, gift shop and picnic areas are open daily.

Pioneer Park
 downtown 1 block N of Lincoln Av. on Cedar St.
The Napa River (a small creek this far upstream) borders this luxuriant little park. Several picnic tables are sequestered under majestic shade trees on expansive lawns that include a children's play area.

Robert Louis Stevenson State Park   *(707)942-4575*
 6 mi. N on Hwy. 29
 parks.ca.gov
In addition to a scenic road through this undeveloped park, there is a five-mile hiking trail to the top of Mt. St. Helena (4,343 feet elevation). From the top of the extinct volcano (Wine Country's highest landmark) the Pacific Ocean, Bay Area, and Sierra Nevada are visible–on a clear day. A memorial one mile up the trail notes the cabin site where Robert Louis Stevenson honeymooned in 1880 and got his inspiration for *The Silverado Squatters.*

Sharpsteen Museum & Sam Brannan Cottage   *(707)942-5911*
 downtown at 1311 Washington St.
 sharpsteen-museum.org
Calistoga's offbeat history is depicted in exhibits and detailed dioramas prepared by Ben Sharpsteen, an Academy Award-winning artist and producer for Walt Disney. An attached authentic 1860 cottage from Sam Brannan's original resort was relocated here. The museum store features regional books and crafts. Nearby is a peaceful creekside garden. Open 11-4 daily.

★ **Warm Water Features**

Calistoga has an abundance of facilities where the public can luxuriate year-round in indoor and outdoor warm mineral water pools and whirlpools in serene, genial settings. Most are affiliated with in-town lodgings. Steam baths, herbal and blanket wraps, and massages can also be reserved. The most unusual feature is the ash bath, in which local volcanic ash is mixed with mud and hot mineral water to fill "mud relaxation tubs." Several places package all of the above features into one sensationally sybaritic session lasting about two hours. Following are the ten best and most complete facilities. All are listed under lodgings, and feature a range of spa treatments and facilities including mineral springs pools.

Calistoga Spa Hot Springs
Calistoga Village Inn & Spa
Dr. Wilkinson's Hot Springs Resort
Eurospa Inn & Spa
Golden Haven Hot Springs Spa & Resort
Indian Springs Resort & Spa
Mount View Hotel & Spa
Nance's Hot Springs
Roman Spa Hot Springs Resort
Silver Rose Inn & Spa

★ *Wineries*

Calistoga, at the warm northern end of the world famous Napa Valley wine district, is surrounded by outstanding wineries featuring cabernet sauvignon and chardonnay. Delightful tasting and sales facilities and tours attract visitors year-round.

Chateau Montelena   *(707)942-5105*
2 mi. N at 1429 Tubbs Lane
montelena.com
Chateau Montelena put California on the map as a world class wine-making region in 1976, when their 1973 chardonnay ranked best among all international white wines during a blind tasting by French judges in Paris. This renowned winery was established in 1880 in a castle-like building with imported facing stone, and side walls built of native stone up to twelve feet thick. Nearby, Oriental water gardens distinguish a pretty little five acre lake. (Fee) tours by appointment. Premium cabernet sauvignon, chardonnay and zinfandel are featured for (fee) tasting. Open 9:30-4 daily.

Clos Pegase   *(707)942-4981   (800)366-8583*
2 mi. SE at 1060 Dunaweal Lane
clospegase.com
Architect Michael Graves' post-modern Greco-Roman stucco complex and caves house museum-quality sculptures, paintings

and reliefs, as well as a diverse selection of premium wines including notable cabernet sauvignon, chardonnay and merlot. In addition to memorable tours, there is a regular (fee) tasting room and reserve (fee) tasting rooms that reflect the stylish austerity of the complex. Open 10:30-5 daily.

Cuvaison   *(707)942-6266*
3 mi. E at 4550 Silverado Trail
www.cuvaison.com
Established in 1970, this winery uses state-of-the-art equipment to concentrate on premium wines–notably cabernet sauvignon, chardonnay, merlot, and pinot noir. Idyllic vineyard views can be enjoyed in oak-shaded picnic grounds next to the winery. Tours by appointment. (Fee) tasting 10-5 daily.

Frank Family Vineyards   *(707)942-0859   (800)574-9463*
1 mi. S at 1091 Larkmead Ln.
An 1885 stone building amid gardens and vineyards is the keystone of this winery featuring chardonnay, cabernet sauvignon, merlot, and sparkling wines. A picnic area adjoins. Free tastes (almost unique for Napa Valley) are generously poured. Open 10-5 daily.

Schramsberg Vineyards   *(707)942-4558   (800)877-3623*
2 mi. S at 1400 Schramsberg Rd.
schramsberg.com
Several of America's most renowned "méthode champenoise" sparkling wines including the superb J Schram are produced here. All are stored in nearly two miles of post-Civil War-era hand-carved tufa caves which are used for storing and riddling the bottles. By appointment, fascinating tours of the historic caves and beautifully landscaped grounds followed by (fee) tasting in the caves are available 10-2:30 daily.

Silver Rose Cellars   *(707)942-9581   (800)995-9381*
1 mi. SE at 351 Rosedale Rd.
silverrose.com
Premium cabernet sauvignon, merlot, chardonnay and blends are the hallmark of this young winery that opened in 2000 next to the **Silver Rose Inn & Spa** (see listing). A delightful tour of the winery surrounded by colorful gardens and vineyards is offered daily, and a barrel tasting is included free of charge. The fee for wines poured in the tasting room is refunded with purchase of one or more bottles. Open 10-5 daily.

Sterling Vineyards   *(707)942-3344   (800)726-6136*
2 mi. SE via Hwy. 29 at 1111 Dunaweal Lane
sterlingvyds.com
In 1973, a monastery-like winery with a resplendent white facade opened on a 400-foot knoll overlooking much of Napa Valley. Worthwhile self-guided tours of the post-modern aerie are reached

by parking at the base and riding a (fee) aerial tram up the hill. Sterling concentrates on premium cabernet sauvignon, chardonnay, merlot and sauvignon blanc in one of the largest estate-bottled wineries in the country. On the hill, visitors can relax indoors or outdoors in a stellar setting for a seated tasting. There is also a store well-stocked with related gifts. Open 10:30-4:30 daily.

Zahtila Vineyards   *(707)942-9251*
1 mi. NE at 2250 Lake County Hwy.
zahtilavineyards.com
Zinfandel is the primary focus (supported by cabernet sauvignon) of this small hillside winery surrounded by rose gardens and picnic areas. (Fee) tasting 10-5 daily.

RESTAURANTS

★ **All Seasons Cafe & Wine Shop**   *(707)942-9111*
downtown at 1400 Lincoln Av.
allseasonswineshop.com
L-D. No L Mon.-Wed.   *Expensive*
Creative California cuisine is showcased in dishes like seared day boat scallops with truffle-scented risotto or red wine-braised beef short ribs with seasonal mushrooms that work well with the excellent assortment of regional and European premium wines available from the retail wine shop ((800)804-9463) tasting bar in back. The simply stylish dining room and bar provide picture-window views of the heart of town.

Boskos Trattoria   *(707)942-9088*
downtown at 1364 Lincoln Av.
boskos.com
L-D.   *Moderate*
Contemporary California/Italian fare includes creative and traditional pastas, and pizzas from an almond-wood-fire oven. The relaxed trattoria is in a historic Victorian building. Rock walls, windows that open to main street, and a horseshoe bar featuring California micro-brews and local wines are accents.

★ **Brannan's Grill**   *(707)942-2233*
downtown at 1374 Lincoln Av.
brannansgrill.com
L-D.   *Expensive*
One of Napa Valley's bright young sources of innovative Wine Country cuisine gives serious attention to seasonal fresh ingredients. The grazing menu features entrees like grilled thick-cut pork loin with mustard spaetzle and braised red cabbage with shallot-cider sauce. The inviting firelit dining room overlooks a bustling expo kitchen. A warm wood-trimmed bar also contributes to the easygoing upscale decor.

Cafe Sarafornia   *(707)942-0555*
downtown at 1413 Lincoln Av.
B-L.   *Expensive*
Designer or build-your-own omelets and scramblers are featured
for breakfast, with contemporary California dishes like portabello
burger or chicken chili for lunch. The casual wood-trimmed cafe
includes an enclosed porch with windows by the main street.
Calistoga Inn Restaurant & Brewery   *(707)942-4101*
downtown at 1250 Lincoln Av.
calistogainn.com
L-D.   *Expensive*
Updated American fare is served to diners at a cozy congestion of
tables in relaxed rooms of a restored inn with aVictorian feeling.
A garden patio by a creek (the Napa River) is next to the wine bar
and micro-brewery. An adjoining English-style pub has periodic
live entertainment, and there are overnight lodgings upstairs.
Calistoga Roastery   *(707)942-5757*
just E at 1631 Lincoln Av.
B-L.   *Moderate*
Assorted coffee varieties are prepared on site in a 1919 roaster
along with many other beverages. Tasty cinnamon rolls and other
housemade pastries and light fare are also served in the
coffeehouse and on a jasmine-bordered deck with a town view.
★ **Catahoula Restaurant & Saloon**   *(707)942-2275*
downtown at 1457 Lincoln Av.
catahoularest.com
D only. Plus B-L Sat.-Sun.   *Expensive*
Catahoula, in the historic Mount View Hotel, is Wine Country's
source of Louisiana-inspired cuisine. From spicy rooster gumbo
through cornmeal fried catfish to traditional Louisiana desserts
like bananas foster with rum cream–here is a dining adventure.
The simply snazzy dining room is highlighted by a mirrored expo
kitchen, colorful wall hangings and a woodburning oven. Next
door is a festive saloon with frequent live entertainment.
★ **Checkers**   *(707)942-9300*
downtown at 1414 Lincoln Av.
L-D.   *Moderate*
Calistoga's gourmet pizza parlor also offers some creative
California cuisine including housemade desserts featuring fresh
fruits of the season. The dining room/bar is festooned with fun-
loving folk art and an expo kitchen.
Flatiron Grill   *(707)942-1220*
downtown at 1440 Lincoln Av.
flatirongrill.com
L-D. No D Sun.   *Expensive*

18

Steaks, apple cider-mushroom reduction pork chops, roasted half chicken, grilled salmon and other California classics are featured. Diners have a choice of a modish dining room overlooking the main street, secluded padded booths, or a warm, wood-trimmed wine bar.

Hydro Bar and Grill   *(707)942-9777*
   downtown at 1403 Lincoln Av.
   B-L-D.   *Expensive*
California and Italian comfort foods are served in a brick-walled dining room with a close-up view of main street and a bar serving many microbrews on tap.

Pacifico Restaurante   *(707)942-4400*
   downtown at 1237 Lincoln Av.
   pacificorestaurante.com
   L-D. Sat. & Sun. brunch.   *Moderate*
Seafood sautés and grilled meats highlight many adaptations of Mexican dishes. A big colorful dining room and cantina include a waterfall and windows that open onto the main street.

★ **Schat's Bakkery**   *(707)942-0777*
   downtown at 1353 Lincoln Av.
   B-L. Closed Tues.   *Moderate*
A wide assortment of tasty breakfast pastries, plus desserts, are made fresh daily and displayed in this storefront bakery. They can be enjoyed with coffee at a couple of tables, or to go. There are also assorted designer breads like their cheddar cheese loaf–ideal for wine-soaked picnics.

Smokehouse Cafe   *(707)942-6060*
   downtown at 1458 Lincoln Av.
   B-L-D.   *Moderate*
They make their own sausages and create their own smoked barbecued meats and sauces for zesty barbecued beef, pork, chicken and fish dishes generously served with Southern support dishes in bright casual dining areas of a historic train depot and (in summer) on a patio.

★ **Wappo Bar & Bistro**   *(707)942-4712*
   downtown at 1226-B Washington St.
   wappobar.com
   L-D. Closed Mon-Tues. in winter.   *Expensive*
Global cuisine featured in selections from the diverse menu is flavorful and notably imaginative. Consider rosemary-scented rabbit with mustard cream and baby spinach, or braised osso bucco with porcini mushrooms. Beyond the simply handsome little dining room with copper-topped tables and a wine bar with redwood interior is a delightful fountain courtyard with a grapevine-covered arbor.

19

LODGINGS

Lodgings downtown all reflect Calistoga's intimate human scale and are oriented around a full range of hot springs spa facilities. Nearby, elaborate bed-and-breakfasts and upscale small inns are proliferating. High season is March through November and weekends year-round. Mid-week winter rates are often reduced at least 30%.

★ **Calistoga Spa Hot Springs**   *(707)942-6269*
downtown at 1006 Washington St. - 94515
calistogaspa.com
57 units   *(866)822-5772*   *Moderate*
The Palisades cliffs above Calistoga are a dramatic backdrop to this contemporary motel with the region's most elaborate complex of mineral water pools. Guests have free use of four nicely landscaped outdoor mineral pools (a big whirlpool, two hot pools, and a large warm pool in a palm-oriented courtyard) plus exercise equipment. These and complete (fee) spa facilities (including volcanic ash mud baths) as well as their own line of health care body products are also available to the public. Spacious, comfortably furnished rooms have kitchenettes and a queen bed.

Calistoga Village Inn & Spa   *(707)942-0991*
just NE at 1880 Lincoln Av. - 94515
greatspa.com
41 units   *Moderate-Expensive*
This single-level motel features warm mineral water for a large outdoor pool and a hot indoor whirlpool. A complete (fee) spa facility is available with a range of treatments and their own line of body products. Each room is simply furnished and has a double, queen or king bed.
    "deluxe room"–spacious, Roman-tiled or whirlpool
        tub, kitchenette, queen or king bed.

★ **Christopher's Inn**   *(707)942-5755*
just W at 1010 Foothill Blvd. - 94515
chrisinn.com
22 units   *(866)876-5755*   *Expensive-Very Expensive*
This recently expanded contemporary bed-and-breakfast and conference center offers upscale touches amid colorful gardens. Expanded Continental breakfast served to your room is complimentary. Each attractively furnished room includes antiques, a private bath, extra amenities, and a queen bed. Most have a gas fireplace. Several suites also have an in-room two-person whirlpool and a garden patio.
    "Ultimate Suite"–spacious, big whirlpool in view of
        gas fireplace, private garden patio, canopy queen bed.

Comfort Inn   *(707)942-9400*
just NE at 1865 Lincoln Av. - 94515
comfortinn.com
54 units   *(800)221-2222*   *Moderate-Expensive*
A hot springs mineral water pool and whirlpool distinguish this
contemporary chain motel. There is also a sauna and steam room,
and it's a short pleasant walk to the heart of town. Each room is
comfortably furnished and has two queens or a king bed.

★ **Cottage Grove Inn**   *(707)942-8400*
downtown at 1711 Lincoln Av. - 94515
cottagegrove.com
16 units   *(800)799-2284*   *Very Expensive*
Cottage Grove Inn is the most romantic cottage complex in Napa
Valley. The sybaritic sanctuary opened in 1996 amid a grove of
towering elms within an easy stroll of the heart of the village.
Expanded Continental breakfast and outstanding afternoon wine
and appetizers are complimentary. So is use of the two first-come,
first-served bicycles. Each playfully themed cottage was designed
for fun-loving couples. The beautifully furnished rooms are
outfitted with individual decor and contemporary and extra
conveniences. A wet bar/refrigerator, woodburning fireplace, an
alcove with a deep in-bath two-person whirlpool tub, and a king
bed complete each idyllic adult escape.

★ **Dr. Wilkinson's Hot Springs Resort**   *(707)942-4102*
downtown at 1507 Lincoln Av. - 94515
drwilkinson.com
42 units   *Expensive*
This well-maintained Calistoga institution includes a modern
motel with indoor and outdoor mineral pools free to guests. Since
1946, extensive (fee) men's and women's bathhouse and spa
facilities have catered to natural, simple relaxation and the
restorative power of hot mineral springs water and volcanic ash
mud. Recently renovated lodgings range from comfortably
furnished rooms with (optional) kitchen and two twins or a queen
bed, through spacious rooms with refrigerator and two queens or
a king bed, to the "Victorian House" where well-furnished rooms
have a refrigerator, queen bed and extra amenities.

★ **The Elms Bed & Breakfast Inn**   *(707)942-9476*
downtown at 1300 Cedar St. - 94515
theelms.com
7 units   *(888)399-3567*   *Expensive-Very Expensive*
A Mansard-style Victorian mansion (circa 1871) on the National
Historic Register now serves as a gracious bed-and-breakfast
surrounded by gardens in a quiet spot by the stream and city park
next to downtown. Multicourse breakfast; afternoon wine and

appetizers accompanied by classical music; and a nightcap of port and chocolate are complimentary. Each room is attractively, individually furnished with a private bath, personal touches and antiques, and a queen or king bed.

"Carriage House"–large, gas fireplace, kitchenette, private patio, in-bath two-person whirlpool and two-person shower, king bed.

"Private Domain"–cozy hideaway, gas fireplace, in-bath whirlpool, canopy queen bed.

Eurospa Inn & Spa   *(707)942-6829*
just S at 1202 Pine St. - 94515
eurospa.com
13 units   *Expensive-Very Expensive*
A pool and whirlpool overlooking vineyards are features of this little complex a stroll from downtown. Expanded Continental breakfast is complimentary. The (fee) spa offers a wide range of health and beauty treatments including some unusual ones like a green tea wrap. Each individually comfortably furnished room has a gas-burning pot-bellied stove, an in-bath (one- or two-person) whirlpool tub, and microwave/refrigerator, plus two queens or a king bed.

★ **Foothill House**   *(707)942-6933*
just NW at 3037 Foothill Blvd. - 94515
foothillhouse.com
5 units   *(800)942-6933*   *Expensive-Very Expensive*
Foothill House is a skillfully transformed Victorian farmhouse sequestered among towering trees and colorful gardens that include an outdoor whirlpool. Gourmet breakfast and afternoon wine and cheese are complimentary. Each individually decorated room is well furnished, including country antiques, a private bath and entrance, small refrigerator, a woodburning or gas fireplace, and queen or king bed.

"Quails Roost"–spacious, in-bath two-person whirlpool with waterfall view, kitchen, private patio, large gas fireplace in view of king bed.

"Redwood Room"–cozy, private patio with redwood tree, two-person whirlpool, woodburning fireplace, queen bed.

"Evergreen Suite"–private deck with waterfall, wood- burning fireplace, deep in-bath whirlpool, king bed.

★ **Golden Haven Hot Springs Spa & Resort**   *(707)942-6793*
just NE at 1713 Lake St. - 94515
goldenhaven.com
27 units   *Moderate-Expensive*
A quiet locale is a feature of this modern motel near downtown. Amenities include a warm indoor mineral pool plus a hot

whirlpool. Complete (fee) bathhouse/spa facilities offer an unusual feature–private volcanic ash mud baths for couples. All rooms are comfortably furnished including a refrigerator, and have a queen or king bed. Some have a private sauna.

"Jacuzzi Room" (8 of these)–in-room
   raised large whirlpool, king bed.

Indian Springs Resort & Spa   *(707)942-4913*
downtown at 1712 Lincoln Av. - 94515
indianspringscalistoga.com
17 units   Expensive-Very Expensive
The oldest continuously-operated thermal pool and spa facility in California includes a restored historic bungalow complex built around Calistoga's largest outdoor hot springs pool. The Olympic-sized mineral water pool next to a picturesque knoll is open to the public (free to guests). On-site thermal geysers and pure volcanic ash are used in the vintage 1913, completely restored (fee) bathhouse with full-service spa facilities. Each comfortably furnished bungalow-style unit along "palm row" has a partial kitchen, gas fireplace, and a queen bed.

★ **Mount View Hotel & Spa**   *(707)942-6877*
downtown at 1457 Lincoln Av. - 94515
mountviewhotel.com
32 units   (800)816-6877   Expensive-Very Expensive
A large pool, whirlpool and a cabana bar enhance a garden courtyard with fountain sculptures behind this small landmark hotel. There is also gourmet dining (see listing for Catahoula), an entertainment lounge, and a full service (fee) health and beauty spa catering to singles and couples. Bottles of Calistoga's famous water are complimentary, as is Continental breakfast delivered to your room. Carefully restored and updated rooms are individually well furnished with antiques and contemporary touches, and have a double, queen or king bed.

"Cottages" (3 of these)–private patio with
   a whirlpool, queen bed.
#221–corner, nice view over pool to town and
   mountains, fine period furnishings, king bed.

Nance's Hot Springs   *(707)942-6211*
downtown at 1614 Lincoln Av. - 94515
nanceshotsprings.com
24 units   (800)201-6211   Moderate
This homespun, vintage motel features a large enclosed hot mineral water whirlpool. Vintage, no-nonsense men's and women's (fee) bathhouse facilities featuring volcanic ash mud baths are available. Each simply furnished unit has a kitchenette and two twins or a king bed.

★ **Roman Spa Hot Springs Resort**   *(707)942-4441*
downtown at 1300 Washington St. - 94515
romanspahotsprings.com
60 units   *(877)208-9444*   *Expensive- Very Expensive*
Luxuriant semitropical gardens are a delightful complement to
tile-and-stucco villa-style buildings, an outdoor mineral pool and
whirlpool, plus a hot indoor mineral whirlpool and saunas for
guests. Complete (fee) spa facilities and services featuring
immersion mud baths (a mixture of volcanic ash, peat moss and
warm mineral water) for both couples and individuals are located
in the adjoining modern **California Oasis Spa** ((800)404-4772).
Each room was recently remodeled and upgraded and is well
furnished including a refrigerator and a queen or king bed.
#130,#134–end units, in-bath large mineral-springs-water
    whirlpool tub with shower, king bed.

★ **Silver Rose Inn & Spa**   *(707)942-9581*
1 mi. SE at 351 Rosedale Rd. - 94515
silverrose.com
20 units   *(800)995-9381*   *Expensive-Very Expensive*
The Silver Rose Inn is one of the Wine Country's most elegant
and romantic bed-and-breakfasts. Stylish contemporary buildings
crown a well-landscaped knoll and are sequestered in vineyards
below. Amenities include two tennis courts, two warm mineral
water pools and whirlpools and exercise equipment, plus state-of-
the-art (fee) spa facilities. The estate also includes their own
Silver Rose Cellars (see listing). Fresh, light breakfast and
afternoon wine and cheese are complimentary. Each spacious,
themed room is beautifully, individually furnished and has
tranquil mountain or vineyards views and a queen or king bed.
"Vineyard Suite"–two rooms, gas fireplace, big
    in-room whirlpool, private balcony, queen bed.
"Cleopatra's Room," "Hello Hollywood," "The Library"–
    gas fireplace, big in-room whirlpool, private patio, king bed.
"Garden Room"–spacious, gas fireplace, big in-room
    whirlpool, large private deck, queen bed.
"Western Room"–gas fireplace, big in-room
    whirlpool, large private balcony, queen bed.

Stevenson Manor Inn - Best Western   *(707)942-1112*
just NE at 1830 Lincoln Av. - 94515
bestwestern.com
34 units   *(800)780-7234*   *Expensive-Very Expensive*
This contemporary motel has a pool, whirlpool, steam room and
sauna. Each spacious room is well furnished including a
refrigerator and microwave, and has a king bed. Some rooms have
an in-bath whirlpool tub or a gas fireplace.

Carmel

Carmel is one of the world's loveliest collaborations between man and nature. Homes and businesses are sequestered in a forest of rare Monterey cypress on the southern side of the Monterey Peninsula. The unique seaside village borders a slope of fine white sand that extends into the surf of Carmel Bay. Almost as remarkable as the setting is the mild climate where snow and frost are as rare as hot days. Flowery landscapes and a wealth of outdoor activities are enjoyed year-round.

Father Junipero Serra built a mission here in 1770. Well over a century later, artists and dreamers attracted by the captivating location, fine weather, and potential for a simple lifestyle began to build homes among the pines. The sensitivity of these bohemians fostered the charm that is still being nurtured.

Fairy tale cottages and fanciful houses and shops are a highly visible part of the legacy today. Another is the residents' continuing determination to retain the beauty of this place. In spite of its overwhelming popularity, the village still does *not* have: traffic lights, parking meters, neon signs, billboards, street lights outside the business district, or tall buildings. It *does* have a compact downtown with a remarkable concentration of fascinating places to stroll, shop, eat, drink and sleep. An area smaller than one square mile has more than seventy galleries and studios displaying everything from local to international fine arts and crafts. Unique speciality shops also compete for the stroller's attention. Here, too, is one of the nation's greatest concentrations of gourmet restaurants and romantic lodgings.

Carmel

WEATHER PROFILE

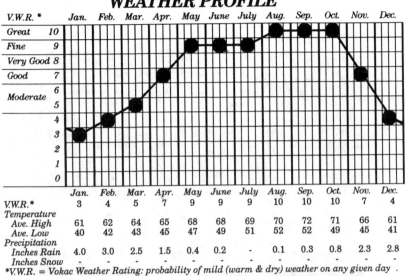

V.W.R. *	Jan.	Feb.	Mar.	Apr.	May	June	July	Aug.	Sep.	Oct.	Nov.	Dec.
V.W.R.*	3	4	5	7	9	9	9	10	10	10	7	4
Temperature												
Ave. High	61	62	64	65	68	68	69	70	72	71	66	61
Ave. Low	40	42	43	45	47	49	51	52	52	49	45	41
Precipitation												
Inches Rain	4.0	3.0	2.5	1.5	0.4	0.2	-	0.1	0.3	0.8	2.3	2.8
Inches Snow	-	-	-	-	-	-	-	-	-	-	-	-

*V.W.R. = Vokac Weather Rating: probability of mild (warm & dry) weather on any given day .

BASIC INFORMATION

Population: 4,080
Elevation: 200 feet
Location: 125 miles South of San Francisco
Airport (regularly scheduled flights): Monterey - 8 miles

Carmel Business Association   (831)624-2522
   downtown on San Carlos between 5th & 6th Avs. (Box 4444) - 93921
   carmelcalifornia.org
Monterey County Convention & Visitors Bureau   (888)221-1010
   Box 1770 - 93942
   montereyinfo.org

ATTRACTIONS

★ **Bicycling**

One of America's finest auto/bicycle rides–the Seventeen-Mile Drive–and other scenic routes provide access to the coastline, mountains and bucolic valleys around Carmel. Rental bicycles by the hour are available in nearby Monterey (see listing).

★ **Big Sur Coast**

S for approximately 80 mi. on Highway 1

California Highway 1 is one of the world's most exhilarating scenic drives. A narrow, paved two-lane road winds and dips along the flanks of a mountain wilderness rising precipitously from an unspoiled shoreline. Numerous hiking trails lead from roadside parking areas into groves of the southernmost coast redwoods and fern-shaded canyons, and to remote sandy beaches and coves. Well-located state parks along the route offer memorable camping and picnicking opportunities. Unique galleries, restaurants and lodgings blend harmoniously into the countryside in the village of Big Sur (25 miles south) and beyond (see listings). South of Big Sur Village are three outstanding showcases of regional arts and crafts. By Nepenthe (see listing) the **Phoenix** shop has fine local arts, crafts and books. Six miles south is the **Coast Gallery** (coastgalleries.com), itself an art object where the original 34-foot circular gallery was built of redwood with the same diameter as the trunk of the General Sherman, the world's largest tree. It, and the avant-garde **Hawthorne Gallery** (hawthornegallery.com) nearby, are two of America's great showcases for museum-quality regional arts and crafts. Also nearby are **Ventana Inn** and the **Post Ranch Inn** (see listings), quintessential examples of affinity between civilization and nature.

★ **Carmel Beach Park**

just W at the foot of Ocean Av.

A picturesque beach is backed by a pine-studded slope of fine, dazzlingly white sand. Cold water and undertow preclude swimming, but it is a wonderful place for strolling, picnicking, and sunbathing. Don't miss the inspiring (albeit sedate) local custom of sunset-watching here. Participants have been known to burst into applause at the gorgeous spectacle each evening.

★ **Carmel Mission Basilica**   *(831)624-1271*

1 mi. S off Highway 1 at 3080 Rio Rd. (at Lasuen Dr.)
carmelmission.org

A key link to early California history was established on this site overlooking the mouth of the Carmel River in 1771 by Father Junipero Serra ("father of the California missions"). It was his residence and headquarters until his death in 1784. He is buried beneath the church floor in front of the altar of the present sandstone church, which was completed in 1797. The carefully restored mission's museum has a notable collection of his memorabilia and other historic relics. It is open daily.

Carmel River State Park   *(831)624-4909*
1 mi. S on Scenic Rd.
A photogenic ocean beach composed of fine white sand beckons beachcombers, sunbathers and picnickers. It is unsuitable for swimming because of cold water and currents.

★ *Golf*
Carmel is surrounded by coastal, valley and forested golf courses. Collectively those have been designated as the world's #1 golf destination according to *Golf Digest Magazine*. Three courses are ranked in the top ten internationally. Several of the most renowned are open to the public by reservation year-round with all facilities and rentals. The best include:

Pebble Beach Golf Links   *(831)624-3811   (800)654-9300*
2 mi. NW on Seventeen-Mile Dr. - Pebble Beach
The home course of a renowned pro-am tournament is always ranked as one of the best championship golf courses in the nation. The oceanfront site is also one of the most picturesque (and expensive) anywhere.

Rancho Cañada Golf Course   *(831)624-0111*
2 mi. SE at 4860 Carmel Valley Rd. - Carmel Valley
Two well-regarded 18-hole championship golf courses feature reasonable green fees in scenic and often-sunny Carmel Valley.

Spyglass Hill Golf Course   *(831)624-3811   (800)654-9300*
3 mi. NW on Stevenson Dr. - Pebble Beach
This Robert Trent Jones-designed championship golf course in Pebble Beach is ranked among the nation's top forty. Cypress forests and panoramic seascapes distinguish the difficult, spectacular course. All facilities and rentals are available.

★ *Horseback Riding*
Horses can be rented by the hour or longer for guided scenic rides in Pebble Beach, Carmel Valley, or Big Sur. Horseback riding by the surf is a truly memorable experience. For information and reservations, contact:

The Holman Ranch   *Carmel Valley*   *(831)659-6054*
holmanranch.com
Molera Horseback Tours *Big Sur*   *(831)625-5486*
molerahorsebacktours.com   *(800)942-5486*
Pebble Beach Equestrian Center *Pebble Beach* *(831)624-2756*
ridepebblebeach.com

★ **Point Lobos State Reserve**   *(831)624-4909*
3 mi. S off Highway 1
One of the most beautiful reserves on the Pacific coast includes

six miles of headlands, secluded coves, tidepools, sea lion rocks, and a natural grove of rare Monterey cypress. The setting inspired Robert Louis Stevenson's *Treasure Island*. Picnic areas, hiking and nature trails and world class diving access are provided. Whale watching is also popular when the awesome animals pass close to shore on their 12,000-mile winter migration to Baja California. Hikers should be wary of poison oak.

Scenic Drive
★ **Scenic Road**
   S for approximately 2 mi. from foot of Ocean Av.
Whether walking, bicycling, or driving, this aptly named street delights everyone who uses it. Through green tunnels created by overhanging branches of majestic pines, past tiny rockbound coves and white sand beaches, unusual residences and colorful flower gardens, the route follows the shoreline. Take a short detour along the way to 26304 Ocean View Avenue to visit Tor House and Hawk Tower, the home and refuge of Robinson Jeffers (a famous American poet). The drive ends at a panoramic viewpoint overlooking the mouth of Carmel River and the Big Sur beyond.

Specialty Shops
★ **The Barnyard**   *(831)624-8886*
   thebarnyard.com
   1 mi. SE off Highway 1 & Carmel Valley Rd.
The Barnyard is the region's premier destination for recreational shopping apart from downtown Carmel. Profusions of flowers, music, and intriguing fountains and sculptures lend enchantment to a cluster of rustic barn-style buildings housing about fifty fine specialty shops, galleries, and restaurants, including the peerless **Thunderbird Bookshop & Cafe**–California's quintessential combination bookstore and dining experience (see listing).

   Crossroads Shopping Village   *(831)625-4106*
   1 mi. SE off Highway 1 & Rio Rd.
A prominent Westminster chiming clock/bell tower is the centerpiece for an array of about seventy distinctive specialty shops and restaurants amid a colorful mosaic of contemporary California architecture and gardens. The **Bountiful Basket** (bbandb.net) is a super source for worldwide extra-virgin olive oils and premium wines.

★ ***Wineries***   *(831)375-9400*
   montereywines.org
Carmel Valley is an increasingly important source of vineyards among more than 40,000 acres now planted in Monterey County–now the largest producer of premium wine grapes in America.

Bernardus Vineyards & Winery *(831)659-1900 (800)223-2533*
12 mi. E at 5 W. Carmel Valley Rd. - Carmel Valley
bernardus.com
Bernardus concentrates on producing wines with "superior mouth-feel." The full range is sold and available for (fee) tasting in an attractive little tasting room/gift shop. A new demonstration vineyard fronts the enchanting Bernardus Lodge (see listing) two miles west. Open 11-5 daily.

Château Julien *(831)624-2600*
5 mi. E at 8940 Carmel Valley Rd. - Carmel Valley
www.chateaujulien.com
Château Julien is the premier winery in Carmel Valley and still the valley's most complete facility. Tasting and sales of assorted "Château Julien," "Goodland Ranch," and "Emerald Bay Coastal" bottlings are offered in a handsome chateau-style winery building, and there are picnic tables in a garden patio, plus a gift shop. Tours by reservation. Open 8-5 weekdays; 11-5 weekends.

Heller Estate *(831)659-6220 (800)625-8466*
12 mi. E at 69 W. Carmel Valley Rd. - Carmel Valley
hellerestate.com
Heller Estate is one of the region's premier growers of premium varietals–including chenin blanc. All of their wines from dry-farmed, organically grown grapes are available for purchase or (fee) tastings in a handsome roadside room with a gift shop and adjoining sculpture garden. Open 11-5 daily.

Talbott Vineyards *(831)659-3500*
12 mi. E at 53 W. Carmel Valley Rd. - Carmel Valley
talbottvineyards.com
Estate-grown chardonnay and pinot noir are featured, with (fee) tasting and sales in an early-California-style shop that also offers the handmade neckware and silk accessories of the Robert Talbott Company. A garden patio adjoins for picnics and relaxing. Open 11-5 daily. Closed Tues.-Wed. in winter.

RESTAURANTS

★ **Anton & Michel** *(831)624-2406*
downtown on Mission St. between Ocean & 7th Avs.
carmelsbest.com
L-D. *Very Expensive*
For more than twenty years, fresh seafoods like Pacific salmon or Monterey Bay sand dabs have been featured along with an appealing selection of contemporary dishes and luscious desserts in the flagship of a burgeoning local restaurant group. Informally elegant dining rooms give guests a choice of romantic firelight or courtyard fountain views.

★ **Bahama Billy's**   *(831)626-0430*
1 mi. SE at 3690 The Barnyard
bahamabillys.com
L-D.   *Expensive*
The flair and flavors of the Caribbean are now available in the
Barnyard in dishes like barbecued pork spareribs with guava
sauce, and spiced butternut squash and mango bisque with crab.
All meals begin with hot calypso cheesebread, and can end with
housemade desserts like authentic key lime pie served amid
colorful upbeat tropical ambiance.

★ **Bernardus Lodge**   *(831)658-3400*
10 mi. E at 415 Carmel Valley Rd. - Carmel Valley
bernardus.com
B-L-D.   *Very Expensive*
Marinus Restaurant (D only) is the landmark dining room of
the Bernardus Lodge. One of Monterey Peninsula's legendary
chefs is now overseeing the meticulous creation of superb
traditional and innovative French and California cuisine. Top-
quality seasonally fresh products of the region enhanced by the
resort's extensive gardens of herbs, vegetables and (new in 2002)
chardonnay and pinot noir grapes complement the kitchen's
talent with truffles, foie gras and other gourmet ingredients. The
pastry chef also prepares desserts of the season that are as
delicious as they are beautiful. The dining room is a tour-de-force
of comfortable country decor with widely spaced tables, a
monumental raised stone fireplace and colorful floral sprays.
Tables are set with fine linen, crystal, silver, designer candle,
fresh flowers and a distinctive sea salt holder. **Wicket** (B-L-D) is
a comfortably casual restaurant with views of the adjoining
gardens and world class croquet court.

Big Sur Lodge   *(831)667-3100*
26 mi. S on Highway 1 at Pfeiffer State Park - Big Sur
bigsurlodge.com
B-L-D.   *Expensive*
Contemporary California cuisine includes dishes like sautéed fillet
of salmon with ginger soy glaze, or hickory-smoked baby back ribs
with chipotle barbecue sauce. Hardwood tables and armchairs
enhanced by candlelight are surrounded on three sides by views
of the redwood forest. There is also a shaded dining deck.

Big Sur River Inn   *(831)667-2700*   *(800)548-3610*
24 mi. S on Highway 1 at Pheneger Creek - Big Sur
www.bigsurriverinn.com
B-L-D.   *Expensive*
Banana-walnut pancakes, omelets, or pan-fried trout are
breakfast highlights. Black Angus beef steaks star later with

homemade apple pie in a historic wood-trim dining room with a river-rock fireplace and a window-wall view of Big Sur River. The redwood-shaded deck is especially popular when weather permits. A small motel and gift shop adjoin.

★ **Bouchée**   *(831)626-7880*
downtown at Mission St. between Ocean & 7th Avs.
bouchee.biz
D only. Closed Mon.   *Very Expensive*
Bouchée is one of California's best young restaurants. A renowned chef does superb work with top-quality seasonal ingredients of the region. Consider Monterey Bay red abalone with black truffle sauce, roasted salmon with braised artichokes, or Sonoma duck leg confit with Chinese black rice, or venison loin with sour cherry red wine sauce. The plush, firelit dining room and bar are backed by whimsical wall art that contributes to the cosmopolitan appeal–as does the adjoining upscale wine store.

Buon Giorno   *(831)624-0221*
downtown on W. Junipero St. between 5th & 6th Avs.
B-L.   *Expensive*
Buon Giorno is a deservedly popular bakery/coffeehouse. Big cinnamon-caramel pullaparts, apple strudels and turnovers, plus other pastries and desserts made here are served with designer beverages in the spiffy little coffee shop or garden terraces.

Cafe Rustica   *(831)659-4444*
12 mi. E at 10 Delfino Place - Carmel Valley
B-L-D. Closed Wed.   *Expensive*
Morning pizzas, berry pancakes, or ciabatta bread french toast are among breakfast specialties. Wood-fired pizzas, pastas, fresh country fare and housemade desserts are served later. Dining areas with stone floors, rock walls and polished hardwood tables and chairs and a heated patio carry off the warm rustic theme.

★ **Carmel Bakery**   *(831)626-8885*
downtown on Ocean Av. between Dolores & Lincoln Sts.
B-L-D.   *Moderate*
Delicious morning delights like sticky buns, cinnamon rolls and raspberry sticks or several kinds of croissants can be enjoyed with assorted hot beverages at tables by loaded display cases. Several kinds of big soft pretzels and bagels star later along with designer sandwiches using bread baked on-site.

★ **Carmel Chop House**   *(831)625-1199*
downtown at 5th Av. & San Carlos St.
carmelchophouse.com
D only.   *Very Expensive*
A well-thought-out selection of contemporary chophouse cuisine ranges from prime Nebraska corn-fed filet mignon to lamb sirloin

steak, and seafood dishes like tomato-crusted local halibut grilled over almond and oak wood. The urbane dining room with nicely spaced tables and sophisticated wall art is a perfect complement to the chef's style.

★ **Carmel Valley Ranch**   *(831)625-9500*
4 mi. E at One Old Ranch Rd.
B-L-D.   *Very Expensive*
At the heart of the resort, the **Oaks Dining Room** features coastal ranch cuisine blending regional fish, fowl, beef and game with fresh herbs and vegetables of the season from the resort's own garden. Outstanding possibilities include wild boar with mashed sweet potatoes, or house-smoked chicken/wild mushroom ravioli with baby spinach and white truffle oil. Tables set with full linen and crystal, and armchair comfort, distinguish a gracious firelit dining room with romantic views of surrounding oaks.

★ **Casanova Restaurant**   *(831)625-0501*
downtown on 5th Av. between Mission & San Carlos Sts.
casanovarestaurant.com
L-D. Sun. brunch.   *Very Expensive*
Casanova Restaurant is one of Carmel's best and most enduring special-occasion destinations. Classic French, Spanish and Italian cuisine receives creative California topspin in dishes that showcase fresh regional ingredients and the talent of a classically trained chef in three-course dinners and hearty lunches. Homemade desserts are also inspired. Romantic dining adventures for adults are featured in an expansive complex that includes a series of intimate dining rooms around a heated garden patio.

The Cottage Restaurant   *(831)625-6260*
downtown on Lincoln St. between Ocean & 7th Avs.
cottagerestaurant.com
B-L-D. No D Sun.-Wed.   *Moderate*
Breakfast is featured at the Cottage in assorted eggs benedicts, design-your-own omelets, crepes, pancakes, pannetone french toast, waffles and support dishes. Light lunches and dinners are also served in the cozy casual dining rooms in a cottage.

★ **Flaherty's**   *(831)625-1500*
downtown on 6th Av. between Dolores & San Carlos Sts.
carmelsbest.com
L-D.   *Expensive*
All kinds of seafood from clam or crab chowder to sea bass or salmon have been featured in the Grill (for dinner) and the oyster bar (lunch or dinner) since 1975. Homemade pies and other desserts are other reasons to be here in spite of the light bright little room's casual congested lunch counter and plain, closely spaced tables.

★ **Flying Fish Grill**   *(831)625-1962*
downtown at Carmel Plaza (on Mission bet. Ocean & 7th Avs.)
D only. Closed Tues.   *Expensive*
Innovative Asian cuisine is featured in dishes like salmon fillet
steamed in a paper pouch or seafood clay pots, and in desserts like
green tea sundae in a simply sophisticated wood-trim cellar
restaurant enhanced by a wealth of whimsical art–much of it
oriented toward flying fish.

★ **The Forge in the Forest**   *(831)624-2233*
downtown at 5th Av. & Junipero St.
forgeintheforest.com
L-D. Sun. brunch.   *Expensive*
One of Carmel's most unusual and venerable watering holes
features an ornate wooden bar in a saloon with nostalgic
blacksmith antiques and intriguing copper walls that gleam in the
light of the room's fireplace. A tasty pub menu is served in this
romantic adult respite, and in three other distinctive dining
rooms. Outside is a classic-Carmel garden patio with firepits.

★ **The French Poodle**   *(831)624-8643*
downtown at Junipero St. & 5th Av.
D only. Closed Sun.   *Expensive*
The French Poodle is one of California's great gourmet havens.
The chef's classic French background and his expertise with fresh
top-quality ingredients of the season treated with the light, lively
flair of creative California cuisine is apparent in every dish.
Consider Dungeness crab legs out of the shell with champagne
sauce, saffron and caviar to begin a meal that might include
provimi veal T-bone for an entree, and a sumptuous dessert made
here like the signature "floating island for two." The intimate,
gracious dining room is accented by colorful paintings and fresh
roses on each table. Widely spaced tables, a rarity in Carmel, add
to the romantic ambiance.

Ginna's   *(831)659-7770*
12 mi. E at 19 E. Carmel Valley Rd. - Carmel Valley
B-L. Closed Mon.-Tues. Plus D on Fri.   *Expensive*
Baked goods each morning include Ginna's giant popovers and a
range of light breakfast items. Soup, salad and sandwiches can be
enjoyed with tasty housemade desserts in a unique century-old
milkhouse tower or by live oaks in an adjoining garden patio.

★ **Grasing's**   *(831)624-6562*
downtown at 6th Av. & Mission St.
grasings.com
L-D.   *Very Expensive*
Coastal cuisine has another important young showcase in Carmel
with dishes like rack of lamb with roasted artichokes, pearl onion

and Yukon golds in a mustard sauce, or grilled artichoke with blue crab and lemon vinaigrette. Housemade desserts are delicious, too, like pear and huckleberry tart. Wall art and town- and garden-view windows enhance intimate dining areas set with linen and flowers.

★ **The Grill on Ocean Avenue**   *(831)624-2569*
downtown on Ocean Av. between Lincoln & Dolores Sts.
carmelsbest.com
L-D.   *Expensive*
An oakwood-fired grill is used for a limited selection of contemporary California dishes with a Pacific Rim flair. Consider Asian crabcakes with spicy mango chutney, or signature duck ravioli in an orange buerre blanc. Affiliated with Anton & Michel, the relaxed but stylish firelit dining room complements the cuisine.

★ **Highlands Inn**   *(831)622-5445*
5 mi. S on Highway 1 at 120 Highlands Dr. - Big Sur
highlands-inn.com
B-L-D.   *Very Expensive*
The resort's incomparably-sited **Pacific's Edge Restaurant** (D only–Very Expensive) serves California cuisine with a window-wall awe-inspiring ocean view. Precisely prepared bounty of the region complements the sophisticated elegance of the newly remodeled dining room and the coastal panorama beyond. Nearby, a plush firelit lounge shares the romantic seascape, and features live grand piano music. **California Market** (B-L–Expensive) offers contemporary California fare amid upscale rusticity by an expo kitchen or on a sea-view terrace.

Hog's Breath Inn   *(831)625-1044*
downtown off San Carlos St. between 5th & 6th Avs.
hogsbreathinn.net
L-D.   *Expensive*
The California pub grub hasn't changed much in Clint Eastwood's one-time watering hole. Neither has decor like free-form redwood tables in a rustic little bar with a corner fireplace and (no surprise) hogs staring down from the walls. The courtyard features hogs in sculptures and a colorful full-wall mural of Carmel Valley toward Big Sur.

Jack London's   *(831)624-2336*
downtown off Dolores between 5th & 6th Avs. (in Su Vecino Court)
jacklondons.com
L-D.   *Moderate*
A popular rendezvous, this wood-paneled bar and dining room pairs tap beers, wines by the glass, etc. with the most eclectic assortment of tasty dishes imaginable into the wee hours.

Jeffrey's Grill & Catering   *(831)624-2029*
8 mi. E at 112 Mid-Valley Center - Carmel Valley
B-L. Closed Mon.   Moderate
Jeffrey's is a good bet for breakfasts like fresh ripe persimmon
pancakes or designer omelets (consider pasilla chilis, ham, cheese
and avocado), plus assorted housemade muffins. The cheerful
coffee shop and adjoining dining deck overlook colorful gardens.
Katy's Place   *(831)624-0199*
downtown on Mission St. between 5th & 6th Avs.
katysplacecarmel.com
B-L.   *Very Expensive*
One of Carmel's oldest breakfast places serves dishes ranging
from several varieties of eggs benedict, or corned beef hash and
eggs to breakfast burritos, waffles, designer pancakes and more.
The cozy, congested cafe has a redwood-shaded dining deck.
La Bohème Restaurant   *(831)624-7500*
downtown at Dolores St. & 7th Av.
laboheme.com
D only.   *Expensive*
Each evening, one three-course prix-fixe menu features French
country cuisine that includes soup, salad and an entree like veal
with mushrooms. Housemade desserts are available a la carte.
The little dining room with a congestion of tables set with full
linen is a convivial reflection of each night's adventure.
★ **La Playa Hotel**   *(831)624-6476*
downtown at Camino Real & 8th Av.
laplaycarmel.com
B-L-D. Sun. brunch.   *Expensive*
Continental cuisine with a disciplined light touch distinguishes
the elegant **Terrace Grill**. Diners have an expansive picture-
window view of manicured grounds backed by Monterey pines
and the ocean. A lovely dining terrace shares the luxuriant garden
view. Polished hardwoods and well-lighted pictoral memorabilia
distinguish the refined adjoining lounge.
★ **Lincoln Court**   *(831)624-6220*
downtown on Lincoln St. between 5th & 6th Avs.
lincolncourt.com
D only. Closed Mon.   *Very Expensive*
Culinary classics are creatively updated in one of Carmel's
gourmet restaurants. Fresh quality ingredients are skillfully
transformed into exciting dishes like breast of maple leaf duck
with wild mushroom sauce. Housemade desserts are similarly
appealing–consider apple-cranberry-macadamia crunch. The
firelit dining room offers widely spaced candlelit tables outfitted
in full linen amid romantic understated elegance.

★ **The Lodge at Pebble Beach**   *(831)625-8519*
2 mi. NW at 1700 Seventeen-Mile Dr. - Pebble Beach
pebblebeach.com
B-L-D.   *Very Expensive*
The world famous Lodge at Pebble Beach includes three
restaurants that showcase the magnificent setting. In the resort's
Club XIX (L-D), gourmet light French cuisine is formally
presented in prix-fixe dinners. Jackets are required for gentlemen
in the opulent setting. The atmosphere is more informal for
lunch, and the romantic bricked patio with fireplaces shares the
grand Carmel Bay view. Upstairs, **The Stillwater Bar and
Grill** (B-L-D) features fresh seasonal seafood that must compete
with a fabulous panorama of the golf course and seascapes. **The
Gallery** (B-L) offers homestyle casual fare with fine views of
fairways and the sea, while **The Tap Room** (L-D) serves steaks
and chops in a warm casual setting amid golf memorabilia.
Lucy's   *(831)625-1915*
downtown on Dolores St. between Ocean & 7th Avs.
B-L-D.   *Expensive*
California country fare is highlighted for breakfast by signature
dishes like croissant french toast and apple-oat pancakes. A good
variety of other comfort foods is served at all meals in this cozy
cafe that opened in late 2002.
Lugano Swiss Bistro   *(831)626-3779*
1 mi. SE at 3670 The Barnyard
swissbistro.com
L-D.   *Expensive*
Creative and traditional Swiss dishes like puff pastry with shitake
and oyster mushrooms, schnitzel or fondue contribute to the
appeal of this Swiss bistro tucked away in the Barnyard. Cozy
dining areas with warm wood-chalet decor reflect the Continental
spirit. So does occasional live Alpine music.
★ **Mission Ranch**   *(831)625-9040*
1 mi. S at 26270 Dolores St.
missionranchcarmel.com
D only. Sun. brunch.   *Expensive*
The Restaurant at Mission Ranch skillfully pairs a historic
century-old ranch house with contemporary California dishes
with roots going way back. Consider a smoked salmon appetizer
or Dungeness crab soup with local artichokes. Among entrees, the
big slab of roast prime rib of beef, baby back ribs, or New York
strip steak are fine. The firelit dining room and adjoining lounge
with nightly piano bar entertainment exude Carmel conviviality.
Just below, a heated dining deck shares the delightful view of the
Carmel River mouth and nearby Big Sur Mountains.

★ **Nepenthe**   *(831)667-2345*
   29 mi. S on Highway 1 - Big Sur
   nepenthebigsur.com
   L-D.   *Expensive*
For more than half a century, classic and creative American
dishes have included treats like their ambrosia burger (a ground
steak sandwich with secret sauce on a french roll) or deep-dish
apple pie. A wood-trimmed window-walled dining room and
lounge maximize the view through live oaks to the Big Sur Coast
more than eight hundred feet below. Adjoining firelit patios share
the view. At **Cafe Kevah** (B-L), American and Mexican casual
fare and a couple of fine crumb-topped fruit pies are served on an
umbrella-shaded terrace overlooking the mountains and the sea.
The **Phoenix** gift shop is a long-established source of top-quality
arts, crafts, books and treats of the region.

Patisserie Boissiere   *(831)624-5008*
   downtown at Carmel Plaza on Mission St. near Ocean Av.
   L-D. Sat. & Sun. brunch. No D Mon. & Tues.   *Moderate*
For many years, pastries, cakes, tarts, and breads from their
bakery have been served with light meals with a Continental flair
in a snazzy little firelit dining room.

★ **Post Ranch Inn**   *(831)667-2800*
   27 mi. S on Highway 1 - Big Sur
   postranchinn.com
   L-D.   *Very Expensive*
Sierra Mar Restaurant at Post Ranch is one of America's most
enchanting restaurants. An architectural jewel of wood, stone and
glass crowns a rugged bluff more than a thousand feet above the
heart of the Big Sur Coast. Four-course prix-fixe dinners (or a la
carte, on request) are featured on a dinner menu (by reservation
only) that changes daily. Inspired creations prepared from top-
quality seasonal ingredients result in cutting-edge California
cuisine. Caviar, foie gras, truffles and other epicurean ingredients
are used for exciting presentations of dishes like curried mussel
bisque, or roast venison loin with chestnut puree. Housemade
desserts are similarly delicious. Full-length floor-to-ceiling
windows maximize the awe-inspiring view from simply elegant
tables adjacent to window alcoves along the blufftop.

★ **Rio Grill**   *(831)625-5436*
   1 mi. SE at 101 Crossroads Blvd. (in the Crossroads)
   riogrill.com
   L-D.   *Expensive*
Rio Grill is one of America's premier sources of New California
cuisine. Emphasis is on fresh regional ingredients innovatively
prepared in a flavorful array of appetizers through desserts

described on a grazing menu. For example, consider center-cut pork chops with grilled mushrooms and Point Reyes blue cheese with roasted garlic butter, or balsamic-chile marinated pork with honey-onion-chipotle marmalade. Avant-garde art enlivens a series of cheerful Santa Fe style alcoves beyond a colorful firelit bar.

★ **Robata Grill & Sake Bar**   *(831)624-2643*
  1 mi. SE at 3658 The Barnyard
  restauranteur.com
  D only.   *Expensive*
Robata is the best Japanese restaurant on the Peninsula. The long-established restaurant gives careful attention to an extensive selection of classic and creative Japanese dishes from sushi to green tea ice cream. Massive polished redwood tops a dramatic sushi bar, and rough or polished woods are used for a series of intimate booths and dining areas. There is also a popular bar and a heated courtyard backed by a Japanese garden and a raised firepit.

Rocky Point Restaurant   *(831)624-2933*
  10 mi. S on Highway 1 - Big Sur
  rocky-point.com
  B-L-D.   *Very Expensive*
Charcoal-grilled steaks and fish have long been served with an old-fashioned relish tray and other traditional support dishes. But, it's the view that is extraordinary. Dozens of fully linened tables line picture windows overlooking rocky headlands and coves that seem to be immediately below. The lounge and heated terrace share the unforgettable scene.

Thunderbird Bookshop   *(831)624-1803*
  1 mi. SE at The Barnyard
  thunderbirdbooks.com
  L-D. No D Sun.-Wed.   *Moderate*
Tasty contemporary California fare like turkey pot pie or chicken quesadillas or salmon-broccoli-sesame stir can be enjoyed along with a princely popover with assorted beverages and desserts in the renowned bookstore's firelit dining room and fully enclosed atrium deck overlooking luxuriant landscaping of The Barnyard.

Tuck Box   *(831)624-6365*
  downtown on Dolores St. between Ocean & 7th Avs.
  tuckbox.com
  B-L-tea.   *Expensive*
The Tuck Box has been a Carmel tradition for more than half a century. The thatched cottage facade of the tiny English tea room is very photogenic. They feature their own scone mix and preserves in the cozy congestion of an unassuming little tea shop.

★ **Ventana Inn**   *(800)628-6500*
   27 mi. S on Highway 1 - Big Sur
   ventanainn.com
   L-D.   *Very Expensive*
In **Cielo**, fresh flavorful California cuisine is featured on a selected list featuring quality ingredients of the season. Consider mixed greens with a Castroville artichoke confit, or warm Dungeness crab salad with avocado and citrus fruit. Entrees range from oak-grilled prime Kansas City steak with Madeira demi-glaze to carmelized Maine diver scallops, with notable housemade desserts. The luxurious post-modern multilevel dining room provides expansive glass window views of the ocean or mountains. An adjoining umbrella-shaded terrace showcases an inspiring seascape far below. A woodcrafted firelit lounge adjoins.

★ **Village Corner**   *(831)624-3588*
   downtown at 6th Av. & Dolores St.
   carmelsbest.com
   B-L-D.   *Moderate*
Banana pecan pancakes star along with waffles, french toast, plus egg skillet dishes and omelets for breakfast. Creative California dinners (Expensive) prepared over an oak-fired open grill are also featured in this pleasant Mediterranean-style bistro with a heated garden court–a Carmel favorite for over half a century.

Wagon Wheel   *(831)624-8878*
   4 mi. E in Valley Hills Center on Carmel Valley Rd. - Carmel Valley
   B-L.   *Moderate*
One of the region's longest-established breakfast favorites still features biscuits and gravy with a variety of omelets and some designer treats like oatmeal or banana-pecan pancakes. A cozy congestion of tables surrounds an expo kitchen in casual dining areas amidst Western memorabilia.

★ **Will's Fargo**   *(831)659-2774*
   12 mi. E at 4 Carmel Valley Rd. - Carmel Valley
   willsfargo.com
   D only. Closed Tues.   *Moderate*
Nebraska corn-fed properly cut and aged beef stars for all kinds of steaks including a two-pound Porterhouse, and a tender filet mignon. The Valley's brick-and-stone-trimmed landmark restaurant offers the comfortable look and feel of an old-time Western dinner house and saloon as it has since 1959.

LODGINGS

Lodgings in town are abundant, invariably picturesque, and individualistic. Renowned resorts surround the village. High season is May through October, and weekends year-round. Midweek in winter, rates may be as much as 20% less.

Adobe Inn   *(831)624-3933*
downtown at Dolores St. & 8th Av. (Box 4115) - 93921
adobeinn.com
20 units   *(800)388-3933*   *Expensive-Very Expensive*
This contemporary motor inn in an oak-shaded garden features a small pool and sauna, and has a covered garage. Complimentary Continental breakfast is delivered to your room. Each spacious, beautifully furnished room was recently remodeled, and has a gas fireplace, wet bar with refrigerator, private deck nestled among oaks and pines, extra amenities, and two queens or a king bed.
#29,#30,#37–some ocean view, king bed.

★ **Bernardus Lodge**   *(831)658-3400*
10 mi. E at 415 Carmel Valley Rd. (Box 80) - Carmel Valley 93924
bernardus.com
57 units   *(888)648-9463*   *Very Expensive*
The spectacular young Bernardus resort is sequestered among oaks and pines on a gentle slope of the Carmel River Valley. In this romantic adult hideaway, a luxuriant chardonnay and pinot noir vineyard lies just beyond beautiful gardens that surround contemporary California-style low-rise buildings, two tennis courts, a large outdoor pool, a professional-class bocce ball and croquet court, and a full-service (fee) spa and salon. The main lodge includes enchanting gourmet dining (see listing). Guests are greeted at check-in with a glass of fine Bernardus wine. Distinctive introductory treats and wine are also complimentary. Each spacious, luxuriously appointed unit is individually furnished and includes all contemporary and extra amenities, a gas fireplace, two-person soaking tub and spacious walk-in shower, refrigerator, large balcony or deck with a view of gardens and mountains beyond, and a king featherbed.
#1,#6–extra-large, vaulted ceiling, raised gas fireplace, spacious private patio with garden/mountain view and large whirlpool, two-person soaking tub and walk-in high-tech shower.

Big Sur Lodge   *(831)667-3100*
26 mi. S on Hwy. 1 at Pfeiffer State Park - Big Sur 93920
bigsurlodge.com
61 units   *(800)424-4787*   *Expensive-Very Expensive*
Recently remodeled cabins and lodge rooms surrounded by a luxuriant redwood forest are near trailheads which lead into surrounding forested highlands and down the Big Sur River to the coast. A restaurant (see listing), well-stocked gift shop and grocery store are a stroll from hillside cottage-style rooms. Each is comfortably furnished without distractions, but with a private deck. Several have a woodburning fireplace and kitchen.

Carmel Bay View Inn - Best Western *(831)624-1831*
downtown at Junipero St. between 5th & 6th (Box 3715) - 93921
carmelbayviewinn.com
58 units (800)343-1831 Expensive-Very Expensive
A large courtyard pool and expanded complimentary Continental breakfast are features of Carmel's largest motel. All rooms in the contemporary five-story complex are attractively furnished and have queens or a king bed. Many have a gas fireplace.
"Deluxe View Room" (several)–refrigerator, gas fireplace, private ocean-view balcony, king bed.

Carmel Mission Inn - Best Western *(831)624-1841*
2 mi. SE (off Highway 1) at 3665 Rio Rd. - 93923
carmelmissioninn.com
165 units (800)348-9090 Expensive-Very Expensive
The Mission, the Barnyard, and Crossroad shops are a stroll from Carmel's largest full-service hotel. The four-story contemporary complex on well-landscaped grounds has a garden pool, two whirlpools, a fitness center, restaurant and lounge. Each well-furnished room has all amenities, plus a refrigerator and two queens or a king bed. Some rooms have a private balcony.

★ **Carmel Tradewinds Inn** *(831)624-2776*
downtown at Mission St. & 3rd Av. (Box 3403) - 93921
28 units (800)624-6665 Expensive-Very Expensive
This historic inn in a luxuriant garden is being completely upgraded. Expanded Continental breakfast is complimentary. All units are beautifully furnished and have two queens or a king bed. The first new wing includes deluxe suites noted below.
"Carmel Bay room," "Artists room"–refrigerator/wet bar, in-bath whirlpool tub, gas fireplace, private (full or partial) ocean-view balcony, king bed.
"Serenity Suite," "Poets Suite"–living room with refrigerator/ wet bar, two balconies, (full ocean view in Serenity), bedroom with gas fireplace, in-bath whirlpool tub, king bed.

★ **Carmel Valley Lodge** *(831)659-2261*
12 mi. E on Carmel Valley Rd. (Box 93) - Carmel Valley 93924
valleylodge.com
31 units (800)641-4646 Expensive-Very Expensive
Ancient oak trees surround this country inn with acres of lovely gardens. An extra-long pool and whirlpool in a landscaped courtyard are complimentary to guests, as is a generous buffet breakfast. Each attractive room has individual Shaker-style furnishings, a refrigerator, all contemporary amenities, and queens or a king bed.
"Fireplace Suite" (4 of these)–spacious, kitchenette, raised woodburning fireplace, private patio, king bed.

★ **Carmel Valley Ranch-A Wyndham Luxury Resort** *(831)625-9500*
8 mi. E via Carmel Valley Rd. at One Old Ranch Rd. - 93923
wyndham.com
144 units *(800)422-7635* *Very Expensive*
Carmel Valley Ranch is one of California's most delightful hideaway resorts. Noble oak trees shade the grounds of this exclusive adult playground high on a hill overlooking a Shangri-La valley a few miles from the ocean. Amenities include a (fee) 18-hole championship golf course (where deer and turkeys roam when duffers don't); four tennis courts and all related facilities; in-room spa services; plus hiking trails, a fitness center, two large pools, six whirlpools, sauna, and a resort shop. The romantic restaurant (see listing) blends regional gourmet cuisine with the easygoing elegance of contemporary California decor at its best. Nearby is a stylish entertainment lounge. Each spacious, luxuriously furnished suite has a woodburning fireplace, a private deck with a pastoral valley view, honor bar/refrigerator, a wealth of extra amenities, and two doubles or a king bed. Many also have a large in-bath whirlpool.

"Luxury Spa Suite" (#157,#158,#152,#142,#184, plus 9 more)–extra-large one bedroom; living room with woodburning fireplace; bathroom with large two-person whirlpool and walk-in shower; huge private deck with big whirlpool and grand valley view; bedroom with woodburning fireplace and window-wall view of valley from king bed.

★ **Carriage House Inn** *(831)625-2585*
downtown on Junipero St. between 7th & 8th Avs. (Box 101) - 93921
innsbythesea.com
13 units *(800)433-4732* *Very Expensive*
Carriage House Inn is one of California's most romantic bed-and-breakfast inns. The charming adult retreat in a garden captures the spirit of Carmel in quality arts and crafts and thoughtful embellishments. Expanded Continental breakfast served to the room, afternoon wine and appetizers, and evening cappuccino or espresso, port and cookies are complimentary. Each spacious, luxuriously furnished room has all contemporary amenities plus refrigerator and honor bar, either a whirlpool tub or soaking tub, a gas fireplace and a king bed.

#3,#2–extra-large, in-bath two-person whirlpool, gas fireplace in sight of canopy king bed.

Coachman's Inn *(831)624-6421*
downtown at San Carlos St. & 7th Av. (Box C-1) - 93921
coachmansinn.com
30 units *(800)336-6421* *Expensive-Very Expensive*
Old English pleasantries and contemporary conveniences blend

comfortably in a little complex with a whirlpool, sauna, and patio with a fireplace. Morning Danish and evening sherry hour are complimentary. Each spacious, well-furnished room has a refrigerator, microwave, and king bed.

#302–gas fireplace, in-bath two-person whirlpool tub.

★ **The Cobblestone Inn**   *(831)625-5222*
downtown at Junipero St. & 8th Av. (Box 3185) - 93921
foursisters.com
24 units   *(800)833-8836*   *Expensive-Very Expensive*
The garden courtyard in this bed-and-breakfast inn is nearly surrounded by more than two dozen rooms. A complimentary full breakfast is served in the dining room, along with wine and appetizers in the afternoon. Each room is beautifully outfitted with all contemporary amenities plus a refrigerator, a gas fireplace faced with cobblestones from the Carmel River, and a queen or king bed.

#250–spacious, in-bath whirlpool tub, four-poster king bed.

★ **Colonial Terrace Inn**   *(831)624-2741*
1 mi. SW on San Antonio Av. at 13th Av. (Box 1375) - 93921
colonialterraceinn.com
25 units   *(800)345-8220*   *Expensive-Very Expensive*
Located in a quiet residential area near the beach is a small romantic inn comprised of several buildings (circa 1925) amid luxuriant garden terraces. All rooms were completely redecorated and upgraded in 2001. Expanded Continental breakfast is complimentary. Each well-furnished unit is individually decorated and has a queen or king bed. Most have a gas fireplace.

#26,28–spacious, in-bath whirlpool tub,
   gas fireplace, some ocean view, king bed.

Cypress Inn   *(831)624-3871*
downtown at Lincoln St. & 7th Av. (Box Y) - 93921
cypress-inn.com
33 units   *(800)443-7443*   *Expensive-Very Expensive*
The lovely little Cypress Inn, a landmark since 1929 with a brilliant white facade and Spanish-tiled roof, is built around a garden courtyard. A fruit basket, sherry, and expanded Continental breakfast are complimentary. A gracious, intimate cocktail lounge is surrounded by posters of Doris Day, one of the owners. Each individually beautifully furnished room has all contemporary amenities, and double, queen, or king bed.

#215–spacious, gas fireplace, private distant
   ocean-view veranda, king bed.

Deetjen's Big Sur Inn   *(831)667-2377*
30 mi. S at 48865 Highway 1 - Big Sur 93920
deetjens.com

20 units   *Moderate-Expensive*
A historic complex of redwood cottages (on the National Historic Register) has settled into luxuriant natural forests and gardens in a little canyon by the highway. Trails lead nearby to mountains and the sea. The dining room offers creative cuisine amid stylish rusticity that still epitomizes the artistic spirit of Big Sur in the 1960s. Each room is truly rustic, funky, and unique, the way they were built many years ago; and is simply furnished with heat provided by wood fireplaces, woodburning stoves and electric heaters. Hand-hewn doors have no keys and can be locked from the inside only. There are no phones, TVs, nor soundproofing between rooms. Each simply furnished room has a shared or private bathroom and a double or queen bed.

Dolphin Inn   *(831)624-5356*
downtown at San Carlos St. & 4th Av. (Box 1900) - 93921
innsbythesea.com
27 units   *(800)433-4732*   *Expensive-Very Expensive*
An outdoor pool is a feature of this contemporary motel. Complimentary Continental breakfast is brought to your door. Each well-furnished room has a refrigerator and all amenities, plus two doubles or a king bed. Some also have a gas fireplace.
    #15–gas fireplace, in-bath whirlpool tub, king bed.

★ **Highlands Inn - Park Hyatt Carmel**   *(831)620-1234*
5 mi. S (on Highway 1) at 120 Highlands Dr. - 93923
highlands-inn.com
143 units   *(800)682-4811*   *Very Expensive*
One of the world's best coastal panoramas is the highlight of this delightfully updated resort hotel high above the Big Sur coast. Lush grounds sequester a large pool, three whirlpools, exercise room, and bicycles. All are complimentary. Other facilities include a resort shop, and newly upgraded restaurants (see listing) where the sophisticated elegance of the dining room and the panoramic seascape view blend seamlessly. Nearby, a plush firelit lounge shares the romantic view. Each spacious unit offers all luxurious contemporary furnishings, a private deck, and two doubles or a king bed. Most also have a kitchenette, spacious whirlpool bath, a woodburning fireplace, and an unforgettable seascape view (with binoculars provided).
    #422,#439,#208,#209–spacious, vaulted ceiling, woodburning
       fireplace, kitchenette, large private sea-view balcony, raised
       in-bedroom two-person whirlpool, floor/ceiling windows with
       awesome coastal view from king bed.

Horizon Inn/Ocean View Lodge   *(831)624-5327*
downtown at Junipero St. & 3rd Av. (Box 1693) - 93921
horizoninncarmel.com

29 units   *(800)350-7723*   *Expensive-Very Expensive*
Fine distant ocean views are a feature of this motel-and-cottage complex. A breakfast basket (expanded Continental) delivered to the room and use of an outdoor whirlpool are complimentary. Each well-furnished room in the recently upgraded Horizon Inn has extra amenities plus a refrigerator and microwave, and doubles, a queen or king bed. Some rooms have a gas fireplace, in-bath oversized whirlpool tub and/or ocean view.

"Horizon Inn Jacuzzi Suites" (3 of these)–spacious, gas fireplace, in-bath oversized whirlpool tub, private balcony with distant ocean view, king bed.

★ **La Playa Hotel**   *(831)624-6476*
downtown at Camino Real and 8th Av. (Box 900) - 93921
laplayahotel.com
80 units   *(800)582-8900*   *Expensive-Very Expensive*
The La Playa Hotel is Carmel's Grande Dame hideaway. The four-story landmark with its distinctive Mediterranean style was built in 1904 on the edge of downtown near the beach. It is now surrounded by impeccably landscaped grounds with a pool, an assortment of (fee) spa services, lounge and restaurant (see listing) where fresh innovative California cuisine is served in a plush dining room and on a heated open terrace with a spectacular view of the ocean and gardens. Each room is beautifully furnished and has twins, doubles, queen or king bed. Some have an ocean view. Five storybook cottages with kitchens and one to three bedrooms are also available.

#441–full ocean view beyond lawn, king bed.
#170,#172–gas fireplace, near the pool, king bed.

Lobos Lodge   *(831)624-3874*
downtown at Ocean Av. & Monte Verde St. (Box L1) - 93921
loboslodge.com
30 units   *Expensive*
Several buildings comprise this small modern motor inn amid colorful gardens on the main street a few blocks up from the beach. A complimentary Continental breakfast is served to your room. Each attractively furnished room has a gas fireplace, refrigerator, a private deck, and twins, queen or king bed.

#37–spacious, private walled balcony, ocean view, king bed.
#25–private walled balcony, partial ocean view, king bed.

★ **The Lodge at Pebble Beach**   *(831)647-7500*
2 mi. NW at 1700 Seventeen-Mile Dr. - Pebble Beach 93953
pebblebeach.com
161 units   *(800)654-9300*   *Very Expensive*
The world famous Lodge at Pebble Beach has an incomparable oceanfront location and a remarkable variety of resort amenities.

In addition to the beach, there is a pool, whirlpool and sauna; the legendary 18-hole (fee) golf course (see listing); a large state-of-the-art tennis complex; complete health and fitness center; horseback riding (see listing) and bicycling; nature trails; plus a promenade of resort shops and fine restaurants (see listing). Each spacious room is luxuriously furnished and has a private balcony, stocked honor bar/refrigerator, gas fireplace, and a king bed. Some have a superb ocean view.

"Spa Suite" (5 of these)–woodburning fireplace,
  private enclosed patio with a large whirlpool.
★ **Mission Ranch**   *(831)624-6436*
1 mi. S at 26270 Dolores St. - 93923
missionranchcarmel.com
31 units   *(800)538-8221*   *Expensive-Very Expensive*
Mission Ranch is Carmel's great in-town resort. A historic 1850s farmhouse is the heart of a collection of charming cottages and lodge buildings on flowery grounds. Beyond, a meadow extends to the spectacular coastline at the mouth of Carmel River. Expanded Continental breakfast is complimentary. Amenities include six (fee) tennis courts, an exercise room, piano bar, and restaurant (see listing) offering fine contemporary American classics amid elegant rusticity. Each beautifully furnished unit has all contemporary conveniences and a queen or king bed. Most have a fireplace and a large in-bath whirlpool tub. Many have an ocean view.

"Meadowview triplex" (9 of these)–gas fireplace, in-bath
  two-person whirlpool tub, private porch with distant
  ocean view, king bed.
Pine Inn   *(831)624-3851*
downtown on Ocean Av. at Lincoln St. (Box 250) - 93921
pine-inn.com
49 units   *(800)228-3851*   *Expensive-Very Expensive*
Carmel's main street landmark is a three-story inn (circa 1889) surrounded by gardens. Plush Victorian furnishings distinguish common areas, while a dramatic greenhouse atrium houses a link in a chain of upscale Italian restaurants and a lounge. Breakfast is complimentary during the week. Rooms and suites are well furnished and have two queens or a king bed.

#64–gas fireplace, refrigerator, king bed.
★ **Post Ranch Inn**   *(831)667-2200*
27 mi. S on Highway 1 (Box 219) - Big Sur 93920
postranchinn.com
30 units   *(800)527-2200*   *Very Expensive*
Post Ranch Inn is the quintessential Big Sur luxury retreat. The grandeur of a site high above a rugged coast is perfectly matched by tranquil post-modern architecture and artistic decor

seamlessly blended into luxuriant natural surroundings. A glass of wine upon arrival, bountiful gourmet breakfast buffet, and stocked wet bar/refrigerator (including a half-bottle of wine) are complimentary. Amenities include two pools (both are "infinity" pools that seem rimless and overlook a breathtaking coastline), whirlpool, exercise room, hiking trails to memorable "secret spots," (fee) full-service spa treatments (like outdoor massage from a table with an eagle's-eye view of the coastline far below), a quality mercantile shop and restaurant (see listing) where gourmet New California cuisine is as sophisticated as the artful dining room and as appealing as the panoramic coastal view. Each uniquely decorated room is luxuriously furnished, including a private view deck, woodburning fireplace and large whirlpool bath, and a king bed.

"Ocean" (5 of these)–single structure, two-sided fireplace, ocean views from whirlpool, window seat, terrace and king bed.

"Coast" (10 of these)–circular duplex with ocean view from the whirlpool, terrace, or king bed.

★ **Quail Lodge Resort & Golf Club**   *(831)624-2888*
4 mi. SE via Carmel Valley Rd. at 8205 Valley Greens Dr. - 93923
quaillodge.com
97 units   *(888)828-8787*   *Very Expensive*
Quail Lodge opened in 1967 as the premier resort in Carmel Valley. Manicured grounds provide a serene setting for a championship (fee) 18-hole golf course and all related facilities, four tennis courts, and a full-service spa with a wide range of treatments, plus fitness room, hiking trails, putting green, two pools, whirlpool, resort shop and **The Covey** (D only–Very Expensive) where contemporary California dishes are served in an elegant dining room overlooking a scenic pond. Each beautifully furnished unit has a private deck overlooking the small lake, golf course or gardens, stocked refrigerator/honor bar, plus extra amenities, and two queens or a king bed.

"Executive Villa"–gas fireplace, large patio with two-person whirlpool, two queens or a king bed.

★ **Tickle Pink Inn**   *(831)624-1244*
5 mi. S on Highway 1 at 155 Highlands Dr. - 93923
ticklepink.com
35 units   *(800)635-4774*   *Very Expensive*
Spell-binding coastline views distinguish this gracious contemporary motel high above the ocean. Pine-studded grounds shade a view-terrace whirlpool. An expanded, fresh-baked Continental breakfast, afternoon wine and cheese, and binoculars-on-request are complimentary. The beautifully furnished units have a private view balcony, extra amenities, a small refrigerator and a king bed.

Some also have a woodburning fireplace and large in-room whirlpool tub.

> #30 through #35 (6 of these)–sitting area with wood-burning fireplace, two-person in-room whirlpool that shares grand ocean view with large private balcony and king bed.
>
> #21,#20–top floor, spacious, woodburning fireplace, large balcony, private seascape view.

★ **Ventana Inn & Spa**   *(831)667-2331*
27 mi. S on Highway 1 - Big Sur 93920
ventanainn.com
62 units   *(800)628-6500*   *Very Expensive*
Ventana is the progenitor of posh post-modern architecture and decor in California lodgings. The enchanting country inn for adults blends seamlessly into mountain meadows high above the Big Sur coast. Amenities include paved walking paths and nature trails through woodlands to coastal overlooks, two large pools (one is clothing-optional), serene Japanese-style hot baths open to moonlight, sauna, exercise room, new full-service (fee) spa and boutique, art gallery, gift shop, and a restaurant (see listing). The dining room is informally elegant, while the expansive garden terrace offers a stunning panoramic seascape. Gourmet Continental breakfast and the manager's afternoon wine and appetizers reception are complimentary. Adjoining is the **Store at Ventana** featuring arts, crafts, books, music and resort wear. Each room is a luxuriously furnished study in elegant rusticity. Many have a private deck (some with a distant ocean view), fireplace, and two-person whirlpool, plus a queen or king bed.

> #3,#4–extra-large, woodburning fireplace, two-person whirlpool on large private ocean-view deck, separate tub and shower with glass wall ocean view, king bed.
>
> #54,#55,#56–spacious, woodburning fireplace, two-person whirlpool on large private ocean-view deck, king bed.

Wayside Inn   *(831)624-5336*
downtown at Mission St. & 7th Av. (Box 1900) - 93921
innsbythesea.com
22 units   *(800)433-4732*   *Expensive-Very Expensive*
Colonial Williamsburg decor contributes to the warm appeal of this contemporary motel in the pines. Continental breakfast and cookies and coffee in the afternoon are complimentary. Each well-furnished room has all conveniences plus a refrigerator and two doubles, a queen or king bed. Some have a kitchen, gas fireplace, or in-bath whirlpool tub.

> #21,#23–private deck, in-room two-person whirlpool, gas fireplace, king bed.

Eureka

Eureka is the keystone of the Redwood Coast. Most of the world's tallest trees are within an hour's drive. This prime site on Humboldt Bay, sheltered along one of the Pacific Coast's largest natural harbors, is only two miles from the open ocean beyond a long narrow sandspit.

Shortly before the Civil War, Eureka began to develop as a seaport. Lumbering, farming, fishing and shipbuilding soon followed. Eureka was a rough and tumble boom town from the "Gay 90s" (1890s, that is) through the "Roaring 20s" when it was linked to the rest of the nation by both a railroad and a major highway. The Great Depression ended the boom times of the largest and wealthiest coastal port north of San Francisco. But, there was no "bust" because of its key location.

Eureka's proud heritage is being revitalized, and the town is embracing its ultimate destiny as a major recreation and leisure destination catering to travelers. Hundreds of ornate Victorian commercial buildings and houses have been skillfully restored and embellished with verdant landscapes in and around Old Town. In a historic district with the look and feel of a city several times as large, galleries, studios and shops feature regional fine arts and crafts, antiques and keepsakes. Numerous restaurants (including some of gourmet stature) are close to the revitalized waterfront as are several charming bed-and-breakfasts and a landmark hotel. One of the West's great town parks–complete with giant sequoias–is nearby. Just beyond, ocean beaches, clear rivers, rugged mountains, and majestic redwood forests beckon.

Eureka

WEATHER PROFILE

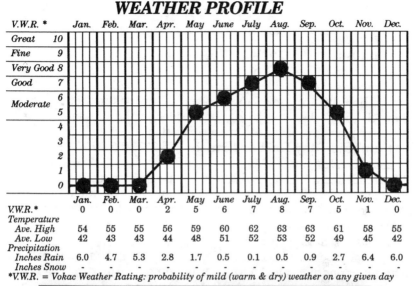

V.W.R. *		Jan.	Feb.	Mar.	Apr.	May	June	July	Aug.	Sep.	Oct.	Nov.	Dec.
Great	10												
Fine	9												
Very Good	8												
Good	7												
Moderate	6												
	5												
	4												
	3												
	2												
	1												
	0												

	Jan.	Feb.	Mar.	Apr.	May	June	July	Aug.	Sep.	Oct.	Nov.	Dec.
V.W.R.*	0	0	0	2	5	6	7	8	7	5	1	0
Temperature												
Ave. High	54	55	55	56	59	60	62	63	63	61	58	55
Ave. Low	42	43	43	44	48	51	52	53	52	49	45	42
Precipitation												
Inches Rain	6.0	4.7	5.3	2.8	1.7	0.5	0.1	0.5	0.9	2.7	6.4	6.0
Inches Snow	-	-	-	-	-	-	-	-	-	-	-	-

*V.W.R. = Vokac Weather Rating: probability of mild (warm & dry) weather on any given day

BASIC INFORMATION

Population: 26,128
Elevation: 44 feet
Location: 270 miles Northwest of San Francisco
Airport (regularly scheduled flights): McKinleyville - 15 miles

The Greater Eureka Chamber of Commerce   (707)442-3738
   2 mi. S at 2112 Broadway - 95501   (800)356-6381
   eurekachamber.com
Humboldt County Convention & Visitors Bureau   (707)443-5097
   just E at 1034 Second St. - 95501   (800)346-3482
   www.redwoodvisitor.org

ATTRACTIONS

Boat Rides
Hum-Boats *(707)443-5157*
downtown at foot of F St.
humboats.com
From here you can take a water-taxi to any destination on the bay. Sailboat charters, tours, boat rides, sailing lessons, boat rentals, kayaks and canoes are also available.
Humboldt Bay Harbor Cruise *(707)445-1910*
downtown at foot of C St.
The Madaket, a 1910 ferry, is the oldest passenger-carrying vessel in operation in the United States. A 75-minute narrated tour of the colorful harbor can be enjoyed from March to October.
★ Carson Mansion
downtown at Second & M Sts.
This monumental tribute to "gingerbread" architecture may be the most photographed Victorian building in America. It's not open to the public, but the well-kept building and grounds still reflect the full grandeur of the era of lumber barons.
Food Specialties
Mr. Fish Seafoods *(707)443-2661* *(800)736-5921*
2 mi. SW at 2740 Broadway
King and silver salmon and other regional seafoods are smoked on the premises. Alder-smoked salmon fillet in a foil pouch is a specialty. In the little highway-fronting shop, delicious gourmet canned seafoods are also displayed and sold for picnics, and shipment as gifts. Closed Sun.
Fort Humboldt State Historic Park *(707)445-6567*
3 mi. SW via US 101 at Highland Av.
A Civil War era white clapboard hospital serves as the visitor center for Fort Humboldt circa 1853-1866. The surgeon's two-story frame home is nearby on a blufftop site overlooking the bay. U.S. Grant spent some lonely months here as a captain in 1854. Nearby, a young forest shades many massive pieces of historic logging equipment and buildings with exhibits describing redwood cutting operations in the area.
★ Humboldt Bay
downtown along Waterfront Dr.
Now that California's second largest natural deep-water harbor is no longer dominated by heavy, polluting industries, its pleasures are becoming more accessible to everyone. Waterfront drives offer great nautical views and access to public fishing piers and parks, picnic areas and wildlife viewing sites. Nearby, Woodley Island has an egret rookery in cypress trees, a full-service marina, and "The Fisherman," a twenty-five-foot copper

sculpture dedicated to those who lost their lives at sea.

Humboldt State University   *(707)826-4402*
8 mi. N via US 101 - Arcata
humboldt.edu

Humboldt State University is one of the schools that comprise the California State University system. About 7,000 students use the handsome 160-acre campus crowning a hill overlooking Humboldt Bay. Features include the largest library in California north of San Francisco, a marine laboratory and fish hatchery, art exhibits, live theater, concerts, and lectures open to the public.

★ **Old Town**
downtown around Second & H Sts.

Just up from the Humboldt Bay waterfront is a mile-long enclave of Victorian commercial structures that is one of the most extensive and unspoiled in the West. A highlight among many public art displays is **Romano Gabriel Sculpture Garden** at 315 Second St. The whimsical wooden garden is a tribute to the late folk artist. Art galleries, studios, craft shops, collectibles stores and other places featuring regional specialties are beginning to fill in the substantial area that had once been the heart of town and the most dynamic business district in Redwood Country. Scruffy edges and absence of upscale chain stores is genuinely appealing to people who can enjoy the difference between this unaffected downtown and the more cosmetic upscale settings that are now part of more famous (but no more impressive) historic urban enclaves.

★ **Patrick's Point State Park**   *(707)677-3570*
28 mi. N via US 101 at 4150 Patrick's Point Dr.

Patrick's Point State Park is one of the West's finest recreation sites. Two miles of spectacular beaches are backed by a dramatic peninsula shrouded in luxuriant pines. Numerous trails including a two-mile-long rim trail that extends above the beach around the entire peninsula, a visitor center, three full-service campgrounds, plus some unusual overnight facilities like a cabin and yurt, are extremely popular in summer. Semi-precious agates are the feature of an appropriately named beach and can be found here along with driftwood of all kinds. Picnic sites are abundant and often sited to maximize the luxuriant forest or grand seascapes.

★ **Prairie Creek Redwoods State Park**   *(707)464-6101*
52 mi. N on US 101

Here is the quintessential place to experience the solemn grandeur of a primeval redwood forest. More than seventy miles of hiking and (designated) biking trails meander through luxuriant woodlands punctuated by giant trees towering more than 300 feet high. Clear fern-shrouded streams tumble out of gentle hills to wild and scenic beaches. Idyllic camping and picnic sites include some near the surf. Beachcombers and hikers frequently get intimate views of deceptively mild-mannered herds of magnificent Roosevelt Elk. There is a visitor center and store.

★ **Redwood National Park**   *(707)464-6101*
   47 mi. N on US 101
The world's tallest tree, a redwood towering more than 367 feet, is sequestered deep within a park that (since 1968) has grown to encompass more than 150 square miles. In addition to dense forests of old-growth (virgin) redwoods, there are clear rivers and streams extending to a rugged coastline with delightfully remote sandy beaches. More than 150 miles of leisure and hiking trails beckon. Developed or primitive campgrounds are well sited and scenic. Very cold water and heavy undertows preclude ocean swimming and surfing, but fresh and saltwater fishing, horseback riding and whale watching are popular. The Redwood Information Center one mile south of Orick has maps, books and permits.

Samoa Dunes State Recreation Area   *(707)825-2300*
   5 mi. W via CA 255
Beachcombing, hiking, surf fishing and (for the really rugged) surfing are enjoyed in a park distinguished by an abundance of low coastal sand dunes.

★ **Sequoia Park & Zoo**   *(707)442-6552*
   3 mi. SE at W St. & Glatt St.
One of America's best town parks is tucked away, but well worth finding. Like all great town parks, there is a unique stellar attraction. In this urban jewel, it is a grove of primeval redwood giants with a paved mile-long scenic loop that is as satisfying as any access to a natural wonder can be. Numerous hiking trails lead to a pond and lush fern canyons deep in the preserve. Features include an attractively landscaped zoo, (summer) petting zoo and aviary. The zoo is small but well organized, with distinctive displays of popular and unusual animals. Nearby are colorful formal gardens, picnic areas and playgrounds.

★ **Six Rivers National Forest**   *(707)442-1721*
   44 mi. E via US 101 on CA 299
   http://www.r5.fs.fed.us/sixrivers
Six wild and scenic rivers run through a million-plus acres of luxuriant national forest lands that also feature several designated wilderness and botanical areas. Rafting, kayaking and fishing for salmon and steelhead star. Hundreds of miles of dirt roads and hiking trails provide access to spectacular whitewater (and some notable swimming holes), plus camping, hunting, biking and nature study opportunities. The Supervisor's Office is at 1330 Bayshore Way.

★ **Trinidad** *(707)677-0223*
22 mi. N via US 101 - Trinidad
trinidadcalif.com
If you are here on a calm sunny day, you'll wonder why this village isn't many times as large. Vacant lots are still numerous in the tiny blufftop hamlet surrounded by lovely parks and forests that extend on two sides to a spectacular seamount and shoreline with sandy beaches ideal for hiking. **Memorial Lighthouse** park is the local landmark and a great spot for photographers, strollers and whale-watchers (March through May). Nearby, **Katy's Smokehouse** ((707)677-0151) features smoked and canned salmon and other seafoods. Below, a tiny sheltered harbor offers excursion and sportfishing boats, while the **Seascape Restaurant** ((707)677-3762) has served seafood at the pier for half a century. **Larrupin Cafe** ((707)677-0230) four miles north of the village features barbecued crabs and oysters in season in a landmark dinner house with a fine view and a handsome deck and lounge. Nearby, **The Lost Whale** (see listing), the region's finest lodging, offers real comfort and memorable seascapes.

RESTAURANTS

Abruzzi *(707)826-2345*
8 mi. N at 791 Eighth St. - Arcata
abruzzicatering.com
D only.   *Moderate*
Housemade pastas and robust sauces contribute to the appeal of a wide variety of Southern Italian dishes. The large trattoria with an exposition kitchen is in a historic building on Arcata Plaza.

★ **Avalon** *(707)445-0500*
downtown at Third & G St.
avaloneureka.com
L-D. Closed Mon.   *Expensive*
Avalon, opened in 2000, is already a great dining destination. Fresh local ingredients coupled with culinary talent assure memorable flavors and presentations–from heirloom tomato soup through farmer's market baby organic lettuce salad to cedar-planked wild salmon and desserts like frozen praline mousse. A simply stylish expansive dining room with a handsome little backbar supports each cosmopolitan adventure.

★ **Bon Boniere** *(707)268-0122*
downtown at 215 F St.
L-D.   *Moderate*
More than two dozen ice creams including seasonal treats like egg nog and sorbets (try the pear) star in this spiffy reconstruction of a classy old-time ice cream parlor. Belly-up to the marble-topped

bar to place your order, then dine in the nostalgic parlor or out front with an Old Town view. Light meals are also offered.

Cafe Marina   *(707)443-2233*
1 mi. N on Startare Dr.
B-L-D.   *Moderate*
Generous portions of American standards are served in dining rooms and a bar with intimate views of the inner harbor and Old Town from Woodley Island. There is also a large umbrella-shaded deck sharing the fine waterfront view.

Cafe Waterfront   *(707)443-9190*
downtown at 102 F St.
B-L-D.   *Moderate*
Steamed clams, clam fritters and oyster burgers are among seafood dishes featured in a nifty old-timey corner bar and grill with a picture-window view of boats in the nearby bay.

Carl's Fine Omelettes   *(707)443-5342*
1 mi. SW at 1023 Broadway (US 101)
B-L. Closed Mon.   *Moderate*
This classic Western diner is *the* place to go for omelets in Eureka, along with biscuits and gravy and other comfort foods, served at a counter or tables in a bright little corner room.

★ **Carter House**   *(707)444-8062*
just E at 301 L St.
carterhouse.com
D only.   *Very Expensive*
Restaurant 301 is the Northern Redwood Coast's premier landmark for gourmet dining. Seasonally fresh organic herbs, vegetables, fruits, and edible flowers from their own extensive gardens complement fresh seafood including local kumamoto oysters, wild salmon and other specialties. All are prepared with skill and verve into innovative cuisine that celebrates the memorable flavors and textures of the Northwest. Elegant tables set with full linen, candles, flowers and crystal overlook the harbor and nostalgic nearby buildings.

★ **Eureka Inn**   *(707)442-6441*
downtown at 518 Seventh St.
eurekainn.com
B-L-D.   *Moderate-Expensive*
In the historic hotel's **Rib Room** (D only–Expensive), prime rib and traditional Continental dishes are served in a posh firelit dining room enhanced by cozy leather banquettes and polished wood tones. The **Bristol Rose Cafe** (B-L–Moderate) offers contemporary American fare and comfortable booths in a stylish coffee shop with snazzy chandeliers, or alfresco on a courtyard patio. The **Palm Lounge** features occasional live entertainment.

★ **Folie Douce**   *(707)822-1042*
8 mi. N at 1551 G St. - Arcata
holyfolie.com
D only. Closed Sun.-Mon.   *Expensive*
A tasty assortment of wood-fired brick oven pizzas is featured along with creative American dishes like grilled chicken with wild mushrooms in merlot sauce, or scallops in a macadamia nut crust on a menu that changes seasonally. Linen contributes to the sophisticated ambiance of this deservedly popular little trattoria.

Gabriel's   *(707)445-0100*
downtown at 216 E St.
L-D. Closed Sun.   *Moderate*
A historic pizza parlor has been transformed into an Italian restaurant where calzones and whole wheat crust pizza are offered along with a range of updated Italian entrees. Assorted desserts are made here. Diners have a choice of casual upstairs dining or a downstairs lounge.

Gill's by the Bay   *(707)442-2554*
8 mi. SW at 77 Halibut - King Salmon
B-L.   *Moderate*
At the end of the road in raffish little King Salmon is a nifty harborfront restaurant. Hearty American breakfasts include regional treats like bay shrimp omelets and distinctive scrambles as well as humongous buttermilk biscuits. Later, try a griddled sole fillet or a clam cutlet with a bayfront view from the shaped-up cafe or umbrella-shaded terrace.

★ **Hurricane Kate's**   *(707)444-1405*
downtown at 511 Second St.
hurricanekate.com
L-D. Closed Sun.-Mon.   *Expensive*
Hurricane Kate's fusion cuisine is showcased in tapas-style dishes that skillfully blend fresh seasonal regional produce with culinary flourishes from around the world. Designer pizzas from a wood-fired oven (itself an art statement) are popular, along with all sorts of appetizers. Pecan-crusted pork tenderloin with cherry compote typifies entrees. Desserts are all housemade and delicious. Minimalist table settings and colorful avant-garde folk art paintings contribute to the easy sophistication.

Los Bagels   *(707)442-8525*
downtown at 403 Second St.
losbagels.com
B-L. Closed Tues.   *Moderate*
All kinds of bagels plus assorted morning delights like sticky buns are served in a casual corner shop with a few tables overlooking a small plaza in the heart of Old Town.

Lost Coast Brewery   *(707)445-4480*
downtown at 617 Fourth St.
lostcoast.com
L-D.   *Moderate*
A wide variety of contemporary beer-battered pub grub can be
enjoyed with a full range of their popular tap beers, plus draft
root beer. The high-ceilinged hangout in a historic building
usually attracts a boisterous younger crowd.

★ **Ramone's Bakery & Cafe**   *(707)445-2923*
downtown at 209 E St.
ramonesbakery.com
B-L.   *Moderate*
The best bakery in town offers assorted morning delights like
pecan sticky buns and oatmeal scones with coffees (brewed from
their on-premises roastery) that can be enjoyed in a relaxed coffee
house that is the original among several area outlets.

★ **Rolf's Park Cafe & Motel**   *(707)488-3841*
42 mi. N on US 101 - Orick
B-L-D. Call for winter hours.   *Moderate*
Rolf's continues a long run as a culinary beacon of the Redwood
Coast. Rolf's German country omelet, served family-style, is one
of the truly legendary breakfasts of the West. This hearty
monster-of-a-meal delights all who have walked among some of
the world's tallest trees nearby. Dinner is special, too, featuring
buffalo, elk and wild boar with a German accent. The cheerful
wood-trimmed roadside restaurant complements the country
cuisine, and there is a sunny deck overlooking redwoods and wild
elk. Their motel with cozy, simply furnished rooms adjoins.

Roy's   *(707)442-4574*
downtown at 218 D St.
L-D. Closed Sun.-Mon.   *Expensive*
Traditional Italian dishes have been the mainstay of this dining
room/bar/deli for more than a half century. Crisp linens
contribute to the old-fashioned clubby decor in the dining room,
and there is a bar and well-stocked Italian deli/market.

★ **Samoa Cookhouse**   *(707)442-1659*
3 mi. N across the Samoa Bridge on Samoa Rd. - Samoa
humboldtdining.com/cookhouse
B-L-D.   *Low*
Samoa Cookhouse (circa 1893) is the last lumber-camp-style
cookhouse in operation in North America. Meals have been served
here continuously for well over a century. Visitors enjoying
abundant family-style traditional American fare can get some of
the feel of the days when this vast multiroom cookhouse was
where mill workers ate. A museum and gift shop are also here.

★ **The Sea Grill**   *(707)443-7187*
  downtown at 316 E St.
  L-D. No L Sat. & Mon. Closed Sun.   *Moderate*
Contemporary California cuisine with an emphasis on fresh
seafood is showcased in dishes that are carefully sautéed, grilled,
broiled, poached, beer-battered, or fried and complemented by
appropriate sauces. Properly aged, charbroiled steaks and prime
rib are also featured. Tables set with bouquets of fresh flowers
contribute to the easy sophistication of casually elegant dining
rooms often full of happy natives and guests.

Six Rivers Brewing Company   *(707)268-3893*
  downtown at 325 Second St.
  L-D.   *Moderate*
Since early 2001, Six Rivers Brewing Company has featured an
expansive menu of contemporary pub grub as support for their
full range of beers and ales. The big multilevel beer hall offers a
choice of comfortable settings overlooking the bar or Old Town.

LODGINGS

Accommodations are numerous. Several of the best are in historic
buildings. US 101 west and east of downtown is sprinkled with
modern motels including some bargains. High season is summer.
Rates are often reduced 20% or more at other times.

Abigail's - An Elegant Victorian Mansion   *(707)444-3144*
  1 mi. S at 1406 C St. - 95501
  4 units   *Expensive*
One of the most rococo landmark homes in town (circa 1888) now
serves as an unabashedly old-fashioned inn. Ornate Victorian
flourishes and bric-a-brac are everywhere. Continental breakfast
is complimentary, as are bicycles and a sauna. Each room teems
with nostalgia. Some rooms share a bath, and all have a queen
bed.

Bayshore Inn - Best Western   *(707)268-8005*
  3 mi. SW (on US 101) at 3500 Broadway - 95501
  bayshoreinn.com
  82 units   *(888)268-8005*   *Expensive*
One of the area's nicest contemporary motels has an indoor/
outdoor pool, whirlpool, sauna; exercise room, game room, and a
coffee shop on site. The town's largest mall adjoins. Full breakfast
is complimentary. Each spacious room is well furnished, and also
has a refrigerator, microwave, and two queens or a king bed.
  #307,#207–peek-a-boo bay view, in-room two-
    person whirlpool, gas fireplace, king bed.

Bayview Motel   *(707)442-1673*
  2 mi. S (off US 101) at 2844 Fairfield St. - 95501

bayviewmotel.com
17 units   *(866)725-6813*   *Moderate-Expensive*
A bay view is a feature of this recently built small motel on a bluff
rim. Each unit is spacious, well furnished, including a dual
shower and wet bar/refrigerator, and has queens or a king bed.
   "Romantic Getaway Room" (2 of these)–gas
   fireplace, in-room two-person whirlpool, king bed.
★ **Carter House**   *(707)444-8062*
   just E at 301 L St. - 95501
   carterhouse.com
   32 units   *(800)404-1390*   *Expensive-Very Expensive*
The Carter House, an enclave of four charming tributes to
Victoriana, is Eureka's premier lodging. Skillfully crafted interiors
and gracious furnishings beautifully reflect period and contemporary good taste. So do flowery surrounding landscapes, and the
large prolific kitchen garden. Old Town and the bayfront are
within an easy stroll. The sophisticated gourmet restaurant (see
listing) is among the best in Northern California. Full gourmet
breakfast is well worth the nominal fee, while afternoon wine and
appetizers and evening cookies and tea are complimentary. Each
romantic room is luxuriously furnished and is individually
decorated with original local artwork, contemporary and extra
amenities, and has a private bath and a queen or king bed.
   "Carter Cottage" ("the Love Shack")–spacious, state-of-the-
   art demo kitchen, living room, two gas fireplaces, large
   marble whirlpool, big private bayview deck, king bed.
   "Hotel Carter Suites" (#301-#304)–sitting room, marina
   or Victorian view, gas fireplace, raised in-room two-
   person whirlpool, queen bed.
   Carter House #508, #506–spacious, gas fireplace,
   loveseat/corner alcove view of Carson Mansion,
   two-person whirlpool tub, ornate queen bed.
   Bell Cottage #601,#603–gas fireplace, marble
   whirlpool tub for two, queen bed.
★ **The Cornelius Daly Inn**   *(707)445-3638*
   just S at 1125 H St. - 95501
   dalyinn.com
   5 units   *(800)321-9656*   *Moderate-Expensive*
A large whitewashed Colonial revival mansion in a luxuriant
garden with enormous rhododendron and azalea bushes is one of
the region's most impressive bed-and-breakfasts. The 1905
building has been lovingly restored. Full gourmet breakfast and
afternoon wine and appetizers are complimentary. Each beautifully furnished room is individualized with some fine turn-of-the-
century antiques. Most have a private bath and a queen bed.

"Garden View Suite"–spacious, romantic,
sitting room, private bath, queen bed.
"Annie Murphy's Room"–woodburning fireplace, overlooks
garden, shared bath (private if inn not full), queen bed.

★ **Eureka Inn**   *(707)442-6441*
downtown at 518 Seventh St. - 95501
eurekainn.com
99 units   *(800)862-4906*   *Expensive*
Eureka's landmark lodging since 1922 is being skillfully retained
as an urbane hotel with an understated Continental flair. The
four-story complex has an outdoor pool, whirlpool, sauna, stylish
restaurants and entertainment lounge (see listing), and a baronial
half-timbered lobby worthy of an English manor house. Each
room is attractively furnished with contemporary decor and all
conveniences including a queen or king bed.
Honeymoon Suite–spacious, refr./wet bar, gas fireplace,
extra-large in-bath whirlpool in view of king bed.

Halcyon Inn Bed & Breakfast   *(707)444-1310*
1 mi. S at 1420 C St. - 95501
halcyoninn.com
3 units   *(888)882-1310*   *Moderate-Expensive*
Dozens of rhododendron and camellia bushes surround this
handsome 1920s guest house that was recently lovingly
transformed into a bed-and-breakfast. Full breakfast, evening
truffles, and other treats are complimentary. Each room is
individually well furnished to reflect the spirit of a peaceful earlier
time, and has a private bath and queen bed.
"Rose Room"–original 1920 six-foot tub with shower.
"Camellia Room"–garden view, six-foot clawfoot tub with shower.

Humboldt Bay Inn - Best Western   *(707)442-2234*
just W (on US 101) at 232 W. Fifth St. - 95501
humboldtbayinn.com
115 units   *(800)521-6996*   *Expensive*
Old Town is a few blocks from this contemporary motel with a
pool, whirlpool and recreation area. Continental breakfast buffet
is complimentary. Each well-furnished room has doubles, queens,
or a king bed. Two rooms have an in-bath whirlpool.

★ **The Lost Whale Bed & Breakfast Inn**   *(707)677-3425*
26 mi. N at 3452 Patrick's Point Dr. - Trinidad 95570
lostwhaleinn.com
8 units   *(800)677-7859*   *Expensive*
California's most spectacular coastal lodging north of Eureka is
the Lost Whale. The contemporary Cape-Cod-style bed-and-
breakfast inn is surrounded by gardens and lawns on a bluff high
above the sea. A wooded trail leads to a secluded private beach

and cove. The ocean view from the hot tub is outstanding. Bountiful gourmet breakfast and afternoon beverages and appetizers are complimentary. Each room is beautifully furnished with private bath and queen bed. Two have private ocean-view balconies.

Motel 6   *(707)445-9631*
2 mi. SW (on US 101) at 1934 Broadway - 95501
motel6.com
98 units   *(800)466-8356*   Low
The thrifty chain's two-story local edition is a large modern motel. Simply furnished rooms have two double or two queen beds.

The Old Town Bed & Breakfast Inn   *(707)443-5235*
just E at 1521 Third St. - 95501
oldtownbnb.com
6 units   *(888)508-5235*   *Moderate-Expensive*
The original home (circa 1871) of the William Carson family (of Carson Mansion fame) has become a bed-and-breakfast. Full gourmet breakfast is complimentary. Each well-furnished room has many nostalgic artifacts, contemporary conveniences, a private bath, and double, queen, or king bed.
    "Lavender Room"–glass-front gas wood stove, sitting
    area, large clawfoot soaking tub, king bed.

Quality Inn Eureka   *(707)443-1601*
just E (on US 101) at 1209 Fourth St. - 95501
qualityinneureka.com
60 units   *(800)772-1622*   *Moderate*
This modern motel has a small pool, whirlpool, and sauna. Each room is nicely furnished including a refrigerator and has one or two queens or a king bed.
    "executive room" (15 of these)–in-bath
    whirlpool tub, two queens or king bed.

Red Lion Hotel   *(707)445-0844*
1 mi. E (on US 101) at 1929 Fourth St. - 95501
redlion.com
176 units   *(800)325-4000*   *Expensive*
Red Lion's three-story contemporary motor hotel has a small pool, whirlpool, exercise room, coffee shop, and lounge with periodic live entertainment. Each room is well furnished. Most have a small private patio or balcony, and a queen or king bed.

Town House Motel   *(707)443-4536*
just E at 933 Fourth St. - 95501
20 units   *(800)445-6888*   Low
The bayfront and Old Town are within strolling distance of this small main street motel. Each compact room is simply furnished including a queen or king bed. Some have a one- or two-person whirlpool.

Ferndale

Ferndale is California's classic Victorian village. Only four miles inland from the ocean on the broad flat Eel River delta, it is sheltered by mountains that rise abruptly to the south. In this idyllic setting between lush pasturelands and gentle highlands with a rare Sitka spruce forest, the village has successfully avoided both urban sprawl and contrived "old town" renewal.

Settlement began in 1852 with dairying and cattle farming. By 1890, Yankees, Danes, Swiss and Germans had established a dozen creameries. Substantial, sustained wealth led to the construction of many elaborate commercial buildings, churches, and elegant homes–called "butterfat palaces." Growth stopped nearly ninety years ago, when the main north-south highway and railroad were completed several miles to the east.

Now off the beaten path, Ferndale continues in gracious serenity thanks to the captivating locale, relatively mild climate, and prosperous bucolic heritage. The whole main street is on the National Historic Register. There are still no traffic lights, parking meters, buildings over three stories tall, or look-alike chain stores. Meticulously-tended ornate Victorian buildings accented by colorful floral landscapes display a wealth of regional fine arts and crafts and collectibles. Restaurants are relatively scarce but diverse, and delightfully old-fashioned. Lodgings, including several bed-and-breakfasts in splendid "butterfat palaces," celebrate the genteel heritage. Attractions like walks in a primeval forest or hikes on a nearby isolated beach reflect the unique tranquility of this special place.

WEATHER PROFILE

V.W.R. *		Jan.	Feb.	Mar.	Apr.	May	June	July	Aug.	Sep.	Oct.	Nov.	Dec.
Great	10												
Fine	9												
Very Good	8												
Good	7												
Moderate	6												
	5												
	4												
	3												
	2												
	1												
	0												

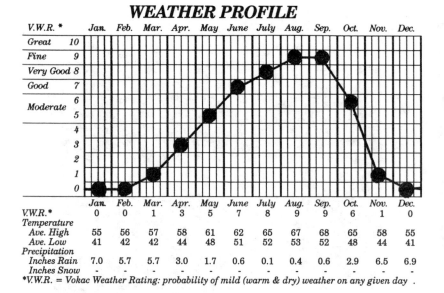

	Jan.	Feb.	Mar.	Apr.	May	June	July	Aug.	Sep.	Oct.	Nov.	Dec.
V.W.R.*	0	0	1	3	5	7	8	9	9	6	1	0
Temperature												
Ave. High	55	56	57	58	61	62	65	67	68	65	58	55
Ave. Low	41	42	42	44	48	51	52	53	52	48	44	41
Precipitation												
Inches Rain	7.0	5.7	5.7	3.0	1.7	0.6	0.1	0.4	0.6	2.9	6.5	6.9
Inches Snow	-	-	-	-	-	-	-	-	-	-	-	-

*V.W.R. = Vokac Weather Rating: probability of mild (warm & dry) weather on any given day .

BASIC INFORMATION

Population: 1,400
Elevation: 30 feet
Location: 257 miles Northwest of San Francisco
Airport (regularly scheduled flights): McKinleyville - 38 miles

Ferndale Chamber of Commerce   (707)786-4477
  Box 325 - 95536   (no office)
  victorianferndale.org/chamber

ATTRACTIONS

America's Tallest Living Christmas Tree   *(707)786-4477*
downtown on Main St.
At the south end of Main Street near a nifty town park is a 150-foot-tall spruce. Since 1934, volunteer firemen have decked it out for the holidays. On the first Sunday of December, the lighting festivities are memorable, and the tree sparkles through the month as a towering tribute to the Christmas spirit.

★ **Centerville Beach County Park**
4 mi. W on Centerville Rd.
Ferndale is surprisingly close to wild ocean beaches that are among California's least used. An unimproved dirt parking lot provides access to fine-sand beaches up to one-quarter mile wide and nine miles long, backed by dairy farms and the Eel River delta to the north. Dramatic bluffs to the south provide fine whale-watching sites in winter.

★ **Downtown**   *(707)786-4477*
along Main St.
The heart of the village is an unspoiled classic of nineteenth-century Americana. A wealth of colorful human-scaled buildings all celebrate the Victorian style that earned Main Street a designation on the National Register of Historic Places. Strollers and photographers are delighted by authentic architectural flourishes. Shoppers are rewarded with a wealth of fine regional arts, crafts, antiques and food specialties. Everyone loves the convenient public restroom and drinking fountain, and the complete absence of parking meters, stoplights, and chain stores.

Ferndale Cemetery
just S between Ocean Av. and Eugene St.
The town cemetery attracts visitors because of the unusual appearance of the graves and markers (many dating back to Victorian times) and a site that offers panoramic views of the village, bucolic valley and ocean to the west.

Ferndale Museum   *(707)786-4466*
downtown at 515 Shaw Av. (at 3rd St.)
Period room displays and farming and dairy equipment illustrate the rich Victorian heritage of the "Cream City" area. Exhibits are changed frequently. There is a gift shop. Closed Mon. and closed Tues. in winter.

Ferndale Repertory Theatre   *(707)786-5483*
downtown at 447 Main St.
Humboldt County's oldest community theater presents a wide variety of live productions year-round. The popular little showcase for the performing arts has featured both local and guest artists for more than thirty years.

Food Specialties
★ **Loleta Cheese Factory**   *(707)733-5470   (800)995-0453*
7 mi. NE at 252 Loleta Dr. - Loleta
Visitors are always welcome to sample their full line of delicious
award-winning Monterey jack and cheddar cheeses (including a
distinctive smoked salmon cheddar) in their tasting room. The
manufacturing of their quality natural cheeses can be observed
through large viewing windows. Picnic-sized (and larger) cheese
bricks are sold to go, along with selected beverages and gourmet
deli items, or enjoy them at tables in their lovely garden out back.
Gift packs can be shipped. Open 9-5 daily.
★ **Humboldt Redwoods State Park**   *(707)946-2409*
15 mi. SE on US 101
The largest remaining stand of ancient redwoods in the world
makes this the heart of California's entire 500-mile redwood belt.
The oldest known coastal redwood, dating back more than 2,000
years, is here. Many of the park's spectacular redwood groves are
accessible to all. The 33-mile renowned **Avenue of the Giants**
scenic two-lane roadway winds the entire length of the park.
Along the way, the **Founders Grove** and **Rockefeller Forest**
have self-guided nature trails to trees up to 363 feet tall. More
than seventy miles of hiking trails provide access to remote
groves, while horseback riders and mountain biking are enjoyed
along fire roads throughout the steep hills. Photogenic little Eel
River winds throughout the park and provides many swimming
and fishing holes. There are several developed and primitive
campgrounds. The **Visitor Center** (2 mi. S of Weott) does a fine
job of interpreting the redwood environment.
★ **Kinetic Sculpture Race Museum**   *(707)786-9259*
downtown at 393 Main St.
Don't miss the area's most unusual (and amazing) museum.
Ferndale is the southern terminus of the annual Kinetic
Sculpture Race. Many of the most delightfully ingenious and
colorful of the wild and wacky people-powered all-terrain floating
vehicles from years past are on display. Open daily.
Russ Park
just SE on Ocean Av. & Bluff St.
A rare Sitka spruce forest on a steep hillside, and three miles of
(appropriately) fern-lined hiking trails are highlights of
Ferndale's 110-acre wilderness park and bird sanctuary.
Scenic Drive
★ **The Lost Coast**
15 mi. SE along Mattiole Rd.
The "Lost Coast" is California's most isolated–and one of the
state's most spectacular–shorelines. A narrow paved highway

winds through scenic hill country and finally reaches the Pacific coast south of Cape Mendocino (the most westerly point in the coterminous United States). For the next several miles, the road follows the remarkably untamed shoreline. Bring a picnic and take a hike–the isolated splendor will linger long among your memories. Soon after the road turns inland, you'll cross the scenic little Mattole River, the northern boundary of California's longest roadless coastline. For more than thirty miles to the south, there are no roads along the Pacific Ocean. Most of the shoreline, forests and mountains are in the King Range National Conservation Area. Many miles of trails provide access to pristine recreation areas and a choice of developed or primitive campsites.

RESTAURANTS

Candy Stick Fountain & Grill   *(707)786-9373*
  downtown at 361 Main St.
  L-D.   *Moderate*
Hamburgers and other American grill fare and assorted ice cream/fountain treats are served in a cheerful cafe or to go.

★ **Curley's Grill**   *(707)786-9696*
  downtown at 400 Ocean Av.
  restaurant.com/curleysgrill
  L-D. Plus B Sat.-Sun.   *Expensive*
Curley's Grill is the best restaurant for miles around. Creative California cuisine is highlighted on a grazing menu. Here on the wild North Coast, regional dishes like grilled salmon topped with raspberry vinaigrette and steamed clams are especially satisfying. Local seasonal vegetables and fruits support dishes like a delightful tomato-basil signature soup, followed by decadent delights including carrot cake with lemon-zest frosting. The simply sophisticated cuisine is complemented by a large wood-trimmed dining room with some old-fashioned curtained tables and a friendly lounge.

★ **Ferndale Pizza Company**   *(707)786-4345*
  downtown at 607 Main St.
  L-D. Closed Mon.   *Moderate*
All sorts of hand-tossed, carefully prepared pizzas with lots of local cheeses are featured. They can be enjoyed with a salad bar, selected Italian dishes and sandwiches with homemade bread, plus assorted tap beers in several small rooms, or at picnic tables by the main street.

Hotel Ivanhoe   *(707)786-9000*
  downtown at 315 Main St.
  hotel-ivanhoe.com
  D only. Closed Mon.-Tues.   *Moderate*

67

Several kinds of steaks and pastas top traditional Southern Italian/American dishes served in generous portions. The split-level red-hued dining room is often filled with guests at fully linened candlelit tables.

Vern's Blue Room   *(707)786-9980*
   1 mi. N at Arlynda Corners on Market St.
   B-L. Closed Sun.-Mon.   *Moderate*
A historic four-corners gas station is now a deservedly popular little cafe featuring breakfasts and lunches. The specialty is "hoppel poppel" (a mixture of bacon, ham, scrambled eggs, home fries and onions), and Ingrid makes her own pies and biscotti. The shaped-up little dining area offers a choice of tables or the counter, all in view of the kitchen.

★ **Village Baking & Catering**   *(707)786-9440*
   downtown at 468 Main St.
   B-L. Closed Mon.-Tues. in winter.   *Moderate*
One of the nicest additions to Ferndale's culinary scene is the Village Baking & Catering. Classics and creative updates of an appealing range of Continental and American pastries and breads are made and displayed in a handsome little shop in the heart of town. You can design your own sandwiches with a wealth of ingredients coupled with their delicious breads, or enjoy their fine pastries and desserts with assorted beverages. A giant mural enhances their pleasant garden court and a few tables inside are backed by a whimsical "mooving" mural.

LODGINGS

Accommodations are relatively scarce, but delightfully distinctive, with no chain motels for many miles. High season is late spring into fall. Rates usually stay the same year-round.

Collingwood Inn Bed & Breakfast   *(707)786-9219*
   just N at 831 Main St. (Box 1134) - 95536
   collingwoodinn.com
   4 units   *(800)469-1632*   *Expensive*
Careful restoration to its Victorian origins has made Collingwood Inn a gracious bed-and-breakfast amid well-tended gardens. A gift shop and art gallery are also in the building. Full buffet breakfast and evening wine and cheese, desserts, and bedtime port and chocolates are complimentary. All rooms are well furnished in Victorian style, including antiques, and have a private bath and queen featherbed.
   "Renaissance Room"–private garden/town-
      view balcony, in-room clawfoot tub.
   "Hart Room"–in-room clawfoot tub for two,
      private garden view, sitting porch.

Fern Motel   *(707)786-5000*
downtown at 332 Ocean Av. (Box 121) - 95536
10 units   *Moderate*
The only motel in town is a modern winner in a tranquil location
just off main street. Each carefully maintained unit is attractively
furnished and fully equipped, including a refrigerator and
microwave, and has a queen bed.
    suite—full kitchen, living/dining areas.
★ **Gingerbread Mansion Inn**   *(707)786-4000*
downtown at 400 Berding St. (Box 40) - 95536
gingerbread-mansion.com
11 units   *(800)952-4136*   *Expensive-Very Expensive*
The Gingerbread Mansion Inn is one of America's most romantic
bed-and-breakfasts. The stately three-story Queen Anne-style
Victorian, built in 1899, is on the National Historic Register. In
a quiet setting amid showy English gardens, the yellow and peach
extravaganza of turrets, gables, porches and gingerbread is one of
the most photographed buildings in California. The masterfully
restored interior is completely outfitted with quality antiques.
Full gourmet breakfast, afternoon tea with homebaked culinary
delights and evening port are complimentary. Each spacious,
individually decorated room is luxuriously furnished with
meticulously coordinated quality antiques seamlessly blended
with contemporary conveniences that include a distinctive private
bath, and queen or king bed.
    "Fountain Suite"—large, front, corner bay window,
        village/garden view, his-and-hers clawfoot tubs
        with view of raised tiled gas fireplace, queen bed.
    "Empire Suite"—extra-spacious, marble and glass
        multihead shower, clawfoot soaking tub by fire-
        place, second fireplace in living area, king bed.
    "Rose Suite"—large, front corner veranda with hills
        and town view, two gas fireplaces, raised clawfoot tub
        with town and fireplace view visible from queen bed.
    "Gingerbread Suite"—large, private garden deck,
        his-and-hers clawfoot tub in view of queen bed.
Hotel Ivanhoe   *(707)786-9000*
downtown at 315 Main St. (Box 458) - 95536
hotel-ivanhoe.com
4 units   *Moderate-Expensive*
Ferndale's original hotel still welcomes travelers with a popular
restaurant (see listing) and saloon downstairs. Victorian decor
and antiques contribute to the nostalgic spirit of each well-
furnished room which also has a private bath, all contemporary
amenities, and a queen or king bed.

"Valsacchi Room"–spacious, windows overlook
main street and hills, king bed.

★ **Shaw House Inn Bed & Breakfast**   *(707)786-9958*
downtown at 703 Main St. (Box 1369) - 95536
shawhouse.com
8 units   *(800)557-7429*   *Moderate-Expensive*
A large, luxuriant garden surrounds this 1854 Carpenter Gothic-style building on the National Historic Register. Ferndale's oldest residence is now a charming bed-and-breakfast inn. Full breakfast and afternoon tea and treats are complimentary, and there is a gift shop. All of the attractively furnished rooms include period decor, quality antiques, a private bath (some are down the hall), and all but one have a queen bed.

"Shaw Suite"–private balcony with garden view, skylit
clawfoot tub in view of queen bed.
"Fountain Suite"–parlor with electric fireplace,
in-room clawfoot tub.
"Garden Room"–big garden-view private balcony,
clawfoot tub/shower next door.
"Isabella Room"–very private, garden-view private
porch, vaulted skylit ceiling, clawfoot tub.

The Stewart Inn & Gallery   *(707)786-9687*
just N at 1099 Van Ness Av. (at Main St.) (Box 1067) - 95536
jstewart.com
2 units   *Expensive*
A large Victorian house surrounded by lawns, gardens and a creek now serves as a combination bed-and-breakfast and quality art gallery. Original works (many for sale) and antiques are everywhere. A full breakfast and afternoon live piano/appetizer hour are complimentary. Each beautifully furnished room has peaceful pastoral views, a private bath and queen bed.

★ **Victorian Inn**   *(707)786-4949*
downtown at 400 Ocean Av. at Main St. (Box 96) - 95536
a-victorian-inn.com
12 units   *(888)589-1808*   *Moderate-Expensive*
One of the most impressive buildings on main street has been carefully transformed to include a Victorian-style inn upstairs. For fine dining, Curley's Grill (see listing) and bar are below. A full breakfast is complimentary. Each room is attractively outfitted, including vintage fixtures and furnishings and has a private bath, all contemporary amenities, and a double, queen or king bed. Some have a clawfoot tub.

"Ira Russ Suite"–unique five-sided turret window
with a superb view of main street, king bed.
"Pacifica Room"–corner room with bay window
seating, woodburning fireplace, king bed.

Fort Bragg

Fort Bragg is a village with a hard-working past and a fun-loving future. The Pacific Ocean is less than one-half mile from the heart of town. But it has always been separated by a giant redwood mill. On the south end of town is tiny sheltered Noyo Harbor, a picturesque hub of maritime activity. North beyond the mouth of a scenic creek are miles of rugged beaches, coves, and low sand dunes. Low rolling mountains east of town are blanketed with near-rain-forest overgrowth.

The first lumber mill was established on the Noyo River in 1857. Growth was rapid, especially after California Western Railroad ("the Skunk Train") formed to haul freight inland, and Noyo Harbor developed into a major commercial fishing port.

Today, commercial fishing is much diminished, the giant mill is closed, and the uncertain future of freight hauling threatens the continuing existence of the railroad. But, the outlook (while murky) is golden thanks to improving tourist facilities and the grand setting. The splendid little harbor is a prime destination for travelers seeking bracing nautical scenery, fresh seafood restaurants, sportfishing and whale-watching cruises, and harbor-view lodgings. Hopefully, the unique "Skunk Train" will continue as the single most important attraction on the North Coast. Finally, the mill site can become the key link between the ocean and downtown (as it did years ago in Mendocino). The legacy of unassuming Victorian redwood commercial buildings and houses are already serving nicely as shops featuring local arts, crafts and collectibles, and nostalgic lodgings.

WEATHER PROFILE

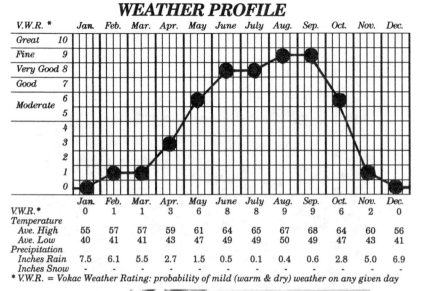

V.W.R. *		Jan.	Feb.	Mar.	Apr.	May	June	July	Aug.	Sep.	Oct.	Nov.	Dec.
Great	10												
Fine	9												
Very Good	8												
Good	7												
Moderate	6												
	5												
	4												
	3												
	2												
	1												
	0												

	Jan.	Feb.	Mar.	Apr.	May	June	July	Aug.	Sep.	Oct.	Nov.	Dec.
V.W.R.*	0	1	1	3	6	8	8	9	9	6	2	0
Temperature												
Ave. High	55	57	57	59	61	64	65	67	68	64	60	56
Ave. Low	40	41	41	43	47	49	49	50	49	47	43	41
Precipitation												
Inches Rain	7.5	6.1	5.5	2.7	1.5	0.5	0.1	0.4	0.6	2.8	5.0	6.9
Inches Snow	-	-	-	-	-	-	-	-	-	-	-	-

* V.W.R. = Vokac Weather Rating: probability of mild (warm & dry) weather on any given day

BASIC INFORMATION

Population: 7,026
Elevation: 80 feet
Location: 165 miles Northwest of San Francisco
Airport (regularly scheduled flights): San Francisco - 175 miles

City of Fort Bragg   (707)961-2823   fortbragg.com
Fort Bragg-Mendocino Coast Chamber of Commerce (707)961-6300
downtown on Hwy. 1 at 332 N. Main St. (Box 1141) - 95437
mendocinocoast.com   (800)726-2780
Mendocino County Alliance   (707)462-7417   (866)466-3636
525 S. Main St., Suite E - Ukiah 95482   gomendo.com

ATTRACTIONS

Brewery

★ **North Coast Brewing Company**   *(707)964-2739*
downtown at 455 N. Main St.
northcoastbrewing.com
Tours of the award-winning brewery are offered on Saturdays, and there is a gift shop with beer-related gifts.

★ **California Western Railroad**   *(707)964-6371   (800)777-5865*
downtown at foot of Laurel St.
skunktrain.com
The "Skunk" line offers one of America's most scenic train rides. Departing from California Western Railroad's "Skunk" Depot downtown, it twists through forty miles of rugged mountains highlighted by groves of redwoods along the picturesque Noyo River. The eastern terminus is Willits, in a gentle interior valley. More than thirty bridges, trestles, and tunnels are along the route—which is inaccessible by car. Diesel and steam trains operate daily year-round for one-way and round trips, but schedules vary. The round trip takes six hours. Half-day tours in summer months feature open observation cars to Northspur, a midway stop deep in the redwoods. By reservation, you can even arrange to ride in the cab with engineer and fireman. The depot includes a large shop with railroad-related gifts and souvenirs of regional arts and crafts.

★ *Festivals*
    (see listing in Mendocino)

★ *Fishing Charters*
    1 mi. S on Hwy. 1 - Noyo Harbor
Sportfishing is the major year-round attraction in Noyo. The tiny village in a sheltered site near the mouth of the Noyo River has a hard-working, authentically scruffy appeal enhanced by several casual restaurants along the waterfront. The **Noyo Fishing Center** (32440 N. Harbor Dr. - Noyo, fortbraggfishing.com, (707) 964-3000) has charters, information, tackle sales/rentals, food/drinks and souvenirs. Several other oceangoing fishing charters and equipment rentals are also especially popular during summer and fall salmon runs. Winter California Grey Whale watching trips can also be arranged. For details and reservations, contact:

All Aboard Adventures   *(707)964-1881*
allaboardadventures.com
Anchor Charter Boats   *(707)964-4550*
anchorcharterboats.com
Telstar Charters   *(707)964-8770*
gooceanfishing.com

Food Specialties

★ **Harvest Market**   *(707)964-7000*
just S at 171 Boatyard Dr. (corner of Hwys. 1 & 20)
harvestmarket.com
This long-time landmark showcases local gourmet foods and all regional wines, and a full-line bakery and deli. Free tastes are available at the remarkably diverse olive and artichoke bar. In 2003, Harvest Market opened a crab cooker out front to prepare local Dungeness from winter through spring. The freshness, price and quality can't be beat on the Redwood Coast.

★ **Hot Pepper Jelly Co.**   *(707)961-1899   (866)737-7379*
downtown at 330 N. Main St.
hotpepperjelly.com
Samples are generously offered of jams and jellies as well as many other local food specialties in a well-organized shop.

★ **Mendocino Chocolate Company**   *(707)964-8800 (800)722-1107*
just N at 542 N. Main St.
mendocino-chocolate.com
Luscious truffles and chocolates on display are made here and sold worldwide. One of the delights is usually available for tastes. Open 10-5 daily.

Fort Bragg Depot   *(707)964-6261*
downtown at 401 Main St.
A small museum showcasing the area's history in pictures and exhibits is part of this popular little shopping complex near the historic Skunk Depot, which also has a large gift shop.

Horseback Riding

★ **Ricochet Ridge Ranch**   *(707)964-7669   (888)873-5777*
2 mi. N at 24201 Hwy. 1
horse-vacation.com
Guided trail rides along the coast or Ten-Mile Beach are offered by appointment several times daily year-round. Rides last 1½ hours. Four-hour and longer rides can be arranged that include both the beach and redwood forest as part of the tour. Splashing through ocean surf aboard a steed matched to your ability is a truly exhilarating experience.

★ **MacKerricher State Park**   *(707)937-5804*
2 mi. N on Hwy. 1
The region's largest coastal park has about eight miles of Pacific Ocean beaches. There are also many miles of biking, hiking and horseback (see listing) trails. One path (including an elevated wooden gangway) extends to a viewpoint overlooking a colony of harbor seals (and whales during their winter migration). In addition to scenic beachfront picnic areas, four full-service campgrounds are deservedly popular.

★ **Mendocino Coast Botanical Gardens**   *(707)964-4352*
  3 mi. S at 18220 Hwy. 1
  gardenbythesea.org
Here is the only public garden in the Continental United States
fronting directly on the ocean. Miles of self-guided (fee) nature
trails wind through woodlands and meadows interspersed with a
profusion of colorful ornamental rhododendrons, camellias, wild
lilac, fuchsias, and other seasonal blooms. A superabundant fern
canyon and rustic bridges extend to a rustic cliff house with an
enchanting view of the rugged coast. The gardens are open daily
year-round. A nursery and a gift shop are at the gardens'
entrance.

★ **Old Haul Road Trail**
  1 mi. N by Hwy. 1
A delightfully scenic freight-line railroad has been torn out and
replaced with a paved hiking/biking trail, with horse access too,
overlooking meadows and dunes and ocean coves and beaches for
several miles from town into MacKerricher State Park. Two
parking lots near the south end provide easy access to the trail
and the coast.

RESTAURANTS

Cliff House Restaurant   *(707)961-0255*
  1 mi. S at 1011 S. Main St.
  fortbragg.org
  D only.   *Expensive*
Traditional American fare featuring a wide assortment of seafood
is served along with housemade desserts in a comfortable
multilevel dinner house with a window-wall view of the narrow
inlet to Noyo Harbor from the ocean.

★ **Eggheads Restaurant**   *(707)964-5005*
  downtown at 326 N. Main St.
  eggheadsrestaurant.com
  B-L.   *Moderate*
One of the area's best breakfast places has featured a wide range
of omelets and hearty American fare for many years in a cozy
comfortable cafe.

Headlands Coffeehouse   *(707)964-1987*
  downtown at 120 E. Laurel St.
  headlandscoffeehouse.com
  B-L-D.   *Moderate*
Light meals can accompany a wide range of coffee drinks in this
relaxed wood-trimmed coffee house. It's locally popular as a
meeting place and hangout with easygoing atmosphere, art
displays, books and live entertainment most nights.

★ **Mendo Bistro**   *(707)964-4974*
downtown at 301 N. Main St.
mendobistro.com
D only.   *Expensive*
Bistro classics with a contemporary California topspin are
featured in one of Fort Bragg's best restaurants. A selection of
seasonally fresh support dishes and housemade pastries enhance
top-quality chicken, pork, fish and beef dishes skillfully cooked
any of five ways with sauces ranging from barbecue to dijon
tarragon cream. Seasonal specialties like the award-winning
Dungeness crabcakes are also delicious. Enjoyable housemade
desserts include gelatos and a signature "chocolate volcano" with
molten chocolate flowing from a baked-to-order cake. The
expansive comfortable dining room upstairs in the Old Mill Store
overlooks the main street.

★ **North Coast Brewing Company**   *(707)964-3400*
11 mi. N at 444 N. Main St.
northcoastbrewing.com
L-D.   *Moderate*
Pub grub becomes cuisine through creative use of seasonal
ingredients and fresh local seafood in dishes like sautéed local
rock fish and chips, steamed clams steeped in their wheat beer,
and Tex-Mex red and green pork chili. Desserts like key lime pie
and chocolate-orange-walnut pie are made here. Lotus cream ice
cream, unique to this restaurant, is sensationally refreshing–don't
miss it. The wood-trim pub and dining room are separated by a
shop with regional gifts.

Old Coast Hotel   *(707)961-4488*   *(888)468-3550*
downtown at 101 N. Franklin St.
oldcoasthotelmendocino.com
L-D. No L Mon.-Thurs. Closed Wed.   *Moderate*
Traditional American fare includes a variety of seafood dishes
served in casual whitewashed wood dining areas of a small
Victorian-era hotel. A popular bar adjoins.

★ **Rendezvous Inn & Restaurant** *(707)964-8142* *(800)491-8142*
downtown at 647 N. Main St.
rendezvousinn.com
D only. Closed Mon.-Tues.   *Expensive*
Rendezvous is Fort Bragg's premier culinary destination. Fresh
seasonal produce is skillfully transformed into flavorful creative
cuisine. Consider dishes like local wild king salmon sautéed and
served with a pan sauce of lemon and whole grain mustard, or
roasted farm quail served with cranberry glaze. Luscious desserts
are also housemade. A historic home showcases a dark-wood-
trimmed dining room with tables set with full linen surrounding

an island fireplace. Upstairs are several comfortably furnished moderately priced inn rooms. Full gourmet breakfast is complimentary and might include the chef's legendary fresh-baked muffins or scones.

The Restaurant *(707)964-9800*
downtown at 418 Main St.
therestaurantfortbragg.com
D only. Closed Wed. Sun. brunch. Expensive
Contemporary California cuisine like lemon chicken or sautéed crabcakes with jalapeño star on an eclectic menu that also includes housemade desserts like sorbets and ice creams. This restaurant, a long-time locals' favorite, offers comfortable little art-filled dining rooms.

The Wharf - Anchor Lodge *(707)964-4283*
2 mi. S via Hwy. 1 at 32260 N. Harbor Dr. - Noyo Harbor
wharf-restaurant.com
L-D. Expensive
The Wharf is the biggest among several casual family-oriented eateries along the little Noyo River harbor. "Fisherman's Wharf style" seafood is featured. The extra-large casual dining room and adjoining deck overlook the busy waterfront. Several simply furnished (moderate) motel rooms share the view from downstairs in the Wharf's Anchor Lodge.

LODGINGS

Accommodations are numerous. Several of the best are in historic buildings near the depot. A few motels on Highway 1 north of downtown have ocean views and access. The area's only moderately priced rooms are in older local motels south and east of downtown. High season is May through September weekends. Winter and spring weekdays are often reduced 25% or more.

★ **Avalon House** *(707)964-5555*
downtown at 561 Stewart St. - 95437
theavalonhouse.com
6 units *(800)964-5556* Moderate-Expensive
A historic Craftsman-style home amid dense gardens has become a romantic haven. A beach is within an easy stroll. Full breakfast is complimentary. Each well-furnished room is individually decorated and has a private bath and double or queen bed.
"Yellow Room"–private ocean-view deck, skylights,
   gas fireplace, in-room whirlpool, queen bed.
"Quilt Room"–private ocean-view deck, refrigerator,
   gas fireplace, in-bath whirlpool, queen bed.
"Blue Room"–skylight and stained glass, gas
   fireplace, in-bath whirlpool, queen bed.

★ **The Beach House Inn**   *(707)961-1700*
1 mi. N (on Hwy. 1) at 100 Pudding Creek Rd. - 95437
beachinn.com
30 units   (888)559-9992   Moderate-Expensive
One of Fort Bragg's finest lodgings opened in 1998 on a bluff
above a creek. It is an easy stroll to Pacific Ocean tidepools,
beaches, and the Old Haul Road hiking/biking trail. Most of the
beautifully furnished rooms have a microwave and refrigerator,
a private balcony with a creek view, and one or two queens or a
king bed.
    #105,#205,#305,#405–gas fireplace, big
        soaking tub, private balcony, king bed.
    upper floors–gas fireplace, private balcony, two queen beds.
★ **Beachcomber Motel**   *(707)964-2402*
1 mi. N at 1111 N. Main St. - 95437
thebeachcombermotel.com
75 units   (800)400-7873   Expensive-Very Expensive
A small motel was transformed into a much-larger upgraded
lodging in 1999. It is located at the beginning of the Old Haul
Road hiking/biking trail in full view of the ocean and an adjoining
expansive beach. Each well-furnished unit has a refrigerator and
most have a spectacular seascape beyond floor-to-ceiling windows
and a choice of doubles, queens, or king bed.
    "suite" (4 of these)–in-room large whirlpool with
        ocean view, microwave, raised gas fireplace and
        private ocean-view balcony in view of king bed.
Emerald Dolphin Inn   *(707)944-6699*
1 mi. S at 1211 S. Main St. - 95437
emeralddolphin.com
43 units   (866)964-6699   Moderate-Expensive
This highway-side motel opened in 2001 within walking distance
of ocean bluffs and the bridge over Noyo Harbor. Each room is
well furnished and has a refrigerator and a queen or king bed.
Five units also have an in-room two-person whirlpool.
★ **The Grey Whale Inn**   *(707)964-0640*
downtown at 615 N. Main St. - 95437
greywhaleinn.com
14 units   (800)382-7244   Expensive
Fort Bragg's turn-of-the-century hospital became the area's first
bed-and-breakfast inn more than a quarter-century ago. It
remains one of the town's best. A first-rate full breakfast buffet
and use of the game room is complimentary. Each well-
maintained room is attractively furnished with comfortable
nostalgic decor, a private bath, all contemporary amenities, and
a queen or king bed.

"Sunrise"–penthouse, town view from private
  deck, refr., large in-bath whirlpool, king bed.
"Sunset"–ocean view, private deck, refr., king bed.
"Railway," "Campbell"–spacious, Skunk Train Depot
  view, gas fireplace, refrigerator/microwave, king bed.
"Navarro Ridge"–romantic, woodburning
  fireplace, queen bed.
★ **Harbor Lite Lodge**   *(707)964-0221*
1 mi. S (on Hwy. 1) at 120 N. Harbor Dr. - 95437
harborlitelodge.com
  79 units   *(800)643-2700*   *Moderate-Expensive*
Motel rooms along a blufftop above Noyo Harbor provide
excellent views of the waterfront activity far below. A trail leads
to the beach and village. There is a sauna and complimentary
breakfast bar. Most of the well-furnished units have a private
balcony with an intimate view and queens or a king bed.
"King Deluxe" (6 of these)–woodburning stove,
  private harbor-view balcony, king bed.
Hi-Seas Inn   *(707)964-5929*
1 mi. N at 1201 N. Main St. - 95437
  15 units   *(800)990-7327*   *Moderate*
This single-level small motel has a shaded deck with a good ocean
view beyond a broad lawn. Guests have a choice of compact or
standard-sized simply furnished rooms with one or two queen beds.
Holiday Inn Express   *(707)964-1100*
2 mi. S at 250 Hwy. 20 - 95437
sixcontinentshotels.com/hiexpress
  54 units   *(800)465-4329*   *Moderate-Expensive*
New in 2001, this chain motel overlooks a small natural canyon
and has an indoor pool, whirlpool and exercise room. Expanded
Continental breakfast is complimentary. Each attractively
furnished room has two queens or a king bed.
"suite" (3 of these)–gas fireplace, private
  balcony overlooking canyon, king bed.
★ **The Lodge at Noyo River**   *(707)964-8045*
2 mi. S (via Hwy. 1) at 500 Casa del Noyo Dr. - 95437
noyolodge.com
  16 units   *(800)628-1126*   *Expensive*
A luxuriant cypress forest backs a romantic hillside bed-and-
breakfast overlooking picturesque Noyo Harbor. The carefully
preserved complex includes a residence (dating from 1868)
trimmed with heartwood redwood. Garden paths lead down to the
waterfront. A full breakfast is complimentary. All well-furnished
rooms are individually decorated, and have a private bath and
queen or king bed.

"Carriage House"–romantic in-room soaking tub with close-up
river view, private deck, gas fireplace, skylit king bed.
"The Captain's Berth"–cozy, woodburning
fireplace, private river-view deck, king bed.
"The Harbor Hideaway"–sunroom, private deck,
harbor and river view, woodburning fireplace, king bed.
"A–F" (6 of these)–private bridge-view deck, gas
fireplace, two-person soaking tub, queen bed.

★ **North Cliff Hotel** *(707)962-2500*
1 mi. S (on Hwy. 1) at 1005 S. Main St. - 95437
fortbragg.org
39 units   (866)962-2550   Expensive-Very Expensive
One of Fort Bragg's finest lodgings is a three-story complex that
opened in 2000 on a bluff immediately above Noyo River near its
mouth at the Pacific Ocean. Each room is beautifully furnished.
All have dramatic harbor and ocean views, a small private
balcony, gas fireplace, refrigerator/microwave with expanded
Continental breakfast, and queens or a king bed.
"Master Deluxe" (21 of these)–spacious,
two-person whirlpool by window with ocean
view and raised gas fireplace, king bed.

★ **Ocean View Lodge** *(707)964-1951*
1 mi. N (on Hwy. 1) at 1141 N. Main St. - 95437
oceanviewlodging.com
30 units   (800)643-5482   Expensive-Very Expensive
Sandy beaches are just beyond a grassy meadow and a paved
ocean-view hiking/biking path bordering this contemporary motel.
All attractively furnished units have a full ocean view and a large
private balcony or deck and queens or a king bed.
"King Bed with whirlpool and fireplace" (15 of these)–
in-room two-person whirlpool, raised gas fireplace,
large view balcony, king bed.

★ **Surf 'n Sand Lodge** *(707)964-9383*
1 mi. N (on Hwy. 1) at 1131 N. Main St. - 95437
surfsandlodge.com
30 units   (800)964-0184   Moderate-Expensive
For beachcombers, Fort Bragg's nicest lodging is the Surf 'n
Sand. This posh little motel is separated from the sandy ocean
beaches by only a grassy meadow and the scenic paved Old Haul
Road hiking/biking trail. Each unit is beautifully furnished
including a refrigerator, and has queens or a king bed. Most have
a delightfully up-close ocean view.
"Spa/gas fireplace room" (6 of these)–spacious, large
private deck with fine ocean view, gas fireplace,
in-room two-person whirlpool tub, king bed.

Fort Bragg

Tradewinds Lodge   *(707)964-4761*
just S at 400 S. Main St. - 95437
fortbragg.org
92 units   (800)524-2244   Moderate-Expensive
The area's largest lodging is this contemporary motel with an
indoor pool, whirlpool, exercise facilities, a family restaurant (with
big housemade cinnamon rolls featured for breakfast), a bar and
a gift shop. Each nicely furnished unit–up to two bedrooms–has
doubles, queens or a king bed.

Vista Manor Lodge - Best Western   *(707)964-4776*
1 mi. N (on Hwy. 1) at 1100 N. Main St. - 95437
bestwesterncalifornia.com
55 units   (800)937-8376   Moderate-Expensive
The ocean is nearby across a highway from this hilltop motel.
Landscaped grounds include a beach-access path and an indoor
pool. Many of the well-furnished rooms have an ocean view and
queens or a king bed.

★ **The Weller House Inn**   *(707)964-4415*
downtown at 524 Stewart St. - 95437
wellerhouse.com
10 units   (877)893-5537   Expensive
A three-story wood-trimmed mansion on the National Historic
Register is further distinguished by a landmark water tower that
is the tallest structure in Fort Bragg. The estate, a block north of
the Skunk Train Depot, was lovingly transformed into a
delightful bed-and-breakfast inn in 1998 surrounded by colorful
statue-filled gardens. The water tower now includes a complimentary whirlpool and ocean-view top deck for guests, plus two
fine rooms completed in 2003. A full complimentary breakfast is
served in the dramatic polished-redwood top-floor ballroom, as is
wine in the afternoon. Each room is beautifully individually
accented with romantic Victorian artifacts and nostalgic touches,
plus a private bath and a queen or king bed.
    "Raven"–in water tower, town/ocean view,
        gas fireplace, in-bath whirlpool, king bed.
    "Heather"–in water tower, cozy, town/ocean
        view, gas fireplace, queen bed.
    "Aqua"–spacious, overlooks gardens toward
        ocean, large in-bath whirlpool, queen bed.
    "Tulip"–spacious, delightful garden view, stained-glass
        bay windows, big clawfoot tub/shower, queen bed.
    "Minuet"–woodburning fireplace in view of queen bed.
    "Tuscany"–big corner windows, large
        gas fireplace in view of queen bed.

Gualala

Gualala is the civilized hub of one of the most wildly beautiful shorelines in America. The village is on a sloping bench above the ocean at the outlet of the gentle Gualala River. Rising abruptly to the east are dense, forested mountains punctuated by redwoods. With this bewitching location and a temperate climate, the village is beginning to fulfill its destiny as a major getaway.

Russians, Germans, and Spanish settled here, sporatically, during the early 1800s. They were followed by Americans after a redwood mill was established. The San Francisco earthquake of 1906 gave the village a boost when as many as four sawmills were operating at once to provide some of the wood necessary to rebuild the city. The last mill closed in the 1960s, and with its removal, visitors began stopping in increasing numbers to enjoy the restored beauty of this remote locale.

Today, travelers come here to get away from the congestion, noise and smog of cities. Relaxation reigns, along with gentle recreation like boating and fishing on the peaceful little river, or hiking along picturesque headlands and beaches. In the village, a few galleries, studios and specialty shops feature local arts and crafts. The town's art center offers polished performances and exhibits in an inspiring structure which blends seamlessly into the woodland setting. Several restaurants offer ocean views, and nearby dinner houses showcase some of the finest gourmet cuisine on the coast. Lodgings in town and nearby extol the spectacular locale with romantic decor and stirring picture-window views of this magic stretch of shoreline.

WEATHER PROFILE

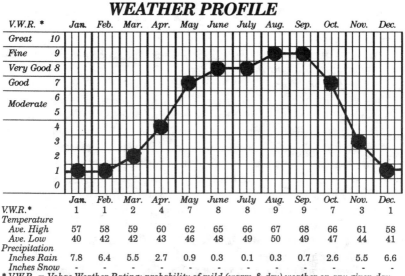

V.W.R. *	Jan.	Feb.	Mar.	Apr.	May	June	July	Aug.	Sep.	Oct.	Nov.	Dec.
V.W.R.*	1	1	2	4	7	8	8	9	9	7	3	1
Temperature												
Ave. High	57	58	59	60	62	65	66	67	68	66	61	58
Ave. Low	40	42	42	43	46	48	49	50	49	47	44	41
Precipitation												
Inches Rain	7.8	6.4	5.5	2.7	0.9	0.3	0.1	0.3	0.7	2.6	5.5	6.6
Inches Snow	-	-	-	-	-	-	-	-	-	-	-	-

* V.W.R. = Vokac Weather Rating: probability of mild (warm & dry) weather on any given day

BASIC INFORMATION

Population: 595
Elevation: 60 feet
Location: 106 miles Northwest of San Francisco
Airport (regularly scheduled flights): San Francisco - 115 miles

The Redwood Coast Chamber of Commerce   (707)884-1080
  P.O. Box 199 - 95445 (no office)   (800)778-5252
  redwoodcoastchamber.com

ATTRACTIONS

Boat Rentals

★ **Adventure Rents**   *(707)884-4386   (888)881-4386*
downtown in Cantamare Center
adventurerents.com
The Gualala River is naturally blocked each summer from entering the ocean. A sandbar dam turns it into a lagoon several miles long until the rainy season washes out the bar each fall. It is ideal for self-guided paddling (no motorized watercraft) past sandy beaches, salt marshes and into redwood forests. A variety of canoes and kayaks and related gear are available for guided or unguided trips, along with transport to the launch site. They also provide free instruction for beginners, and sponsor summer moonlight flotillas including a river beach picnic.

★ **Fort Ross State Historic Park**   *(707)847-3286*
27 mi. S on Highway 1
Fort Ross was built on a coastal headland in 1821 as Russia's prime fur-trading outpost in California. They sold it to John Sutter (of later gold-rush fame) twenty years later, after depleting the coast of seals and otters. In 1850 the area became part of the new state of California. The reconstructed redwood stockade, Russian Orthodox Chapel, officers' barracks and block house are open daily. The museum has extensive exhibits documenting area history.

★ **Gualala Arts Center**   *(707)884-1138*
just SE at 46501 Old State Highway
gualalaarts.org
Tucked away in a second-growth redwood forest next to town is an unexpected cultural bonus–a large and sophisticated center for the visual and performance arts. Gallery displays and performances on a changing schedule are showcased year-round in handsome settings backed by picture-window views of woodlands and sculptures in surrounding natural gardens and picnic areas.

★ **Gualala Point Regional Park**   *(707)785-2377*
1 mi. S on Highway 1
The junction of a hilly peninsula where the Gualala River empties into the ocean is a romantic headland shaded by mature cypress. World-class seascapes can be enjoyed from the visitor center that also has a small museum of regional artifacts. In summer, the mouth of the river gets blocked by a sandbar. The surprisingly clear and warm river/lagoon becomes a favorite destination of sunbathers, swimmers, canoeists, kayakers, and fishermen. Trails lead to scenic overlooks that are ideal (in winter) for whale watching; long sandy beaches; and to secluded picnic sites by the stream and ocean.

Point Arena Lighthouse   *(707)882-2777*
16 mi. N at 45500 Highway 1 - Point Arena
The U.S. Lighthouse Service operated this facility from 1870 to 1939, followed by the U.S. Coast Guard from 1939 to 1984. The Lighthouse Keepers now maintain it as a historic museum with a gift shop and rental lodgings (open daily varying hours) that share the dramatic ocean view from the isolated peninsula. The 115-foot tower is open for tours on most days for several hours.
Scenic Drive
★ **The North Coast Scenic Highway**
Highway 1 from Jenner to Rockport (110 miles)
The "Shoreline Highway" (California 1) between Jenner where the highway begins to parallel the shore at the mouth of the Russian River to where it turns inland at Rockport north of Fort Bragg is one of the world's great coastal drives. It winds and dips through hundreds of curves, high above and close by the ocean. Travelers are rewarded with almost constant panoramas of sheltered ocean coves, sandy beaches, and dramatic headlands. Numerous parks with campgrounds (**Salt Point State Park**, (707)847-3221, 18 miles south), beaches and picnic areas scattered along the captivating coastline are accessed by Highway 1.
★ **The Sea Ranch Chapel**   *(707)785-2444*
4 mi. S at 40033 Highway 1 - Sea Ranch
The intimate Sea Ranch Chapel is one of the world's most inspired religious structures. This remarkable nondenominational sanctuary was designed by renowned artist and master craftsman James Hubbell in 1985 in a meadow near the sea. His ingenious use of stained glass, inlaid ceramics, freeform hardwood and wrought iron is nonpareil. The net effect is genuinely inspirational.

RESTAURANTS

★ **The Food Company**   *(707)884-1800*
just N at 38411 Highway 1
B-L.   *Moderate*
Fresh seasonal ingredients are skillfully transformed into a delightful array of light salads, pastas, and meat items like honey and apricot pork loin, plus several pastries, cookies, cakes, and pies. All are displayed in deli cases and served in a cheerful little dining room by the cases, or on a garden deck.
Gualala Bakery   *(707)884-4055*
downtown at 39225 S. Highway 1 (in Sundstrom Mall)
B-L-D.   *Moderate*
Tucked away in a plain little shopping center is a bakery with breads, sticky buns, other fine pastries (superb bear claws!), cookies, cakes and desserts. An enclosed dining court adjoins.

Gualala Hotel   *(707)884-3441*
downtown at 39301 S. Highway 1
D only.   Moderate
Traditional American fare is served in hearty helpings in the
casual dining room of a historic (1903) little hotel. The adjoining
bar is a long-established major hangout with a skylit pool room
and well-worn fireplace and backbar.

★ **Inn at Victorian Gardens**   *(707)882-3606*
24 mi. N at 14409 S. Highway 1 - Manchester
innatvictoriangardens.com
D only. Closed Mon.-Wed.   Very Expensive
Victorian Gardens is one of America's great dining experiences.
Far away from the maddening crowds, in a nostalgic farmhouse
near the sea, a meticulous and multitalented chef creates culinary
masterpieces derived from top-quality seasonal ingredients raised
on the estate. Each night, sixteen people in one seating are served
amid the Victorian opulence of an enchanting firelit dining room
outfitted with museum-quality linens, crystal, china and silver.
Each multicourse meal is complemented by appropriate wine and
completed by extraordinary desserts.

Oceansong   *(707)884-1041*
downtown at 39350 S. Highway 1
breakersinn.com
L-D.   Moderate
Oceansong is one of the area's most popular restaurants. The
Swiss-born chef uses fresh quality ingredients for contemporary
Continental cuisine in creative updates of traditional seafood, beef
and poultry entrees. The split-level dining room and heated
alfresco deck have a panoramic view of the inlet and ocean below.

Pangaea   *(707)882-3001*
14 mi. N at 250 Main St. (Highway 1) - Point Arena
www.pangaeacafe.com
D only. Closed Mon.-Tues.   Expensive
Current owners maintain a tradition of adventurous dishes with
bold flavors and unusual textures. A casually artistic dining room
and lounge complement the "lusty, zaftig, soulful food."

★ **Point Arena Bakery**   *(707)882-3770*
14 mi. N on Main St. - Point Arena
B-L. Closed Mon.-Tues.   Moderate
Point Arena Bakery is the hidden gem among Coastal California
artisan bakers. Outstanding calzones, small pizzas, and bread
loaves and twists with assorted cheeses, vegetables and herbs are
perfect for picnics, as are traditional and innovative brownies and
shortbread cookies. Pies like rhubarb meringue are also superb
from this unpretentious gourmet takeout in the heart of little
Point Arena.

★ **St. Orres**   *(707)884-3335*
2 mi. N at 36601 S. Highway 1
saintorres.com
D only. Closed Tues.-Wed.   *Expensive*
St. Orres is an exquisite exemplar of cuisine as theater. Top-quality seasonal ingredients of the region set the stage for a nightly culinary tour de force by an extraordinary chef with a flair for both drama and fun. Each course stars as a spectacular presentation served by a gracious staff in a dramatic dining room beneath a three-story clerestory tower with stained-glass accents, an ocean view and luxuriant cascades of exotic greenery tumbling from balconies on three sides. White linen accented by a single white candle and a long-stemmed rose complete the romantic production. There is also a firelit lobby bar with an ocean-view deck, and a garden solarium for appetizers and desserts.

The Sea Ranch Lodge   *(707)785-2371*
8 mi. S on Highway 1 - Sea Ranch
searanchlodge.com
B-L-D. Sun. brunch.   *Expensive*
Seasonally fresh North Coast cuisine stars in the Lodge's dining room in dishes like herb-roasted wild salmon with artichoke and chanterelle ragout. Housemade desserts are also served in a casually elegant dining room with a window-wall view of nearby headlands and the sea.

Timber Cove Inn   *(707)847-3231*
23 mi. S at 21780 N. Highway 1 - Jenner
timbercoveinn.com
B-L-D.   *Very Expensive*
Contemporary California and Continental cuisine, rock walls and a circular see-through center fireplace enhance tables set with full linen in Timber Cove's dining room. A window wall provides an aesthetic view of the distant sea. The adjoining lobby lounge overlooks a fountain/sculpture garden and a baronial stone fireplace.

Top of the Cliff   *(707)884-1539*
downtown (on Highway 1) in the Seacliff Center
L-D. No L Thurs. Closed Mon.-Wed.   *Expensive*
A contemporary menu is given creative California topspin. A panoramic ocean view on three sides distinguishes a casually posh dining room. An adjoining raised lounge shares the view.

The Upper Crust Pizzeria   *(707)884-1324*
downtown at 39331 Highway 1
D only. Closed Mon.   *Moderate*
A full range of well-made pizzas can be enjoyed in the little parlor, on an adjoining flowery deck by the highway, or to go.

LODGINGS

There are about a dozen lodgings in and around Gualala. All are individualistic, with a decidedly romantic orientation. Some feature ocean views. High season is May through October. Winter weekdays may be reduced 10%.

★ **Breakers Inn**   *(707)884-3200*
   downtown at 39300 S. Highway 1 (Box 389) - 95445
   breakersinn.com
   30 units   *(800)273-2537*   *Expensive-Very Expensive*
The Breakers is one of the most delightful lodgings on the California coast. An expanded Continental breakfast is complimentary and the popular Oceansong restaurant (see listing) is on the property. Most of the beautifully furnished units have a superb view from a bluff rim overlooking the mouth of the Gualala River and the ocean. All are individually themed and have a private deck, pressed-wood fireplace and queen or king bed.

"Oceanfront Luxury Spa" (4 of these)–spacious,
   two-person whirlpool with picture-window ocean view,
   wet bar, refrigerator, sitting area by fireplace, large private
   ocean-view deck (two have a private sauna), king bed.
"Deluxe Corner Oceanfront" (12 of these) –spacious, two-
   person in-bath whirlpool, large private ocean-view deck,
   corner fireplace, wet bar, refrigerator, king bed.

Gualala Country Inn   *(707)884-4343*
   downtown on Highway 1 (Box 697) - 95445
   gualala.com
   18 units   *(800)564-4466*   *Moderate-Expensive*
This small New England-style motel by the highway has several individually well-furnished compact rooms with an ocean view (across the highway), a queen bed, and romantic features.

"Surf," "Sea Spray," "Sunset"–gas fireplace,
   in-room two-person whirlpool.

★ **Inn at Victorian Gardens**   *(707)882-3606*
   24 mi. N at 14409 S. Highway One - Manchester 95459
   innatvictoriangardens.com
   4 units   *Very Expensive*
Sequestered on a slope by foothills of the Coast Range Mountains is one of America's most enchanting lodgings. Well back from the highway in a lush pastoral setting is a Victorian country mansion that has been meticulously transformed into the quintessential bed-and-breakfast getaway. The manor house is surrounded by colorful flower gardens and an acre of year-round herb and vegetable gardens backed by small buildings housing pheasants, game hens, and other exotic birds and animals that are all part of the country dining experience. Additions in 2003 include an

"enoteca" (unique Italian wine cellar) and firelit dining area, and a new room with a Tuscan-style pizza oven. Amenities include a bocce court and paths leading to nearby hills and the rugged coastline. Impeccably furnished common rooms and porches provide picturesque seascapes and pastoral views as well as charming spaces for playing games, sharing conversations and relaxing. Complimentary full gourmet breakfast is enhanced by a unique opportunity–to gather around a great fireplace in the ultimate kitchen for a gourmet chef. World class romantic dinners (see listing) are served in a plush firelit dining room or on a lovely dining porch. Each spacious, individually decorated room is luxuriously furnished with fine pieces from the owners' worldwide travels and includes a private bath and king bed.

"Master Bedroom"–pastoral/ocean views on three sides, private standing balcony, clawfoot tub beneath dramatic stained-glass window, separate shower.

"Northwest Bedroom"–spectacular ocean/pastoral view, two-person soaking tub, separate shower.

"Golden Bedroom"–octagonal turret room with ocean/garden view, handsome private tub/shower across hall.

★ **The Old Milano**   *(707)884-3256*
  1 mi. N at 38300 Highway 1 - 95445
  oldmilanohotel.com
  6 units   *Expensive-Very Expensive*
High on a bluff amid luxuriant gardens is one of the North Coast's most romantic bed-and-breakfast inns. Several garden cottages rise above emerald lawns that seem to tumble precipitously to the sea. Full breakfast served to the room is complimentary. So is one of the most spectacularly-sited hot tubs anywhere. Beautifully furnished rooms include some gracious Victorian antiques and a double or queen bed.

"Iris," "Applegate"–spacious, two-person whirlpool, gas fireplace, ocean view from queen bed.

"The Caboose"–rustic, authentic train caboose with private bath and wood stove, two upstairs brakeman's seats with view, double bed.

★ **St. Orres**   *(707)884-3303*
  1 mi. N at 36601 S. Highway 1 (Box 523) - 95445
  saintorres.com
  20 units   *Moderate-Very Expensive*
St. Orres is a classic extension of the romantic freeform era of the 1960s. The complex in a "naturalized garden" includes a three-story handcrafted wood building with strong Russian influences housing one of California's great restaurants (see listing). A hot

tub and sauna are available to guests. Full breakfast is complimentary. Each room or cabin is spacious and attractively furnished with local art and plants, and has a double, queen or king bed. Most have a fireplace. Some have a soaking tub and ocean view. Eight small handcrafted rooms in the hotel share baths.

"Blue Iris"–forest/ocean view from two-person whirlpool tub, sauna, refrigerator/wet bar, private view deck, wood stove visible from queen bed.

"Sequoia"–sitting area with wood stove, soaking tub, refrigerator/wet bar, private deck, ocean view from king bed.

"Treehouse"–sitting area with Franklin fireplace, ocean-view deck, refrigerator/wet bar, soaking tub with a view, skylight, king bed.

★ **The Sea Ranch Lodge**   *(707)785-2371*
8 mi. S on Highway 1 (Box 44) - Sea Ranch 95497
searanchlodge.com
20 units   *(800)732-7262*   *Expensive*
A grey weathered-wood complex in a meadow above the nearby sea includes fine dining (see listing) with a view. A complimentary buffet breakfast is served in the dining room. Each spacious, well-furnished wood-trimmed room has an ocean view and a queen bed. Most also have a pressed-wood fireplace.

"Garden-View Suite" (2 of these)–fireplace, two-person hot tub on deck, queen bed.

★ **Seacliff on the Bluff**   *(707)884-1213*
downtown off Highway 1 (Box 1317) - 95445
seacliffmotel.com
16 units   *(800)400-5053*   *Expensive*
Well off the highway in the heart of town, this contemporary wood-trimmed motel crowns a bluff with a grand overview of the river, beach and ocean. In winter, you might be lucky enough to see California grey whales up close when they come to the sandbar to shed their barnacles. All of the romantically oriented, well-furnished units have binoculars, a gas fireplace, refrigerator with complimentary champagne or sparkling cider, and fine surf views from a large private deck, two-person whirlpool, and king bed.

Surf Motel at Gualala   *(707)884-3571*
downtown at 39170 S. Highway 1 (Box 695) - 95445
gualala.com
16 units   *(888)451-7873*   *Moderate-Expensive*
This contemporary single-level motel has a scenic blufftop picnic area. Each comfortably furnished room has a refrigerator and microwave, and two doubles, queen, or king bed.

★ **Timber Cove Inn**   *(707)847-3231*
23 mi. S at 21780 N. Highway 1 - Jenner 95450
timbercoveinn.com
53 units   *(800)987-8319*   *Expensive-Very Expensive*
Timber Cove crowns one of the great coastal overlooks in America. The handcrafted wood complex atop a bluff with trails above half a mile of rocky ocean frontage includes a sophisticated sea-view dining room (see listing). Each unit is individually well furnished including appealing art and handicrafts and a queen or king bed. Most have an outstanding ocean view, gas fireplace, and in-room whirlpool bath.

#50,#56–corner; two-person in-room whirlpool, circular gas fireplace and large private balcony all share awesome ocean/cove view with king bed.

#32,#34–raised two-person tiled shower with floor-to-ceiling window to ocean, freestanding gas fireplace, large in-bath whirlpool, private deck beyond window wall with ocean view, full ocean view from king bed.

#36–two-person whirlpool and shower stall share ocean view, freestanding gas fireplace, private ocean-view deck, king bed.

#91–corner; sauna, two-person in-room whirlpool, gas fireplace, big private balcony share ocean view with king bed.

★ **Whale Watch Inn**   *(707)884-3667*
4 mi. N at 35100 Highway 1 - 95445
whalewatchinn.com
18 units   *(800)942-5342*   *Expensive-Very Expensive*
Whale Watch Inn is the Gualala area's premier coastal lodging. The contemporary woodcrafted complex includes five buildings secluded amid cypress and gardens perched on the edge of a cliff with breathtaking seascapes. A private stairway descends to secluded sandy beaches, rocky points and tidepools. Homemade gourmet breakfast delivered to the room is complimentary. Each romantic unit is fully, luxuriously furnished including a pressed-wood fireplace, private deck, and superb ocean views. Many have a refrigerator and a large in-room whirlpool near the queen bed.

"Crystal Sea"–fireplace, two-person whirlpool, dual showerheads, awesome private ocean-view deck, skylit queen bed.

"Ocean Sunrise"–as above, but downstairs.

"Silver Mist"–multilevel; two-person whirlpool and fireplace share ocean view with private deck and skylit queen bed.

"The Bath Suite"–spiral stairway to ocean-view two-person whirlpool with skylit roof, fireplace, surf-view private deck.

"Pacifica"–romantic ocean-view window seat and private deck, mirrored 2-person whirlpool, fireplace, refrigerator, skylight.

Healdsburg

Healdsburg is uniquely centered around great wine and running water. The Russian River and its largest tributary–Dry Creek–flow through town. Both are flanked by more than fifty wineries ensconced among lush vineyards that extend to redwood forests in hills to the west. The river is large enough to foster a diversity of water-oriented recreation almost year-round, thanks to a warm mild climate.

During the 1860s, Healdsburg was platted as a town complete with a central Spanish-style plaza. Growth accelerated once farmers and vintners recognized the potential for premium grapes. Prohibition ended the boom times, and the village languished for more than half a century.

Today, the plaza is fully developed–a classic among the few intact examples of early California town planning. Healdsburg's peaceful unaffected charm is apparent in the luxuriant palm-and-redwood-shaded plaza that remains the heart of town, and in a riverside park popular for swimming, canoeing, fishing and picnics. Buildings around the plaza feature shops full of regional art, handicrafts, antiques, gourmet wines and edibles, plus several fine restaurants. Century-old buildings blend comfortably with Healdsburg's post-millennial avant-garde landmarks like the new anchor hotel on the historic plaza. Numerous historic buildings have been transformed into romantic bed-and-breakfast inns amid gardens or vineyards perfectly suited to adult visitors here to enjoy a town that celebrates the pleasures of wines, and the river that runs through it.

WEATHER PROFILE

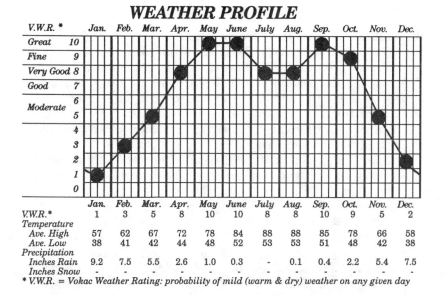

V.W.R. *		Jan.	Feb.	Mar.	Apr.	May	June	July	Aug.	Sep.	Oct.	Nov.	Dec.
V.W.R.*		1	3	5	8	10	10	8	8	10	9	5	2
Temperature													
Ave. High		57	62	67	72	78	84	88	88	85	78	66	58
Ave. Low		38	41	42	44	48	52	53	53	51	48	42	38
Precipitation													
Inches Rain		9.2	7.5	5.5	2.6	1.0	0.3	-	0.1	0.4	2.2	5.4	7.5
Inches Snow		-	-	-	-	-	-	-	-	-	-	-	-

* V.W.R. = Vokac Weather Rating: probability of mild (warm & dry) weather on any given day

BASIC INFORMATION

Population: 10,722
Elevation: 104 feet
Location: 70 miles North of San Francisco
Airport (regularly scheduled flights): San Francisco - 80 miles

Healdsburg Chamber of Commerce & Visitors Bureau (707)433-6935
    downtown at 217 Healdsburg Av. - 95448   CA:(800)648-9922
www.healdsburg.org

ATTRACTIONS

★ **Armstrong Redwoods State Reserve** *(707)869-2015*
18 mi. SW via Westside Rd. & Armstrong Woods Rd.
Redwoods reaching 300 feet are at the heart of this awe-inspiring
forest in lush coastal foothills. Nature, hiking and riding trails
provide access to more than 800 acres of cool, quiet reserve.

★ *Ballooning*
  Aerostat Adventures *(707)258-8889 (800)579-0183*
  aerostat-adventures.com
  The pastoral grandeur of the Russian River Valley is memorably
  revealed in an early morning balloon flight followed by
  champagne and picnic brunch at their choice launch site out of J
  Vineyards & Winery and Rodney Strong Vineyards.
  Air Flambuoyant *(707)480-6646 (800)456-4711*
  airflambouyant.com
  A champagne flight in a hot-air balloon provides a serene
  perspective on the Russian River Valley. This family-owned
  business is one of the oldest and most experienced in California.

★ *Bicycling*
  Back roads by vineyards, farms and redwood forests along the
  Russian River are ideal for bicyclists. All kinds of bicycles are
  available for rentals or tours, with related equipment and a map.
  Spoke Folk Cyclery *(707)433-7171*
  downtown at 201 Center St.
  spokefolk.com

★ *Boating*
  The Russian River (see listing) can be enjoyed for boating almost
  year-round. Prime time is when the water is clear and flows
  slowly through this lush peaceful valley in summer. That means
  easy fun for boating, canoeing or rafting. Explore-on-your-own or
  guided trips, hourly, half-day or longer canoe or inflatable rentals,
  boating gear, and shuttles can be reserved at:
  SOAR Inflatables *(707)433-5599 (800)280-7627*
  1 mi. SE at 303 Healdsburg Av. (year-round)
  www.soar1.com
  Trowbridge Canoe Trips *(707)433-7247 (800)640-1386*
  1 mi. SE at 20 Healdsburg Av. (May through October)
  trowbridgecanoe.com

Food Specialties
★ **Kozlowski Farms** *(707)887-1587 (800)473-2767*
  13 mi. SW at 5566 Gravenstein Highway (Hwy. 116) - Forestville
  kozlowskifarms.com
  Tucked away in the heart of a major deciduous fruit and grape
  producing district is Kozlowski Farms. Here is a premier source
  for jams, jellies, syrups and all sorts of 100% fruit-sweetened

chutneys and other condiments made from regional products. Most are available for generous tastes among attractive displays in the well-furnished retail store. They also have a catalog.

★ **Oakville Grocery** *(707)433-3200*
downtown at SE corner of plaza at 124 Matheson St.
oakvillegrocery.com
Wine Country's renowned gourmet grocer has an outpost on the plaza. Numerous jams, sauces, breads, etc. are available for tastes. A wealth of deli items, condiments, and breads, plus wine and upscale beverages, are uniformly first rate and ideal for assembling a picnic. Awning-shaded tables out front are just right for dining (B-L-D) overlooking the plaza.

Healdsburg Veterans Memorial Beach Park *(707)433-1625*
1 mi. SE at 13839 Old Redwood Hwy.
From Memorial Day into September, the town's beach on the Russian River is *the* place to be for swimming and fishing. Nearby are shady picnic sites, a snack bar and canoe rentals.

★ **Lake Sonoma Recreation Area** *(707)433-9483*
11 mi. NW (via Dry Creek Rd.) at 3333 Skaggs Springs Rd.
www.spn.usace.army.mil
An earthfill dam 319 feet high was completed in 1983 to create a lake that extends nine miles into redwood groves and oak woodlands on foothills above Dry Creek. A visitor center and fish hatchery are open year-round. A full-service marina caters to the main attraction–boating. You can use sail, paddle, motor, or waterski boats on most of the lake. Other facilities include a store, swimming beaches, picnic areas, and campgrounds ranging from full-service to primitive campsites accessible only by boat or trail. More than forty miles of hiking, biking, and horseback riding trails provide access to surrounding hills.

★ **Russian River**
The gentle little Russian River offers more than fifty miles of slow-moving water, and a few easy riffles. Natural swimming holes backed by sunny, sandy beaches abound. Handsome, second-growth redwoods line the banks for miles. Swimming, fishing, sunbathing and floating are popular most of the year.

★ *Wineries*
Healdsburg has more wine tasting rooms downtown than anyplace in California. Within a block of the plaza are: **Artisan Cellars, Gallo, Rosenblum, Selby,** and **Windsor**. More than seventy premium wineries surround Healdsburg in the scenic Russian River, Dry Creek and Alexander Valleys. Many have tasting, tours, sales, gift shops and picnic facilities. Unlike Napa Valley wineries, most of these do not charge tasting fees. The best are among the outstanding wineries of America.

95

Alderbrook Winery   *(707)433-9154 (800)405-5987*
just SW at 2306 Magnolia Dr.
alderbrook.com
A handsome old ranch-style building houses a Hospitality Center with premium wine tasting, sales, tours, and a gourmet shop, plus picnic sites and vineyard views from a wrap-around veranda. Open 10-5 daily.

Chateau Souverain   *(707)433-8281 (888)809-4637*
6 mi. N (near US 101) at 400 Souverain Rd. - Geyserville
chateausouverain.com
A landmark chateau crowns a slope surrounded by gardens and vineyards. The main building has (fee) tasting facilities for premium red and white wines with a view, an art gallery, a connoisseur's shop featuring Reidel stemware, and a memorable restaurant (see listing). Open 10-5 daily.

Davis Bynum Winery   *(800)826-1073*
8 mi. SW at 8075 Westside Rd.
davisbynum.com
A luxuriant hillside above the Russian River Valley is a charming site for picnics by this vine-shrouded winery. Organic farming contributes to the appeal of pinot noir and other premium varietals available for tasting and sales. Open 10-5 daily.

Dry Creek Vineyards   *(707)433-1000 (800)864-9463*
4 mi. NW at 3770 Lambert Bridge Rd.
drycreekvineyard.com
Dry Creek Vineyards became (in 1972) the first new winery to be built in Dry Creek Valley following Prohibition. The deservedly popular landmark has a vine-covered building for tasting and sales of classically styled premium varietals, including fume blanc that is a California benchmark. Adjoining gardens and shady picnic areas are surrounded by vineyards. Open 10:30-4:30 daily.

Ferrari-Carano Vineyards & Winery *(707)433-6700 (800)831-0381*
9 mi. NW at 8761 Dry Creek Rd.
ferrari-carano.com
One of America's great premium wineries is showcased in a complex that includes acres of spectacular gardens, fountains and plazas overlooking surrounding vineyards and mountains. Regular and reserve chardonnays are especially notable. A monumental Mediterranean-style chateau crowning a rise includes an expansive (fee) tasting room and retail store. Downstairs is the most elegant wine storage facility in America. Vertical tastings are scheduled frequently in the aromatic cellar. Open 10-5 daily.

Fetzer Vineyards   *(707)744-1250 (800)846-8637*
26 mi. NW at 13601 Eastside Rd. - Hopland

fetzer.com
Fetzer remains the keystone among reasonably priced major premium wine producers in California. Many varietals are available for tastes in both the regular tasting room and a premium reserve (fee) tasting room in a complex that evolved from the (1844) Valley Oaks Ranch and now also includes a plush bed-and-breakfast inn amidst vineyards. There is a well-stocked wine-related gift shop and gourmet deli, plus picnic tables. Open 9-5 daily.

Fritz Winery *(707)894-3389 (800)418-9463*
11 mi. NW at 24691 Dutcher Creek Rd. - Cloverdale
fritzwinery.com
This family-owned and operated winery on a hillside at the top of Dry Creek is ingeniously dug into a slope with tunnels for aging single-vineyard-designated chardonnays, zinfandels, and other premium varietals. A tasting and sales room overlooks lush hillsides and nearby picnic area in a garden. Open 10:30-4:30 daily.

Hartford Family Wines *(707)887-1756 (800)588-0234*
13 mi. SW at 8075 Martinelli Rd. - Forestville
hartfordwines.com
Deep in a narrow valley reached by a winding two-lane road is a splendid chateau-style building surrounded by luxuriant gardens. All around, vineyards extend to redwood-forested hills. The estate's several styles of single-vineyard chardonnay, pinot noir and zinfandel are uniformly excellent. Overlooking a fountain court is one of the most gracious tasting rooms in Wine Country. Open 10-4:30 daily.

Hop Kiln Winery *(707)433-6491*
7 mi. SW at 6050 Westside Rd.
hopkilnwinery.com
At Hop Kiln, three picturesque towering structures rising from a stone base are a 1905 landmark now used for wine production. The tasting room has picture-window views of ponds and vineyards, and many wine-related gifts. Picnic tables are in surrounding gardens. Open 10-5 daily.

Iron Horse Vineyards *(707)887-1507*
15 mi. SW at 9786 Ross Station Rd. - Sebastopol
ironhorsevineyards.com
Iron Horse is an American benchmark for super-premium sparkling and still wines. Both reflect the winemaker's preoccupation with award-winning quality using methode champenoise, chardonnay and pinor noir grapes. Crowning a ridgetop above the lush folds of Green Valley is a gracious complex. An outdoor tasting bar with a grand Wine Country panorama surrounded by gardens, orchards and flourishing vineyards is still (remarkably) complimentary. Open 10-3:30 daily.

J Vineyards & Winery   *(707)431-3646   (888)594-6326*
3 mi. S at 11447 Old Redwood Hwy.
jwine.com
J Winery is a post-modern facility that showcases both premium wine and gourmet regional cuisine in a tour-de-force setting of fiber-optic glass jewels in a mega-wall behind the tasting bar. Famed J sparkling wine and premium varietals are cleverly matched with cutting-edge cuisine in paired (fee) tastes or individual tastes that lend a new dimension to a Wine Country experience. The adjoining shop is similarly sophisticated in wines and related quality products. Open 11-5 daily.

Jordan Vineyard & Winery   *(707)431-5250   (800)654-1213*
4 mi. N at 1474 Alexander Valley Rd.
jordanwinery.com
On a hill above Alexander Valley is one of Wine Country's most grandiose sources of premium chardonnay and cabernet sauvignon. The winery is housed in a baronial building remi-niscent of a French chateau surrounded by beautiful gardens. (Fee) tours and tasting by appointment only. Call Mon.-Fri. 8-5.

Kendall-Jackson Wine Center   *(707)571-8100*
10 mi. SE (near US 101) at 5007 Fulton Rd. - Fulton
kj.com
Lovely flower gardens, a fountain court, a wine sensory garden, an organic culinary garden, and a demonstration vineyard frame a handsome chateau. Facilities include (fee) tastings of premium varietals produced by Kendall-Jackson and smaller wineries encompassed by this estate, garden tours, a wine shop, exhibits, deli, and picnic area. Open 10-5 daily.

Korbel Champagne Cellars   *(707)824-7000*
15 mi. SW at 13250 River Rd. - Guerneville
korbel.com
Korbel, founded in the 1870s by natives of Bohemia, produces "methode" sparkling wines nationally known as fair-price-bench-marks. Tastes, sales, tours, a museum, deli and shop are housed in vine-covered stone buildings with a tower right out of Medieval Bohemia. Old Country gardens can also be toured in season. Open 9:30-4:30 daily.

Lambert Bridge Winery   *(707)431-9600   (800)975-0555*
5 mi. NW at 4085 W. Dry Creek Rd.
lambertbridge.com
Premium wine (chardonnay, sauvignon blanc and zinfandel are especially notable) tasting and sales are in a notably romantic tasting room. Picnic areas are also charming, and there is a gourmet gift shop with generous tastes of their premium mustards and grapeseed oil specialties. Open 10:30-4:30 daily.

Lancaster Estate   *(707)433-8178   (800)799-8444*
13 mi. E at 15001 Chalk Hill Rd.
lancaster-reserve.com
The Hospitality Center opened in 2001 in an elegant salon setting
with comfortable sofas and easy chairs for guests to enjoy the
latest vintage of Lancaster's single remarkable release—a super-
premium bordeaux-style red wine. The gracious (fee) tasting is
enhanced by expansive views of organic gardens and vineyards on
adjoining hillsides. The cave and vineyard tour is very
worthwhile. Open only by appointment Mon.-Sat.

Mazzocco Vineyards   *(707)431-8159   (800)501-8466*
6 mi. NW at 1400 Lytton Springs Rd.
mazzocco.com
Mazzocco's family-owned winery tasting room/gift shop crowns a
ridge in a stylish wood-trimmed building. A twenty-foot-high
window wall provides outstanding views of oak-covered hills,
surrounding vineyards and gardens. The picnic area is well-
positioned to share the scene. Premium estate wines are
generously available for tastes. Open 10-4:30 daily.

Quivira   *(707)431-8333   (800)292-8339*
6 mi. NW at 4900 W. Dry Creek Rd.
quiverawine.com
In 2002, Quivira introduced a charming expanded facility that
includes a tasting room with a fine vineyard view and barrel-
vaulted ceiling to enhance enjoyment of handcrafted, estate-
grown varietals (especially zinfandel and sauvignon blanc)
produced here. The adjoining gardens feature a choice of sunny
or shaded picnic tables surrounded by vineyards. Open 11-5 daily.

Rodney Strong Vineyards   *(707)431-1533 (800)678-4763*
3 mi. S at 11455 Old Redwood Hwy.
rodneystrong.com
A dramatic, post-modern building houses a recently remodeled
hospitality center with a stylish skylit premium wine tasting
room, well-stocked gift shop, and wine gallery tours. Special
musical and other events are staged in a picturesque greensward
that is also used for picnicking adjacent to a building alcove
surrounded by vineyards. Open 10-5 daily.

Roshambo Winery   *(707)431-2051   (888)525-9463*
3 mi. SW at 3000 Westside Rd.
winery.cc
Roshambo, opened in 2002, features glass, stone, metal and wood
combined in post-modern ways that make the expansive tasting
room and adjoining art gallery a compelling sensual experience.
A window wall beyond a handsome tasting bar where premium
chardonnays and sauvignon blancs are poured overlooks

umbrella-shaded picnic tables on a terrace that shares a lovely view of the winery and vineyards. Open 10:30-4:30 Wed.-Mon. Closed Tues.

Simi Winery   *(707)433-6981   (800)746-4880*
2 mi. N at 16275 Healdsburg Av.
simiwinery.com
Founded in 1876, Simi offers excellent tours involving a historic stone building, (fee) tastes of all premium wines, and gift specialties in a handsome shop. Picnic facilities are well sited on luxuriant grounds beneath towering redwoods. Open 10-5 daily.

Sonoma Cutrer   *(707)528-1181*
11 mi. S at 4401 Slusser Rd. - Windsor
sonomacutrer.com
The winery, founded in 1973, is dedicated to the production of estate-bottled chardonnay from their own vineyards. Resulting benchmark chardonnays are often ranked #1 in annual restaurant polls of most popular wine. Grounds include manicured lawns where World Croquet championships are held; umbrella-shaded tables on a terrace next to a genteel tasting/reception room, and a picnic area in a redwood grove by a pond. Winery tours, tasting and sales by appointment Mon.-Sat.

RESTAURANTS

★ **Applewood Inn & Restaurant**   *(707)869-9093*
18 mi. SW at 13555 Hwy. 116 - Guerneville
applewoodinn.com
D only. Closed Sun.-Mon.   *Very Expensive*
Bold colorful dishes with unusual flavors, textures and combinations of ingredients are the hallmark of "adventure cuisine" in the Applewood Inn. The creative compositions prepared with seasonally fresh regional ingredients are served in a simply comfortable candlelit dining room enhanced by a river-rock fireplace.

Bear Republic Brewing Co.   *(707)433-2337*
downtown at 345 Healdsburg Av.
bearrepublic.com
L-D.   *Moderate*
A nifty selection of pub grub includes some distinctive dishes like clams steamed in house ale or shepherd's pie. The big, boisterous brew pub includes a nifty display of brewing apparatus behind a bar, all sorts of colorful bric-a-brac, periodic live music and a lattice-shaded dining deck by a park.

★ **Bistro Ralph**   *(707)433-1380*
downtown at 109 Plaza St.
L-D. Closed Sun.   *Expensive*

Bistro Ralph is a long-established source for California cuisine. A short menu offers dishes emphasizing fresh seasonal ingredients in presentations that can taste as good as they look. The casual avant-garde little bistro dining area and bar are popular.

Catelli's The Rex   *(707)433-6000*
downtown at 241 Healdsburg Av.
catellistherex.com
L-D. No L Sat. & Sun. Closed Mon.   *Expensive*
This long-popular area restaurant recently settled into downtown Healdsburg. New York steak and sautéed mushrooms or tiger prawns sautéed with white wine are among favorites that suggest continuing interest in traditional California/Italian dishes. Full white linen and flowers further distinguish dining areas.

★ **Chateau Souverain Winery Cafe** *(707)433-3141 (888)809-4637*
6 mi. N (near US 101) at 400 Souverain Rd. - Geyserville
chateausouverain.com
L-D. No D Mon.-Thurs.   *Expensive*
Chateau Souverain Cafe is one of the best restaurants-in-a-winery in California. Seasonally fresh regional ingredients are expertly prepared into innovative cuisine in a luxurious firelit dining room. The romantic window-wall view of surrounding vineyards and mountains is exceeded only by the view from the terrace.

★ **Costeaux French Bakery**   *(707)433-1913*
downtown at 417 Healdsburg Av.
cousteaux.com
B-L.   *Moderate*
Fine assortments of breakfast pastries, award-winning sourdough and other breads, cakes, pies and cookies are attractively displayed. Light fare and beverages are also served in the large spiffy coffee shop or streetside patio, or to go.

Downtown Bakery & Creamery   *(707)431-2719*
downtown at 308-A Center St.
B-L.   *Moderate*
All sorts of American and European-style breads, desserts, and breakfast pastries are served to go from this popular long-established bakery fronting on the plaza.

★ **Dry Creek Kitchen**   *(707)431-0330*
downtown at 25 Matheson St.
hotelhealdsburg.com
L-D.   *Very Expensive*
Wine Country dining recently got edgier, thanks to Charlie Palmer, a renowned Manhattan chef. His preoccupation with top-quality seasonal ingredients emphasizing the region and artisan products is now ensconced in Healdsburg. "Adventure cuisine" is presented in an ever-evolving selection of cutting-edge dishes that

will surprise, and may delight–or dismay. Even the uber-cool upscale dining room offers a surprisingly unique take on the expo kitchen. Next door, the **Cafe Newsstand** (301 Healdsburg Avenue) offers the restaurant's fine pastries along with an extensive newspaper and magazine selection in a spiffy little cafe.

★ **Farmhouse Inn & Restaurant**   *(707)887-3300*
12 mi. SW at 7871 River Rd. - Forestville
farmhouseinn.com
D only. Closed Mon.-Wed.   *Very Expensive*
The Farmhouse Restaurant is a sterling destination for Wine Country cuisine. Remarkably diverse bounty from the nearby sea and farmlands is translated with skill and passion into culinary delights that smoothly complement the wealth of world class wines produced nearby. Ever-changing seasonal dishes like pan-seared tenderloin of venison with roasted French butter pears and a wildflower honey curry sauce are among California's finest, as are desserts like apple and pear in a cornmeal crust with vanilla bean gelato. Details–a polished presentation of classic local and international cheeses; a wide choice of coffee infusions; and black, green or herbal teas–enrich the experience. An intimate dining room with informally elegant candlelit tables, a corner fireplace, murals, and wine display captures the romantic spirit of Wine Country at its very best.

Felix & Louie's   *(707)433-6966*
downtown at 106 Matheson St.
D only, plus L on Sat. Sun. brunch.   *Very Expensive*
California fare with an Italian slant is presented on a grazing menu. A wood-fired pizza oven and a handsome ever-popular bar enliven big simply decorated dining areas. A grand piano is played occasionally, along with live entertainment.

★ **Flying Goat Coffee Roastery**   *(707)433-9081 (800)675-3599*
downtown at 324 Center St.
flyinggoatcoffee.com
B-L.   *Moderate*
The Flying Goat Coffee Roastery is one of the best sources of gourmet coffee in Wine Country. Their spacious coffeehouse by the plaza also features their own delicious mighty muffins, scones, and other morning delights in a snazzy setting of hardwood floors, funky seating, and avant-garde local artwork.

★ **John Ash & Co.**   *(707)527-7687*
11 mi. S on Hwy. 101 at 4330 Barnes Rd. - Santa Rosa
vintnersinn.com
L-D. No L Sat.   *Very Expensive*
John Ash & Co. was one of California's first sources of Wine Country cuisine like roasted breast of Sonoma duck with

portabello mushroom dorados and mango/tangerine barbecue sauce. International culinary styles are skillfully blended into bold and beautiful gourmet delights, from exotic appetizers to superb desserts. The posh firelit vineyard-view dining room is a peaceful backdrop with full linen, designer candles and objects of art.

★ **Madrona Manor**   *(707)433-6831*
1 mi. W at 1001 Westside Rd.
www.madronamanor.com
D only.   *Very Expensive*
Madrona Manor is once again a major destination for New California cuisine. Greens, herbs, fruits and vegetables from their adjoining garden are skillfully combined with top-quality regional products. Diners can opt for a la carte or a prix-fixe tour-de-force tasting menu. The mansion's comfortably elegant dining rooms capture a serene Victorian spirit.

★ **Manzanita Restaurant**   *(707)433-8111*
downtown at 336 Healdsburg Av.
D only. Closed Mon.-Tues.   *Very Expensive*
Manzanita, opened in 2001, features innovative Wine Country cuisine in dishes like flatbread or roasted half-chicken with wild mushroom ragout. Meyer lemon cake with mascarpone sorbet and strawberries typifies housemade desserts. A raised mesquite-fired oven distinguishes a kitchen extension by tables set with candles and full linen. A stylish bar adjoins.

★ **Ravenette**   *(707)431-1770*
downtown at 117 North St.
L-D. Closed Mon.-Tues. No D Sun.   *Expensive*
The more casual offshoot of Ravenous Cafe remains in the original location. Creative California cuisine might include smoked trout salad or grilled salmon with an Asian noodle salad and baby bok choy served in an intimate informal setting.

★ **Ravenous**   *(707)431-1302*
downtown at 420 Center St.
D only. Closed Mon.-Tues.   *Expensive*
Creative cuisine is expertly prepared. A short menu changes frequently to assure quality and seasonal freshness. Housemade desserts like apple rhubarb crisp with vanilla rosemary gelato can be delicious. Candles, a fireplace, and a bar enhance intimate dining areas in a cottage behind a lovely garden.

Singletree Inn Cafe   *(707)433-8263*
just S at 165 Healdsburg Av.
B-L.   *Moderate*
All-American breakfasts like biscuits and gravy with omelets, pancakes, and french toast are served in a coffee shop with a choice of padded booths or chairs.

★ **Tastings Restaurant & Wine Bar**   *(707)433-3936*
downtown at 505 Healdsburg Av.
tastingsrestaurant.com
L-D. Closed Tues.-Thurs.   *Very Expensive*
Tastings is a progenitor of a new style of "adventure cuisine."
Fresh quality seasonal ingredients from the region are skillfully
transformed into piquant dishes that are deliberately different.
Minimalist decor in a dining room overlooking the kitchen does
not detract from the bold adventurous offerings. In keeping with
the restaurant's name, a five-course tastings menu is an option
that is paired with local wines.

★ **Zin Restaurant & Wine Bar**   *(707)473-0946*
downtown at 344 Center St.
zinrestaurant.com
L-D.   *Expensive*
A thoughtful grazing menu of creative California dishes has
distinguished Zin since it opened in 1999. Dishes on the changing
menu might be topped with a (seasonally fresh) fruit crisp with
fresh berry sauce and toasted almond ice cream. Wine Country's
most comprehensive selection of zinfandels by the bottle, glass or
sampler is another feature offered in a minimalist bistro setting
with exposed beams, folk art murals and an expo kitchen.

LODGINGS

Conventional lodgings by the freeway are surprisingly scarce.
Happily, fine bed-and-breakfast inns emphasizing historic
buildings or Wine Country scenery are numerous. High season is
April through October. Apart from weekends, rates may be as
much as 20% less at other times.

★ **Applewood Inn & Restaurant**   *(707)869-9093*
18 mi. SW at 13555 Hwy. 116 (Pocket Canyon) - Guerneville
applewoodinn.com
19 units   *(800)555-8509*   *Very Expensive*
Tucked away on a slope within walking distance of the Russian
River is one of Wine Country's distinctive country inns. Gardens,
a fountain court, a pool and whirlpool enhance a Tuscan-style
cluster of buildings shaded by luxuriant young redwoods. Full
gourmet breakfast is complimentary. Culinary adventures are
assured in the sophisticated dining room (see listing). Each
spacious, beautifully furnished room in the historic mansion and
newer complex has all contemporary amenities and a queen bed.
Some also have a raised gas fireplace and a private patio.
    #10–fine redwoods view, large tile two-head shower,
        private patio with a fountain and redwood view,
        raised gas fireplace in view of queen bed.

★ **Belle de Jour Inn**   *(707)431-9777*
2 mi. N at 16276 Healdsburg Av. - 95448
belledejourinn.com
5 units   *Expensive-Very Expensive*
Bucolic surroundings contribute to the tranquil feeling of this
bed-and-breakfast inn built around a Victorian farmhouse. Full
breakfast is complimentary. Each unit is individually beautifully
furnished in contemporary country decor with a private bath,
extra amenities, a refrigerator and a queen or king bed.
    "The Terrace Room"–gas fireplace, two-person
    valley-view whirlpool in view of king bed.
    "The Carriage House"–spacious, upstairs, gas
    fireplace, two-person whirlpool room, king bed.
    "The Caretaker's Suite"–cottage, in-bath two-person
    whirlpool, cast-iron fireplace in view of canopy king bed.
★ **Calderwood**   *(707)431-1110*
just NW at 25 W. Grant St. - 95448
calderwoodinn.com
6 units   *(800)600-5444*   *Expensive-Very Expensive*
A gracious bed-and-breakfast (circa 1902) is ensconced among
mature redwood and cedar trees and luxuriant gardens planted
by Luther Burbank a century ago. Full gourmet breakfast,
afternoon appetizers and wine, and evening cookies and port are
complimentary. Each beautifully decorated room is individually
furnished with antiques and most contemporary amenities, a
private bath, plus a queen bed.
    "Cambria"–large in-bath whirlpool, upstairs
    with garden view, antique brass queen bed.
    "Springkell"–spacious, gas fireplace, clawfoot tub/shower.
★ **Camellia Inn**   *(707)433-8182*
just NE at 211 North St. - 95448
camelliainn.com
9 units   *(800)727-8182*   *Expensive- Very Expensive*
A villa-style swimming pool is a feature of this bed-and-breakfast
in an impeccably restored Italianate Victorian townhouse
surrounded by lush gardens and camellia bushes. Full buffet
breakfast and afternoon wine and cheese are complimentary.
Each individually decorated room is beautifully furnished with
period touches and contemporary conveniences, a private bath,
and a double or queen bed.
    "Tower West," "Tower East"–spacious, gas fireplace,
    two-person whirlpool, queen bed.
    "Tiffany"–gas fireplace, two-person whirlpool, queen bed.
Dry Creek Inn - Best Western   *(707)433-0300*
1 mi. N (near Hwy. 101) at 198 Dry Creek Rd. - 95448

drycreekinn.com
104 units   *(800)222-5784*   *Moderate-Expensive*
Healdsburg's biggest lodging is a contemporary motel with a pool, whirlpool, exercise room and restaurant. A split of wine and Continental breakfast are complimentary. Each room is well furnished including a refrigerator and two queens or a king bed.

★ **Duchamp**   *(707)431-1300*
downtown at 421 Foss St. - 95448
duchamphotel.com
10 units   *(800)431-9341*   *Very Expensive*
Duchamp is an avant-garde newer lodging. European-style villas and cottages artistically combine minimalist sensibilities and whimsical touches. Features include a long lap pool, whirlpool, and (fee) evening wine bar. Expanded Continental breakfast is complimentary. Each villa and cottage is beautifully furnished in stark, simple decor and has a private terrace, mini-bar, oversized walk-in shower, gas fireplace, and a king bed.

★ **Farmhouse Inn**   *(707)887-3300*
12 mi. SW at 7871 River Rd. - Forestville 95436
farmhouseinn.com
8 units   *(800)464-6642*   *Expensive-Very Expensive*
The Farmhouse Inn is one of the most romantic getaways in California. Off the beaten path by oak-and-redwood-shrouded hills at the western edge of Wine Country is a series of cottages sprinkled up a tiny canyon. A historic farmhouse centerpiece amid luxuriant gardens has been transformed into an outstanding dinner house (see listing). A garden pool (May-October) and (fee) spa services are other features. Bicycles for touring and full gourmet breakfast are complimentary. Each beautifully furnished room is individually decorated to convey the peaceful charm of Wine Country, and includes all contemporary amenities plus (in most rooms) a woodburning or gas fireplace, a two-person whirlpool tub with a view of a lush hillside, and a queen or king bed. Some units also have a two-person sauna.

   #2,#8–sitting area, in-bath two-person whirlpool/
     shower, woodburning fireplace, king bed.
   #1,#3,#4–in-bath two-person whirlpool/shower,
     sauna, woodburning fireplace, queen bed.

The George Alexander House   *(707)433-1358*
just E at 423 Matheson St. - 95448
georgealexanderhouse.com
4 units   *(800)310-1358*   *Expensive-Very Expensive*
This low-rise 1905 gingerbread mansion on a quiet street is newly renovated and furnished with antiques to serve as a bed-and-breakfast inn amid gardens. Full breakfast is complimentary, as

is a sauna. Each attractively furnished room has a private bath and queen or king bed.
"Back Porch Suite"–small garden-view deck, wood-
burning stove and large whirlpool in view of king bed.

★ **Grape Leaf Inn**   *(707)433-8140*
just N at 539 Johnson St. - 95448
grapeleafinn.com
12 units   (866)732-9131   Expensive-Very Expensive
A Queen Anne Victorian home has been transformed and skillfully expanded into a gracious bed-and-breakfast surrounded by gardens. Full gourmet country breakfast is complimentary. So is a quintessential Wine Country adventure–you're invited into the owner's handsome wine cellar via a secret door hidden in a bookcase to experience an assortment of premium wines of Sonoma County paired with selected top-quality cheeses and breads. Frequently, a winemaker is invited to present his varietals. Period pieces and contemporary decor including private bathrooms and a queen or king bed distinguish each beautifully furnished room. All are enhanced by numerous flourishes like skylights, stained-glass windows, dormers and sconces, gas fireplaces, and some unusual extras like a full-tile steam/shower, authentic Japanese soaking tub or push-button-control skylight closures in various rooms. Most also have a whirlpool bath for two.
"Syrah"–spacious, large full-tile two-person steam room,
shower and authentic Japanese soaking tub, gas fireplace, skylight with push-button control, king bed.
"Roussanne"–fireplace, in-bath two-person whirlpool
under skylit gable, skylit gable above king bed.
"Mourvedre"–two-person in-bath whirlpool, antique gas
fireplace faces eight-sided turret with ornate king bed.
"Viognier"–gas fireplace, in-bath two-person
whirlpool under skylighted window, king bed.
"Chardonnay Suite"–big romantic hideaway, two-person in-
bath whirlpool, two skylight ceiling windows over king bed.

★ **Healdsburg Inn on the Plaza**   *(707)433-6991*
downtown at 110 Matheson St. (Box 1196) - 95448
healdsburginn.com
11 units   (800)431-8663   Expensive-Very Expensive
A historic bank building right on the plaza has been transformed to include a boutique on the first floor and a bed-and-breakfast upstairs. Full complimentary breakfast, afternoon wine with appetizers, and evening refreshments are served in a solarium overlooking the plaza. Each well-furnished room has period touches, all contemporary conveniences and a queen or king bed. Most have a gas fireplace and clawfoot tub.

"Carriage House"–corner gas fireplace, private balcony,
in-bath heart-shaped two-person whirlpool, king bed.
"Garden Suite"–corner gas fireplace, private balcony,
in-bath two-person whirlpool, king bed.

★ **Honor Mansion**   *(707)433-4277*
1 mi. NW at 14891 Grove St. - 95448
honormansion.com
11 units   *(800)554-4667*   *Expensive-Very Expensive*
Honor Mansion is one of America's most romantic bed-and-breakfast inns. The expansive complex surrounded by an artistic white picket fence includes a handsome Victorian mansion and compatible recent additions. Luxuriant gardens showcase a magnificent 120-year-old magnolia and daphne, a bush with an unforgettably delicate sweet scent in late winter, tranquil ponds, a waterfall, walking paths, and a landscaped lap pool. Full gourmet breakfast, afternoon refreshments, appetizers and wine hour, evening sherry and cookies, 24-hour espresso/cappuccino machine access, and concierge service are complimentary. There is also (fee) massage and a shop full of quality gifts. Each luxuriously furnished room is individually decorated and has a private bath, a wealth of extra amenities, plus a queen or king bed. Some rooms also have a gas fireplace and refrigerator.
"Vineyard Suite I"–gas fireplace, soaking tub, big private
patio with two-person whirlpool in view of king bed.
"Vineyard Suite II"–large gas fireplace in view of soaking
tub, private patio with large whirlpool in view of king bed.
"Garden Suite"–gas fireplace, three private decks/porches,
patio with two-person whirlpool, dual-head shower, king bed.
"Tower Suite"–in historic water tower by the pool,
private sundeck, gas fireplace upstairs, two-person
garden whirlpool, dual-head shower, queen bed.

★ **Hotel Healdsburg**   *(707)431-2800*
downtown at 25 Matheson St. - 95448
hotelhealdsburg.com
55 units   *(800)889-7188*   *Very Expensive*
Healdsburg's charming plaza accented by towering redwoods is now complete with the Hotel Healdsburg, established in 2001 on the west side. The three-story complex reflects the town's recent evolution toward "big city" themes. Amenities include a spa with an exercise room, a large landscaped pool, (fee) wide range of beauty and body treatments, and famed Dry Creek Kitchen (see listing). A complimentary expanded Continental breakfast is available in the lounge or you can take it to your room. Each spacious room is beautifully furnished in a minimalist, postmodern way, and includes a six-foot soaking tub and walk-in

shower, private standing balcony, mini-refrigerator with complimentary beverages, and feather queen or king bed.

★ **Madrona Manor**   *(707)433-4231*
1 mi. W at 1001 Westside Rd. (Box 818) - 95448
www.madronamanor.com
22 units   (800)258-4003   Expensive-Very Expensive
Madrona Manor is a major Wine Country landmark. The three-story Victorian mansion (circa 1881) is surrounded by lovely gardens, orchards, and a lush forest on a hill above Dry Creek. Amenities include a pool and gourmet restaurant (see listing). Full breakfast buffet is complimentary. Each room is romantically well furnished with a blend of stately antiques and contemporary decor. All have private baths and a queen or king bed. Most have a gas or woodburning fireplace.
"Schoolhouse East and West Suites"–beautifully furnished
    sitting room, private garden-view deck, two-person
    whirlpool with open-shutter view of gas fireplace, king bed.
"Suite 400"–large in-bath whirlpool tub in view of wood-
    burning fireplace, private hillside-view deck, king bed.

★ **Villa Messina**   *(707)433-6655*
3 mi. NW at 316 Burgundy Rd. - 95448
villamessina.com
5 units   Very Expensive
The historic Simi reservoir site is now a hilltop bed-and-breakfast villa. Colorful surrounding gardens also sequester a pool and whirlpool. Full breakfast and afternoon wine and appetizers are complimentary. Each beautifully furnished room blends antiques, artworks, extra amenities, Wine Country views, and a queen or king bed. Most have a whirlpool tub and/or gas fireplace.
"Asti Room"–fine view from private deck, gas fireplace,
    in-bath two-person whirlpool with view, king bed.

★ **Vintners Inn**   *(707)575-7350*
11 mi. S (on Hwy. 101) at 4350 Barnes Rd. - Santa Rosa 95403
vintnersinn.com
44 units   (800)421-2584   Expensive-Very Expensive
This French-style country inn, surrounded by vineyards, has a fine restaurant next door (see John Ash & Co.), and a tranquil garden whirlpool. Full gourmet breakfast is complimentary. Each spacious room is beautifully furnished including an honor bar/refrigerator, and has a king bed. Many also have a pressed-wood fireplace and private deck overlooking vineyards.
"Upstairs Junior Suite" (2 of these)–vaulted ceiling,
    spacious, private vineyard-view balcony, large in-bath
    whirlpool, pressed-wood fireplace in view of king bed.
"Downstairs Junior Suite" (2 of these)–spacious, patio, large
    in-bath whirlpool, pressed-wood fireplace in view of king bed.

Mendocino

Mendocino is the most romantic seaside village in America. It celebrates a dreamy appeal out of place and time. The "place" is an isolated verdant promontory overlooking a wildly beautiful coastline that could be in Maine. The "time" would be Victorian, since the whole village seems to be of whitewashed wooden buildings and tidy gardens unchanged from the 19th century.

Not surprisingly, the town was settled in the 1850s by lumbermen from New England. They recognized the commercial potential for a sawmill on the headlands above a deep-water anchorage by a river with access to vast adjacent redwood forests. After nearly a century, the last mill closed during the Depression. Mendocino's demise was averted by artists and dreamers attracted by the natural beauty and isolation of the area. They were followed by more affluent urban escapists who also helped preserve and restore this authentic cluster of clapboard relics. The future as a romantic getaway was secured when the state acquired the blufftop meadow that had been the mill site between downtown and the ocean.

Today, Mendocino's Yankee-Victorian relics and manicured gardens flourish. Weathered whitewashed structures house unique specialty shops and galleries displaying fine local arts and crafts, and romantic restaurants offering regional gourmet cuisine. Charming bed-and-breakfast inns romance guests here to browse artistic gems throughout the village; explore headlands and redwood forests by canoe, bicycle, foot or car; or seek tranquility in secluded coves and inspiring overlooks.

WEATHER PROFILE

V.W.R. *		Jan.	Feb.	Mar.	Apr.	May	June	July	Aug.	Sep.	Oct.	Nov.	Dec.
Great	10												
Fine	9												
Very Good	8												
Good	7												
Moderate	6												
	5												
	4												
	3												
	2												
	1												
	0												

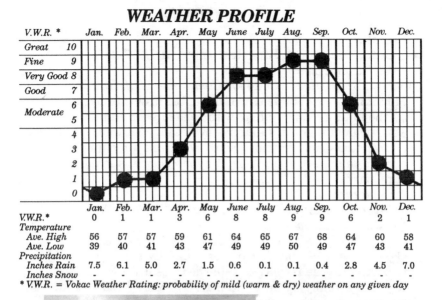

	Jan.	Feb.	Mar.	Apr.	May	June	July	Aug.	Sep.	Oct.	Nov.	Dec.
V.W.R.*	0	1	1	3	6	8	8	9	9	6	2	1
Temperature												
Ave. High	56	57	57	59	61	64	65	67	68	64	60	58
Ave. Low	39	40	41	43	47	49	49	50	49	47	43	41
Precipitation												
Inches Rain	7.5	6.1	5.0	2.7	1.5	0.6	0.1	0.1	0.4	2.8	4.5	7.0
Inches Snow	-	-	-	-	-	-	-	-	-	-	-	-

* V.W.R. = Vokac Weather Rating: probability of mild (warm & dry) weather on any given day

BASIC INFORMATION

Population: 1,100
Elevation: 60 feet
Location: 155 miles Northwest of San Francisco
Airport (regularly scheduled flights): San Francisco - 165 miles

Fort Bragg-Mendocino Coast Chamber of Commerce
  11 mi. N at 332 N. Main St. (Box 1141) - Fort Bragg 95437
mendocinocoast.com   (707)961-6300   (800)726-2780
Mendocino County Alliance (707)462-7417   (866)466-3636
  525 S. Main St., Suite E - Ukiah 95482
  gomendo.com

ATTRACTIONS

Bicycling

★ **Catch-a-canoe & Bicycles, Too** *(707)937-0273*
catchacanoe.com
1 mi. S (off Hwy. 1) at 44850 Comptche-Ukiah Rd.
Mountain or road bicycles can be rented in this full-service shop by the hour or longer along with related gear and information. Tour coastal highways and byways that are always scenic, but often narrow and winding. Better yet, rent a mountain bike to explore the redwood and fern canyons via trails in surrounding state parks.

Boat Rentals

★ **Catch-a-canoe & Bicycles, Too** *(707)937-0273*
catchacanoe.com
1 mi. S (off Hwy. 1) at 44850 Comptche-Ukiah Rd.
Canoe rentals are available year-round by the hour or day for trips up into the recently established Big River State Park. Big River is actually a gentle little river lined by redwood and fir interspersed with sandy beaches and swimming holes. Because the river is tidal for several miles (it is the longest undeveloped estuary in California), you can allow the flow of the tides to carry you up and back for a rare experience–if you time it right!

★ *Festivals*
gomendo.com *(866)466-3636*
Mendocino is the base camp for delightfully creative annual festivals that celebrate crabs, mushrooms, wine and whales among superb bounties of the secluded setting. These well-organized events have become so popular that most businesses in both Mendocino and Fort Bragg participate, especially romantic bed-and-breakfasts, gourmet provisioners and talented chefs, and the legendary Skunk Train.

Food Specialties

★ **The Apple Farm** *(707)895-2333*
31 mi. SE (via Hwy. 128) on Philo-Greenwood Rd.
Bates & Schmitt's outstanding organic apple juice and other gourmet treats like chutneys and jams are sold at a display by a seasonal fruit pressing and packing shed. Their sophisticated contemporary cooking school and related four-unit inn adjoins.

★ **Mendocino Jams & Jellies** *(707)937-1037 (800)708-1196*
downtown at 440 Main St.
mendojams.com
Samples are available of first-rate jams and other products displayed for sale in this small gourmet shop. Open 10-5 daily.

★ *Galleries*
Quality art and handcrafted pieces, most produced by regional

artisans, are showcased in sophisticated galleries throughout town. The best are:

Highlight Gallery   *45052 Main St.*   *(707)937-3132*
thehighlightgallery.com
Mendocino Art Center   *45200 Little Lake St.*   *(707)937-5818*
mendocinoartcenter.org
Panache   *45110 Main St.*   *(707)937-0947*
thepanachegallery.com
William Zimmer Gallery   *Kasten & Ukiah*   *(707)937-5121*
williamzimmergallery.com

Golf

Little River Inn Golf Course   *(707)937-5667*
3 mi. S at 7750 Hwy. 1 - Little River
This challenging 9-hole course overlooking the ocean is open to the public. Facilities include a pro shop, driving range, putting greens, cart rentals, and a restaurant.

Horseback Riding

★ **Ross Ranch**   *(707)877-1834*
17 mi. S (via Hwy. 1) on Greenwood Rd. - Elk
elkcoast.com/rossranch
Ross Ranch offers private guided horseback rides through redwood forests in the coastal mountains above Elk. For an even more memorable adventure, reserve their two-hour ride on the wet packed sand of spectacular Manchester Beach.

★ **Jug Handle State Reserve**   *(707)937-5804*
5 mi. N on Hwy. 1 - Caspar
At Jug Handle Creek is a remarkable "ecological staircase" phenomenon. Five wave-cut terraces form a staircase with each step holding an ecosystem much older than the one below. On the partially submerged bottom terrace are tidepools with a wealth of marine life. A self-guided nature trail explores all five terraces from the coast to a pygmy forest two and a half miles inland.

★ **Mendocino Headlands State Park**   *(707)937-5397*
surrounding town on S, W, N sides
This park was created to protect natural meadows, wave-carved bluffs, coves, and natural bridges of a promontory that juts into the Pacific around town, and a picturesque sandy beach at the mouth of Big River. Hiking trails, overlooks, picnic sites, and restrooms are well located. **The Ford House Visitor Center** on Main Street provides current and historic information in the converted home (circa 1854) of Mendocino's founder.

Mendocino Theatre Company   *(707)937-4477*
downtown at 45200 Little Lake St.
lmtc.org

Mendocino's recently renovated intimate theater (founded in 1977) showcases a talented cast (including some members of Actors Equity Association) in at least six classic and avant-garde productions through most of the year.

Old Masonic Hall Sculpture
downtown on Lansing St.

Atop a historic building at the heart of town, the whimsical sculpture of Father Time braiding a maiden's hair captures both the artistic and romantic spirit of Mendocino in a century-old piece of whitewashed redwood.

★ **Russian Gulch State Park**   *(707)937-5804*
2 mi. N off Hwy. 1

One of the West's great coastal parks includes an idyllic sandy beach where a shallow creek empties into the ocean. Beyond the sand, wave-sculpted headlands reveal rocky coves and tidepools to hikers and beachcombers. Ocean fishing and diving are also popular. In the nearby canyon are shady campsites. A waterfall in a fern-edged grotto highlights an easy five-mile trail.

Shopping

A highlight among numerous one-of-a-kind shops is **Lark in the Morning Music Shoppe** at 10460 Kasten St. *((707)964-5569) larkinam.com* with all kinds of hard-to-find musical instruments, related recordings, compact disks, and books.

★ **Van Damme State Park**   *(707)937-5804*
2 mi. S off Hwy. 1

Inland from the highway along Little River is a large campground sequestered in a luxuriant pine forest. Hike-in, recreational vehicle, and tent sites are available in this full-service facility. A splendid sandy beach by the stream's outlet is a short stroll. The ocean is inevitably cold for swimming, but ocean kayaking, sport diving and shore fishing are popular. Miles of trails access ocean views, a sword fern canyon, and an ancient pygmy forest of stunted conifers.

Warm Water Feature

★   **Sweetwater Spa & Inn**   *(707)937-4140   (800)300-4140*
downtown at 955 Ukiah St.
sweetwaterspa.com

Guests can rent a private room by the hour with a hot tub, sauna, and tiled bath; small private tubs; or a large communal hot tub in this serene, artistic facility adjoining a fine organic restaurant. Massage is also available by appointment. Upstairs above the communal hot tub is the romantic, rustic "Sweetwater Tower," an overnight room with a double bed. Windows on all sides provide town and ocean views. The downstairs bathroom, hot tub and sauna are private for this room after hours and evenings.

★ **Wineries**   *(707)895-9463*
  avwines.com
Vineyards and premium wineries are the major attraction in
pretty little Anderson Valley inland from the Mendocino coast.
The best produce world class still or sparkling wines, and are
sprinkled along Highway 128 near Philo.
  Fetzer   *(707)937-6190   (800)846-8637*
  downtown at 45070 Main St.
  fetzer.com
Fetzer Vineyards (fee) tasting room in the heart of Mendocino is
a small showcase for selected varietals. Open 10-6 daily. The
winery (see listing in Healdsburg) is 68 miles east in Hopland.
  Husch Vineyards   *(707)895-3216   (800)554-8724*
  29 mi. SE at 4400 Hwy. 128 - Philo
  huschvineyards.com
A wooden cabin houses a pleasant tasting and sales room where
premium wines produced exclusively from family-owned
vineyards may be sampled. Grape-arbor-shaded picnic tables are
nearby. Open 10-6 daily (summer); 10-5 daily (winter).
  Navarro Vineyards   *(707)895-3686   (800)537-9463*
  30 mi. SE at 5601 Hwy. 128 - Philo
  navarrowine.com
Since 1974, Navarro Vineyards has consistently produced super-
premium wines (especially chardonnay and pinot noir) that are
among the author's favorites in America. A handsome woodcrafted building with idyllic vineyard views is used for tasting and
sales of the full line of acclaimed benchmark wines. An outdoor
deck has picnic tables overlooking gardens and vineyards. Open
10-6 spring through early fall; 10-5 late fall and winter.
  Pacific Echo Cellars   *(707)895-2065   (800)824-7754*
  33 mi. SE at 8501 Hwy. 128 - Philo
  www.pacific-echo.com
A gracious house in a lovely garden is the setting for (fee) tasting
and sales of five traditional sparkling wines by one of the valley's
premier producers of sparklers made in the classic French
method. A vine-trellis-covered picnic table overlooks vineyards
and hills. Open 11-5 daily.
  Roederer Estate   *(707)895-2288*
  29 mi. SE at 4501 Hwy. 128 - Philo
  roederer-estate.com
The American extension of the famed French champagne house
produces three award-winning sparkling wines using only estate-
grown grapes and traditional methode champenoise artistry. All
are available for (fee) tasting in a refined hilltop setting
surrounded by gardens and vineyards. Open 11-5 daily.

RESTAURANTS

★ **Albion River Inn** *(707)937-1919*
7 mi. S on Hwy. 1 at 3790 N. Hwy. 1 - Albion
albionriverinn.com
D only.   *Expensive*
Albion River Inn Restaurant is one of the best shoreline dinner houses on the West Coast. Creative California cuisine is expertly prepared using the freshest quality regional ingredients. Inspired possibilities might include Oregon blue cheese salad with organic greens and red grapes in a raspberry vinaigrette; pan-roasted grouper with rock shrimp; and delectable housemade desserts like fresh wild berry-rhubarb cobbler with lemon-poppyseed ice cream. The dining room, perched near the rim of a high bluff, has a window-wall view of gardens and a rocky coast far below. Tables set with full linen, flowers and candles; a stone fireplace; and tony bar also contribute to the romantic ambiance.

Bay View Cafe *(707)937-4197*
downtown at 45040 Main St. (upstairs)
B-L-D. No D Sun.-Thurs.   *Moderate*
Assorted contemporary California dishes are served in an upstairs dining room and bar with an ocean view and an alfresco ocean-view deck.

★ **Bridget Dolan's Pub & Dinner House**   *(707)877-3422*
16 mi. S at 5910 S. Hwy. 1 - Elk
griffinn.com
D only.   *Moderate*
Bridget Dolan's well-earned popularity derives from dishes like hearty soups, fish & chips, barbecued baby-back pork ribs, and delightfully decadent housemade bread pudding with whiskey. The snug dining room is enhanced by tables set with full linen and fresh flowers around a pot-bellied iron stove/fireplace. **Griffin House at Greenwood Cove** (7 units–Expensive) is also on the premises and offers romantic cottages with woodburning fireplaces and a full Bridget's breakfast delivered to the door.

★ **Cafe Beaujolais** *(707)937-5614*
downtown at 961 Ukiah St.
cafebeaujolais.com
D only.   *Expensive*
One of the area's earliest sources of organic North Coast cuisine is a now-famous crowd-pleaser with assorted brick-oven breads (available for sale by the loaf), seasonally fresh appetizers and entrees, and desserts like housemade fruit sorbets with toasted almond butter cookies. A congestion of tables with full linen and candles fills cozy wood-trim dining areas in a converted cottage with an enclosed garden dining room.

★ **Greenwood Pier Inn**   *(707)877-9997*
16 mi. S at 5928 Hwy. 1 - Elk
greenwoodpierinn.com
B-L-D. No D Tues. & Wed.   Expensive
Innovative North Coast cuisine features vegetables and herbs
from their garden, plus housemade desserts like huckleberry ice
cream. The warm plant-filled cafe has a picture-window coast
view past colorful gardens.

★ **Heritage House**   *(707)937-5885*
5 mi. S at 5200 N. Hwy. 1 - Little River
heritagehouseinn.com
B-D.   *Very Expensive*
Heritage House, one of America's most celebrated and historic
inns, puts culinary emphasis on fresh regional products for
creative country cuisine, breads, and desserts. Three elegant
dining rooms share a magnificent ocean view. So does the
handsome firelit lounge and a sunny deck.

The Hill House Inn   *(707)937-0577*
just N at 10701 Palette Dr.
hillhouseinn.com
B-D. No D. Sun.-Tues.   Expensive
Rick's of Mendocino offers California fare with a touch of
Casablanca in the hotel's large split-level dining room with a
distant panoramic ocean view on three sides.

★ **The Ledford House Restaurant**   *(707)937-0282*
7 mi. S at 3000 N. Hwy. 1 - Albion
ledfordhouse.com
D only. Closed Mon.-Tues.   *Very Expensive*
Innovative seasonally fresh California cuisine is expertly prepared
into dishes like crisp roasted duckling with blackberry zinfandel
sauce. All breads and desserts are homemade (try the avocado
cream pie when available). Plush widely spaced tables enhance a
large dining room and lounge with a grand window-wall view to
the ocean.

★ **Little River Inn**   *(707)937-5942*
3 mi. S at 7751 N. Hwy. 1 - Little River
littleriverinn.com
B-D.   Expensive
The landmark inn has a nice way with Swedish pancakes and
other breakfast specialties. Fresh regional seafood, steaks, and
housemade desserts are featured each evening. The gracious
dining room (the focal point of a pre-Civil War mansion) has an
intimate picture-window view of an enchanting garden.

Little River Market   *(707)937-5133*
3 mi. S on Hwy. 1 beside post office - Little River

B-L-D. *Low*

The old market has been retooled to present a window-wall view of a beautiful coastline close-by. Calzones, pastas and light fare can be enjoyed beyond the deli cases at a few tables in a rustic deli setting by the window, or to go.

★ **MacCallum House Inn** *(707)937-5763*
downtown at 45020 Albion St.
maccallumdining.com

D only. *Expensive*

Quality organic ingredients become North Coast cuisine in seasonally fresh flavorful dishes like pan-seared duck breast with shitake mushrooms and ginger plum sauce, and luscious homemade desserts like a praline cookie taco with a sampling of six ice creams. The inn's firelit dining room is intimate and charming, as is the cozy bar with an enclosed dining porch.

★ **Mendocino Bakery** *(707)937-0836*
downtown on Lansing St.

B-L-D. *Moderate*

The area's original gourmet bakery (circa 1980) continues to offer a tempting display of pastries, bagels, breads and desserts. These and (later in the day) create-your-own or their specialty pizzas (plus deep-dish pizza by the slice), along with a variety of coffees, teas and other beverages attract natives and visitors alike to the cozy coffee shop, courtyard patio or takeout.

Mendocino Hotel *(707)937-0511*
downtown at 45080 Main St.
mendocinohotel.com

B-L-D. *Very Expensive*

Contemporary California fare is served amidst casual elegance in a dining room evoking some of the spirit of a gracious earlier time. There is also a posh little Victorian saloon and a greenery-laden cafe with marble tables used for breakfast and lunch.

★ **The Moosse Cafe** *(707)937-4323*
downtown at 10390 Kasten St.
theblueheron.com

L-D. *Expensive*

Light and lively California cuisine like pork chop house-cured in a spiced apple brine is served with luscious desserts. The blackout cake is a must for chocoholics. A fireplace lends cheer to warm wood tones in the popular little cafe. Upstairs, **The Blue Heron Inn** (Moderate-Expensive) has three cozy, comfortable village- or ocean-view rooms.

★ **955 Restaurant** *(707)937-1955*
downtown at 955 Ukiah St.
955restaurant.com

D only. Closed Mon.-Tues. *Expensive*

The 955 consistently offers fine cuisine. Seasonally fresh quality ingredients from the region are skillfully transformed into dishes like boneless salmon fillets with apple cider vinaigrette, leg of lamb in stew, and exotic desserts like bread pudding with huckleberry compote or mango sorbet. A lofty wood-trim dining room is enhanced by tables set with full linen, and pots brimming with healthy greenery overlooking a luxuriant garden.

★ **The Stanford Inn by the Sea** *(707)937-5615*
1 mi. SE at Hwy. 1 & Comptche-Ukiah Rd.
stanfordinn.com
B-D. No D Tues. & Wed. *Expensive*

At **The Ravens**, creative vegetarian cuisine inspired by the inn's extensive organic gardens is expertly prepared for gourmet dishes like calzone with carmelized onions, sautéed chard and two cheeses, or grilled portabella mushroom burger, or housemade focaccia, or lasagne with roasted tomato sauce, spinach, squash, portabello mushrooms, red bell pepper and aged asiago. The handsome wood-trimmed dining room has a fine view overlooking prolific gardens and the distant sea.

★ **Stevenswood Lodge** *(707)937-2810*
2 mi. S at 8211 N. Hwy. 1
stevenswood.com
D only. Closed Wed. *Very Expensive*

Stevenswood Lodge features one of the Redwood Coast's best restaurants. Year-round fresh regional produce is celebrated in an eclectic selection of creative dishes that are as colorful as they are delicious. Consider mushroom consomme with white truffle essence and pheasant ravioli, pine-nut-crusted salmon fillet with basil oil, or herb-crusted lamb loin with morel mushrooms. The elegant dining room showcases avant-garde wall hangings and views of surrounding luxuriant gardens and forests.

★ **Tote Fête** *(707)937-3140*
downtown at 10450 Lansing St.
B-L. *Moderate*

Excellent artisan breads and assorted pastries, pizza and sandwiches are as delicious as they look in tempting displays. The little bakery in a courtyard with a few tables in a garden also has a nearby main street carryout.

LODGINGS

In Mendocino and along the nearby coast is one of America's great concentrations of romantic inns. The area's only moderately priced rooms are in motels in nearby Fort Bragg. High season is May through October. Winter weekdays may be 10% less.

Agate Cove Inn   *(707)937-0551*
1 mi. N at 11201 N. Lansing St. (Box 1150) - 95460
agatecove.com
10 units   (800)527-3111   Expensive-Very Expensive
A historic farmhouse on a slope across a road from an ocean cove
has become an appealing bed-and-breakfast. Full complimentary
breakfast is served with a delightful ocean view, and there is a gift
shop. All of the attractively furnished units have a private bath
and contemporary amenities, plus a queen or king feather bed.
    "Emerald," "Obsidian"–whitewater view, large dormered
    room with gas fireplace, soaking tub/shower for two,
    private deck shares ocean view with king bed.
★ **Albion River Inn**   *(707)937-1919*
7 mi. S at 3790 N. Hwy. 1 (Box 100) - Albion 95410
albionriverinn.com
20 units   (800)479-7944   Very Expensive
Albion River Inn is one of California's great getaways. The stylish
contemporary wood-trim complex blends gracefully into lush
gardens along a bluff high above a picturesque little harbor. Their
gourmet restaurant (see listing) maximizes the enchanting view,
and serves a full breakfast to guests. A bottle of premium local
wine and use of binoculars in your room are also complimentary.
Each luxuriously furnished room is a study in tasteful individual
decor that captures the romantic feeling of the historic site, and
has an outstanding ocean view, woodburning or gas fireplace, and
a queen or king bed. Some also have a large ocean-view whirlpool
and private surf-view deck.
    #17 through #20–woodburning fireplace; ocean view
    from two-person whirlpool, large deck and king bed.
★ **Alegria**   *(707)937-5150*
downtown at 44781 Main St. (Box 803) - 95460
oceanfrontmagic.com
5 units   (800)780-7905   Expensive-Very Expensive
Alegria is the only oceanfront lodging in town. The romantic
wood-trimmed bed-and-breakfast crowns a bluff overlooking Big
River and the coast. Beyond lovely gardens, there is a private trail
to the nearby beach. A sumptuous breakfast served in the ocean-
view room or to your room by request is complimentary, as is use
of an outdoor hot tub. Each uniquely designed room is beautifully
furnished. All rooms have a private entrance, deck, private bath,
fireplace, refrigerator, microwave, and a queen or king bed.
    "Pacific Suite"–spacious, semi-private view deck,
    ocean view from shower and queen bed.
    "Cove Cottage"–soaking tub with ocean view, large private
    deck overlooking beach, water view from queen bed.

★ **Brewery Gulch Inn**   *(707)937-4752*
1 mi. S at 9401 N. Hwy. 1 - 95460
brewerygulchinn.com
10 units   *(800)578-4454*   *Expensive-Very Expensive*
Brewery Gulch Inn is one of the North Coast's most romantic
adult getaways. Giant redwood logs painstakingly eco-salvaged
from a nearby river have been artistically permuted into an
elegant contemporary redwood bed-and-breakfast on extensive
grounds in a lush forest. Full gourmet organic breakfast is
complimentary as are afternoon wine and epicurean appetizers
and evening treats. Each spacious room is individually beautifully
furnished including extra amenities, and has a gas fireplace and
queen or king bed. Most also have a private ocean-view deck and
two-person whirlpool or large soaking tub.
   "Osprey"–in-bath soaking tub for two, corner room
      with ocean view from private deck and king bed.
   "Madrone"–in-bath two-person whirlpool, corner room
      with ocean view from private deck, queen bed.
Dennen's Victorian Farmhouse   *(707)937-0697*
3 mi. S at 7001 N. Hwy. 1 (Box 661) - 95460
victorianfarmhouse.com
10 units   *(800)264-4723*   *Expensive*
A historic farmhouse (once painted by artist Thomas Kinkade)
has been upgraded into a photogenic bed-and-breakfast complex.
Full breakfast to your room is complimentary. Each cozy room is
well furnished and includes some antiques, a private bath, and a
queen or king bed. Some also have a woodburning fireplace.
★ **Elk Cove Inn**   *(707)877-3321*
16 mi. S at 6300 S. Hwy. 1 (Box 367) - Elk 95432
elkcoveinn.com
14 units   *(800)275-2967*   *Expensive-Very Expensive*
Elk Cove Inn is one of California's most romantic–and
dramatic–bed-and-breakfast inns. It is sequestered in an intimate
natural amphitheater high above the picturesque outlet of Elk
Creek into the ocean. Complimentary full gourmet breakfast
buffet is served in a woodcrafted room with a window wall
overlooking an offshore sea mount with a wave-formed tunnel.
Epicurean appetizers like philo-wrapped mushroom pillows are
served with wine in the afternoon. A welcome basket of wine,
fresh fruit and cookies, and a decanter of port and chocolates are
also complimentary. A new European-style day spa offers an
appealing selection of (fee) spa treatments. Each beautifully
furnished room celebrates romantic possibilities with a plush
private bath, a wealth of artistic expressions, contemporary
amenities, and queen or king featherbeds. Almost all rooms have

a gas fireplace or wood stove and/or enchanting view deck or whirlpool tub for two.

"Sam McCanse Suite," "L.E. White Suite"–large living room with window wall to superb ocean/cove view shared by large private balcony, raised gas remote-control fireplace, refrigerator, microwave, two-person whirlpool, ocean view from king bed and intimate second balcony.

★ **Glendeven**   *(707)937-0083*
   2 mi. S at 8205 N. Hwy. 1 - Little River (Box 914 - 95460)
   glendeven.com
   11 units   *(800)822-4536*   *Expensive-Very Expensive*
An elegant, beautifully furnished bed-and-breakfast inn is centered around a large Victorian residence that has overlooked the headland meadows near the bay at Little River for well over a century. Grounds also house a fine local arts gallery. A complimentary breakfast is served in the morning in a charming garden-view sitting room, and wine and appetizers are offered by the fire in the evening. Each room is beautifully furnished and has a private bath, and queen or king bed. Most have a woodburning fireplace, private deck, and distant ocean view.

"Eastlin Suite"–spacious, ocean-view porch, woodburning fireplace, king bed.

"Briar Rose"–vaulted ceilings, woodburning fireplace, private balcony shares ocean view with queen bed.

★ **Greenwood Pier Inn**   *(707)877-9997*
   16 mi. S at 5928 Hwy. 1 (Box 336) - Elk 95432
   greenwoodpierinn.com
   13 units   *(800)807-3423*   *Expensive-Very Expensive*
Coastal views of sea-carved arches from Greenwood Pier Inn are unsurpassed. The romantic woodcrafted complex atop an ocean bluff includes a fine cafe (see listing), first-rate country store, garden shop, and cottages in a luxuriant garden by the sea. A whirlpool perched on a bluff above the coast is complimentary, as is Continental breakfast delivered to your room. Each beautifully furnished room has a private bath, artistic expressions everywhere, and a queen or king bed. Most have an awesome sea view and a fireplace. Several also have a view bathtub or whirlpool.

"Cliff House"–redwood cabin atop cliff, refrigerator, metal woodburning fireplace, private ocean view from big deck, spiral staircase to two-person whirlpool with awesome seascape, king bed.

"North Sea Castle," "South Sea Castle"–clifftop, spacious, glassed center woodburning fireplace, spiral stairs to two-person whirlpool that shares awesome ocean view with large deck and king or queen bed.

"Starfish"–big brick woodburning fireplace, refrigerator,
two-person whirlpool shares ocean view with queen bed.
"Tower"–connected water tower, gas fireplaces on two
levels, two-person whirlpool, third floor sleeping loft
(mattress) with ocean view, queen bed.

★ **The Harbor House Inn**   *(707)877-3203*
15 mi. S at 5600 S. Hwy. 1 (Box 369) - Elk 95432
theharborhouse.com
10 units   *(800)720-7474*   *Expensive-Very Expensive*
The blufftop setting of this classic country inn in a lovely garden
provides sensational views of the rugged coastline. A garden path
descends to a small private beach far below. The stately
Craftsman-style main house (built in 1916) is a marvel of hand-
fitted virgin redwood from nearby Albion forests. Each
luxuriously individually furnished room has a private bath, gas
fireplace or Franklin stove, extra amenities and a queen or king
bed. Modified American plan rates include a gourmet breakfast
and four-course dinner for two in an elegant, intimate dining
room that showcases an incomparable seascape.

"Cypress"–spacious, large clawfoot tub, fireplace, panoramic
ocean/garden views from private deck and king bed.
"Harbor"–top floor, fireplace, grand private seascapes
(windows on three sides) in view of king bed.
"Sea View," "Oceansong"–private cottage; fireplace;
grand ocean view from private deck, in-bath
clawfoot tub, and king bed.

★ **Heritage House**   *(707)937-5885*
5 mi. S at 5200 N. Hwy. 1 - Little River 95456
heritagehouseinn.com
66 units   *(800)235-5885*   *Expensive-Very Expensive*
Heritage House is one of the most celebrated inns along
California's north coast. Luxurious and romantic New England-
style cottages are sprinkled among lawns and gardens on a hillside
above a picturesque ocean cove. Amenities include scenic hiking
trails, an elegant ocean-view restaurant (see listing) and lounge,
and a fine country store. Spacious units range from individually
beautifully furnished traditional rooms to luxuriously furnished
suites. All have a private bath and a queen or king bed. Most have
a woodburning fireplace or wood stove, and a grand ocean view.
Some also have a whirlpool tub and private deck.

"Carousel" (5 of these)–suite, two-sided fireplace,
in-bath two-person whirlpool and dual shower,
great ocean view, private deck, king bed.
"Sea Cliff" (4 of these)–spacious, fireplace, in-bath two-
person whirlpool, great sea view, private deck, king bed.

"Meadow 1"–fireplace, close to cove, awesome
private ocean view, in-bath whirlpool, king bed.
"Vista 3"–end suite, woodburning iron fireplace, superb
private ocean views, two-person whirlpool, king bed.
"Next Year"–ocean/cove view, fireplace, in-bath
whirlpool, private deck, king bed.
"Same Time"–ocean/cove view, fireplace,
large tub, private deck, king bed.

The Hill House Inn   *(707)937-0554*
just N at 10701 Palette Dr. (Box 625) - 95460
44 units   (800)422-0554   Expensive-Very Expensive
This modern wood-trim motor lodge is a replication of a sprawling
Victorian inn with period decor. The restaurant (see listing) has
a distant ocean view. Complimentary Continental breakfast is
served to the room. Each spacious, well-furnished room has all
contemporary conveniences and doubles or a king bed. Some have
ocean views and a woodburning fireplace.

#201–corner, fine view across town to ocean,
woodburning fireplace, in-bath two-person
whirlpool, king bed.

★ **Inn at Schoolhouse Creek**   *(707)937-5525*
3 mi. S at 7051 N. Hwy. 1 (Box 1637) - Little River 95456
schoolhousecreek.com
16 units   (800)731-5525   Expensive-Very Expensive
A historic complex of buildings has been thoroughly upgraded into
a delightful bed-and-breakfast inn amid gardens and meadows
high on a slope above the sea. A forest/ocean-view hot tub is
complimentary, as is a bountiful breakfast buffet and afternoon
wine and appetizers. Each attractively furnished room has all
contemporary amenities and doubles, queen or king bed. Several
have a gas fireplace and/or whirlpool, refrigerator, and view deck.

"Captain's Watch"–spacious, large whirlpool tub,
microwave/refrigerator, ocean-view deck in view
of fireplace and king featherbed.
"Water Tower Cottage"–cozy, private ocean-view
deck on top of tower, two-person hot tub, woodburning fireplace, queen featherbed.

John Dougherty House Bed & Breakfast   *(707)937-5266*
downtown at 571 Ukiah St. (Box 817) - 95460
jdhouse.com
7 units   (800)486-2104   Expensive-Very Expensive
One of the oldest houses in Mendocino (circa 1867) has been
transformed into a bed-and-breakfast inn outfitted with period
country antiques. Full breakfast is complimentary. All of the cozy,
attractively furnished rooms have a private bath and a queen or

king bed. Several also have a refrigerator and fireplace.

"Osprey," "Raven"–two-person in-bath whirlpool,
refrigerator, gas fire stove, outstanding village/ocean
view from shared deck and king bed.

★ **Joshua Grindle Inn**   *(707)937-4143*
downtown at 44800 Little Lake Rd. (Box 647) - 95460
joshgrin.com
10 units   *(800)474-6353*   *Expensive-Very Expensive*
A landmark 1879 home is now a lovely bed-and-breakfast
surrounded by gardens. Full breakfast, cookies and a bottle of
wine in each room are complimentary. Each beautifully furnished
room has American antiques, a private bathroom and a queen or
king bed. Many have a fireplace and an ocean/town view.

"Master"–spacious, fireplace, skylit in-bath
two-person whirlpool, queen bed.
"Grindle"–views of town and ocean, king bed.
"Saltbox Cottage" (2 of these)–fireplace, in-bath
whirlpool, queen bed.

★ **Little River Inn**   *(707)937-5942*
3 mi. S at 7750 N. Hwy. 1 (Drawer B) - Little River 95456
littleriverinn.com
65 units   *(888)466-5683*   *Expensive-Very Expensive*
The area's only 9-hole golf course (with a driving range, putting
green, pro shop and fine ocean view) and two tennis courts are
features of this historic New England-style resort on extensive
well-landscaped grounds overlooking the nearby ocean. There is
also a fine restaurant (see listing) and nostalgic lounge. Each
beautifully furnished unit has a country-modern flair, an ocean
view, all contemporary conveniences, and queens or a king bed.
Newer spacious rooms also have a view deck, woodburning
fireplace and a large in-bath whirlpool.

#263-#264,#268-#271–spacious, vaulted ceiling, refr./wet bar,
in-bath two-person whirlpool, woodburning fireplace,
fine ocean view from large private deck and king bed.

★ **MacCallum House Inn**   *(707)937-0289*
downtown at 45020 Albion St. (Box 206) - 95460
maccallumhouse.com
20 units   *(800)609-0492*   *Expensive*
One of Mendocino's premier inns includes a stately 1882 home
that may be the most photographed building in the heart of the
village. The recently upgraded complex amid colorful gardens has
a fine restaurant (see listing) and lounge. A gourmet breakfast
served in the formal dining room and the afternoon wine hour are
complimentary. Each compact, beautifully furnished room has a
private bath and artistic period touches, and a double, queen or

king bed. Many also have a gas or woodburning fireplace, whirlpool, or clawfoot tub for two.

    #19–spacious, woodburning raised stone fireplace,
        refrigerator, wet bar, big ocean-view deck, queen bed.
    #13 "Watertower"–three level, fine ocean view
        from top floor, queen and king beds.
    #18 "Upper Barn"–semi-private flowered deck, in-bath
        two-person whirlpool/shower, woodburning stone
        fireplace, ocean view, queen bed.
    #17 "Barn Studio"–big woodburning stone fireplace,
        kitchenette, tiled tub with shower, private deck, king bed.
    "The Gwen MacCallum"–clawfoot tub for two,
        ocean view, queen bed.

Mendocino Hotel   *(707)937-0511*
downtown at 45080 Main St. (Box 587) - 95460
mendocinohotel.com
51 units   *(800)548-0513*   *Moderate-Very Expensive*
Perhaps the most visible symbol of Mendocino's Yankee heritage is this three-story clapboard hotel built in 1878. The firelit lobby, bar and dining room (see listing) decorated with Victorian antiques, reproductions and artifacts have a kind of movie-set pizzazz. Rooms with a choice of private or shared bath and double, queen, or king bed range from small and comfortably furnished to large suites with a woodburning fireplace and ocean view.

    "Suites"(4 of these)–spacious, in garden behind hotel,
        woodburning fireplace, parlor, private bath, king bed.

★ **Packard House Bed & Breakfast**   *(707)937-2677*
downtown at 45170 Little Lake St. (Box 1065) - 95460
packardhouse.com
5 units   *(888)453-2677*   *Expensive-Very Expensive*
A graceful "Carpenters Gothic" Victorian home (circa 1878) in a garden is now a bed-and-breakfast with a pleasing mix of antique and modern furnishings. Full breakfast is complimentary, along with evening wine. Each beautifully furnished room has a gas fireplace, private bath with limestone floors and whirlpool tub, all contemporary amenities and a queen or king bed.

    "Pacific View," "Chapman Point"–ocean/village views,
        gas fireplace, in-bath two-person whirlpool, king bed.

★ **Reed Manor**   *(707)937-5446*
just N at 44950 Palette Dr. (Box 127) - 95460
reedmanor.com
5 units   *Expensive-Very Expensive*
One of Mendocino's most beguiling landmarks built to serve as an elegant bed-and-breakfast inn tops a hill above town. Light breakfast served to the room and evening beverage are

complimentary. Each spacious room is luxuriously furnished with a seamless blend of period pieces and all contemporary conveniences, plus a gas fireplace, refrigerator, large in-bath whirlpool, private deck, and queen or king bed. Most have a town/ocean view.

"Napoleon"–spacious, gas fireplace, in-bath two-person
   whirlpool, big ocean-view deck, telescope, king bed.

★ **Sea Rock Bed & Breakfast Inn**   (707)937-0926
   just N at 11101 N. Lansing St. (Box 906) - 95460
   searock.com
   14 units   (800)906-0926   Expensive-Very Expensive
Sea Rock Inn is an enchanting adult getaway. It has evolved into a romantic cottage complex in a luxuriant garden overlooking the ocean and Mendocino headlands. The complimentary expanded Continental breakfast buffet can be enjoyed with a remarkable panoramic seascape. Each beautifully furnished unit has all contemporary amenities, some ocean view, a private deck, and a queen or king bed. Some also have a woodburning fireplace and large soaking tub with a picture-window view.

#12, #11–large, grand ocean/headlands view from living
   room with woodburning fireplace, private balcony,
   large soaking tub with ocean view, king bed.
#18,#17–grand ocean/headlands view from private
   balcony, Franklin fireplace, queen bed.
#1–superb ocean/headlands view from front bedroom,
   deck, gas fireplace, two queen beds.
#5–delightful full knotty pine trim and decor, plus
   ocean view, gas fireplace, deck, queen bed.

★ **The Stanford Inn by the Sea**   (707)937-5615
   1 mi. SE at Hwy. 1 & Comptche-Ukiah Rd. (Box 487) - 95460
   stanfordinn.com
   40 units   (800)331-8884   Expensive-Very Expensive
The Stanford Inn by the Sea is the Mendocino region's most complete bed-and-breakfast resort. Contemporary wood-trimmed buildings crown a spacious slope above the sea, where luxuriant gardens of certified organic herbs, vegetables, fruit trees, and edible flowers–and a herd of curious llamas–contribute to an enchanting scene. The Ravens (see listing) features creative gourmet vegetarian fare in a congenial setting. Hiking trails lead down to rental canoes that can be enjoyed in Big River State Park (on California's longest undeveloped estuary) and beyond to the nearby village and ocean. Other amenities include complimentary bicycles, an authentically tropical greenhouse pool, whirlpool, sauna, exercise room, and (fee) massage studio. Full gourmet breakfast and evening beverages and appetizers are compli-

mentary. Each luxuriously furnished room has numerous artistic touches, all contemporary conveniences including a refrigerator, and a queen or king bed. Most have a private ocean-view deck and a woodburning fireplace or wood stove.

#240–vaulted ceiling, woodburning fireplace, romantic
town/ocean view from private deck, king bed.

#241–one-bedroom suite, vaulted ceiling, woodburning
fireplace in living room, fine ocean view from large
private deck, king bed.

★ **Stevenswood Lodge**   *(707)937-2810*
2 mi. S at 8211 N. Hwy. 1 (Box 170) - 95460
stevenswood.com
10 units   *(800)421-2810*   *Expensive-Very Expensive*
Stevenswood Lodge is one of the best of the North Coast's newer bed-and-breakfast inns. The urbane wood-trimmed complex is tucked amid colorful gardens enhanced by avant-garde sculptures in a luxuriant forest a short hike from the ocean. Full gourmet breakfast and evening wine and appetizers are complimentary. So is use of private forest spa pools. The restaurant (see listing) is outstanding. Each spacious, luxuriously furnished room blends handcrafted hardwood furniture; fine contemporary art; picture-window views of forests, gardens, and (some) distant ocean; a woodburning fireplace; all contemporary conveniences; a refrigerator/honor bar; and a queen bed.

"Grand Suite" (2 of these)–living room,
fine view of garden/forest to ocean.

★ **Whitegate Inn**   *(707)937-4892*
downtown at 499 Howard St. (Box 150) - 95460
whitegateinn.com
6 units   *(800)531-7282*   *Expensive-Very Expensive*
A handsome century-old residence on the National Historic Register has been meticulously transformed into a charming bed-and-breakfast inn. Full breakfast in the elegant dining room or lovely garden porch with an ocean view is complimentary, as are wine and appetizers served in the early evening and cookies, chocolates and sherry later. Each room is beautifully, individually furnished with Victorian antiques and contemporary amenities, and has down comforters and a queen or king featherbed.

"Cypress Room"–woodburning fireplace, in-bath whirlpool, garden/ocean views from bay windows, queen bed.

"French Rose Room"–woodburning fireplace, refrigerator,
corner windows with ocean view from queen bed.

"Enchanted Cottage"–spacious, secluded room
with private garden deck, refrigerator, woodburning fireplace, clawfoot tub, king bed.

Monterey

Monterey is a treasury of superlative history and geography. Located by Monterey Bay in what has been called one of the most beautiful natural amphitheaters in the world, this seaport has played a major role in the development of the West Coast for more than two centuries.

The idyllic site became the first permanent settlement in California when in 1770 Gaspar de Portola established the first of Spain's four presidios and Father Junipero Serra dedicated the second mission in Alta California. Monterey was a capital for Spain until 1822, and for Mexico until 1846 when the United States annexed California. For the next hundred years, the town served as a maritime center. It wasn't until after World War II that its destiny as one of the West's most playful towns was fulfilled.

Today, Cannery Row and Fisherman's Wharf are ingenious, fun-loving transformations from an earlier hard-working era. Nowhere is this more apparent than in the superstar of Cannery Row–the Monterey Bay Aquarium. From outside, it looks like the sardine cannery it once was. Inside, the smell, noise and toilers are gone, replaced by some of the finest maritime exhibits anywhere. Downtown, a collection of historic landmarks blends with urbane shops and galleries. Gourmet and view restaurants are plentiful, and nightlife is diverse and exuberant. Accommodations of all kinds are abundant. So are year-round crowds, due to an unusually mild climate and seemingly endless opportunities for offshore and onshore recreation and leisure fun.

WEATHER PROFILE

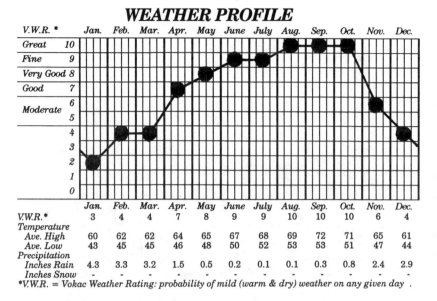

V.W.R. *		Jan.	Feb.	Mar.	Apr.	May	June	July	Aug.	Sep.	Oct.	Nov.	Dec.
Great	10												
Fine	9												
Very Good	8												
Good	7												
Moderate	6												
	5												
	4												
	3												
	2												
	1												
	0												

	Jan.	Feb.	Mar.	Apr.	May	June	July	Aug.	Sep.	Oct.	Nov.	Dec.
V.W.R.*	3	4	4	7	8	9	9	10	10	10	6	4
Temperature												
Ave. High	60	62	62	64	65	67	68	69	72	71	65	61
Ave. Low	43	45	45	46	48	50	52	53	53	51	47	44
Precipitation												
Inches Rain	4.3	3.3	3.2	1.5	0.5	0.2	0.1	0.1	0.3	0.8	2.4	2.9
Inches Snow	-	-	-	-	-	-	-	-	-	-	-	-

*V.W.R. = Vokac Weather Rating: probability of mild (warm & dry) weather on any given day .

BASIC INFORMATION

Population: 29,674
Elevation: 40 feet
Location: 120 miles South of San Francisco
Airport (regularly scheduled flights): in town

Monterey County Convention & Visitors Bureau (831)649-1770
  downtown at 150 Olivier St. (Box 1770) - 93942 (888)221-1010
  Info Center just E at Franklin St. & Camino El Estero
  montereyinfo.org

ATTRACTIONS

★ **Bicycling**

There are many miles of scenic waterfront trails, bike lanes and off-road tracks in and around Monterey. The best are the bayside Monterey Peninsula Recreation Trail which extends eighteen miles from Castroville to Pacific Grove and the renowned Seventeen-Mile Drive between Pacific Grove and Carmel. Assorted bicycles (and canopy-covered four-wheeled surreys outfitted with two sets of bicycle pedals) are offered at:

Adventures by the Sea   *(831)372-1807*
www.adventuresbythesea.com
downtown at 201 Alvarado Mall
2nd location: 1 mi. NW at 299 Cannery Row
Bay Bikes   *(831)646-9090*
montereybaybikes.com
1 mi. NW at 640 Wave St. (2+ person surreys featured)
2nd location: by Fisherman's Wharf (831)655-8687

★ **Boat Rentals**

Sailboats can be rented, and boating instruction is available here.
Monterey Municipal Yacht Club   *(831)372-9686*
downtown at Wharf #2

Kayaks are especially popular here as a way to get an intimate look at sea otters, sea lions, harbor seals and other denizens of the **Monterey Bay National Marine Sanctuary** (see listing). One- and two-person kayaks can be rented, along with accessories, at:

A B Seas Kayaks   *(831)647-0147   (866)824-2337*
1 mi. NW at 32 Cannery Row #5
montereykayak.com
Adventures by the Sea   *(831)372-1807*
1 mi. NW at 299 Cannery Row
adventuresbythesea.com

★ **Cannery Row**

starts just NW along Cannery Row
canneryrow.com

A few hulking cannery buildings and overpasses across Cannery Row still capture some of the flavor of the times before sardines vanished from Monterey Bay around 1950. The noise and smell described in John Steinbeck's *Cannery Row* are gone–replaced by a world class aquarium (see listing), imaginative shops, restaurants and night spots that have brought bright lights, the sound of music, and the smell of good food to ingeniously renovated old buildings and elaborate new structures. The Row is also a staging area for one of America's best beach dives. The continent's deepest near-shore underwater canyon, a vast kelp forest and abundant sea life are nearby offshore from San Carlos Beach.

★ **Fisherman's Wharf**   *(831)649-6544*
downtown at the N end of Alvarado St.
montereywharf.com
Original commercial fishing activities that operated here since 1845 are long gone. The wharf remains and the over-water buildings have evolved into a colorful potpourri of shops, restaurants, and open-air fish markets. Swarms of visitors are drawn by the bracing nautical atmosphere, marine views, close-up glimpses of harbor seals, sea otters, aquatic birds, and the peninsula's major terminus for sportfishing and sightseeing boats.

★ *Fishing Charters*
downtown on Fisherman's Wharf
Several sportfishing boats leave daily year-round for deep sea fishing, and salmon fishing in season. Memorable winter whale watching excursions and narrated sightseeing cruises are also featured. The following operators, located on Fisherman's Wharf, offer these services and all necessary equipment:

Chris' Fishing Trips   *(831)375-5951*
chrissfishingtrips.com
Monterey Sport Fishing   *(831)372-2203*   *(800)200-2203*
montereywhalewatching.com
Randy's Fishing Trips   *(831)372-7440*   *(800)251-7440*
randysfishingtrips.com

Food Specialties
The Giant Artichoke   *(831)633-3501*
12 mi. N at 11261 Merritt St. - Castroville
Artichokes reign in Castroville–the world's largest producing region. This tourist landmark features them in cans and jars of all sizes. The cafe (B-L-D–Moderate) serves them in scrambles, omelets, salad, bread and steamed or deep-fried as an appetizer.

★ **Jack's Peak Regional Park**   *(831)755-4899*
5 mi. SE via Hwy. 68 & Olmstead Rd.
Panoramic views of the peninsula, miles of hiking trails, and picnic sites in the pines are features of the high forested hills south of town. A mile-long nature trail provides a scenic loop to the top of the peak. At 1,068 feet, it is the highest summit on the peninsula.

★ **Lake El Estero Park**   *(831)646-3866*
just E on Pearl St.
This big park next to downtown has walkways and picnic areas around a small lake with paddleboat rentals. For family fun, Dennis the Menace Playground is where Hank Ketcham, creator of "Dennis the Menace," helped develop free-form "hands-on" play equipment. Narrow tunnels, balanced roundabouts, swinging bridges, giant slides, and other unusual devices entice children of all ages. Closed Mon. from November to May.

Live Theater

Wharf Theater *(831)649-2332*
downtown on Fisherman's Wharf
For more than a quarter century, Wharf Theater (designed and built by Bruce Ariss) has been pleasing theater-goers with exuberant performances of musicals and dramas in an intimate showcase on the Wharf. Dark Mon.-Wed.

★ **Monterey Bay Aquarium** *(831)648-4888*
1 mi. NW at 886 Cannery Row
mbayaq.org
One of the world's biggest and best aquariums opened in 1984 in an ingeniously remodeled cannery complex that extends into the ocean at Monterey Bay. Visitors are given a unique and exciting view of the native inhabitants of Monterey Bay–sea otters, octopus, salmon, sharks, jellyfish, and hundreds of other species of flora and fauna in an interactive naturalistic setting. A highlight is feeding time in a three-story kelp forest in a towering glass-walled tank. More than one hundred close-up viewing tanks and six giant tanks display near-shore-to-outer-bay environs and creatures ranging from starfish to schools of sardines (in a truly hypnotic circular tank) and giant sea turtles. "Jellies: Living Art" is an enchanting combination of exotic jellies and fine art in a crowd-pleasing new exhibit. "Splash Zone" is an ingenious child-oriented area full of interactive marine exhibits. The complex also includes **Portola Cafe** (L only–Moderate), where contemporary California fare is served with a remarkable ocean view. A window wall adjoins, and the binoculars on each table can bring offshore birds, seals, even dolphin and grey whales into view. In winter, storm surf splashing against the windows provides high drama. The adjoining cafeteria offers pizza and pasta, and shares marine views. Near the entrance is an excellent gift-and-book shop.

★ **Monterey Bay National Marine Sanctuary** *(831)647-4201*
just N
The nation's largest marine preserve covers 5,312 square miles. The Monterey Peninsula and Big Sur coasts provide spectacular gateways to offshore areas teeming with colorful vegetation, fish, crustaceans and marine mammals. Access is as close as the beaches adjoining downtown Monterey. The centerpiece of the offshore sanctuary is an underwater canyon a few miles out that is nearly twice as deep as the Grand Canyon.

★ **Monterey State Historic Park** *(831)649-7118*
downtown at #20 Custom House Plaza
www.inbay.net/~mshp/
California's European colonial history began here. More than two centuries of impressive history and architectural heritage in

California's oldest town are carefully preserved and enhanced by period gardens on a seven acre site near Fisherman's Wharf, and in numerous downtown buildings that have been restored and furnished in period antiques. **Pacific House** is a recently opened museum with interactive pre-statehood exhibits. The **Custom House** (1827) is the oldest government building in California. The **First Theater** (1846) was a sailors' lodging house and the first place in California to charge admission for theatrical performances. **Larkin House** (1834), combining Spanish-Colonial and New England architectural features, became a prototype copied throughout California. Robert Lewis Stevenson boarded and wrote in the **Stevenson House** in 1879. **Colton Hall** (1848), the first American public building in California, was where the state's first constitution was written in 1849. **Cooper-Molera Adobe** includes fruit and vegetable gardens, barns and farm animals, a visitor center, and gift shop on expansive grounds behind adobe walls. **Royal Presidio Chapel**, the only one of California's four Spanish presidio chapels still standing, has been used since 1795, making it the state's oldest church in continuous use.

★ *Moped Rentals*
Motorized bicycles provide an exhilarating and relatively effortless way to tour the scenic peninsula. For hourly and longer rentals of mopeds or bikes, plus information, maps and instruction, call:
Monterey Moped Adventures   *(831)373-2696*
1 mi. E at 1250 Del Monte Av. (Closed Wed.-Thurs.)
★ **National Steinbeck Center**   *(831)796-3833*
18 mi. NE at One Main St. - Salinas
www.steinbeck.org
The National Steinbeck Center opened in 1998 as a large state-of-the-art museum and archive dedicated to one of America's most renowned authors. The center, at the head of main street in downtown Salinas (Steinbeck's birthplace), presents a wealth of interactive multi-sensory exhibits. Seven themed theaters showcase his life and work featuring excerpts from *Cannery Row*, *East of Eden*, and other movies from his books. The original camper that was home to the author and his poodle while they researched *Travels With Charley* is a highlight. An orientation theater shows a brief biographical film of Steinbeck's life, while a changing gallery displays a variety of related art exhibits. Other features include comprehensive archives, a well-stocked museum store, and an indoor/outdoor cafe. The Center is open 10-5 daily. A large wing will house the "Valley of the World" agricultural history center in 2003. Nearby in Salinas is The Steinbeck House, his birthplace. The Victorian is now a luncheon restaurant (closed Sun.–Moderate) and gift shop featuring Steinbeck memorabilia.

★ *Wineries*
montereywines.org   *(831)375-9400*
Many good wineries are within an hour's drive of Monterey. Two have tasting facilities in town.

A Taste of Monterey   *(831)646-5446*   *(888)646-5446*
1 mi. NW at 700-KK Cannery Row (upstairs)
tastemonterey.com
Taste selections from among thirty-five Monterey County wineries for a (refundable) fee and purchase from one hundred-plus regional wines while watching ocean swells roll under your waterfront table. Tour wineries via their film. A well-stocked Monterey-themed gift shop is also worth a visit. Open 11-6 daily.

Bargetto Winery Tasting Room   *(831)373-4053*
1 mi. NW at 700-L Cannery Row
bargetto.com
Natural fruit wines, as well as premium varietals, are offered for tastes and sales daily in a pleasant facility (Monterey's oldest tasting room) with a notable gift shop. Open 10:30-6 daily.

Ventana Vineyards   *(831)372-7415*
5 mi. SE on Hwy. 68 at 2999 Monterey/Salinas Hwy. #10
ventanawines.com
Various premium wines including estate-grown chardonnay, chenin blanc, sauvignon blanc and more are available for tasting and sales in an atmospheric old limestone building that also has a gift shop and garden patio for your picnic. Open 11-5 daily.

RESTAURANTS

★ **Billy Quon's**   *(831)647-0390*
5 mi. SE (via Hwy. 68) at 1 Harris Ct. at Ryan Ranch
restauranteur.com/billyquons
L-D. No L Sat. & Sun.   *Expensive*
Pacific Rim cuisine is given a light and lively edge in dishes ranging from heirloom tomatoes and basil pizzas through tempura-style coconut jumbo prawns to rotisserie half duck seared with a ginger-plum glaze. Imaginative desserts and drinks contribute to the fun spirit of the comfortably upscale bistro with an expo kitchen.

★ **Cafe Fina**   *(831)372-5200*   *(800)843-3462 outside CA*
downtown at 47 Fisherman's Wharf
cafefina.com
L-D.   *Expensive*
A smooth blend of classic Italian and innovative California cuisine is showcased in fresh fish; homemade pastas and raviolis; wood-fired small pizzas; and housemade desserts. Intimate dining areas have tables set with full linen and fresh flowers. Harbor-view tables upstairs are especially romantic.

Chart House   *(831)372-3362*
1 mi. NW at 444 Cannery Row
chart-house.com
D only.   *Expensive*
Contemporary California seafoods and steaks compete for each
diner's attention with spectacular Monterey Bay views. Playful
sea otters and other marine animals are often seen from
waterfront tables set amid comfortably retro-rustic decor.

Cibo Ristorante   *(831)649-8151*
downtown at 301 Alvarado St.
cibo.com
D only.   *Expensive*
Pasta, pizza and grill dishes with a Sicilian emphasis are well
regarded on a grazing menu offered in a large modish dining
room. Jazz and other live music is featured nightly.

★ **Domenico's on Fisherman's Wharf**   *(831)372-3655*
downtown at 50 Fisherman's Wharf
pisto.com
L-D.   *Expensive*
Seasonally fresh fish star–like delightful pan-fried local sand dabs
or salmon filet grilled on an open mesquite-wood hearth.
Additionally, assorted homemade pasta and luscious desserts like
tiramisu and crème brûlée made here distinguish this long-time
favorite. Many dining room tables outfitted with full linen,
candles and flowers overlook boats in the inner harbor.

The Fish Hopper   *(831)372-8543*
1 mi. NW at 700 Cannery Row
fishhopper.com
L-D.   *Expensive*
Contemporary American fare is offered on a grazing menu, but
the most compelling reason to be here is the view. Some tables are
actually over water, and there is a sunny heated bay-view deck.

★ **Fresh Cream Restaurant**   *(831)375-9798*
downtown at Heritage Harbor - 99 Pacific St. #100-C
freshcream.com
D only.   *Very Expensive*
Fresh Cream is one of California's premier dining landmarks.
Splendid traditional French cuisine like full roast rack of lamb has
shared billing with creative California delights like poached
salmon on a bed of spinach and artichoke with saffron-thyme
sauce for more than twenty years. Housemade desserts like
Grand Marnier soufflé or tarte tatin with carmelized apples baked
under flaky puff pastry are similarly memorable. Many widely
spaced tables in the elegant dining rooms have an intimate,
romantic view of Fisherman's Wharf and the bay.

★ **Gianni's Pizza**   *(831)649-1500*
1 mi. NW at 725 Lighthouse Av.
giannispizzamonterey.com
L-D. No L Mon.-Thurs.   Moderate
The Peninsula's best pizza is Gianni's. Since 1974, the family-owned restaurant has featured all kinds of thick-crust pizza lavishly outfitted with designer or you-select toppings. Assorted calzones are also excellent. Fresh tender bread sticks and garlic sticks displayed for sale at the front entrance and tempting desserts–pies and gelatos–are also served in big warm dining rooms set around an exposition kitchen.

★ **Hula's**   *(831)655-4852*
1 mi. NW at 622 Lighthouse Av.
L-D. No L Sun. Closed Mon.   Moderate
Monterey's nod to Hawaii is a light lively bar and dining room with Island classics like shrimp and pork stuffed potstickers, a luau pork plate with sticky rice and slaw, or macadamia nut or coconut-encrusted ahi, ono, mahi mahi, and other fish flown in from Hawaii. Rattan, bamboo, surfboards, and related wall art contribute to the pleasing casual "Islands" spirit.

Lallapalooza   *(831)645-9036*
downtown at 474 Alvarado St.
D only.   Expensive
Beyond a big sports and martini bar is a snazzy dining room next to an expo kitchen serving a fine range of all-American updates like smoked ribs with firecracker fries or one-pound baseball-cut prime sirloin through crab cannelloni. A dessert highlight is their really big apple pie or chocolate gorilla cake.

★ **Loulou's**   *(831)372-0568*
just E on Municipal Wharf #2
www.loulousgriddle.com
B-L. Plus D on Fri.-Sat.   Moderate
Loulou's lively little cafe on the bay is a locals' favorite. Perched on the second wharf with a view of historic Fisherman's Wharf, fine specialties include tender pancakes filled with bananas or strawberries or a sizable seafood omelet. All breakfasts get a hearty helping of their flavorful tomato-herb skin-on potatoes that you can enjoy while viewing nifty nautical surroundings.

★ **Massaro & Santos**   *(831)649-6700*
just N at 32 Cannery Row, Suite H-1
massaroandsantos.com
L-D. Closed Mon.   Expensive
Massaro & Santos is a seafood house that is deservedly popular with locals. From silky Boston clam chowder to delicate local sand dabs or giant Monterey prawns, each dish is fresh and flavorful.

Most glass-topped tables set with fresh flowers around three sides of the upstairs dining room have a pleasing view of Monterey and the harbor. An adjoining heated dining porch shares the view.

★ **Monterey Plaza Hotel & Spa**   *(831)646-1700*
1 mi. NW at 400 Cannery Row
montereyplazahotel.com
B-L-D.   *Expensive-Very Expensive*
The Duck Club (B-D–Very Expensive) is the hotel's main dining room. Fresh seafood, prime meats and top-quality seasonal produce are skillfully transformed into signature dishes like wood-roasted duck, Colorado lamb chops with huckleberry sauce, and oak-grilled salmon. The comfortably elegant dining room, backed by an exhibition kitchen, offers panoramic views of Monterey Bay from a location over the water. **Schooners** (L-D–Expensive) serves regional fare like grilled Castroville artichoke, and fresh fish with preparations ranging from herb-roasted to macadamia-crusted. The warm, mahogany-trimmed lounge and umbrella-shaded deck share a fine bay view.

★ **Montrio Bistro**   *(831)648-8880*
downtown at 414 Calle Principal
montrio.com
D only.   *Expensive*
Expert attention given to a grazing menu of European-inspired contemporary American dishes (like artichoke fritters) has made this restaurant one of the best downtown. Stylish dining rooms have been fashioned within a historic Monterey firehouse along with an expo kitchen, rotisserie and whimsical bar.

★ **Morgan's**   *(831)373-5601*
downtown at 498 Washington St.
B-L-D.   *Moderate*
Morgan's is the Monterey Peninsula's best coffee house. They make a terrific almond galette and a delightful selection of scones, cookies and other pastries that can be enjoyed with beverages from a huge selection of coffees and teas, hot or iced drinks, beer and wine. Lush greenery, a fireplace, funky art in stone-wall rooms, sunny patio, and coffee roastery/beans on display and live music on weekends all contribute to deserved popularity.

★ **The Mucky Duck**   *(831)655-3031*
downtown at 479 Alvarado St.
L-D.   *Moderate*
Mucky Duck is Monterey's best pub. Consider fresh giant artichokes with a choice of stuffings, or thick homemade onion rings in imported beer batter with half-pound pub burgers or Porterhouse steak. Purists can choose an English banger sampler (in three styles), or beef Guinness and oyster pie. All can be

washed down with a remarkable range of English and American (including local) tap beers. Classic pub decor includes lots of hardwood and brass railings, stained glass, bronze knickknacks and wall hangings, plus a fire-ring room and a traditional cozy fireplace dining area. Live entertainment happens most nights. Out back is a large shaded patio with a big central fireplace.

Old Fisherman's Grotto   *(831)375-4604*
   downtown at 39 Fisherman's Wharf
   fishermansgrotto.com
   L-D.   *Moderate*
For more than half a century, Old Fisherman's Grotto has been pleasing visitors, especially families, with all sorts of traditional seafoods plus steaks, poultry and pastas. The casual dining rooms include many window tables with bayfront views.

★ **Paris Bakery**   *(831)646-1620*
   downtown at 271 Bonifacio Place
   B-L.   *Moderate*
Sequestered on a side street is one of the best and most comprehensive bakeries on the Peninsula. Bear claws, cinnamon rolls, scones, and other morning delights are uniformly excellent, while croissants with ham and cheese or spinach make delicious lunches or picnics. Assorted breads and luscious desserts are also on display in many cases backed by several tables where baked goods can be enjoyed with coffee, or to go.

Phil's Fish Market & Eatery   *(831)633-2152*
   16 mi. NE at 7600 Sandholdt Rd., on the island - Moss Landing
   philsfishmarket.com
   L-D.   *Moderate*
At Phil's cavernous funky fish market/deli/restaurant, you can get your fill of regional fresh seafood charbroiled, breaded, grilled, fried or in pastas and sandwiches. You can also get artichokes steamed, stuffed, french-fried or Sicilian style. There is plenty of really casual indoor and outdoor seating, or you can get it to go.

★ **Sardine Factory**   *(831)373-3775*
   1 mi. NW at 701 Wave St.
   sardinefactory.com
   D only.   *Very Expensive*
Fresh local seafood has distinguished the peninsula's longest-established gourmet dinner house for more than three decades. Traditional dishes include peerless abalone bisque or Cannery Row cioppino, and there are contemporary specialties like local sand dabs with lemon-thyme sauce. Save room for a selection from a long list of luscious desserts. The capacious restaurant offers a variety of elegant dining settings, including a gilt and rococo firelit Victorian room and grand glass-domed conservatory.

★ **Stokes Restaurant & Bar**   *(831)373-1110*
   downtown at 500 Hartnell St.
   stokesadobe.com
   L-D. No L Sun.   *Expensive*
Southern Mediterranean classics are skillfully translated into a
flavorful selection of cutting-edge California cuisine with clean
bold flavors. Consider grilled lavender pork chop with leek-lemon
bread pudding and plum chutney. Meticulous emphasis is on
freshness, quality, and local sources who bring wild mushrooms,
organic produce and herbs directly from fields to the kitchen door.
The culinary appeal is coupled with warmly unpretentious dining
rooms in a historic adobe dating from 1833.

★ **Tarpy's Roadhouse**   *(831)647-1444*
   5 mi. SE at 2999 Monterey-Salinas Hwy. (Hwy. 68)
   tarpys.com
   L-D.   *Expensive*
Zesty New California cuisine is described on a grazing menu
ranging from smoky barbecue baby back ribs to luscious housemade desserts. A historic rock-sided roadhouse now has several
whimsically romantic firelit dining areas and a garden patio.

★ **Turtle Bay Taqueria**   *(831)333-1500*
   downtown at 431 Tyler St.
   L-D.   *Low*
Seafoods of coastal Mexico are featured in fresh and flavorful
tacos, burritos, and wraps, plus soups and salads. The self-serve
salsa bar with mild or hot, green or red sauces is a nice addition.
Big colorful wall hangings and padded booths are the backdrop for
this nifty place-your-order-at-the-counter taqueria.

★ **Whaling Station**   *(831)373-3778*
   1 mi. N at 763 Wave St.
   restauranteur.com/whalingstation
   D only.   *Expensive*
Oak-grilled prime meat specialties like a nearly two-pound
Porterhouse steak and fresh seafoods like Monterey sand dab
fillets highlight a grazing menu of contemporary and traditional
California cuisine. The large, fully-linened restaurant remains one
of the peninsula's long-time favorite dinner houses.

★ **Wild Plum Cafe & Bakery**   *(831)646-3109*
   downtown at 731-B Munras Av.
   restauranteur.com/wildplum
   B-L. Closed Sun.   *Moderate*
A large case displays the day's delicious fresh muffins, cinnamon
rolls, and turnovers that can be enjoyed with scrambles, omelet
specialties, and more. Fresh deli items are also available to go or
at tables overlooking the cases and colorful wall murals.

LODGINGS

Lodgings are abundant and diverse including resorts, beachfront motor inns, and gracious bed-and-breakfasts. Fremont Street (less expensive) and Munras Avenue (upscale) are the peninsula's motel rows. June-to-October is high season. Non-weekend winter rates may be 30% less.

★ **The Beach Resort - Best Western**   *(831)394-3321*
   2 mi. E at 2600 Sand Dunes Dr. - 93940
   montereybeachhotel.com
   196 units   *(800)242-8627*   *Moderate-Expensive*
The Beach Resort is the Peninsula's only oceanfront lodging directly on miles of sandy beach. This modern four-story hotel also has a pool, whirlpool, exercise room, and lounge (live entertainment on weekends), and a gift shop. The top floor restaurant offers a window-wall panorama of Monterey and the bay. Many of the well-furnished rooms have a dramatic view of the beach and bay, and downtown in the distance. All have a refrigerator, extra amenities, and two queens or a king bed.
   #304,#308,#312,#316–fine view of beach/bay
      to Cannery Row, king bed.

Clarion Hotel Monterey   *(831)373-1337*
   just S at 1046 Munras Av. - 93940
   clarionhotelmonterey.com
   52 units   *(800)821-0805*   *Moderate-Very Expensive*
An attractive indoor pool is the center of interest, and there is also a whirlpool and sauna in this stylish motel. Each room is spacious and well furnished including a microwave/refrigerator, extra amenities, and queens or a king bed.
   "Honeymoon Suite"–gas fireplace and two-
      person whirlpool in view of canopy king bed.
   "King Executive" (6 of these)–gas fireplace, kitchen, king bed.

Colton Inn   *(831)649-6500*
   downtown at 707 Pacific St. - 93940
   coltoninn.com
   50 units   *(800)848-7007*   *Moderate-Expensive*
This modern motel has a convenient downtown location and a sauna. Each room is nicely furnished and has two queens or a king bed. Some have a pressed-wood fireplace, or kitchenette, or jet-tub.

★ **Doubletree Hotel**   *(831)649-4511*
   downtown at 2 Portola Plaza - 93940
   doubletreemonterey.com
   380 units   *(800)222-8733*   *Expensive-Very Expensive*
This modern convention-oriented hotel is a six-story landmark

occupying most of the choice location between downtown and Fisherman's Wharf. Amenities include a pool, whirlpool, (fee) day spa, fitness center, restaurant, lounge, on-premises micro-brew pub, shops, and (fee) parking. Each room is well furnished and has doubles, queen, or king bed. Some have a fine bay view.
6th floor (8 of these)–panoramic bay/town views, king bed.

Econo Lodge   *(831)372-5851*
2 mi. E at 2042 N. Fremont St. - 93940
47 units   *(877)424-6423*   *Low-Expensive*
A pool and whirlpool are features of this modern motel. Kitchenettes are available. Each nicely furnished unit has a queen or king bed.

El Dorado Inn   *(831)373-2921*
just S at 900 Munras Av. - 93940
15 units   *(800)722-1836*   *Moderate-Expensive*
Downtown is an easy stroll from this convenient, contemporary little motel. Continental breakfast is complimentary. Each attractively furnished room has a double, queen, or king bed.
#14–pressed-log fireplace, some bay view, queen bed.

Embassy Suites Hotel Monterey Bay   *(831)393-1115*
2 mi. E at 1441 Canyon Del Rey - Seaside 93955
embassymonterey.com
225 units   *(800)362-2779*   *Very Expensive*
An indoor pool, whirlpool, sauna, fitness center, restaurant and lounge are features of this business-oriented twelve-story hotel, as are the complimentary breakfast and afternoon manager's reception. A beach is only two blocks away. Each well-furnished suite has extra amenities, a kitchenette, and a separate bedroom with two doubles or a king bed.

Hilton Monterey   *(831)373-6141*
1 mi. S at 1000 Aquajito Rd. - 93940
www.hilton.com
204 units   *(800)234-5697*   *Expensive-Very Expensive*
Amenities of the three-story convention-oriented complex include a large garden pool, two tennis courts, saunas, fitness room, putting green, ping pong, restaurant, and lounge. Each spacious, well-furnished unit has a private deck, extra amenities and two doubles or a king bed.

★ **Hotel Pacific**   *(831)373-5700*
downtown at 300 Pacific St. - 93940
hotelpacific.com
105 units   *(800)232-4141*   *Expensive*
Downtown Monterey's best lodging is a four-story all-suites hotel. Graceful adobe buildings reflecting the Spanish-Colonial legacy are enhanced by intimate garden courtyards with whirlpools. An

expanded Continental breakfast buffet and afternoon refreshments are complimentary. Each spacious, beautifully furnished suite has a gas fireplace, honor bar, refrigerator, and private patio or terrace, plus queens or a king bed.

★ **Hyatt Regency - Monterey Resort**   *(831)372-1234*
1 mi. SE at 1 Old Golf Course Rd. - 93940
hyatt.com
575 units   *(800)233-1234*   *Expensive-Very Expensive*
A scenic 18-hole golf course adjoins this well-landscaped four-story resort and conference center. Amenities include (fee) golf, six tennis courts, and rental bicycles, plus two pools, two whirlpools, a fully equipped fitness center, ping pong, gift shop, restaurant, and entertainment lounge. All well-furnished rooms and suites were recently redecorated and have golf course views and two doubles or a king bed.

★ **The Jabberwock**   *(831)372-4777*
1 mi. NW at 598 Laine St.
jabberwockinn.com
7 units   *(888)428-7253*   *Expensive-Very Expensive*
A convent above Cannery Row has been charmingly transformed into an antique-filled bed-and-breakfast inn surrounded by gardens. Extras include goose down pillows and comforters, fresh flowers, a hearty complimentary breakfast and evening appetizers and aperitifs. Each well-furnished room has a queen or king bed.
"Borogrove"–spacious, gas fireplace, in-room two-person
    whirlpool, windows on 3 sides, superb bay view, king bed.
"Mome Rath"–bay-view windows, gas fireplace,
    in-room two-person whirlpool, king bed.

Lone Oak Motel   *(831)372-4924*
2 mi. E at 2221 Fremont St. - 93940
loneoaklodge.com
46 units   *(800)283-5663*   *Moderate-Expensive*
Whirlpool, sauna and exercise equipment are features of this single-level motel. Each recently redecorated room is comfortably furnished including a refrigerator, and queen or king bed.
#38,#39–spacious, gas fireplace, whirlpool in
    separate room, in-bath steam bath, king bed.

★ **The Mariposa**   *(831)649-1414*
1 mi. S at 1386 Munras Av. - 93940
50 units   *(800)824-2295*   *Expensive*
The best lodging on either of Monterey's "motel rows" is the Mariposa. It is a contemporary motel with a garden court pool and whirlpool that caters to romance. Expanded Continental breakfast is complimentary. Most of the well-furnished units have a raised gas fireplace. All have extra amenities and either a queen or king bed.

#321,#223 "Spa Suites"–spacious, beautifully
   furnished, gas fireplace, in-room raised whirlpool,
   refrigerator, double shower, king bed.
Marina Dunes Resort   *(831)883-9478*
8 mi. NE (via Hwy. 1) at 3295 Dunes Dr. - Marina 93933
marinadunes.com
60 units   *(877)944-3863*   *Very Expensive*
One of the area's newest bayfront lodgings shares a remote sandy
beach and (restricted) windswept dunes with an upscale time-
share complex. Guests have (restricted) access to the shoreline, a
pool and whirlpool, (fee) massage and spa services, and on-site
A.J. Spurs (L-D–Expensive), a link in an Old West-style
restaurant chain. All of the spacious, attractively furnished units
have a gas fireplace, refrigerator/wet bar, private deck with a view
of the bay or dunes, and a king bed.
★ **Monterey Bay Inn**   *(831)373-6242*
1 mi. N at 242 Cannery Row - 93940
montereybayinn.com
47 units   *(800)424-6242*   *Very Expensive*
Monterey's finest motel has a spectacular site by a sandy cove and
the National Marine Sanctuary on the bay at the quiet end of
Cannery Row. The posh, post-modern four-story complex also
features a rooftop bay-view whirlpool, plus (fee) day spa and
garage. Expanded Continental breakfast delivered to your door is
complimentary, as are apples and cookies in the afternoon. Most
of the beautifully furnished rooms have a window wall and large
private balcony with an ocean view, binoculars and honor bar,
extra amenities, plus a (feather) king bed. Waves lap under the
enchanting rooms on the bay side.
   #411 thru #414–top floor, private super views of the bay.
   #410,#409–top floor, fine views of the yacht harbor.
The Monterey Hotel   *(831)375-3184*
downtown at 406 Alvarado St. - 93940
montereyhotel.com
45 units   *(800)727-0960*   *Expensive-Very Expensive*
The only small hotel in downtown Monterey is a four-story hotel
(circa 1904) on the main street that has been skillfully restored.
Expanded Continental breakfast and afternoon refreshments are
complimentary. Each attractively furnished room has all
contemporary amenities plus a double, queen or king bed.
   "Master Suite" (4 of these)–spacious, gas fireplace,
      refrigerator/wet bar, king bed.
Monterey Marriott   *(831)649-4234*
downtown at 350 Calle Principal - 93940
marriotthotels.com
341 units   *(800)228-9290*   *Very Expensive*

Monterey's tallest landmark is a plain, modern ten-story convention-oriented hotel in the heart of downtown and near the waterfront. Amenities include a pool, whirlpool, exercise room, (fee) parking, restaurant, sports bar and gift shop. The well-furnished rooms have extra amenities and doubles, queen or king bed. Many have a bay view.

★ **Monterey Plaza Hotel & Spa**   *(831)646-1700*
  1 mi. NW at 400 Cannery Row - 93940
  woodsidehotels.com
  290 units   (800)631-1339   Expensive-Very Expensive
The five-story Monterey Plaza Hotel is a perfect paradigm of urbane renewal. Monterey's most sumptuous full-service hotel is on a choice bayfront location on Cannery Row. There is beach access, an elegant rooftop full-service (fee) spa with a complete range of body/beauty treatments and facilities, resort shops, view bistro/ lounge plus the delightful Duck Club (see listing) and (fee) valet parking. Each recently upgraded, spacious room is beautifully furnished including a wealth of upscale amenities, an honor bar, and two queens or a king bed. Many have a large private balcony that is literally over the bay/ocean. Three extra-large two-bedroom top-floor suites have a gas fireplace and an in-bath whirlpool.
  #1302,#1202,#1102,#1002–corner, balcony over bay/wharf,
    floor-to-ceiling windows with superb water view, king bed.

Munras Lodge   *(831)646-9696*
  just S at 1010 Munras Av. - 93940
  munraslodge.com
  29 units   (800)472-6480   Moderate-Very Expensive
An easy stroll from downtown, Munras Lodge is a contemporary motel. It has a sheltered courtyard with a whirlpool and sauna. Each room is spacious, well furnished (including a microwave and refrigerator) and has two queens or a king bed. Most have a gas fireplace.
  "Deluxe Room" (4 of these)–spacious, in-room
    two-person whirlpool, gas fireplace, king bed.

★ **Old Monterey Inn**   *(831)375-8284*
  just SW at 500 Martin St. - 93940
  oldmontereyinn.com
  10 units   (800)350-2344   Very Expensive
Old Monterey Inn is the most enchanting bed-and-breakfast in town. A 1929 Tudor-style mansion has been meticulously transformed, and is now sequestered amid luxuriant English gardens on a hillside a stroll from downtown. Bountiful gourmet breakfast, tea and fresh-baked cookies, evening wine and appetizers are complimentary. Each spacious, romantically decorated room is beautifully furnished with antiques; contemporary amenities; a

145

private bath, sitting area, and queen or king featherbed. Many rooms also have a gas or woodburning fireplace.

"Garden Cottage"–private cottage with in-room two-person whirlpool with skylight, woodburning fireplace, king bed.

"Library"–large oak-view windows on three sides, private sundeck, stone woodburning fireplace facing king bed.

"Mayfield Suite"–romantic, wisteria view, two-person in-room whirlpool, gas fireplace in view of king bed.

"Rookery"–cozy, skylight, private garden view, fireplace facing queen bed.

Sand Dollar Inn   *(831)372-7551*
just S at 755 Abrego St. - 93940
sanddollarinn.com
63 units   *(800)982-1986*   *Moderate-Expensive*
Conveniently located next to downtown, this contemporary motel has a pool and whirlpool. Expanded Continental breakfast is complimentary. Each room is attractively furnished including a wet bar/refrigerator, and two queens or a king bed. Most have a balcony or patio.

"Deluxe Rooms" (9 of these)–spacious, gas fireplace, private balcony, king bed.

★ **Spindrift Inn**   *(831)646-8900*
1 mi. N at 652 Cannery Row - 93940
spindriftinn.com
42 units   *(800)232-4141*   *Very Expensive*
The Spindrift Inn is a gracious contemporary getaway above a picturesque beach in the midst of Cannery Row. Valet (fee) parking and waterfront dining are available. Expanded Continental breakfast delivered to your room and afternoon wine and cheese reception are complimentary. Each individually decorated, beautifully furnished room has a refrigerator, honor bar, extra amenities, woodburning fireplace and window seat or private deck, plus a goosedown feather queen or king bed. Many have a bayfront view.

#407,#307–grand bay view, window alcove seats, king bed.

The Victorian Inn - Best Western   *(831)373-8000*
1 mi. NW at 487 Foam St. in Cannery Row - 93940
victorianinn.com
68 units   *(800)232-4141*   *Expensive-Very Expensive*
This contemporary Victorian-themed motel is a block from the bay in Cannery Row. There is a whirlpool in the patio, and underground (fee) parking. Continental breakfast and afternoon wine and cheese are complimentary. Each compact rooms is well furnished with good reproductions and has a gas fireplace, honor bar, a window seat, and two doubles or a king bed.

#301,#305,#307,#308–two-person whirlpool tub, king bed.

Murphys

Murphys is the newest bonanza in California's Mother Lode. The historic Gold Camp is sequestered in a fold of gentle foothills of the Sierra distinguished by a clear stream and lush natural woodlands. A sterling mild climate, a golden legacy, and a liquid asset–wine–are fueling a rush of fun-seekers, not fortune-hunters, to this latter-day boomtown.

Placer gold mining and a trading post were established by John and Daniel Murphy in 1848. With the luck of the Irish, they were among the first Californians to strike it rich. By 1852, 3,000 people lived here, attracted by some of the state's richest gold placers. Boom times eventually ended, leaving a rich legacy of businesses, churches and homes. More than a century of peaceful prosperity followed, as the village was sustained by agriculture, sawmills, trade and tourism.

Today, nearby caverns and giant redwood forests (popular since the 1850s) have been joined by burgeoning local wineries as this area's major attractions. Increasing numbers of visitors pursue recreation and leisure opportunities, and explore remnants of Murphys' golden past. Mature trees shade a main street full of historic buildings and tasteful new replicas housing a proliferation of regional arts, crafts, antiques, and gourmet specialties including several winery tasting rooms. Nostalgia buffs can pan for gold, enjoy a horse-drawn carriage ride, then settle into the landmark hotel (made famous by luminaries like U.S. Grant and Mark Twain) for unspoiled Gold Camp decor, warm meals, cold beer, and a cozy bed (including the one Grant slept on).

WEATHER PROFILE

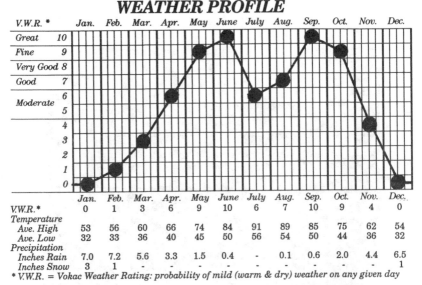

V.W.R. *		Jan.	Feb.	Mar.	Apr.	May	June	July	Aug.	Sep.	Oct.	Nov.	Dec.
Great	10												
Fine	9												
Very Good	8												
Good	7												
Moderate	6												
	5												
	4												
	3												
	2												
	1												
	0												

	Jan.	Feb.	Mar.	Apr.	May	June	July	Aug.	Sep.	Oct.	Nov.	Dec.
V.W.R.*	0	1	3	6	9	10	6	7	10	9	4	0
Temperature												
Ave. High	53	56	60	66	74	84	91	89	85	75	62	54
Ave. Low	32	33	36	40	45	50	56	54	50	44	36	32
Precipitation												
Inches Rain	7.0	7.2	5.6	3.3	1.5	0.4	-	0.1	0.6	2.0	4.4	6.5
Inches Snow	3	1	-	-	-	-	-	-	-	-	-	1

* V.W.R. = Vokac Weather Rating: probability of mild (warm & dry) weather on any given day

BASIC INFORMATION

Population: 1,500
Elevation: 2,171 feet
Location: 130 miles East of San Francisco
Airport (regularly scheduled flights): Sacramento - 92 miles

Calaveras Visitors Bureau   (209)736-0049   (800)225-3764
   8 mi. SW at 1192 S. Main St. - Angels Camp 95222
   visitcalaveras.org
Murphys Business Associates
   (no office) Box 2034 - 95247
   visitmurphys.com

ATTRACTIONS

Boating

Sierra Nevada Adventure Co. *(209)795-9310 (888)900-7622*
11 mi. NE at 2293 Hwy. 4 - Arnold
snacattack.com
One of the largest selections of rental flat-water kayaks and canoes in the Sierra are available in the shop. All necessary equipment is available, but you have to provide your own transportation to get the craft to one of several of California's most scenic reservoirs less than an hour away.

★ **Calaveras Big Trees State Park** *(209)795-2334*
15 mi. NE via Hwy. 4
bigtrees.org
Two magnificent groves of giant sequoias are the world class highlight of the park. They distinguish more than six thousand acres of mixed forests filling both sides of a scenic Stanislaus River canyon. Trails up to four miles long provide access for hikers from spring through fall, while cross-country and snow-shoe tours are popular in winter. An interpretive center and complete campground are near the North Grove. The mile-long well-marked loop trail in the North Grove is a must. As an added treat, a six-mile scenic drive from the entrance provides access to the Stanislaus River at the bottom of a deep canyon. Staircases from a parking lot extend to boulder-strewn deep clear pools.

Caves

Murphys is the epicenter of California's most impressive caverns. All are cool, scenic, and offer a choice of easy tours or rugged spelunking adventures. Each has a gift shop and picnic tables.

★ **California Caverns** *(209)728-2101 (866)762-2837*
18 mi. N via Sheep & Mountain Ranch Rds.
caverntours.com
Opened to the public in 1850, this was the first commercial cave in California. An easy hour-plus "trail-of-lights" walking tour showcases geological delights ranging from delicate soda straws to massive flowstones–plus signatures from Gold Rush days on walls and ceilings. More adventurous spelunkers can opt for guided three- to four-hour "Middle Earth Expeditions" through mud and water where beautiful and pristine formations are illuminated by your cave helmet light. The caverns are open daily from May through October or longer depending on water levels.

★ **Mercer Caverns** *(209)728-2101*
1 mi. N at 1665 Sheep Ranch Rd.
mercercaverns.com
Discovered by a gold prospector in 1885, Mercer Caverns is the longest continuously operating commercial cave in California.

Visitors who can handle 238 steps down (and back up) are rewarded with views of some dazzling crystalline formations like one of the world's largest arrays of aragonite–a rare white mineral that looks like heavy refrigerator frost. Guided forty-five-minute tours on well-lighted walkways leave hourly every day.

★ **Moaning Cavern**   *(209)736-2708   (866)762-2837*
   6 mi. SW via Parrotts Ferry Rd. at 5150 Moaning Cave Rd. - Vallecito
   caverntours.com
Discovered around 1851, this is California's largest public cavern. A guided forty-five-minute walking tour includes a descent on a historic 100-foot spiral wooden staircase into a gigantic chamber with impressive formations and a clear span of 180 feet between floor and ceiling. For the athletic, "the rappel" is another way into the vast chamber (offered on a continuous basis daily–no experience necessary). Three-hour adventure trips can also be arranged. There is also a gift shop, plus picnic tables and a nature trail. The cavern is open every day all year.

★ *Wineries*   *(800)225-3764 x 25*
   calaveraswines.org
After a long hiatus extending back to the Gold Rush era, Murphys is again the heart of a reborn Gold Country wine district. Downtown has one of the few strollable clusters of winery tasting rooms in California. As an added feature, none of the wineries has a fee for tastes.

Black Sheep Winery   *(209)728-2157*
   just W at west end of Main St. at 634 French Gulch Rd.
   blacksheepwinery.com
Some of the region's best premium reds (and two whites) are generously poured for tastes in a handsome little vine-covered building on the outskirts of downtown that captures the spirit of this Gold Country wine district. Open noon-5 weekends and by appointment at other times.

Chatom Vineyards   *(209)736-6500*
   2 mi. SE at 1969 Hwy. 4 - Douglas Flat
   chatomvineyards.com
A handsome wood-trim tasting room and well-stocked gift shop adjoin a beautifully landscaped winery. Tastes are generously offered of the full range of premium red and white wines. The sauvignon blancs and zinfandels are especially notable. Several picnic tables under a grape arbor overlook gardens and the attractive complex. Open 11-5 daily.

Courtyard Wineries   *(209)728-8487*
   downtown at 415 Main St.
   domainebecquetwinery.com
All of the wines of **Domaine Becquet**, **French Hill** and **Le Mulet Rouge** are, since 2002, available for tastes in a handsome courtyard shop on main street. Open 11-6 Thurs.-Sun.

French Hill Winery   *(209)286-1800*
27 mi. NW at 8032 S. Main St. - Mokelumne Hill
frenchhill.com
French Hill is worth going out of the way for in Calaveras County
because the winemaker has done notable work with unusual (for
this area) wines. Port is very good, and the ice wine and barbera
are special in a little shop near the intersection of Highway 49
and Highway 26. Open 11-5 Sat. & Sun. or by appointment.

Ironstone Vineyards   *(209)728-1251*
1 mi. S at 1894 Six Mile Rd.
ironstonevineyards.com
Ironstone Vineyards is one of America's most extraordinary
young wineries. Beautifully landscaped grounds include a Gold
Country museum showcasing the "Ironstone Crown Jewel"–the
world's largest pure crystalline gold leaf nugget–found nearby
recently. Other features in a sprawling complex that is an
unabashed tribute to the California Gold Rush include a handsome tasting room, a memorable tour of the premium winery
(including limestone cellars and luxuriant grounds with elaborate
gardens, ponds and a celebrity-event amphitheater) plus an art
and jewelry gallery, gourmet deli and in-house bakery with fresh-
made breads and desserts, and an expansive gift and wine store.
Open 10-5 daily.

Malvadino Vineyards   *(209)728-9030*
downtown at 457C Algiers St.
malvadino.com
A handsome cottage has been transformed into an inviting tasting
and sales room. The winery buys their grapes primarily from
Calaveras growers. The Lodi Zinfandel is a standout among
premium varietals. Open 11-5 except closed Tues.

Milliaire Winery   *(209)728-1658*
downtown at 276 Main St.
milliarewinery.com
Wine barrels full of flowers distinguish a historic ex-gas station
that now serves as a charming little tasting room/gift shop where
guests can sample from an extensive range of red and white
wines. Zinfandel is from a century-old vineyard. Open 11-5 daily.

Stevenot Winery   *(209)728-3436*
4 mi. N at 2690 San Domingo Rd.
stevenotwinery.com
This award-winning picturesque winery is sequestered among
vineyards at the bottom of a deep gorge. Zinfandel, the Mother
Lode's most famous contribution to wine, and other premium
varietals are poured in a historic tasting room, and there are
tours, sales, gifts and picnic areas. Open 10-5 daily. An attractive
tasting room downtown (458 Main St.) is open 11-5 daily.

Zucca Mountain Vineyards   *(209)728-1623*
downtown at 425 E. Main St.
zuccawines.com

A cozy little tasting and sales room has been fashioned into a rock-rimmed "grotto" cellar in a 150-year-old building off Main Street. Premium cabernets, barbera and old-vine zinfandel star, along with a syrah port. Tastes are accompanied by a unique feature–first-class cheese (and chocolate) fondue. Open 12-5 daily.

RESTAURANTS

★ **Alchemy Market**   *(209)728-0700*
downtown at 191 Main St.
alchemymarket.com
B-L-D. Closed Wed. No D Sun.-Tues.   *Expensive*
Alchemy reflects sophistication that Murphys has achieved post-millennium. Baked goods made here are displayed at the entrance where guests settle into the comfortable wine bar and dining area that includes a fireplace and shaded patio. Designer soups, salads, and sandwiches are enhanced by appetizers in the evening as accompaniments to assorted premium wines. An adjoining charcuterie has in-depth selections of gourmet provisions including some samples. This is *the* place to assemble a fancy picnic.

★ **Auberge 1899**   *(209)728-1899*
downtown at 498 Main St.
auberge1899.com
D only. Closed Mon.-Tues.   *Expensive*
Auberge 1899 is an alluring source of traditional French dining. Classics ranging from escargot or foie gras to chateaubriand for two or crêpes flambé are served in a casual dining room and on a lovely tree-shaded garden court behind the century-old building.

★ **Biga**   *(209)728-9250*
downtown at 458 Main St.
L only. Closed Tues.   *Moderate*
An artisan bakery displays classic and unique breads and pastries handcrafted here each day with results that range from superb to sad, based on the inclinations and availability of a gifted baker. Breads are sold until the baker decides there's not enough dough to make it worth sticking around.

Blue Coyote Cafe   *(209)795-2872*
12 mi. NE at 1224 Oak Circle - Arnold
L-D. Closed Mon.-Tues.   *Expensive*
An eclectic selection of creative California dishes begins with beer-batter chicken tenders with lemon-mustard dipping sauce and ends with bread pudding with various sauces or fruits of the season for dessert. Warm knotty-pine decor and a flowery dining deck contribute to the high country dining adventure.

Firewood   *(209)728-3248*
downtown at 420 Main St.
L-D. Closed Mon.-Tues.   *Moderate*
California comfort food including all kinds of designer wood-fired pizzas, plus tacos, burritos, hamburgers, and barbecued baby back ribs are served with tap beers and local wines. The spiffy little eatery opens up on warm days (except for screening) to a fine view of the heart of town.

★ **Grounds**   *(209)728-8663*
downtown at 402 Main St.
B-L-D. No D Mon. & Tues.   *Expensive*
Light and lively California cuisine is carefully prepared from fresh seasonal vegetables, fruits and seafoods. Breakfast pastries and breads on display up front lend extra appeal. In back, diners can enjoy a comfortable wood-trimmed dining room overlooking an alfresco garden court dining area.

Murphys Historic Hotel & Lodge   *(209)728-3444*
downtown at 457 Main St.
murphyshotel.com
B-L-D.   *Expensive*
Murphys Hotel Dining Room has been a landmark for years. Traditional and updated American fare on a seasonally changing menu is served in a recently renovated nostalgic setting. In the next room, the wood-trim saloon with a pot-bellied stove is an authentic old-time gem with a remarkably long and lively history.

Pick & Shovel Cafe   *(209)728-3779*
downtown at 419-B Main St.
L only. Plus D on Fri. Closed Tues.-Wed.   *Moderate*
The kitchen-sink chili and half a dozen different kinds of hot dogs top a list of comfort foods that can be washed down with assorted premium tap beers or multi-fresh-fruit smoothies. This little main street cafe, remodeled in 2002, features a nifty heated deck under a giant shade tree overlooking the heart of town.

LODGINGS

Lodgings in Murphys are scarce, but now include stylish bed-and-breakfast inns and contemporary motels to supplement the historic landmark hotel (which for decades was the only place to stay in town). There are no bargains, but rates may be reduced 10% apart from weekends in winter and spring.

★ **Angels Hacienda**   *(209)785-8533*
18 mi. SW at 4871 Hunt Rd. - Farmington 95230
angelshacienda.com
8 units   *(800)827-8533*   *Expensive-Very Expensive*
Angels Hacienda is the peerless paragon of splendid isolation in California. The baronial California mission-style hacienda, built

around a beguiling fountain court, has been painstakingly restored to its original 1930s grandeur. It looms over a broad flat valley like the grand centerpiece of a Hollywood western epic. But, it and the extra-starry sky that follows nightly gorgeous sunsets are real. So is the peace and quiet that reigns here–many miles from the nearest freeway or town. Inside, elegant European antiques blend seamlessly with contemporary amenities. Full gourmet breakfast and afternoon refreshments and appetizers are complimentary. Each spacious room and suite is individually luxuriously furnished to complete the glamour of an earlier time with the romantic fun of today's plush possibilities for adult decor, including extra amenities, and a queen or king bed.

#1 "Patron"–extra-large, two-person whirlpool
with sunset views, double spa shower, custom
gas fireplace, canopy king bed.

#2 "Del Sol"–sunroom with two-person whirlpool
with many-window hill view, gas fireplace in view
of canopy queen bed.

"Embarcadero"–sitting area with gas fireplace and
two-person whirlpool with window view, glass-block
shower, hand-carved sleigh queen bed.

★ **Dunbar House 1880**   *(209)728-2897*
downtown at 271 Jones St. - 95247
dunbarhouse.com
5 units   (800)692-6006   Expensive-Very Expensive
Dunbar House 1880 is Murphys' most charming lodging. Majestic elms shade lawns and gardens surrounding an Italianate Victorian home. Gourmet candlelit breakfast, afternoon appetizer plate with local wine and mineral water in your room upon arrival, and handmade chocolates when your bed is turned down are all complimentary. Each individually decorated room is beautifully furnished with antiques; art; refrigerator stocked with a bottle of local wine, mineral water, and an appetizer plate; Norwegian gas-burning stove; private bath; all contemporary amenities plus extras; and a queen or king bed.

"Sequoia"–spacious, in-bath two-person whirlpool
and shower, private porch, king bed.

"Cedar"–two rooms, private sun porch, in-bath
two-person whirlpool and shower, queen bed.

"Sugar Pine"–spacious, private balcony in the trees,
six-foot clawfoot tub and separate shower, queen bed.

★ **Murphys Historic Hotel & Lodge**   *(209)728-3444*
downtown at 457 Main St. - 95247
murphyshotel.com
29 units   (800)532-7684   Moderate
The heart of town has always been the Murphys Hotel. The

picturesque stone building with iron shutters has hosted famous
visitors since 1859, from Mark Twain to U.S. Grant. The actual
bed President Grant slept on at the time of his visit is still here!
So is a casually posh dining room (see listing) and one of
California's most evocative saloons. The nine historic hotel rooms
kindle real nostalgia with authentic period antiques, a bath down
the hall, and a double bed. Twenty modern lodge rooms in a
building reflecting the hotel's historic roots surround an adjoining
lawn and garden. Each has a private bath, all contemporary
motel-style amenities, and a double or queen bed.

Murphys Inn Motel   *(209)728-1818*
   just E at 76 Main St. (Box 882) - 95247
   centralsierralodging.com
   37 units   *(888)796-1800*   *Moderate*
A small pool and an exercise room are features of this
contemporary motel with some extras. Each well-furnished room
has all modern conveniences and two queens or a king bed.
"Mini-Suite"–spacious, refrigerator, microwave, king bed.

★ **Murphys Suites**   *(209)728-2121*
   just E at 134 Hwy. 4 - 95247
   centralsierralodging.com
   70 units   *(877)728-2121*   *Expensive*
Murphys' first all-suites motel opened in late 2002 with a pool,
whirlpool, sauna, and exercise room. Expanded Continental
breakfast served to your room is also complimentary. Each
spacious, well-furnished unit has a refrigerator, microwave, extra
amenities, and two queens or a king bed. Four suites also have an
in-bath whirlpool tub.

★ **Victoria Inn**   *(209)728-8933*
   downtown at 402-H Main St. (Box 2340) - 95247
   4victoriainn.com
   14 units   *Expensive-Very Expensive*
The Victoria Inn is a large contemporary bed-and-breakfast in the
heart of the village. Expanded buffet breakfast is complimentary
as are cookies all day. All of the rooms are individually well
furnished and have two doubles, queen or king bed.
   #2 "Anniversary Suite"–spacious, private balcony,
      wet bar, two-sided woodburning fireplace,
      in-bath two-person whirlpool, sleigh king bed.
   #12 "Wisteria Cottage"–spacious, woodburning
      fireplace in living room, in-bath two-person whirl-
      pool, wet bar/refrigerator, private porch, king bed.
   #7 "Blue Doris"–balcony, in-bath
      two-person whirlpool, king bed.
   #5 "Sweetwater"–big bay window, clawfoot
      slipper tub and wood stove in view of queen bed.

Napa

Napa is the urbane gateway to America's most renowned Wine Country. It is situated where the Napa River's current meets ocean tides about twenty miles upriver from an extension of San Francisco Bay. Lush vineyards of legendary wineries that fill the little valley nearly surround the city which is further complemented by a semitropical climate.

By good luck, Napa was founded in the right place (a warm valley by a river with ocean access) at the right time (1848–just before the great California gold rush). Disenchanted miners came here to warm up and find work. They did, at farms, cattle ranches, sawmills, and stores serving the mining camps. Before the Civil War, the town became the business and government center of the valley. It still is, 150 years later.

With the 21st century, boom times have returned. Napa's only historic environmental problem–flooding–has been resolved. Major improvements have followed to the riverfront in the heart of town including parks; walkways; a dock for cruise yachts; and a historic mill transformed into upscale shops, restaurants, and lodgings. Downtown is vital again with new restaurants, specialty shops and cultural facilities like the restored opera house and landmark movie theater. Gateway-to-Wine-Country status is now secure, with both the unique Wine Train and its depot, and Copia–the ultimate cornucopia of California's gourmet food and wine–near the heart of town. A wealth of sybaritic bed-and-breakfasts in surrounding garden districts showcase the town's legacy of magnificent mansions.

Napa

WEATHER PROFILE

V.W.R. *		Jan.	Feb.	Mar.	Apr.	May	June	July	Aug.	Sep.	Oct.	Nov.	Dec.
Great	10												
Fine	9												
Very Good	8												
Good	7												
Moderate	6												
	5												
	4												
	3												
	2												
	1												
	0												

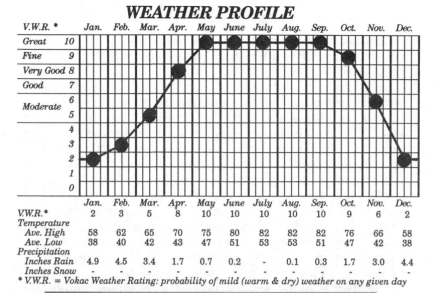

	Jan.	Feb.	Mar.	Apr.	May	June	July	Aug.	Sep.	Oct.	Nov.	Dec.
V.W.R.*	2	3	5	8	10	10	10	10	10	9	6	2
Temperature												
Ave. High	58	62	65	70	75	80	82	82	82	76	66	58
Ave. Low	38	40	42	43	47	51	53	53	51	47	42	38
Precipitation												
Inches Rain	4.9	4.5	3.4	1.7	0.7	0.2	-	0.1	0.3	1.7	3.0	4.4
Inches Snow	-	-	-	-	-	-	-	-	-	-	-	-

* V.W.R. = Vokac Weather Rating: probability of mild (warm & dry) weather on any given day

BASIC INFORMATION

Population: 72,585
Elevation: 17 feet
Location: 46 miles North of San Francisco
Airport (regularly scheduled flights): San Francisco - 57 miles

Napa Valley Conference & Visitors Bureau   (707)226-7459
   downtown at 1310 Napa Town Center - 94559
   napavalley.com
Napa Chamber of Commerce   (707)226-7455
   downtown at 1556 First St. - 94559
   napachamber.org

ATTRACTIONS

★ **American Safari Cruises**   *(888)862-8881*
departs from Pier 40 at Embarcadero & Townsend - San Francisco
amsafari.com   *Very Expensive*
Napa is the most northerly port-of-call, and the only overnight downtown moorage, of a luxury yacht providing a uniquely stylish way to visit Wine Country. The premier cruise focusing on America's most famous wine region features Napa and Sonoma Valleys with itineraries of four or five days days. Approximately twenty guests have the run of a four-deck vessel outfitted with a library, lounge, dining room, hot tub, kayaks and bicycles for shore excursions, and staterooms with queen or king beds and private baths. After sailing from San Francisco, passengers are given a San Francisco Bay orientation with (of course) a fine sparkling wine. Cruise highlights include guided visits to famed sources of premium wines in impressive buildings amid luxuriant vineyards. Premium wines and other alcoholic beverages complement skillfully prepared regional fare of the season served in the casually elegant dining room each night on board and during social hours with appetizers. Gourmet Wine Country cuisine is also featured ashore, including a grand three-course lunch served in a romantically lighted wine cave. A renowned artist, Carlo Marchiori, provides a private tour of his re-created Tuscan villa complete with Romanesque ruins (see listing in Calistoga chapter). While anchored in downtown Napa after cruising up many miles of the scenic little Napa River, a wine escort leads a walk to Copia (see listing), California's ultimate paean to food, wine and art. Later, there is a visit with a major artist in her gallery followed by a tour and barrel tasting in a historic wine cave (see Del Dotto Vineyards listing). Passengers can also explore the city on a bicycle or paddle up the river in a kayak. Others may opt for a relaxing view of the skyline while soaking in the top-deck hot tub of American Safari's unique cruise yacht.

★ *Ballooning*
Fine weather and lovely vineyard-shrouded countryside make Napa Valley one of America's most popular destinations for hot-air balloon flights. Several companies launch at sunrise for memorable morning champagne flights that assure passengers a unique vantage to Wine Country sights and sounds. Most leave from nearby Yountville. The best are:
Napa Valley Aloft, Inc.   *(800)627-2759*
napavalleyaloft.com
Napa Valley Balloons, Inc.   *(800)253-2224*
napavalleyballoons.com

★ **Copia** *(707)259-1600 (888)512-6742*
just E at 500 First St.
copia.org
California's best premium wines and gourmet foods are showcased in a spectacular (new in 2002) complex in Napa, the gateway to California's legendary wine valley. A large post-modern structure overlooks a bend of the Napa River and an extensive demonstration garden displaying the remarkable range of fruits, vegetables and herbs that can be grown throughout the year in this semi-tropical climate. The main building houses extensive exhibits displaying the history and evolution of the culinary arts. Cooking and wine-related demonstrations are featured seasonally with visiting experts in high-tech-oriented lecture halls, and there are state-of-the-art facilities for presentations, meetings, and events that celebrate food and wine. Complimentary wine tastings are scheduled each afternoon (showcasing a different winery every week). Rotating interactive exhibits exalt food as art. Related motion pictures and other entertainments are scheduled year-round. The culmination of this celebration of culinary accomplishments is **Julia's Kitchen** (see listing). Reservations are necessary to experience one of California's best dining adventures. Top-quality seasonally fresh ingredients featuring Copia's gardens and the region's bounty become meals that are as beautiful as they are flavorful. Guests have the added benefit of being able to watch the ballet-like precision of the culinary team at work in the expo kitchen adjoining a simply posh post-modern dining room that also sports a view of the adjoining demonstration gardens. A premium wine tasting bar adjoins, along with a market with gourmet foods and wines, and an expansive store showcasing related arts, crafts and gifts. Tours of the building and gardens are complimentary with admission, and highly recommended. Hours vary seasonally. Copia is closed Tuesday, plus Wednesday in winter.

★ **Di Rosa Preserve** *(707)226-5991*
8 mi. SW at 5200 Carneros Hwy. (Hwy. 12)
dirosapreserve.org
One of America's major collections of California's Bay Area folk art is on display in several buildings and on the luxuriant grounds of a lakeside estate surrounded by vineyards. Intricately festooned automobiles, a hearse and other vehicles stand out among wacky whimsies on display on the expansive grounds. Even the staff reflects over-the-top love of the bizarre–your tour guide may arrive in the "Dragon Wagon." Reservations required for (fee) tours year-round. Closed Sunday (plus Friday in summer, Monday rest of year). A shop at 1142 Main St. in downtown Napa sells some related smaller pieces.

Food Specialties
★ **Anette's Chocolate Factory**   *(707)252-4228*
   downtown at 1321 First St.
   anettes.com

Anette's is the Wine Country's greatest confectionery. Behind a lovely streetfront patio with tables where you can enjoy any of their special drinks or housemade ice creams is an impeccable store. Many cases display superb chocolates in truffles (the novel chardonnay and other wine truffles are a must), brittles, wafers and a host of other styles. Several are generously offered for tastes, along with a couple of their great varietal wine/chocolate syrups. All are available to go, or in gift packs to be shipped. At certain times you can watch them creating syrups, chocolates and other delights in the factory behind the store.

★ **Napa Valley Wine Train**   *(707)253-2111*   *(800)427-4124*
   just E at 1275 McKinstry St.
   winetrain.com

The Napa Wine Train is, along with Copia, the must-see of Napa Valley apart from the wineries. This truly moving experience gives riders (by reservation) an opportunity to experience the lush grandeur of the valley in a unique way. Several kinds of lunches and dinners of various qualities can be reserved–ranging all the way up to fine cuisine coupled with appropriate local premium wines in a vista dome (one of only three in use in America). Train rides averaging about three hours run during the day and at night with food service, or in the lounge car featuring a wealth of regional wines and other beverages. There are also numerous special events coupled with dining and drinking rides–like a monthly jazz concert coupled with a fine dining experience that should be on the list of every visiting gourmet and oenophile. On-board visits by premium wineries are another option coupled with the train ride-and-dine experience. Luncheon-and-tour packages with Domaine Chandon or Grgich Hills wineries provide yet another unique way to enjoy some of the best of Wine Country. Dining rooms set with full linen and orchids on the table in meticulously restored historic cars contribute to memorable experience, as do views of wineries and vineyards passing by. It is not surprising that the Society of International Railroad Travelers voted the Napa Valley Wine Train one of the top twenty railroads in the world.

★ *Wineries*   *(707)963-3388*
   napavintners.com

Napa is the gateway to America's world-famous wine valley. Thousands of acres of premium vineyards and dozens of renowned wineries are within ten miles of the city. Many require an appointment to tour and/or taste. Most charge tasting fees.

Following are the author's favorites among the distinguished premium wineries that offer tastes and tours in landmark facilities that also have scenic picnic sites and related gift shops.

Andretti Winery   *(707)255-3524   (888)460-8463*
5 mi. N at 4162 Big Ranch Rd.
andrettiwinery.com
Mario Andretti, the famed race car driver, built this winery in 1997 in a Tuscan style to reflect his Italian roots. Beyond a stone piazza and fountain, visitors can sample premium cabernet sauvignon, chardonnay, pinot noir, and other varietals at a handcrafted (fee) tasting bar. There is a well-stocked wine/gift shop, and a demonstration vineyard to explore. Open 10-5 daily.

Artesa   *(707)224-1668*
4 mi. SW at 1345 Henry Rd.
artesawinery.com
Crowning a hill overlooking many of the luxuriant vineyards of the Carneros district is Artesa, a remarkable Spanish winery that was designed to blend into the hillside via cut-and-fill. Lawns and stone walls cover a massive earthen structure that is both beautiful and functional in cooling temperatures within the complex. Inside, a fountain court is surrounded by elegant display areas for notable artworks and a museum ideally suited to everyone interested in learning quickly about "methode champenoise." Focus post-1999 is on fine pinot noir, chardonnay, cabernet sauvignon and merlot instead of sparklers that were the original hallmark. The tour (offered twice daily) is well worth doing to further appreciate the inspired architecture and decor. Adjoining the tasting bar, with (fee) tastings at several levels, tables by the fountain courts and on an adjacent expansive terrace overlook miles of lush vineyards. Nearby is a refined wine-related shop. Open 10-5 daily.

Chimney Rock Winery   *(707)257-2641   (800)257-2641*
7 mi. N at 5350 Silverado Trail
chimneyrock.com
Vineyards tumble down precipitous slopes near this young post-modern winery in gleaming white stucco. Chimney Rock is another major paean to cabernet sauvignon, the star of the Stag's Leap appellation. The pleasant (fee) tasting room adjoins a fountain garden court with views of mountains, vineyard, and a massive frieze tribute to the cup-bearer to the gods. Open 10-5 daily.

Del Dotto Vineyards   *(707)256-3332*
3 mi. NE at 1055 Atlas Peak Rd.
deldottovineyards.com
One of Napa Valley's oldest wineries with caves was established in 1885. The historic building serves as a (fee) tasting room for

their premium cabernet sauvignons and other varietals. Don't miss the (fee) cave tour where you can enjoy truly whimsical sculpture and some of the most atmospheric tunnels anywhere. Candlelight and an appealing musical backdrop lend romance to a barrel tasting revealing differences between wine aged in American and French oak. Open daily by appointment only. Also in the historic building is a wine gallery and shop. Next door at **Jessel Gallery** (1019 Atlas Peak Road, jesselgallery.com) are many rooms filled with Bay Area fine arts and crafts.

Domaine Carneros   *(707)257-0101*
5 mi. SW at 1240 Duhig Rd.
domainecarneros.com
Crowning a ridge on the west side of Napa Valley is a splendid chateau with Louis XV architecture amid colorful formal gardens and fountains. Free regularly scheduled tours are especially worthwhile. An elegant tasting room with a beautiful blondewood bar and fireplace shares superb vineyard views with a patio tasting area. This is the home of famed La Rêve, a luscious full-bodied blanc de blancs with a long finish and extra-silky texture that make it one of the consistently greatest methode champenoise sparklers in America. Other methode sparklers and superb pinot noirs can also be enjoyed at (fee) tastings paired with complimentary appetizers. Open 10-6 daily.

Domaine Chandon   *(707)944-2280*   *(800)934-3975*
10 mi. NW at 1 California Dr. - Yountville
dchandon.com
On an oak-studded knoll surrounded by lovely gardens is a strikingly modern winery built in 1973 by Moet-Hennessy of France to make sparkling wines from California grapes in the traditional manner of French champagne production. Their pioneering success led to the rush of European sparkling wine producers into California. Premium blanc de noirs and brut sparkling wines are served in the gracious salon, or, weather permitting, on a lovely garden terrace adjoining the splendid restaurant complex (see listing). (Fee) tasting and memorable tours 10-6 daily. (Closed Mon.-Tues. from Nov.-Feb.)

Hess Collection   *(707)255-1144*
10 mi. W at 4411 Redwood Rd.
hesscollection.com
The Hess Collection is a quintessential Wine Country experience tucked away in gentle mountains west of Napa Valley. Donald Hess' two passions–fine wine and contemporary art–come together in a century-old winery showcasing premium cabernets and chardonnays as well as outstanding art of major living artists. The self-guided tour is a must, ending in a stylish (fee) tasting room, and a wine store. Open 10-4 daily.

Jarvis Winery   *(800)255-5280 x 150*
6 mi. NE at 2970 Monticello Rd.
jarviswines.com
Jarvis is one of California's most extraordinary Wine Country estates. The entire winery is dug into volcanic hills far above Napa Valley. Temperature-controlled naturally cool tunnels provide a perfect environment for cabernet sauvignon and chardonnay that are estate-grown on only thirty-seven of more than 1,300 acres surrounding the winery/caves entrance. An unforgettable tour features fiber-optic lighting (don't miss the ladies' restroom), and a waterfall and stream that are both charming and functional in humidifying French oak barrels. The tour de force, however, lies behind gigantic doors that open into a large chamber distinguished by truly enormous geodes of amethyst and quartz crystals given museum-quality displays. The tasting room, one of the most opulent in Wine Country, is perfect for experiencing ultra-premium wines with appropriate appetizers. Open for (fee) tour/tastes daily by appointment only.

Kirkland Ranch Winery   *(707)254-9100*
7 mi. SE (on Hwy. 12) at One Kirkland Ranch Rd.
kirklandwinery.com
A handsome winery opened in 1997 crowning a hill overlooking the south end of Napa Valley. Rock waterfalls grace an imposing building fashioned from rock and rough-hewn redwood. Premium chardonnay, merlot and cabernet sauvignons are poured at a U-shaped (fee) tasting bar in a capacious firelit room with windows and a porch overlooking vineyards. Massive polished redwood highlight the appealing Old Western motif. A gallery featuring local art extends to views of oak barrel storage areas. Downstairs is an expansive gift shop. Open 10-4 daily.

Pine Ridge Winery   *(707)252-9647*   *(800)575-9777*
8 mi. NW at 5901 Silverado Trail
pineridgewinery.com
Premium cabernet sauvignon, chardonnays, and several other varietals are available for (fee) tastes in a stylish tasting area overlooking the glass-fronted entrance to caves used for storage. Tours into the caves featuring barrel tastings are available by appointment. Lovely picnic grounds are sited amid lawns and gardens adjoining steep forested hills above surrounding vineyards. Open 10:30-4:30 daily.

Robert Sinskey Vineyards   *(707)944-9090*   *(800)869-2030*
9 mi. NW at 6320 Silverado Trail
robertsinskey.com
Robert Sinskey is one of Wine Country's ultimate sources for all-organic estate-grown premium wine. Their Stag's Leap District

cabernet sauvignon and Los Carneros pinot noir, merlot, chardonnay and pinot blanc are superb. At the winery, limestone rock and polished redwood blend in a spectacular cathedral-like complex adjoining extensive caves. A dramatic (fee) tasting room with clerestory windows and a forty-foot ceiling adjoins a woodburning oven and demonstration kitchen used to prepare local cheeses and other products of the region into tasting dishes that complement Sinskey varietals. The wine, cheese and herb tour, by appointment, is deservedly popular. Gardens and picnic areas are sited to enhance views of surrounding hillside vineyards. Open 10-4:30 daily.

Silverado Vineyards   *(707)257-1770   (800)997-1770*
9 mi. N at 6121 Silverado Trail
silveradovineyards.com

The Disney family established one of Wine Country's most delightful premium winery complexes in the 1970s. High on a knoll overlooking vineyards and oak-covered hills is a grand (new in 2000) complex with a perfect California-style look and "feel." Inside are an expansive firelit (fee) tasting room and gift shop with rewarding panoramic views. Premium cabernet sauvignon is a consistent quality/value benchmark. Reserve cabernet sauvignon, merlot, chardonnay, and sauvignon blanc are also consistently excellent. Open 10:30-5 daily.

Stag's Leap Wine Cellars   *(707)944-2020   (866)422-7523*
8 mi. NW at 5766 Silverado Trail
stagsleapwinecellars.com

In 1976, a Stag's Leap 1973 cabernet sauvignon beat venerable French wineries in a major blind tasting in France, which brought California worldwide attention for the first time. The legendary winery now blends into vineyards and an oak-studded hillside in contemporary low-rise buildings surrounded by gardens. Some of the most famous cabernet sauvignons in America are still their hallmark. It is available for (fee) tastes, along with other premium varietals. Free hour-long tours with tastes are available by appointment only. Open 10-4:30 daily.

Trefethen Vineyards   *(707)255-7700   (800)556-4847*
5 mi. NW at 1160 Oak Knoll Av.
www.trefethen.com

Trefethen is one of only a few truly estate-grown wines in Napa Valley. A luxuriant garden with interesting displays of antique agricultural appliances surrounds a substantial wood structure (circa 1886) with a warm and pleasant tasting room and gift shop with picture-window views to barrel storage areas. Cabernet sauvignon, merlot, chardonnay, pinot noir and riesling are featured. Their garden includes well-labeled displays including English and Spanish lavender. (Fee) tasting 10-4:30 daily.

★ **Yountville**   *(707)944-0904   (800)959-3604*
9 mi. NW off St. Helena Hwy. - *Yountville*
Already a bustling hamlet before the Civil War, Yountville is now
the site of several major Napa Valley restaurants and lodgings
(see listings). These, and numerous tourist-oriented shops, are all
clustered within an easy stroll between the village's tree-shaded
park with picnic spots, and **Vintage 1870,** a converted brick
winery complex housing specialty food, wine and wine shops.

RESTAURANTS

★ **Alexis Baking Company & Cafe**   *(707)258-1827*
downtown at 1517 Third St.
B-L.   *Expensive*
One of Napa's best bets for breakfast is Alexis for housemade
English muffins with omelets, scrambles and other contemporary
California dishes, plus assorted baked goods from the display
cases. Designer sandwiches, salads, and mini-pizzas are featured
later (with a wealth of beverages) to go or at tables in a casual
street-view room.

★ **Angèle**   *(707)252-8115*
downtown at 540 Main St.
angele.us
L-D.   *Expensive*
New in 2003, this little bistro adjoining the landmark Hatt
Complex has a choice location overlooking the Napa River
downtown. Authentic French classics are featured from French
onion soup to old-fashioned veal stew or seared salmon with
salsify ragout and mushroom broth, plus luscious housemade
desserts. The casually stylish little dining room and lounge
provide some river view, and there is a dining patio by the river.

★ **Bistro Don Giovanni**   *(707)224-3300*
4 mi. NW at 4110 Howard Lane (at St. Helena Hwy.)
bistrodongiovanni.com
L-D.   *Expensive*
This long-established trattoria is popular for both classic and
creative Italian and country French dishes. Specialties include
wood-oven roasted whole fish, braised lamb shank, or grilled
double-cut pork chop. Desserts made here like tiramisu contribute
to the appeal of the big colorful dining room with a vineyard view
and a hip bar. A romantic firelit dining terrace adjoins.

★ **Bistro Jeanty**   *(707)944-0103*
10 mi. NW at 6510 Washington St. - Yountville
L-D.   *Expensive*
In this classic French bistro, assorted authentic French dishes
like tomato soup in puff pastry, cassoulet, coq au vin, plus
housemade desserts like crèpes Suzette are served amid the cozy

congestion of an intimate lounge and a larger firelit back room.

★ **Bouchon**   *(707)944-8037*
   10 mi. NW at 6534 Washington St. - Yountville
   L-D.   *Very Expensive*
The owner of the legendary French Laundry is partnered in this popular bistro. Authentic French provincial cuisine is served to guests seated at a cozy congestion of tables and chairs with an upscale country ambiance.

★ **Brix**   *(707)944-2749*
   10 mi. NW at 7377 St. Helena Hwy. - Yountville
   brix.com
   L-D.   *Very Expensive*
Brix is major competition for the most engaging restaurant in Wine Country. Seasonally fresh top-quality ingredients are transformed into culinary delights like grouper en papillote with sweet peppers in citrus-chipotle sauce. Delicious housemade bread and all of the luscious desserts (including local fig tart tatin with rum raisin gelato and port sauce) are prepared here. The comfortably elegant dining room overlooks a large expo kitchen, a warm bar and a window-wall view of salubrious herbs and vegetables (growing year-round for use in the restaurant) backed by vineyards and oak-shrouded mountains. In season, the outdoor dining terrace is also deservedly popular, and there is a large well-stocked shop with Wine Country-related gifts.

★ **Butter Cream Bakery & Cafe**   *(707)255-6700*
   1 mi. NW at 2297 Jefferson St.
   B-L. Closed Mon.   *Moderate*
Butter Cream has been Napa's classic all-American bakery for more than four decades. A humongous display showcases all kinds of breads, pastries, donuts, cakes and pies to go or served with traditional diner fare in their spic-and-span coffee shop.

★ **Cafe Lucy Le Petit Bistro**   *(707)255-0110*
   downtown at 1408 Clay St.
   cafelucy.com
   L-D. No D Sat.-Wed. Closed Sun.-Mon.   *Moderate*
Simply delicious French-inspired bistro dishes like roasted pork loin sandwich with caramelized onions or Fuji apple crisp a la mode explain the well-earned popularity of this tiny bistro. Diners have a choice of a cozy congestion of tables inside, or a heated patio with a luxuriant grape arbor.

★ **Celadon**   *(707)254-9690*
   downtown at 500 Main St., Suite G
   celadonnapa.com
   L-D.   *Expensive*
Ensconced in a historic building by the Napa River is a culinary haven where fresh seasonal ingredients are given expert atten-

tion. Creative California cuisine is expressed in unusually bold and colorful dishes. The simply sophisticated dining room and lounge are a pleasing complement, as is a heated umbrella-shaded courtyard with a four-sided fireplace.

★ **Cole's Chop House**   *(707)224-6328*
downtown at 1122 Main St.
coleschophouse.com
D only.   *Very Expensive*
One of Napa Valley's most popular dining experiences is Cole's Chop House. Contemporary American cuisine (starring prime, dry-aged Angus steaks) combines expert preparation and fresh seasonal ingredients in classic crowd-pleasers. Housemade desserts are also fine. The dining room has generously spaced tables set with full linen and candles in a transformed historic building with rock walls, a bar, and a heated patio above a stream.

★ **Domaine Chandon**   *(707)944-2892   (800)736-2892*
10 mi. NW at 1 California Dr. - Yountville
domainechandon.com
L-D.   *Very Expensive*
The power and the glory of America's premier wine-growing region is perfectly presented by Domaine Chandon. The French have produced a gastronomic showplace for their California sparkling wines made here. Disciplined French haute cuisine, from seasonal appetizers to grand desserts, is enlivened by buoyant California ingenuity and fresh local ingredients. Soaring arched ceiling, glass window walls and warm woods distinguish the plush multilevel dining room as a modern architectural tour de force surrounded by pastoral beauty. Gourmet lunches are served on a flower-strewn outdoor patio during warm months.

Downtown Joe's   *(707)258-2337*
downtown at 902 Main St.
downtownjoes.com
B-L-D.   *Expensive*
Housecrafted beers and ales complement a wide selection of pub grub. A raised back room past the brew kettle has a view of the river; a covered porch overlooks a riverside park; and live entertainment happens in the firelit bar of the historic building.

★ **Foothill Cafe**   *(707)252-6178*
2 mi. SW at 2766 Old Sonoma Rd.
D only. Closed Mon.-Tues.   *Expensive*
A short thoughtful selection of contemporary California dishes features items like slow-roasted baby back ribs, braised lamb shank and pan-seared crusted salmon, plus desserts made here. Locals love the casual comfortable little dining room with the uncomplicated fine food tucked away in a little strip mall.

★ **The French Laundry**   *(707)944-2380*
10 mi. NW at 6640 Washington St. - Yountville
relaischateaux.com
L-D. No L Mon.-Thurs.   *Very Expensive*
Thanks to Thomas Keller, the French Laundry is no longer one
of America's quintessential gourmet hideaways. It has been
discovered. New California cuisine reflects the acclaimed
chef/owner's classic French background and his rigorous concern
for finding the freshest seasonal ingredients and distilling their
purest flavors. Multicourse prix fixe meals are served with
precision in intimate country-elegant rooms with a fireplace or
vineyard view in a stone and redwood building that was a French
laundry. There is also a luxuriant "chef's garden" patio.

★ **Gordon's**   *(707)944-8246*
9 mi. NW at 6770 Washington St. - Yountville
B-L.   *Expensive*
Gordon's is the hidden gem among memorable breakfasts in Napa
Valley. Behind a green storefront that says "Market" is a
cornucopia of skillfully prepared Wine Country-appropriate
breakfast dishes showcasing fresh seasonal products of the region.
On display are homemade croissants and other morning delights,
plus similarly delicious cookies and sweet treats for later on. The
congenial, semi-communal warmth of the little dining room favors
first-rate food prepared in an expo kitchen.

★ **Hurley's**   *(707)944-2345*
9 mi. N at 6518 Washington St. - Yountville
hurleysrestaurant.com
L-D.   *Expensive*
Hurley's, opened in 2002, is already one of Wine Country's best
dining destinations. The chef/owner does brilliant work with wild
game and other dishes like Petaluma rabbit two ways or herb-
crusted sea bass with rock shrimp and basil mashed potatoes that
optimize the best seasonal ingredients. Desserts like huckleberry
silk tart with vanilla crème fraîche are also delicious. Guests can
enjoy warm, simply sophisticated dining by a raised stone
fireplace in a room that is a delightful example of "Wine Country
style." There is also a landscaped patio and a spiffy wood-toned
lounge overlooking the heart of Yountville.

★ **Julia's Kitchen**   *(707)265-5700   (888)512-6742*
just E at 500 First St. (inside Copia)
copia.org
L-D. No D in winter. Closed Tues.   *Very Expensive*
Julia's Kitchen opened in late 2001 and has already earned
international stature as a key destination for dining adventures
involving choice foods of the land and sea in Northern California's

famed Wine Country. Seasonal provisions enhanced by Copia's significant on-site gardens of vegetables, fruits and herbs are masterfully prepared in an exposition kitchen overseen by one of California's great chefs. All resulting dishes look like works of art and capture the flavors and textures of the area memorably. The big informal dining room, enhanced by linens, flowers and quality table settings, provides a dining-as-theater backdrop to activity in the exposition kitchen and the ballet-like precision of staff in transporting each work of art to the tables. The dining room also overlooks Copia's increasingly bountiful demonstration garden.

★ **La Boucane**   *(707)253-1177*
   just W at 1778 Second St.
   D only. Closed Sun.   *Expensive*
For many years, authentic French cuisine has distinguished this chef-owned restaurant. Entrees like salmon in champagne sauce are expertly prepared and served in comfortably understated rooms of a house that has become a fine dining landmark.

★ **Mustards Grill**   *(707)944-2424*
   10 mi. NW at 7399 St. Helena Hwy. - Yountville
   mustardsgrill.com
   L-D.   *Expensive*
Mustards is a premier source of New California cuisine. Mesquite-broiled and brick oven-smoked meats are soul-satisfying hallmarks, while fresh, bold support dishes are given a deft light touch. In this ever-popular Wine Country classic, guests are served in a simply au courant dining room, or amid the whitewashed openness of a cool, screened porch.

★ **Pearl**   *(707)224-9161*
   downtown at 1339 Pearl St. #104
   L-D. Closed Sun.-Mon.   *Expensive*
Pearl is an unusually appealing jazzy/classy cafe. Creative cuisine is featured in dishes involving oysters (natch), plus treats like house tortillas with chopped ginger flank steaks, chiles, cilantro, salsa verde and lime cream. Assorted seasonal housemade desserts are also delicious. Colorful hex signs, modern art, an expo kitchen, and a covered patio complement the light lively cuisine.

Piccolino's Italian Cafe   *(707)251-0100*
   downtown at 1385 Napa Town Center
   piccolinoscafe.com
   L-D.   *Expensive*
Southern Italian family cooking is well represented in this family-oriented restaurant in all sorts of traditional dishes and specialties like individual pizzas and housemade tiramisu. The big casually candlelit dining room and bar overlook the heart of town.

★ **Silverado Resort** *(707)257-0200*
4 mi. NE at 1600 Atlas Peak Rd.
silveradoresort.com
B-L-D. *Very Expensive*
The **Royal Oak** (D only–Very Expensive) offers contemporary California cuisine in dishes like triple-cut baby lamb chops in a casually plush dining room with an expansive fairways-and-mountains view. **Vintners Court** (D only. Closed Sun.-Wed.– Very Expensive) features a popular Friday seafood buffet extravaganza in a big comfortably upscale dining room with piano music and fairway views. At **Silverado Bar & Grill** (B-L–Very Expensive), California contemporary fare is served in a golf clubhouse-style dining room with a nifty window-wall view of fairways. **The Main Lounge** serves drinks and appetizers by a great stone fireplace, or on the terrace.

★ **Sweetie Pies** *(707)257-8817*
downtown at 520 Main St.
sweetiepies.com
B-L. *Moderate*
Sweetie Pies is one of California's great bakeries. The classy little shop is tucked into a historic riverfront complex that includes the Napa River Inn. A passion for quality is apparent. Humongous bear claws plus classic cinnamon rolls, sticky buns, scones and other morning delights can be enjoyed with light breakfast dishes, fresh orange juice and coffee at several tables in view of cases full of stellar pastries and desserts. Artisan breads or ham and cheese croissants also make great wine-tasting complements.

★ **Zuzu** *(707)224-8555*
downtown at 829 Main St.
zuzunapa.com
L-D. No L Sat. & Sun. *Expensive*
Classic Spanish and creative California tapas and small dishes star in one of downtown Napa's most popular restaurants. The comfortably upscale dining room on two levels and a nifty wormwood bar have been fashioned into a historic building.

LODGINGS

Napa has finally fulfilled its destiny as the gateway to America's world famous Wine Country. Lodgings are now plentiful from major conference hotels to multifaceted resorts, and a remarkable selection of historic, romantic inns. There are no bargains. Many lodgings are full through summer and fall, and on weekends year-round. Rates are often reduced 25% or more on weekdays in winter and early spring.

★ **Beazley House**   *(707)257-1649*
  just W at 1910 First St. - 94559
  beazleyhouse.com
  11 units   *(800)559-1649*   *Expensive-Very Expensive*
Napa's first bed-and-breakfast opened in 1981 in a (circa 1902) chocolate-wood-trim mansion amid lawns and gardens. Full buffet breakfast, afternoon treats and refreshments, and periodic weekend wine tastings with appetizers are complimentary. Each individually decorated room is beautifully furnished including some fine antiques, a private bath, and a queen or king bed.
  "Enchanted Rose"–spacious, skylight, raised in-room
    two-person whirlpool and gas fireplace in view of king bed.
  "West Loft"–spacious, vaulted ceiling and stained glass, in-
    bath two-person whirlpool, gas fireplace in view of king bed.
  "Blossom View"–garden view, gas fireplace and
    in-room two-person whirlpool in view of queen bed.

★ **Blackbird Inn**   *(707)226-2450*
  just W at 1755 First St. - 94559
  foursisters.com
  8 units   *(888)567-9811*   *Expensive-Very Expensive*
One of Wine Country's best examples of Craftsman architecture is now meticulously restored to serve as an upscale bed-and-breakfast. Full breakfast and afternoon wine and appetizers are complimentary. Each individually decorated room is beautifully furnished with a private bath and all contemporary amenities, and a queen or king bed. Some rooms also have a gas fireplace, in-bath two-person whirlpool, and a private deck.

★ **Blue Violet Mansion**   *(707)253-2583*
  just S at 443 Brown Av. - 94559
  bluevioletmansion.com
  17 units   *(800)959-2583*   *Very Expensive*
One of California's most picturesque Victorian mansions (circa 1886) now serves as a bed-and-breakfast inn. Spacious lawns and gardens showcase an outdoor pool and whirlpool in the most spectacular building in Napa's historic residential district. Full breakfast (served to the room upon request), and evening hot beverages and sweet treats are complimentary. In-room (fee) massage and multicourse candlelit dinners are available April though October, and a complimentary tasting by a different vintner each week is featured on Saturday. Each well-furnished room is individually decorated and has a private bath, most modern amenities, and a queen or king bed. Most rooms also have a gas fireplace and an in-bath whirlpool tub.
  "The Camelot Floor" (4 of these)–romantic, third floor, sitting
    area, gas fireplace, in-bath large whirlpool, queen or king bed.

Bordeaux House   *(707)944-2855*
9 mi. NW at 6600 Washington St. (Box 2766) - Yountville 94599
bordeauxhouse.com
7 units   *(800)677-6370*   *Expensive*
This modernistic little brick inn has rooms decorated with Continental-vogue furnishings and private, sunken baths. Full buffet breakfast and evening cookies and beverage or glass of wine are complimentary. All but one of the modish rooms has a gas or woodburning fireplace, a private deck and a queen bed.

★ **Candlelight Inn of the Dunn Lee Manor**   *(707)257-3717*
2 mi. W at 1045 Easum Dr. - 94558
candlelightinn.com
10 units   *(800)624-0395*   *Expensive-Very Expensive*
An English Tudor-style home by Napa Creek built in 1929 is now a stylish bed-and-breakfast with gardens and a large swimming pool shaded by towering redwoods. Full breakfast and afternoon wine and appetizers are complimentary. Each well-furnished, individually decorated room has all contemporary amenities and a queen bed. Most also have a gas fireplace and a two-person in-room whirlpool.
    "The Garden View"–private garden-view deck, gas fireplace,
        in-room large whirlpool in view of antique queen bed.
    "The Lady Heather"–romantic redwoods view, gas fireplace,
        in-room large whirlpool in view of ornate queen bed.

★ **Castle in the Clouds**   *(707)944-2785*
10 mi. NW at 7400 St. Helena Hwy. - 94558
www.castleintheclouds.com
4 units   *Very Expensive*
Castle in the Clouds is one of the most spectacularly situated bed-and-breakfasts in America. Bacchus himself guards the gate at the bottom of a steep road that winds up to a beautifully landscaped hilltop. The panorama from the estate includes many of Napa's world famous wineries. Public rooms, garden terraces, and a sequestered whirlpool share memorable views. Numerous delightful sculptures further enhance the romantic setting, including a winsome bronze sunbather on the top view deck. Full gourmet breakfast is complimentary to guests, and there may be afternoon treats. Each individually furnished room is luxuriously appointed with museum-quality antiques, whimsical objects of art and all contemporary amenities, and has a queen or king bed. Most have an outstanding vineyard view.
    "Honeymoon Suite"–bay window view of the valley,
        refrigerator, in-bath whirlpool, king bed.
    "Cherub Room,"–spacious, spectacular valley
        views, in-bath whirlpool, king bed.

★ **Cedar Gables Inn**   *(707)224-7969*
just S at 486 Coombs St. - 94559
cedargablesinn.com
9 units   *(800)309-7969*   *Expensive-Very Expensive*
An 1892 house with the look and feel of a gracious English manor is now a well-landscaped bed-and-breakfast in Napa's peaceful historic district. Full breakfast, evening wine and appetizers, and ruby port in your room are complimentary. Each beautifully furnished room is individually decorated, including some antiques, a private bath and queen bed.
"The Gable Suite"–penthouse, two-person
    whirlpool in view of ornate queen bed.
"Count Bonzi's Room," "Lady Margaret's Room,"
    "Churchill Chamber"–spacious, gas fireplace,
    in-bath two-person whirlpool.

Chardonnay Lodge   *(707)224-0789*
1 mi. N at 2640 Jefferson St. - 94559
20 units   *Moderate*
This small no-frills motel is as close to a bargain as you'll get in the valley. Each compact, simply furnished room has a double or queen bed.

★ **Churchill Manor**   *(707)253-7733*
just S at 485 Brown St. - 94559
churchillmanor.com
10 units   *Expensive-Very Expensive*
A magnificent three-story mansion (circa 1889) on the National Historic Register now serves as a charming bed-and-breakfast. The Second Empire-style manor house with massive whitewashed columns around the front entrance is surrounded by an acre of luxuriant trees, rose gardens and lawns and a formal fountain. Croquet on a side lawn and tandem bicycles are complimentary, as are a full breakfast, afternoon fresh-baked cookies and refreshments, and Napa Valley wines and cheeses each evening. Each beautifully furnished room is individually decorated, including some antiques, a private bathroom, and a queen or king bed. Many of the rooms also have a gas fireplace and clawfoot tub.
"Victoria's Room," "Rose's Room"–fine antiques,
    original tiled (gas) fireplace, big in-room clawfoot
    tub, leaded glass shower, king bed.
"Erik's Room"–English (gas) fireplace, skylit two-
    person slate shower, two-person Victorian bathtub
    in bay window in view of iron queen bed.
"Edward Churchill Room"–spacious, exquisite antiques,
    original gold leaf-tiled (gas) fireplace, big in-room
    Victorian bathtub, two-person shower, king bed.

★ **Crossroads Inn**   *(707)944-0646*
10 mi. NW at 6380 Silverado Trail - 94558
crossroadsnv.com
4 units   *Very Expensive*
The panoramic vineyard view is outstanding from this bucolic
bed-and-breakfast inn's lofty perch. Scenic hiking trails, a valley-
view freeform pool, and an enchanting view-oriented whirlpool
with a native stone waterfall are amenities from one of Wine
Country's best adult playgrounds. Breakfast served in your suite,
afternoon tea and evening beverages are complimentary. Each
extra-spacious, beautifully furnished room has a private bath and
all contemporary amenities, an in-room two-person whirlpool
(most with an outstanding view), vineyards and valley panoramas
from the room and private deck, and a king bed.
   "The Hunt Room"–extra-large, raised two-person
      whirlpool with fine window-wall view of valley
      shared by a cherry sleigh king bed.
   "The Victorian Room"–romantic, great valley view
      from corner windows by a raised two-person whirlpool
      in view of a king bed.
★ **The Daughter's Inn**   *(707)253-1331*
just W at 1938 First St. - 94559
thedaughtersinn.com
5 units   *(866)253-1331*   *Very Expensive*
A large century-old home on Napa's charming Mansion Row
became one of Wine Country's most sybaritic bed-and-breakfasts
in 2003. Full breakfast is complimentary as is bottled water and
a sweet treat. Each of the individually beautifully furnished rooms
has a private bath and all contemporary amenities, a gas fireplace,
an in-room two-person whirlpool, and a queen or king bed.
   "Geranium"–private deck over gardens, gas fireplace,
      two-person whirlpool in view of king bed.
   "Lavender," "Canterbury Bell"–gas fireplace, two-
      person whirlpool in view of king bed.
★ **The 1801 Inn**   *(707)224-3739*
just W at 1801 First St. - 94559
the1801inn.com
8 units   *(800)518-0146*   *Expensive-Very Expensive*
A splendid Queen Anne Victorian built in 1903 has been lovingly
transformed into a bed-and-breakfast on a well-landscaped corner
between Napa's historic district and downtown. In-room (fee) spa
services are a feature. Full gourmet breakfast, afternoon wine and
appetizers, and stocked common area mini-bar are complimentary. Each beautifully furnished room is individually decorated, including some antiques and all contemporary amenities,
plus a gas fireplace and sitting area, an in-bathroom oversized tub

or whirlpool, and a queen or king bed.

"The Carriage House"–large private cottage, French doors
to flowery courtyard, refrigerator, two-way gas fireplace
and oversized in-bath whirlpool in view of king bed.

"The Bella Freisa"–raised oversized tub in a turret
in view of gas fireplace, raised canopy king bed.

"Amica Dolcetto"–sitting area, in-bath two-person whirlpool
with skylight, gas fireplace in view of raised king bed.

Elm House Inn - Best Western   *(707)255-1831*
1 mi. W at 800 California Blvd. - 94559
bestwestern.com
22 units   *(888)849-1997*   *Expensive-Very Expensive*
A garden courtyard with a whirlpool is a feature of this refined
wood-trimmed motel. Deluxe Continental breakfast and afternoon
tea and homemade cookies are complimentary. Each of the well-
furnished rooms has extra amenities and a refrigerator, plus a
queen or king bed.

★ **Embassy Suites - Napa Valley**   *(707)253-9540*
1 mi. W (near Hwy. 29) at 1075 California Blvd. - 94559
embassysuites.com
205 units   *(800)362-2779*   *Very Expensive*
The all-suites Wine Country link is a Spanish-Colonial-style
complex surrounded by tranquil palms and gardens. Amenities
include large indoor and outdoor pools, whirlpool, sauna; exercise
room; and a gift shop. A picturesque waterwheel and mill pond
(complete with swans and sculptured animals) are centerpieces of
a courtyard garden by a dining room where the manager's
evening reception is held. It is complimentary, as is a full
breakfast. Each well-furnished two-room unit includes a living
room and galley kitchen with microwave, refrigerator/wet bar,
extra amenities, and doubles or a king bed.

★ **Hennessey House**   *(707)226-3774*
just N at 1727 Main St. - 94559
hennesseyhouse.com
10 units   *Expensive-Very Expensive*
Beautiful gardens surround a handsome 1889 home and carriage
house on the National Historic Register that are now a gracious
bed-and-breakfast. A sauna, full gourmet breakfast, afternoon
tea and cookies, evening wine and cheese, and sherry and
chocolates in the room are complimentary. Each individually,
beautifully furnished room has some quality antiques and most
contemporary conveniences, a private bath and queen or king
bed. Several rooms also have a gas fireplace, private deck and an
in-bath whirlpool.

"Fox's Den"–spacious, private garden patio, gas fireplace,
in-bath two-person whirlpool, feather king bed.

★ **Inn on Randolph**   *(707)257-2886*
  downtown at 411 Randolph - 94559
  innonrandolph.com
  8 units   *(800)670-6886*   *Expensive-Very Expensive*
A Gothic revival Victorian (circa 1860) and three 1930s cottages amid lawns and gardens have been transformed into a bed-and-breakfast. Full breakfast and afternoon treats are complimentary. Each individually decorated room is well furnished, including some antiques, a private bath, contemporary amenities plus extras, a gas fireplace, double or deep in-bath whirlpool, and queen or king bed. Several also have a refrigerator and a private deck.
  "Arbor Cottage"–kitchenette, gas fireplace, bathroom with
    dual showerheads and two-person whirlpool tub, queen bed.
★ **La Belle Epoque**   *(707)257-2161*
  downtown at 1386 Calistoga Av. - 94559
  labelleepoque.com
  9 units   *(800)238-8070*   *Expensive-Very Expensive*
One of Wine Country's most picturesque Victorian mansions (circa 1893) has been skillfully transformed into a delightful bed-and-breakfast amid lovely gardens at the quiet edge of downtown Napa. Full gourmet breakfast served by candlelight, award-winning wine reception with hot and cold appetizers in the host's intimate wine cellar, 24-hour beverage-service bar, cookies and treats, and in-room port are complimentary. In-room (fee) massages and a gift shop with Wine Country specialties are also available. Each beautifully furnished room has a private bath and is individually decorated with antiques, all contemporary and extra amenities, and a queen or king bed. Most rooms also have a gas or woodburning fireplace and in-bath whirlpool in the main house, and in the Victorian Buckley House across the street.
  "Buckley House - Elizabeth's Suite"–refr. & microwave, gas
    fireplace, in-bath two-person whirlpool, four-poster king bed.
  "Pinot Noir"–gas fireplace, in-bath whirlpool,
    double-headed shower, queen bed.
  "Chardonnay"–stained-glass windows, sitting area with
    woodburning fireplace, two-person shower, queen bed.
★ **La Residence**   *(707)253-0337*
  3 mi. NW at 4066 St. Helena Hwy. - 94558
  laresidence.com
  20 units   *(800)253-9203*   *Very Expensive*
Heritage oaks and redwoods shade expansive lawns, gardens, and vineyard at La Residence, a luxurious Wine Country inn. A pool and whirlpool are features. Full breakfast and afternoon wine and appetizers are complimentary. Each room is beautifully,

individually furnished, including a private bath, all contemporary amenities, and queen or king bed. Most rooms also have a pressed-wood fireplace, and French doors to a patio.

"Cottage Suite"–wet bar/refrigerator, private patio
  overlooking vineyards and gardens, queen bed.

"Cellar House Suite Rooms" (3 of these)–wet bar/
  refrigerator, fireplace, in-bath soaking tub, king bed.

★ **Lavender**   *(707)944-1388*
9 mi. NW at 2020 Webber St. - Yountville 94599
foursisters.com
8 units   (800)522-4140   Expensive-Very Expensive
Lavender has the appearance and feel of a French country inn appropriately fronted by lavender bushes in the heart of Yountville. Full breakfast and afternoon wine and appetizers are complimentary. So are bicycles. Each of the individually well furnished rooms has a gas fireplace and large bathtub and a king bed. Several also have a private patio and a whirlpool tub.

★ **Maison Fleurie**   *(707)944-2056*
9 mi. NW at 6529 Yount St. - Yountville 94599
foursisters.com
13 rooms   (800)788-0369   Expensive-Very Expensive
An 1873 three-story inn in a garden became the valley's first bed-and-breakfast in 1971. It has been enhanced with French country furnishings. Guests can enjoy a whirlpool in an enclosed redwood patio, a large garden pool and bicycles. Full buffet breakfast and afternoon wine and appetizers are also complimentary. Each beautifully furnished room has a private bath, all contemporary amenities, and a double, queen or king bed. Four also have a gas fireplace, private deck, and an in-bath whirlpool.

★ **McClelland-Priest Bed & Breakfast Inn**   *(707)224-6875*
downtown at 569 Randolph St. - 94559
mcclellandpriest.com
5 units   (800)290-6881   Expensive-Very Expensive
A stately home (circa 1879) next to the historic residential neighborhood is now an elegant bed-and-breakfast in a garden. Full breakfast and afternoon wine and appetizers are complimentary as are weekend vintner tastings. By advance reservation, a one-hour (fee) "wine pleasures course" is a good introduction to touring and tasting. Each beautifully furnished room is individually decorated, including quality antiques, a private bath, gas fireplace, soaking or whirlpool tub, and queen or king bed.

"The Roma Suite"–marble gas fireplace, oversized
  whirlpool in Victorian bay alcove, queen bed.

"The Carducci Suite"–spacious, marble gas fireplace,
  in-bath whirlpool, king bed.

★ **Milliken Creek**   *(707)255-1197*
1 mi. NE at 1815 Silverado Trail - 94558
millikencreekinn.com
10 units   *(888)622-5775*   *Very Expensive*
Milliken Creek is Wine Country's most romantic riverfront lodging. The boutique luxury inn opened in 2001 amid luxuriant foliage next to the Napa River–a calm meandering stream at this site. Amenities include a (fee) spa offering a wealth of sybaritic treatments like "four hands" or "couples massage" in your room or riverside. Lovely grounds along the riverfront include fountains, ponds, and a waterfall. Breakfast is served in your room upon request and afternoon wine and cheese are complimentary. Each luxuriously furnished room is individually decorated and has all contemporary and extra amenities, a gas fireplace, and a king bed. All but one also have a two-person whirlpool tub in the bathroom or bedroom.
    "Premium Riverfront" (5 of these)–extra-spacious, romantic, private riverfront terrace, in-room two-person whirlpool, gas fireplace in view of king bed.
★ **Napa River Inn**   *(707)251-8500*
downtown at 500 Main St. - 94559
napariverinn.com
66 units   *(877)251-8500*   *Expensive-Very Expensive*
Napa River Inn is downtown Napa's finest lodging and the valley's only riverfront hotel. The full-service upscale property is the cornerstone of the charming Napa Mill, waterfront buildings on the National Historic Register. Amenities in the complex include a fitness room, on-site (fee) health and beauty spa, general store and deli, Celadon (see listing), Angèle for fine dining (see listing) and Sweetie Pies (see listing) where outstanding morning delights, juice and coffee are complimentary to guests. So are evening appetizers and wine in the Victorian lobby. Each beautifully furnished room has all contemporary and extra amenities, a refrigerator, and a queen or king bed.
    "Historic Suite"–extra-large, sitting area with gas fireplace, slipper tub/separate shower, king bed.
    #221,#220,#216,#215–riverfront view from private balcony, gas fireplace in view of king bed.
★ **Napa Valley Lodge**   *(707)944-2468*
9 mi. NW at 2230 Madison St. - Yountville 94599
woodsidehotels.com
55 units   *(800)368-2468*   *Expensive-Very Expensive*
One of the valley's finest motor lodges is this low-rise Tuscan-style complex surrounded by gardens with a large pool and whirlpool by vineyards, and a sauna and fitness center. A champagne buffet breakfast, tea and cookies in the afternoon, and

wine tastings on Fridays are complimentary. Each room is beautifully furnished including an honor bar/refrigerator, extra amenities, a vineyard-view deck, and queens or a king bed. "Fireplace Room" (25 of these)–spacious, pressed-wood fireplace, private view deck, king bed.

Napa Valley Marriott   *(707)253-8600*
2 mi. NW (by Hwy. 29) at 3425 Solano Av. - 94558
marriott.com
272 units   (800)228-9290   Expensive-Very Expensive
The valley's largest lodging is this business-oriented hotel and spa. The recently expanded and renovated property includes a pool, whirlpool, exercise room, restaurant and lounge, and gift shop, plus a full-service (fee) health and beauty spa. Each well-furnished room has all amenities, and two doubles or a king bed.

★ **Oak Knoll Inn**   *(707)255-2200*
5 mi. NW at 2200 E. Oak Knoll Av. - 94558
napavalley.com
4 units   Very Expensive
Oak Knoll Inn is a paragon among Wine Country's most romantic hideaways. A handsome stone building well off main highways is sequestered amid gardens enhanced by a large tranquil pool and whirlpool–and an enchanting hummingbird deck. All around are lush vineyards. An outstanding gourmet breakfast is served in the dining room, outside, or in your room. Sumptuous appetizers and wine in the afternoon (often with a visiting winemaker) are also complimentary. Each spacious, luxuriously furnished room is individually decorated with fine antiques and contemporary furniture, and has a private bath, extra amenities, a woodburning fireplace, and king bed.
#1–extra-large, shared garden/hummingbird
   view deck, stocked (complimentary) refrigerator,
   raised stone woodburning fireplace, king bed.

★ **Silverado Resort**   *(707)257-0200*
5 mi. NE at 1600 Atlas Peak Rd. - 94558
silveradoresort.com
280 units   (800)532-0500   Very Expensive
Silverado is the most complete, self-contained recreational haven in Wine Country. A plantation-style white-pillared mansion built in the 1870s is the landmark of this 1,200 acre resort situated near famed vineyards at the base of gentle mountains. (Fee) amenities include two 18-hole championship golf courses with a driving range and pro shop; fourteen tennis courts; an elegant spa with many health and beauty treatments; a lap pool, whirlpool, steam and sauna, and exercise studio; plus mountain bike rentals. There are also restaurants (see listing) and a lounge, resort shops, jogging trails, ball courts, and ten swimming pools. All well-

furnished units (up to two-bedroom suites) are spacious, have all contemporary amenities and extras, a private deck, and queen or king bed. Many have a woodburning fireplace, kitchen, and a fairways-and-mountains view.

★ **Stahlecker House**   *(707)257-1588*
2 mi. W at 1042 Easum Dr. - 94558
www.stahleckerhouse.com
4 units   (800)799-1588   Expensive-Very Expensive
An expansive ranch-style home in a luxuriant garden shaded by redwoods, palms, and oaks bordering Napa Creek has become a stylish bed-and-breakfast. Some delightfully playful touches include a hobby horse and a table-filling chess set. Full candlelit breakfast, beverages in an antique ice box, afternoon coffee and tea, and homemade cookies are complimentary. Each beautifully furnished room has a private bath, electric or gas fireplace, all contemporary amenities, and a queen bed.
"Kaitlyn's Karousel Room"–private patio, fireplace,
    couple shower, two-person whirlpool in view of queen bed.

★ **Villagio Inn & Spa**   *(707)944-2930*
9 mi. NW at 6481 Washington St. - Yountville 94599
villagio.com
112 units   (800)351-1133   Very Expensive
In 1998, a luxurious state-of-the-art motor inn opened next to the Vintage 1870 specialty shopping complex. Vineyards and gardens surround low-rise clusters of Tuscan-inspired buildings. Amenities include two tennis courts, a lap pool, whirlpools, adjacent fitness center, bicycle rental, a wine bar and (fee) full-service health and beauty spa. Continental champagne breakfast buffet, welcome wine and afternoon tea are complimentary. Each spacious, beautifully furnished unit (up to two bedrooms) has a pressed-wood fireplace, an oversize sunken bath tub, a private balcony or veranda, and two queens or a king bed.
"Upstairs Suite" (13 of these)–pressed-wood fireplace, in-bath
    two-person whirlpool, private balcony, king bed.

★ **Vintage Inn**   *(707)944-1112*
9 mi. NW at 6541 Washington St. - Yountville 94599
vintageinn.com
80 units   (800)351-1133   Very Expensive
This deluxe motor inn near the Vintage 1870 shopping complex has a landscaped courtyard with a pool and whirlpool, plus rental bicycles. A welcome bottle of wine, champagne buffet breakfast and afternoon tea and cookies are complimentary. Each beautifully furnished unit has a fireplace, an in-bath whirlpool, a private balcony or veranda, and two queens or a king bed.
"mini-suite" (13 of these)–spacious, big in-bath whirlpool,
    private balcony, pressed-wood fireplace in view of king bed.

Nevada City

Nevada City is the soul of California's Mother Lode country. Picturesque Victorian homes and businesses line narrow streets that wind through steep forested Sierra foothills.

Placer gold was abundant in 1849 when miners founded the town. By 1856 it was California's third largest city with nearly ten thousand residents. After a disastrous fire that year, more substantial businesses were constructed of brick–with iron doors and shutters. The gold placers soon played out. But, thanks in part to its increasingly prosperous metal foundry, the town survived, albeit at a substantially reduced pace.

Countryside that once teemed with miners is host again to increasing numbers of visitors. This time they're here to enjoy clear streams and scenic reservoirs folded into these gentle mountains, and to explore the residue of a tumultuous past. Vestiges of long-closed gold mines and foundries are still in evidence. But, it is the heart of the village, one of the West's most unspoiled Victorian business districts–still illuminated by gas lamps–that is the priceless legacy of Nevada City's boom era. Downtown, on the National Historic Register, is a bonanza of historic public buildings, theaters and churches; specialty shops featuring Mother Lode artifacts; and blocks of good restaurants, atmospheric bars and saloons; plus the oldest operating hotel west of the Rockies. Victorian mansions serving as bed-and-breakfast inns and mighty draft horses pulling elegant carriages around town also contribute to the romantic spirit. Nearby forests, lakes, rivers and mountains support all kinds of recreation–even gold panning.

WEATHER PROFILE

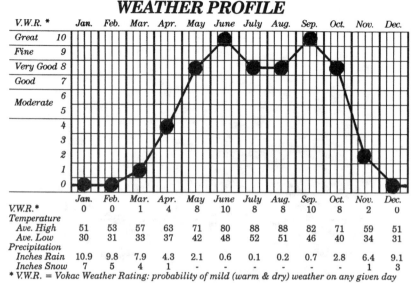

V.W.R. *		Jan.	Feb.	Mar.	Apr.	May	June	July	Aug.	Sep.	Oct.	Nov.	Dec.
Great	10												
Fine	9												
Very Good	8												
Good	7												
Moderate	6 / 5												

	Jan.	Feb.	Mar.	Apr.	May	June	July	Aug.	Sep.	Oct.	Nov.	Dec.
V.W.R.*	0	0	1	4	8	10	8	8	10	8	2	0
Temperature												
Ave. High	51	53	57	63	71	80	88	88	82	71	59	51
Ave. Low	30	31	33	37	42	48	52	51	46	40	34	31
Precipitation												
Inches Rain	10.9	9.8	7.9	4.3	2.1	0.6	0.1	0.2	0.7	2.8	6.4	9.1
Inches Snow	7	5	4	1	-	-	-	-	-	-	1	3

* V.W.R. = Vokac Weather Rating: probability of mild (warm & dry) weather on any given day

BASIC INFORMATION

Population: 2,938
Elevation: 2,535 feet
Location: 155 miles Northeast of San Francisco
Airport *(regularly scheduled flights):* Sacramento - 70 miles

Nevada City Chamber of Commerce (530)265-2692 (800)655-6569
  downtown at 132 Main St. - 95959
  nevadacitychamber.com

ATTRACTIONS

★ *Bicycling*
Tour of Nevada City Bicycle Shop *(530)265-2187*
just S at 457 Sacramento St.
tourofnevadacity.com
Since 1969, this shop has offered a full range of mountain and road bicycle rentals, plus related services, information and maps. They are open every day for any one who would like to tour the hilly streets and inviting byways of the Nevada City area.

★ **Bridgeport Historic State Park**
14 mi. W on Pleasant Valley Rd. - Bridgeport
Built in 1862, the longest single-span wood-covered bridge in the world extends 250 feet across the South Yuba River at Bridgeport. It is a National Historic Landmark. A visitor center and small museum are nearby. Scenic hiking trails lead to secluded picnic sites and picturesque boulder-strewn swimming holes.

★ *Carriage Rides* *(530)265-8778*
downtown at several "carriage for hire" signs
Visitors can tour the gaslit historic district and surroundings in the nostalgic comfort of a beautifully detailed covered carriage pulled by gentle-giant Percheron horses. Rides (conducted by a costumed driver) last for up to an hour and are available daily year-round–weather permitting. The narrated tours are a delightful way to rekindle the spirit of yesteryear while enjoying the bonanza of Victorian structures in town.

★ **Empire Mine State Historic Park** *(916)273-8522*
5 mi. S at 10791 E. Empire St. - Grass Valley
California's oldest and richest gold mine is also one of the deepest (11,000 feet) in the world. From 1852 to 1956, almost six million ounces of gold were extracted from 367 miles of underground shafts. The grounds include a visitor center, mining exhibits including a "gold room," and the baronial Bourn "Cottage"–the former residence of the mine owner. The park also has nearly twelve miles of posted hiking and biking trails. Guided tours of extensive formal gardens (including nearly 1,000 rose bushes) surrounding the mansion are offered daily, except in winter.

★ **Firehouse No. 1** *(530)265-5468*
downtown at 214 Main St.
The Nevada County Historical Society operates a museum in the photogenic 1861 structure. Pioneer implements and garb are exhibited, including relics from the ill-fated Donner Party.

Food Specialties
P.J.'s of Nevada City *(530)265-9091*
1 mi. SE at 106 Argall Way
This long-established hideaway features smoked meats and

sausages to go, or in sandwiches served at a few tables in the shop. The smoked turkey is especially notable. Closed Sun.

★ **The Truffle Shop**   *(530)265-3539   (800)366-3538*
downtown at 408 Broad St.
chocolategod.com
Legendary chocolatier Willem DeGroot's decadent delights–truffles, tortes and other super rich desserts–are displayed and sold here in a cozy storefront, via catalog and the internet.

★ **Malakoff Diggins State Historic Park**   *(530)265-2740*
15 mi. NE off Hwy. 49 at 23579 N. Bloomfield Rd.
Here from the 1850s to the 1880s was the world's largest hydraulic gold mine. The Malakoff Pit is an awesome testament to the destructive power of water under high pressure. It is a vast hole nearly 600 feet deep, and more than a mile long. A former dance hall is now a Park Museum with hydraulic mining exhibits. Nearby is the giant monitor nozzle that controlled the water flow.

★ **Miners Foundry Cultural Center**   *(530)265-5040*
downtown at 325 Spring St.
minersfoundry.org
The historic Miners Foundry (1856) is a group of stone, brick and frame buildings in which the Pelton Wheel (a key link between the water wheel and modern power generation) was first manufactured in 1879. Historic pictures and artifacts are exhibited throughout. Great stone walls provide a unique backdrop for a wealth of theater, musical, and dance perform-ances that are staged here year-round.

★ **Nevada City Carriage House Tour**   *(530)265-8778*
just N at 431 Uren St.
In a fold of forested hills near downtown is a remarkable Victorian carriage house and stables. This beautifully detailed reproduction was constructed with lumber pulled out of local forests by resident horses. The Carriage House tour is a must for history buffs and horse fanciers. During the escorted tour, you'll see up to two dozen "gentle giant" registered Percheron draft horses used to pull the carriages in town. There is also a gift shop.

Nevada County Narrow Gage Railroad Museum *(530)470-0902*
1 mi. SW at 5 Kidder Court
ncngrrmuseum.org
Tucked away in pine-forested hills near town is a new (in 2003) railroad museum complex that includes major exhibits from when the railroad first operated out of Nevada City starting in 1875. One of the first engines is featured, and numerous other cars, model railroad, and related paraphernalia are on display. On adjoining grounds, Northern Queen Inn exhibits (see listing) provide a complement to this museum in the Traction Company.

★ **Nevada County Traction Company** *(530)265-0896*
   just S (by Hwy. 20) at 402 Railroad Av. *(800)226-3090x262*
   northernqueeninn.com
On the grounds of the Northern Queen Inn (see listing) is a
charming tribute to the railroads of yesteryear. You can ride a
narrow-gage railroad on a three-mile round-trip through tall pines
to an authentic Chinese cemetery (used from 1868 to 1939). Along
the way are mining and California/Indian relics, and historic
rolling stock, including Engine #5 from the railroad used in more
than one hundred movies. There is also a depot gift shop.

★ **Nevada Theater** *(530)265-6161*
   downtown at 401 Broad St.
The oldest original-use theater in California was built in 1865.
Today, the building (a National Historic Landmark) still provides
a stage for live plays produced by the Foothill Theatre Company,
plus concerts, films, variety shows, and lectures year-round.

★ **North Star Mining Museum** *(530)273-4255*
   5 mi. SW at the south end of Mill St. - Grass Valley
A giant thirty-foot Pelton waterwheel displayed here was used to
generate power for mining operations. It was the largest of its
type in the world when it was installed in 1895. The massive old
powerhouse is now a museum housing a substantial collection of
artifacts depicting the history and methods of California gold
mining. There is also a creekside picnic area.

Pioneer Park *(530)265-2521*
   just E on Nimrod St.
A public swimming pool, tennis courts, playing fields, and shaded
picnic tables are provided in this town park nestled in the hills.

River Running

★ **Tributary Whitewater Tours** *(530)346-6812 (800)672-3846*
   5 mi. SW at 20480 Woodbury Dr. - Grass Valley
   whitewatertours.com
Tributary has been guiding whitewater rafting trips on Sierra
streams and beyond for more than twenty years. Less than an
hour south of Nevada City is the South Fork of the American
River–perhaps the most popular rafting river in the West. Scenic
half-day and day trips delight beginners and veterans alike.
Nearby to the north, the picturesque North Fork of the Yuba
River appeals to experienced rafters looking for Class V thrills.
Experienced guides, shuttles, equipment, meals, and (for longer
trips) river camps are provided for these and other rivers.

★ **Tahoe National Forest** *(530)265-4531*
   downtown at 631 Coyote St.
   www.r5.fs.fed.us/tahoe
All of the Sierra Nevada mountains between Nevada City and

Lake Tahoe are included in this grand forest. Tahoe National Forest Headquarters in town has detailed maps and information. Features near town include numerous campgrounds, and many miles of maintained trails for hiking and backpacking along scenic canyons of the Yuba and Bear River drainages. Idyllic clear pools attract swimmers as well as fishermen, and long reaches of whitewater rapids appeal to rafters, kayakers, and latter-day Argonauts. In winter, an hour's drive east of town accesses the Royal Gorge Nordic Ski Resort, with the largest system of constantly maintained cross-country ski trails anywhere. Nearby, the historic Donner Pass area is the site of several fully developed downhill skiing complexes. An hour beyond lies Squaw Valley Ski Area (legacy of the 1960 Winter Olympics) and the shore of Lake Tahoe with facilities for every imaginable water and alpine sport (see chapter on Tahoe City).

Wineries
Indian Springs Vineyards   *(530)478-1068   (800)375-9311*
downtown at 303 Broad St.
indianspringsvineyards.com
The downtown tasting room and wine and related gift shop showcase several award-winning varietals from their Gold Country vineyards in a pleasant century-old storefront. Open 11-5 daily.
Nevada City Winery   *(530)265-9463   (800)203-9463*
downtown at 321 Spring St.
ncwinery.com
Nevada County's premier premium winery has a tasting room and a well-stocked gift and gourmet shop above the historic foundry complex. Open 11-5 daily except 12-5 Sunday.

RESTAURANTS

Cafe Mekka   *(530)478-1517*
downtown at 237 Commercial St.
B-L-D.   *Moderate*
Spectacular desserts by Willem DeGroot, a local legendary dessert maker, can be enjoyed with assorted coffees, teas and other beverages in this fancifully funky coffeehouse.
Cirino's Italian Restaurant   *(530)265-2246*
downtown at 309 Broad St.
L-D. No L Mon.-Thurs.   *Moderate*
Traditional pastas, seafood and meat dishes are served in a popular casual dining room backed by a handsome bar.
★ **Citronee**   *(530)265-5697*
downtown at 320 Broad St.
L-D.   *Expensive*
Contemporary California cuisine with a French accent is skillfully

prepared and served in an intimate bistro-style dining room with a bar, or better yet, in tiny rock-walled dining areas beyond. Several delicious desserts are homemade, as is everything else.

Country Rose   *(530)265-6252*
downtown at 300 Commercial St.
L-D.   *Expensive*
Seasonal fresh seafood is featured among country Continental cuisine with an innovative flair served in warm intimate dining areas of a historic brick building and outdoors amid lush greenery.

★ **Friar Tuck's Restaurant**   *(530)265-9093*
downtown at 111 N. Pine St.
www.friartucks.com
D only.   *Expensive*
A fire in 2002 destroyed the Victorian building that housed this landmark dinner house. The Gold Camp's finest fondues star again, along with steaks, seafood and fowl, amid bigger and better wine cellar decor including a "mystical tree," a front room bar with a good street view, and live entertainment.

★ **Happy Apple Kitchen**   *(530)273-2822*
10 mi. S (via Hwy. 49) at 18532 Colfax Hwy. (Hwy. 174) - Chicago Park
L only. Closed Sun.   *Moderate*
Locally grown apples in cupcakes, cookies, and milkshakes, plus housemade apple, French apple and cream cheese apple pies star. All-American burgers, sandwiches, soups and salads are also served in a cheerful dining room, on an orchard-view porch or to go. There is also a (seasonal) produce stand.

★ **Hollywood Sweets**   *(530)272-4470*
2 mi. SE (via Hwy. 20) at 12041 Sutton Way - Grass Valley
hollywoodsweets.com
B-L.   *Moderate*
Hollywood Sweets is a bonanza of baked goods. Many varieties of delicious pastries, pies, cakes, and cookies, breads, rolls and bagels are displayed in capacious cases. Lunches featuring sandwiches using their bread and designer salads are also served in the cheerful wood-trimmed room backed by extensive displays.

★ **Ike's Quarter Cafe**   *(530)265-6138*
downtown at 401 Commercial St.
B-L.   *Moderate*
One of the most successful importations of Louisiana cuisine in the West is Ike's Quarter Cafe. The talented young chef/owner offers assured presentations of classics like jambalaya, gumbo, muffaletta and other hallmarks of the brashly appealing cuisine. All are made from scratch and feature fresh seasonal ingredients of the region. His pies, pastries and desserts are also outstanding. The casual colorful dining room and lush adjoining shaded patio reflect the bon temps food and feeling of New Orleans.

Kirby's Creekside Restaurant & Bar   *(530)265-3445*
downtown at 101 Broad St.
L-D. Sun. brunch.   *Moderate*
Creative California cuisine can work in dishes like seafood ravioli
with roasted bell pepper cream sauce or rolled veal stuffed with
spinach and mushroom. A stylish dining room and bar adjoin
Nevada City's only creekside dining deck.

Main Street Cafe & Bar   *(530)477-6000*
4 mi. S at 215 W. Main St. - Grass Valley
mainstreetcafebar.com
L-D.   *Expensive*
A well-rounded American contemporary menu ranges from pizzas
and pastas to seafoods and grilled meats, and desserts by local
legend Willem de Groot. Art for sale hangs on brick walls in a
historic building that is now a popular local restaurant.

Moore's Cafe   *(530)265-9440*
downtown at 216 Broad St.
B-L.   *Moderate*
Hearty homestyle Western fare includes homemade biscuits and
country gravy, cornmeal pancakes, and a variety of omelets for
breakfast served in the casual coffee shop or at the counter of this
long-popular cafe.

National Hotel   *(530)265-4551*
downtown at 211 Broad St.
B-L-D.   *Expensive*
Old-fashioned dishes including assorted steaks, chicken, fish and
pasta are served in the simply nostalgic dining room of the
landmark hotel. Next door is an authentic saloon full of the
trappings and spirit of the gold camp era.

The New Moon Cafe   *(530)265-6399*
downtown at 203 York St.
thenewmooncafe.com
L-D. No L Sat. & Sun. Closed Mon.   *Expensive*
Natives may tell you that this is one of the two best restaurants
in town. On any given night it might be–or not. Avant-garde food
is served in a simply modish split-level dining room.

Northern Queen Inn   *(530)265-5259*
just S (by Hwy. 20) at 400 Railroad Av.
northernqueeninn.com
B-L-D. No D Mon.-Wed.   *Moderate*
The Inn's **Trolley Junction Restaurant** offers a tempting
selection of California dishes at all meals, and there is a full bar.
A well-appointed dining room and dining cars overlook a
delightful year-round natural waterfall in a lush garden.

Paulette's Country Kitchen   *(530)273-4008*
2 mi. SE (via Hwy. 20) at 11875 Sutton Way - Grass Valley
B-L-D. No D Fri.-Sun.   *Moderate*
American standards and updates are offered in a wide variety of
dishes. Housemade seasonal pies are featured daily in big cheerful
dining rooms with padded booths, and in a bank vault.

The Posh Nosh   *(530)265-6064*
downtown at 318 Broad St.
poshnoshrestaurant.com
L-D. No D Mon.-Thurs.   *Moderate*
Designer burgers, sandwiches and pastas highlight lively, hearty
fare served in a cozy cellar dining room or alfresco on a tree-
shaded patio in season.

Railroad Cafe   *(530)274-2233*
4 mi. S at 111 W. Main St. - Grass Valley
B-L-D. No D Sun.-Thurs.   *Moderate*
Hearty American fare served for breakfast and lunch includes
specials like beef stew in a bread bowl for dinner in winter. A rock
wall, abundant greenery, an enclosed patio, and a model railroad
enhance the nostalgic wood-trimmed cafe.

South Pine Cafe   *(530)265-0260*
downtown at 110 S. Pine St.
B-L.   *Moderate*
California contemporary comfort food plus some appealing
updates like ollaliberry pancakes or breakfast burritos are served
in hearty helpings in a comfortable little cafe.

Sweet Endeavors Bakery   *(530)265-0572*
1 mi. S at 104 Argall Way
B-L. Closed Sat.-Sun.   *Moderate*
This young bakery in a long-established location is doing nice
work with a large variety of traditional American and Continental
pastries and desserts like fruit/nut tarts for desserts.

Tofanelli's   *(530)272-1468*
4 mi. S at 302 W. Main St. - Grass Valley
B-L-D. No D Sun. No L Sat. Closed Mon.   *Expensive*
Contemporary American dishes are given careful attention and
served in a simply stylish grill and better yet, in a handsome
enclosed patio and atrium.

The Willo   *(530)265-9902*
3 mi. NW at 16898 Hwy. 49
L-D. No L Sat.-Mon.   *Low*
You cook your own New York steak of different sizes (or they
will), and there are also chicken, pork chops, or catfish with
appropriate support dishes. A big wood-fired grill adjoins the
casual wood-trimmed dining room and saloon.

LODGINGS

Accommodations are relatively scarce, but distinctive. Many are romantic bed-and-breakfasts in historic buildings. High season is weekends from spring through fall. Winter weekday prices may be reduced at least 15%.

Deer Creek Inn   *(530)265-0363*
downtown at 116 Nevada St. - 95959
deercreekinn.com
6 units   *(800)655-0363*   *Expensive*
A three-story Queen Anne Victorian home is now a bed-and-breakfast amid luxuriant gardens next to Deer Creek. Gourmet breakfast and (most evenings) wine service are complimentary. Each cozy room is attractively furnished to capture the spirit of the Victorian era, and has a private bath and queen or king bed.
"Elaine's Room"–two private creek-view patios, Roman
   tub for two with dual showerheads, canopy queen bed.
"Winifred's Room"–private creek-view balcony,
   clawfoot tub at foot of canopy queen bed.

★ **The Emma Nevada House**   *(530)265-4415*
just N at 528 E. Broad St. - 95959
emmanevadahouse.com
6 units   *(800)916-3662*   *Expensive*
An 1856 Victorian home has been impeccably transformed into a gracious bed-and-breakfast surrounded by gardens and shade trees. A full gourmet breakfast and afternoon tea and cookies are complimentary. Each of the beautifully furnished rooms has a private bath, some stylish antiques and a queen or king bed.
"Nightingale's Bower"–bay window sitting area,
   gas fireplace, in-bath whirlpool, king bed.
"Empress' Chamber"–window-wall sitting area,
   in-bath two-person whirlpool, queen bed.

Flume's End   *(530)265-9665*
downtown at 317 S. Pine St. - 95959
flumesend.com
6 units   *(800)991-8118*   *Expensive*
A charming creek and historic waterflumes, little waterfalls and lush woods distinguish this restored Victorian bed-and-breakfast. Full breakfast is complimentary. Each cozy room is individually well furnished and has a private bath and queen or king bed. Some have a private deck and a peaceful waterfall view.
"The Cottage"–separate cottage with big private
   deck, kitchenette, wood stove, tub/shower, queen bed.
"Master Bedroom," "Garden Room"–private deck by
   waterfalls, in-bath whirlpool tub, queen bed.

Gold Country Inn - Best Western   *(530)273-1393*
2 mi. SE (by Hwy. 49) at 11972 Sutton Way - Grass Valley 95945
bestwestern.com
84 units   *(800)780-7234*   *Moderate-Expensive*
A small pool and whirlpool are features of this conventional motel
by the freeway. Each room is well furnished and has two queens
or a king bed. Some rooms have a refrigerator.

★ **Grandmère's Inn**   *(530)265-4660*
downtown at 449 Broad St. - 95959
grandmeresinn.com
6 units   *Expensive*
A stately whitewashed pre-Civil War mansion (circa 1856) amid
manicured gardens accented by luxuriant shade trees is now a
refined bed-and-breakfast inn. Full gourmet breakfast and
evening cookies and beverages are complimentary. Each
beautifully furnished unit features some period decor and
whimsical touches, a private bath, and a queen bed.
"Senator's Chambers"–spacious suite, elegant fireplace
    in living room, clawfoot tub, private garden-view porch.
"Ellen's Garden Room"–secluded, large,
    garden-view windows, oversized tub.
"Diplomat's Suite"–spacious, deep soaking
    tub, four-poster queen bed.

Holiday Lodge   *(530)273-4406*
4 mi. S at 1221 E. Main St. - Grass Valley 95945
holidaylodge.biz
36 units   *(800)742-7125*   *Moderate*
This contemporary motel has a pool and sauna. Each room is
nicely furnished and has doubles, queen or king bed.

★ **National Hotel**   *(530)265-4551*
downtown at 211 Broad St. - 95959
42 units   *(888)265-4551*   *Moderate-Expensive*
Nevada City's biggest landmark is the three-story National Hotel.
It is also California's oldest lodging–in continuous operation since
1856. On the National Historic Register, it has a pool, Victorian-
style dining room (see listing) and a saloon that truly evokes the
spirit of the Gold Camp era. Each room is simply furnished with
mixed period and modern decor and has a double, queen or king
bed. Some small rooms share baths.
#41–top floor corner, private tiny balcony,
    private bath, town/mountain views, queen bed.
#20–suite, corner, public balcony, private
    bath, some view, 4-poster double bed.
#34–parlor suite, public balcony, sitting
    room, private bath, antique king bed.

★ **Northern Queen Inn**   *(530)265-5824*
   just S (by Hwy. 20) at 400 Railroad Av. - 95959
   northernqueeninn.com
   86 units   *(800)226-3090*   *Moderate-Expensive*
The area's best motel is a modern complex built along a rushing stream in a forest. A big cheerful coffee shop (see listing) provides dramatic waterfall views, and there is a pool and whirlpool. The grounds also house the Nevada County Traction Company (see listing) with museum exhibits, an authentic narrow-gage railroad, depot, and gift shop. Each room is well furnished and has a refrigerator and queen bed.
   cottage (8 of these)–spacious, secluded,
      gas fireplace in living room, kitchenette.

Outside Inn   *(530)265-2233*
   just NW at 575 E. Broad St. - 95959
   outsideinn.com
   14 units   *Moderate-Expensive*
One of the oldest motels in the Mother Lode is now an architectural award-winning, completely renovated 1940s-era motor court with a little pool by a creek. Each compact room is well furnished with contemporary and extra amenities, and has a queen or king bed. Kitchenettes are available.
   "The Cabin"–private deck, kitchen, in-bath
      whirlpool tub, wood fireplace, king bed.

The Parsonage   *(530)265-9478*
   downtown at 427 Broad St. - 95959
   theparsonage.net
   6 units   *(877)265-9499*   *Expensive*
A handsome Victorian parsonage is now a nostalgic bed-and-breakfast rife with heirlooms. Full breakfast set with the family's crystal and Haviland china is complimentary. Each compact room is individually well furnished, including quality antiques and art objects. All have a private bath and double or queen bed.

★ **The Red Castle Inn**   *(530)265-5135*
   just E at 109 Prospect St. - 95959
   www.historic-lodgings.com
   7 units   *(800)761-4766*   *Expensive*
The premier bed-and-breakfast inn in Nevada City is a four-story pre-Civil War brick Gothic Revival landmark overlooking downtown. Lighted paths meander through terraced rustic gardens that include a fish pond. Gourmet breakfast buffet, afternoon tea served on heirloom china and crystal, and desserts are complimentary. Each elaborately furnished room includes quality heirlooms, access to a private or shared veranda with a village view, private bath, and a double or queen bed.
   "Forest View Room"–private deck, clawfoot tub, queen bed.

Pacific Grove

Pacific Grove is a seaside haven of tranquility. Situated along a strikingly beautiful coastline where the waters of the Pacific Ocean and Monterey Bay converge, the town is also favored by a mild year-round climate that is one of America's most temperate. Spectacular displays of flowers and lush green hues distinguish all seasons, culminating at Lovers Point, one of the most romantic pocket parks on the West Coast.

Drawn by the peaceful setting and the idyllic climate, Methodists founded the town in 1875 as a summer retreat. Strict ordinances regulating dancing, drinking, profanity, and even swimming lasted for nearly a century. Residents finally voted to permit the sale of alcohol in California's last "dry" town in 1969. The legacy of the austere settlers was the creation of a genteel haven amidst extravagant surroundings.

Today, shoreline parks, sandy beaches, coves and winding paths frame the entire ocean and bayside perimeters of town. Inland, trim Victorian houses amid gardens line serene tree-shaded streets. The tidy feeling of a Northeastern village center at the turn of the 19th century has been meticulously retained in a highly strollable downtown. Sophisticated galleries, specialty shops, coffee houses, bakeries, and gourmet restaurants are plentiful. To this day, not much happens to disturb tranquil evenings, but two plush bayfront lounges frame seascapes and sunsets through expansive picture windows. Accommodations range from enchanting Victorian bed-and-breakfast inns to refined motels near the forest home of millions of monarch butterflies.

WEATHER PROFILE

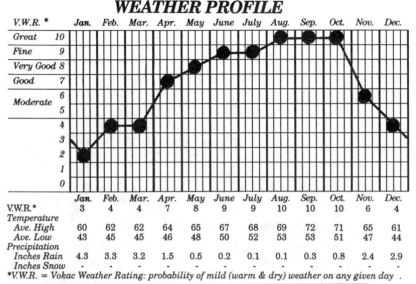

V.W.R.*		Jan.	Feb.	Mar.	Apr.	May	June	July	Aug.	Sep.	Oct.	Nov.	Dec.
Great	10												
Fine	9												
Very Good	8												
Good	7												
Moderate	6												
	5												
	4												
	3												
	2												
	1												
	0												

	Jan.	Feb.	Mar.	Apr.	May	June	July	Aug.	Sep.	Oct.	Nov.	Dec.
V.W.R.*	3	4	4	7	8	9	9	10	10	10	6	4
Temperature												
Ave. High	60	62	62	64	65	67	68	69	72	71	65	61
Ave. Low	43	45	45	46	48	50	52	53	53	51	47	44
Precipitation												
Inches Rain	4.3	3.3	3.2	1.5	0.5	0.2	0.1	0.1	0.3	0.8	2.4	2.9
Inches Snow	-	-	-	-	-	-	-	-	-	-	-	-

*V.W.R. = Vokac Weather Rating: probability of mild (warm & dry) weather on any given day .

BASIC INFORMATION

Population: 15,522
Elevation: 50 feet
Location: 125 miles South of San Francisco
Airport (regularly scheduled flights): Monterey - 5 miles

Pacific Grove Chamber of Commerce (831)373-3304 (800)656-6650
   downtown at Forest & Central Avs. (Box 167) - 93950
   pacificgrove.org
Monterey County Convention & Visitors Bureau   (888)221-1010
   Box 1770 - 93942   montereyinfo.org

194

ATTRACTIONS

★ *Bicycling*

    Adventures by the Sea   *(831)372-1807*
    at the beach at Lovers Point
    adventuresbythesea.com
The Monterey Peninsula Recreation Trail follows one of the most scenic stretches of coastline in California for almost twenty miles from Asilomar in Pacific Grove to Castroville. The separated bikeway accommodates both bicyclists and pedaled surreys as it meanders past colorful parks and popular beaches along Pacific Grove's shoreline. The incomparable Seventeen-Mile Drive, another renowned bike route, extends to the other side of the Peninsula. Rental bicycles, surreys (four-wheeled canopy-covered cycle with side-by-side sets of bicycle pedals), related equipment and information are available daily.

Butterfly Trees
    just W around Lighthouse Av. & Seventeen-Mile Dr.
Pacific Grove is known as "Butterfly Town, U.S.A." because of the annual migration of hundreds of thousands of monarch butterflies to selected groves of trees west of downtown between October and March.

★ *Golf*

    W of downtown
Two public 18-hole golf courses each have an oceanfront location bordering the west side of Pacific Grove. Both are among the most popular on the Peninsula, for different reasons.

    Links at Spanish Bay   *(831)654-9300*   *(800)654-9300*
    2 mi. SW at 2700 Seventeen-Mile Dr. - Pebble Beach
Extraordinary seascapes and a renowned course amid coastal dunes justify huge green fees.

    Pacific Grove Golf Links   *(831)648-5777*
    1 mi. NW via Lighthouse Av.
Ocean-view fairways among low dunes and woodlands are coupled with the Peninsula's lowest green fees.

★ Lovers Point

    just N at the bay end of 17th St.
A small bayside park combines sandy coves, dramatic rock formations, Monterey cypress, and green lawns into one of the peninsula's most romantic and photogenic highlights. It is normally clear and safe, apart from winter storm surf which can be dramatic and dangerous. The water off Bathhouse Beach is a favorite of hearty swimmers in summer.

The Magic Carpet of "Mesembryanthemum"
    just N along the bay
This fanciful tongue-twister is the name for masses of ice plants

that drape a stretch of Monterey Bay shoreline northwest of Lovers Point. From April through August, a solid lavender-pink carpet of tiny flowers provides a brilliant mantle above the rockbound bay.

★ **Pacific Grove Museum of Natural History**   *(831)648-5716*
   downtown at 165 Forest Av.
   pgmuseum.org
Pacific Grove's well-regarded museum has a notable exhibit dealing with the phenomenon of the Monarch butterfly trees. Also, a relief map of the peninsula and bay graphically depicts the great chasm of Monterey Bay, which plummets within a few miles from shore to 8,400 feet below sea level–far deeper than the Grand Canyon. There is also "Sandy," a life-sized bronze sculpture of a grey whale, native plant garden and a well-stocked museum shop. Open 10-5 daily except closed Mon.

Point Piños Lighthouse   *(831)648-3116*
   1 mi. W at west end of Lighthouse Av.
The oldest continuously operating lighthouse on the Pacific Coast has stood at the entrance to Monterey Bay since 1855. It is open to the public on Thursday through Sunday between 1 and 4 p.m.

★ **Seventeen-Mile Drive**   *(831)647-5235*
   starts just W via Lighthouse Av. to Seventeen-Mile Dr.
One of the world's great scenic drives meanders through Pebble Beach and along the splendid coastline between Pacific Grove and Carmel. It is a toll road except to residents. In addition to unforgettable seascapes, highlights include stately homes, legendary golf courses, the Lodge at Pebble Beach, and the Inn at Spanish Bay. Gnarled trees clinging to rocky headlands at The Lone Cypress are among the West's most photographed landmarks.

★ *Shoreline Parks*
   N & W along Ocean View Blvd. & Sunset Dr.
Among picturesque coastline drives, none is more beguiling than Pacific Grove's, which winds for four miles along a variously flower-bordered, rockbound, and sandy shoreline. The road is a boundary between residential portions of town and a continuous series of seaside parks. Along Monterey Bay, beautifully landscaped parks provide access to numerous sandy beaches tucked into coves along rocky headlands. Sun bathing, strolling, bicycling and picnicking are popular. Scuba diving is ideal when the bay is calm and clear. Wetsuits are almost always necessary–the water is cold. On the ocean side beyond Point Piños Lighthouse (see listing), the rugged rocky shoreline is flanked by low grassy sand dunes stopped short by a pine forest that never quite reaches the sea.

RESTAURANTS

★ **Fandango**   *(831)372-3456*
downtown at 223 17th St.
fandangorestaurant.com
L-D. Sun. brunch.   *Expensive*
Fandango is the region's best source of European country-style cuisine. Highlights include dishes from an open mesquite grill like big Black Angus Porterhouse steaks. Braised lamb shank, osso buco, paella, and sautéed sand dabs are other flavorful specialties. Full linen and fresh flowers enliven a series of colorful, romantic little dining rooms, a firelit conservatory, and full bar.

Fifi's Cafe   *(831)372-5325*
1 mi. S at 1188 Forest Av.
fifiscafe.com
L-D. Plus B on Sat. & Sun.   *Moderate*
Country French fare and some nods toward California cuisine like sautéed Monterey sand dabs are featured along with housemade pastries on display out front in a casual little bistro.

First Awakenings   *(831)372-1125*
1 mi. E at 125 Oceanview Blvd.
B-L.   *Moderate*
Assorted humongous pancakes, skillet dishes, and thick french toast highlight breakfasts featured in a light, plant-filled coffee shop and firelit patio in the American Tin Cannery complex.

★ **Fishwife at Asilomar Beach**   *(831)375-7107*
1 mi. SW at 1996 Sunset Dr. at Asilomar Beach
fishwife.com
L-D.   *Moderate*
Fresh seasonal fish are given a light, bright touch on a contemporary California menu with a Caribbean accent. For example, they use 100% canola oil and cornmeal for fried dishes like catfish fillet. Desserts like key lime pie are homemade. Casual little dining areas surround a wood-trimmed bar in this ever-so-popular roadside restaurant.

★ **The Inn at Spanish Bay**   *(831)647-7423*
2 mi. SW at 2700 Seventeen-Mile Dr. - Pebble Beach
pebblebeach.com
B-L-D.   *Expensive-Very Expensive*
At **Roy's at Pebble Beach** (B-L-D–Very Expensive), Hawaiian fusion dishes are prepared combining Asian-Pacific flavors and classic European techniques. A wood-fired oven and exhibition kitchen enhance the relaxed, upscale dining room with a fine window-wall seascape view. **Pèppoli** (D only–Very Expensive) offers gourmet Tuscan-inspired cuisine with an ocean view.

Sticks (B-L–Expensive) offers casual comfort foods in a club-like setting with links and ocean views. **Traps** is a fireplace lounge.

★ **Joe Rombi's**   *(831)373-2416*
downtown at 208 17th St. (at Lighthouse Av.)
joerombis.com
D only. Closed Mon.-Tues.   *Moderate*
Joe Rombi's is the best Italian restaurant in Pacific Grove. From the housemade focaccia through fresh sand dabs and an appealing selection of classic and creative Italian dishes to tiramisu and other delicious desserts made here, it's a winner. The warm stylish little dining room complements the sophisticated cuisine.

Lighthouse Cafe   *(831)372-7006*
downtown at 602 Lighthouse Av.
B-L.   *Moderate*
Hearty all-American fare and homespun atmosphere define this cozy little corner cafe. Breakfasts include a wealth of traditional dishes along with specialties like raisin-walnut pancakes. For lunch, all kinds of half-pound charbroiled burgers and big boneless chicken sandwiches are featured.

★ **Old Bath House**   *(831)375-5195*
just N at 620 Ocean View Blvd.
oldbathhouse.com
D only.   *Very Expensive*
Pacific Grove's most renowned dinner house has a winning way with creative American cuisine that changes seasonally, like pan-seared pheasant breast over mushroom-white truffle raviolis and fresh spinach; or lavender-thyme pork porterhouse, and luscious desserts like Grand Marnier or Belgian chocolate soufflé. But it is the magnificent view of Monterey Bay and Lovers Point, complemented by elegant decor in an ingeniously converted Victorian bathhouse, that assures continuing status as one of California's most romantic restaurants.

★ **Passionfish**   *(831)655-3311*
downtown at 701 Lighthouse Av.
www.passionfish.net
D only. Closed Tues.   *Expensive*
A selection of fresh "sustainable" seafood stars on a creative, ever-changing menu. Examples might include shrimp with spicy orange cilantro dipping sauce or escolar with truffle-citrus soy sauce. There are several dishes for steak and fowl fanciers, as well as unusual desserts served in casual comfortable dining rooms.

★ **Pavel's Bäckerei**   *(831)643-2636*
downtown at 219½ Forest Av.
B-L. Closed Sun.   *Moderate*
Delicious bear claws, Danishes, cinnamon rolls, and bagels are

backed by unusual treats like francesse (white flour pillow), white cheddar cheese bagels and nine-grain rolls and loaves, plus designer cakes. There are a few tables for coffee and morning delights, or get it to go for a grand picnic highlight.

★ **Peppers Mexicali Cafe**   *(831)373-6892*
downtown at 170 Forest Av.
L-D. No L Sun. Closed Tues.   Moderate
Consider innovative Mexican/American dishes like Yucatan snapper with chiles, citrus and cilantro; or chicken caribe with citrus habañero marinade and tropical salsa fresca. These are among a host of grazing goodies served in the cozy congestion of an ever-popular wood-trimmed dining room and bar.

★ **Red House Cafe**   *(831)643-1060*
downtown at 662 Lighthouse Av.
redhousecafe.com
B-L-D. No D Sun.-Wed. Closed Mon.   Moderate
Fresh-squeezed juices and creative light fare can be enjoyed with delicious baked goods on display in the front room of a Victorian cottage with a firelit entry room that is now a deservedly popular cafe. The porch has a lovely view of downtown.

★ **Robert's The White House**   *(831)375-9626*
downtown at 649 Lighthouse Av.
D only. Closed Mon.   Expensive
One of the Peninsula's most renowned chefs opened The White House in 2002. It is already a solid contender for the best-of-the-best among the Monterey Peninsula's top restaurants. Three-course dinners feature top-quality seasonal ingredients meticulously prepared for creative, delectable dishes like salmon and bay shrimp cakes with an avocado sauce, roast chicken Wellington with two sauces, or salmon with scallop mousse in pastry with dill sauce. Luscious housemade desserts can also be enjoyed in casually elegant dining rooms of a transformed landmark mansion in the heart of town.

★ **Taste Cafe & Bistro**   *(831)655-0324*
1 mi. S at 1199 Forest Av.
tastecafebistro.com
L-D. Closed Mon.   Expensive
Taste is one of the Peninsula's most delightful dining experiences. Traditional and creative fare is given expert attention in dishes prepared from scratch like organic red oak leaf salad with blue cheese, balsamic dressing, sliced pears and glazed pecans or grilled marinated rabbit with a juniper berry sauce, or fresh salmon fillet baked in parchment paper. Toothsome desserts made here contribute to the appeal of simply stylish dining rooms with fanciful wall and ceiling art tucked into a shopping complex.

The Tinnery   *(831)646-1040*
just N at 631 Ocean View Blvd.
thetinnery.com
L-D. Sun. brunch.   *Moderate*
American and international favorites are offered on a well-rounded menu. But the highlight of this cheerful restaurant is a superb panoramic view of Lovers Point Park and Monterey Bay. A colorful lounge shares the view.

Toasties Cafe   *(831)373-7543*
downtown at 702 Lighthouse Av.
B-L. Plus D Fri. & Sat.   *Moderate*
Contemporary breakfast specialties continue a long-standing tradition in this country-comfortable cafe.

★ **Wildberries**   *(831)644-9836*
downtown at 212 17th St.
B-L-D. No D Sun. Only B pastry on Thurs. Closed Wed. Moderate
Wildberries ranks among the best coffee houses in California. Consider one of their humongous berry muffins for starters. They're made here, along with assorted coffee cakes and other morning delights, plus light vegetarian fare. Several little rooms of a historic cottage retain their quaint Victorian charm with chandeliers, stamped-tin ceilings, well-worn floors and casual hardwood tables and chairs indoors and on their garden terrace.

LODGINGS

Accommodations are numerous. Most are independent, including several delightful bed-and-breakfast inns and two great resorts in adjacent Pebble Beach. Summer and fall are prime time. Rates are often reduced 20% or more (apart from weekends) in winter.

Asilomar   *(831)372-8016*
1 mi. W at 800 Asilomar Av. - 93950
visitasilomar.com
313 units   *Moderate-Expensive*
Asilomar is a full-service conference center with National Historic Landmark status that has served as a sanctuary-by-the-sea since 1913. Hiking trails extend from thirty buildings through pine-studded dunes to ocean beaches. A pool, bicycle rentals, ping pong and pool tables are available to guests, and there are dining facilities and a gift shop. Each recently upgraded comfortably furnished unit has a private bathroom and double beds. With no phone or TV, the rooms further reflect Asilomar's role as a peaceful retreat.

Beachcomber Inn   *(831)373-4769*
1 mi. SW at 1996 Sunset Dr. - 93950
26 units   *(800)634-4769*   *Moderate-Expensive*
This modern motel is the nearest to Pacific Grove's ocean beaches

and dunes. A pool, sauna, complimentary bicycles, and the popular Fishwife Restaurant (see listing) are features. Each comfortable room has a refrigerator and a queen or king bed.
#24–end, top (2nd) floor, private deck, ocean view, king bed.

Borg's Ocean Front Motel   *(831)375-2406*
just N at 635 Ocean View Blvd. - 93950
60 units   *Moderate-Expensive*
Some of Borg's rooms have views across a street to a bayfront park. Each simply furnished room has a queen bed.
#50–spacious, bayview windows on two sides.

★ **Centrella Bed & Breakfast Inn**   *(831)372-3372*
downtown at 612 Central Av. - 93950
centrellainn.com
26 units   *(800)233-3372*   *Expensive*
A Victorian building (circa 1889) is now a large, well-landscaped bed-and-breakfast inn. Buffet breakfast, and evening beverages, appetizers and cookies are complimentary. Each well-furnished room, suite and cottage combines old with new, and has a private bath. All have a queen bed. Cottages have a gas fireplace.
"Garden View Room"–pot-belly gas stove, two-
    person whirlpool tub, wet bar, canopy queen bed.

Gatehouse Inn   *(831)649-8436*
just E at 225 Central Av. - 93950
sueandlewinns.com
9 units   *(800)753-1881*   *Expensive*
A restored Italianate Victorian mansion constructed in 1884 now captures a bygone era as a bed-and-breakfast inn. Breakfast and afternoon tea, wine and treats are complimentary. Each cozy, well-furnished room is individually decorated, including some antiques, a private bath and queen or king bed.
"Langford Room"–spacious, fine ocean view, pot-belly
    gas stove, clawfoot tub in room, queen bed.

★ **Gosby House Inn**   *(831)375-1287*
downtown at 643 Lighthouse Av. - 93950
gosbyhouseinn.com
22 units   *(800)527-8828*   *Expensive*
An authentic Victorian mansion amid carefully tended gardens in the heart of town now serves as a bed-and-breakfast inn tastefully furnished with original antiques. A full buffet breakfast is included, as are afternoon appetizers and wine, and evening treats. Bicycles are available for the asking. All rooms are individually attractively furnished including some antiques and have most contemporary amenities, a private bath, and a queen or king bed.
"Carriage House Suites" (2 of these)–two-person in-bath
    whirlpool, gas fireplace, private balcony, king bed.

Grand View Inn   *(831)372-4341*
just N at 557 Ocean View Blvd. - *93950*
11 units   *Expensive-Very Expensive*
A landmark Edwardian home across a street from Lovers Point beach was lovingly converted into a gracious bed-and-breakfast in 1994. Full breakfast and afternoon tea are complimentary. Each room is attractively furnished with a blend of period and contemporary decor and a queen bed.
"Seal Rocks"–panorama of park/bay, queen bed.

★ **Green Gables Inn**   *(831)375-2095*
just E at 301 Ocean View Blvd. - *93950*
foursisters.com
11 units   *(800)722-1774*   *Expensive-Very Expensive*
One of California's most beguiling Queen Anne-style mansions (circa 1888) has been meticulously transformed into a romantic bed-and-breakfast. Full breakfast and afternoon wine and appetizers, and use of bicycles, are complimentary. The main house and carriage house are on lovely grounds across a street from the bay. While rooms vary in size, and some share bathrooms, all are beautifully furnished, including fine period decor, most conveniences, and a queen or king bed. Some have a fireplace and/or a bay view.
"Carriage House Rooms" (4 of these)–sitting area,
    some ocean views, in-bath two-person whirlpool
    tub, gas fireplace, king bed.
"Lacey Suite"–parlor, gas fireplace, pvt. bath, queen bed.
"Gable"–cozy loft, shared bath, ocean-view windows, queen bed.

★ **The Inn at Spanish Bay**   *(831)647-7500*
2 mi. SW at 2700 Seventeen-Mile Dr. - *Pebble Beach 93953*
pebblebeach.com
270 units   *(800)654-9300*   *Very Expensive*
One of America's best resorts is the Inn at Spanish Bay. Perched amid tall Monterey pines and sand dunes on a rise above the ocean, the five-story complex includes a (fee) championship 18-hole golf course (see listing), eight tennis courts, and rental bicycles, a fitness club, plus the beach, a large pool, whirlpool, saunas, and miles of scenic trails. Four upscale restaurants provide a wide selection of dining and view options (see listing). Each spacious unit (ranging from a garden-view room to a two-bedroom suite) is luxuriously furnished and has all contemporary amenities plus a stocked refrigerator (complimentary except alcohol), a gas fireplace, and doubles, queen or king bed. Most have a private patio or balcony with a coast or forest view.
"Executive Suites" (22 of these)–one bedroom, in-bath
    whirlpool, gas fireplace, ocean view, private deck, king bed.

★ **Inn at 213 Seventeen Mile Drive** *(831)642-9514*
just W at 213 Seventeen-Mile Dr. - 93950
innat17.com
14 units *(800)526-5666* *Expensive-Very Expensive*
A 1925 Craftsman-style mansion now serves as an appealing bed-and-breakfast inn surrounded by tranquil gardens. Use of a whirlpool in the garden is complimentary to guests, as is a chef-prepared buffet breakfast and evening wine and appetizers. Each spacious, attractively furnished room is individually decorated and has all expected and some extra amenities, a private bath, and a queen or king bed.
"Guillemot"–spacious, dramatic vaulted redwood
   ceiling, gas fireplace, brass king bed.
"Pelican"–secluded garden cottage, sitting
   area, gas fireplace, king bed.
"Blue Heron"–spacious, corner with bay
   views, balcony over garden, brass king bed.

★ **Lighthouse Lodge & Suites** *(831)655-2111*
1 mi. NW at 1150 Lighthouse Av. - 93950
lhls.com
94 units *(800)858-1249* *Expensive-Very Expensive*
The ocean and (in season) Monarch butterflies are a stroll from this contemporary wood-shingled all-suites complex amid pines and gardens. Guests have access to a pool and whirlpool in the lodge (a 63-unit motel) across the street. Full breakfast and evening wine and appetizers are complimentary. Each of the thirty-one spacious, well-furnished suites has a microwave and refrigerator, stocked honor bar, a gas fireplace and a large whirlpool bath, plus a king bed.

★ **Martine Inn** *(831)373-3388*
just E at 255 Ocean View Blvd. - 93950
martineinn.com
24 units *(800)852-5588* *Expensive-Very Expensive*
Martine Inn is a classic California coastal getaway. A large Mediterranean-style villa built in the late 1890s on a rise above the bay is now a luxurious bed-and-breakfast inn in a colorful garden. Full silver-service breakfast, afternoon appetizers and refreshments, and bottled water and sodas any time are complimentary, as is use of the game room billiard table and sheltered hot tub. Authentic, museum-quality period pieces used throughout contribute to the genteel appeal of this romantic retreat. Each beautifully furnished room has a private bath, all contemporary amenities, and a double, queen or king bed. Most have a clawfoot tub and sea view. Some also have a woodburning fireplace.

"The Suite"–corner windows with grand bay view,
corner woodburning fireplace, porcelain tub, king bed.

"Parke"–bay-view windows on 3 sides, corner woodburning fireplace, clawfoot tub, bay view from
four-poster canopy double bed.

"Eastlake"–windows provide fine bay view from both
seven-foot clawfoot tub and raised canopy king bed.

"Maries"–panoramic bay-view windows on two
sides, clawfoot tub and shower, queen bed.

Monarch Resort - Best Western   *(831)646-8885*
1 mi. NW at 1111 Lighthouse Av. - 93950
bwmonarchresort.com
53 units   *(800)992-9060*   *Expensive-Very Expensive*
Amenities of this serene contemporary motel include an outdoor
pool, whirlpool, and sauna. Expanded Continental breakfast and
evening nonalcoholic beverages and appetizers are complimentary. Each well-furnished room has contemporary and extra
amenities, and two doubles, queen or king bed. Most have a
private balcony. Several also have a gas fireplace.

Old St. Angela Inn   *(831)372-3246*
just E at 321 Central Av. - 93950
sueandlewinns.com
8 units   *(800)748-6306*   *Expensive-Very Expensive*
A Craftsman-style home now serves as a bed-and-breakfast inn
with a whirlpool in a garden. Buffet breakfast and afternoon wine
and appetizers are complimentary. All compact, comfortably
furnished rooms have a private bath, and a double or queen bed.

"Whale Watch"–gas fireplace, in-bath whirlpool,
bay view from private balcony, queen bed.

Pacific Gardens Inn   *(831)646-9414*
1 mi. W at 701 Asilomar Blvd. - 93950
pacificgardensinn.com
28 units   *(800)262-1566*   *Expensive*
This recently remodeled motel in the pines is a short walk from
an ocean beach. There are two whirlpools. Expanded Continental
breakfast and wine and cheese in the afternoon are
complimentary. Each of the well-furnished rooms has all
contemporary amenities, plus a refrigerator, a woodburning
fireplace, and a queen or king bed.

Pacific Grove Inn   *(831)375-2825*
just S at 581 Pine Av. - 93950
pacificgrove-inn.com
16 units   *(800)732-2825*   *Expensive*
In 2002, a 1904 mansion on a rise above downtown became an
appealing bed-and-breakfast inn an easy stroll from the heart of

town. In this landmark on the National Historic Register, expanded Continental breakfast and afternoon appetizers and beverages are complimentary. Each well-furnished, compact room has a private bath, all contemporary amenities, mini-bar, and a queen or king bed. Most have a gas fireplace.
   "Forest Pine Room"–spacious, dining room,
      in-bath whirlpool tub, king bed.
★ **Rosedale Inn**　　　*(831)655-1000*
   1 mi. W at 775 Asilomar Av. - 93950
   rosedaleinn.com
   19 units　　　*(800)822-5606*　　　*Expensive*
Asilomar Conference Center is across a street and there are trails leading to an ocean beach only one-quarter mile from this redwood motel in the woods. Expanded Continental breakfast is complimentary. Rustic appearance belies a wealth of contemporary conveniences. Most of the well-furnished rooms include a mini-kitchen, gas fireplace, two-person oval whirlpool bathtub and a king bed.
★ **Seven Gables Inn**　　　*(831)372-4341*
   just N at 555 Ocean View Blvd. - 93950
   www.pginns.com
   14 units　　　　　*Expensive-Very Expensive*
Monterey Bay is across the street from this luxuriously restored Victorian mansion and related nostalgic cottages surrounded by colorful gardens. Full breakfast amid classic elegance and English-style "high tea" with homemade treats and imported cakes are complimentary. A wealth of authentic European antiques blends comfortably with contemporary amenities including a private bath. Each beautifully furnished room has a bay (ocean) view and a queen or king bed.
   "Cypress Room"–romantic, spacious, refrigerator, corner
      window with grand panoramic bay view, king bed.
   "Ocean Mist"–spacious, refrigerator,
      grand panoramic bay view, king bed.
   "Breakers"–corner room with many
      fine bay-view windows, queen bed.
Sunset Inn　　　*(831)375-3529*
   1 mi. W at 133 Asilomar Blvd. - 93950
   montereyinns.com
   21 units　　　*(800)525-3373*　　*Expensive-Very Expensive*
In a quiet pine forest an easy stroll from the ocean is a recently remodeled inn with an outdoor whirlpool and complimentary Continental breakfast. Each individualized well-furnished room has all contemporary amenities and a queen or king bed. Four rooms have both a gas fireplace and in-bath two-person whirlpool.

St. Helena

St. Helena is the heart of America's most illustrious wine-producing valley. In every direction beyond the compact town, a sea of vineyards splashes against gentle oak-covered mountains that frame the flat little valley's floor. Sequestered amid well-tended grapevines are many world famous wineries.

The village, founded in 1853, was flourishing as a farming center when grape growing and wine production began after the Civil War. Talented wine makers and ideal conditions of soil and a mild sunny climate soon established Napa Valley and St. Helena as the center of California's premium wine production.

Napa Valley is still the nation's most renowned wine-making region with more than two hundred wineries. Today, diverse landmark wineries welcome oenophiles in beautiful Victorian mansions and other historic buildings, and in distinctive contemporary complexes around town. St. Helena retains the charm of a Victorian farming village in spite of visiting hordes every weekend. The orderly business district features romantic little parks for picnics beneath noble shade trees. Many carefully restored historic buildings house a delightful array of regional specialty and gourmet shops and sophisticated restaurants. In keeping with the bucolic charm, there are no large conventional hotels or chain motels. Visitors can, however, choose from a notable concentration of stylish bed-and-breakfast inns and plush motor lodges. These adult havens of tranquility, often amidst vineyards, provide romantic bases for serious relaxation and for enjoying hiking, bicycling, ballooning and wonderful wineries.

WEATHER PROFILE

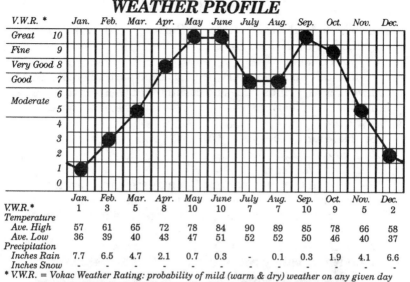

V.W.R. *		Jan.	Feb.	Mar.	Apr.	May	June	July	Aug.	Sep.	Oct.	Nov.	Dec.
Great	10												
Fine	9												
Very Good	8												
Good	7												
Moderate	6												
	5												
	4												
	3												
	2												
	1												
	0												

	Jan.	Feb.	Mar.	Apr.	May	June	July	Aug.	Sep.	Oct.	Nov.	Dec.
V.W.R.*	1	3	5	8	10	10	7	7	10	9	5	2
Temperature												
Ave. High	57	61	65	72	78	84	90	89	85	78	66	58
Ave. Low	36	39	40	43	47	51	52	52	50	46	40	37
Precipitation												
Inches Rain	7.7	6.5	4.7	2.1	0.7	0.3	-	0.1	0.3	1.9	4.1	6.6
Inches Snow	-	-	-	-	-	-	-	-	-	-	-	-

* V.W.R. = Vokac Weather Rating: probability of mild (warm & dry) weather on any given day

BASIC INFORMATION

Population: 5,950
Elevation: 256 feet
Location: 65 miles North of San Francisco
Airport (regularly scheduled flights): San Francisco - 76 miles

St. Helena Chamber of Commerce (707)963-4456 (800)799-6456
   downtown at 1010 Main St., Suite A - 94574
   sthelena.com
Napa Valley Conference & Visitors Bureau   (707)226-7459
   napavalley.com/sthelena (notable link)

ATTRACTIONS

Bale Grist Mill State Historic Park   *(707)942-4575*
3 mi. N on St. Helena Hwy.
cal-parks.ca.gov
A 36-foot-tall wooden waterwheel has been partially restored and
(on weekends) grinds flour and cornmeal at this picturesque mill
built in 1846. Nearby, shady picnic sites overlook a creek.

★ *Bicycling*
    St. Helena Cyclery   *(707)963-7736*
    downtown at 1156 Main St.
    sthelenacyclery.com
Relatively flat terrain, fine Wine Country scenery and attractions,
and usually good weather are all reasons for the enormous
popularity of bicycle touring in Napa Valley. Rentals including all
necessary gear are available by the hour and longer every day,
and they have detailed tour information and maps.

★ **Bothe-Napa Valley State Park**   *(707)942-4575*
5 mi. N on St. Helena Hwy.
Marked hiking trails pass through some of the most easterly
stands of Coast redwoods as well as a luxuriant forest of oak and
madrone. A visitor center, pool, picnic tables and creekside
campsites also contribute to this park's great popularity.

Food Specialties
Regional gourmet foods and local premium wines are superb and
abundant. Essential sources for epicureans are the following:

★   **Dean & Deluca**   *(707)967-9980*   *(877)332-6946*
1 mi. S at 607 S. St. Helena Hwy.
deandeluca.com
Wine Country's single most lavish display of regional and international epicurean foods is Dean & Deluca. A wide selection of
fine breakfast pastries and fresh seasonal fruits, plus exotic
coffees and other beverages are part of the appeal in this expansive highway-side foodie haven. They also have an outstanding
collection of wines for sale and kitchen items. This is an ideal
place to assemble all of the fixings for a memorable gourmet picnic.

★   **Napa Valley Olive Oil Mfg. Co.**   *963-4173*
just S at 835 Charter Oak
One of the valley's historic sources for gourmet provisions is
delightfully unchanged through the years. Fine cheeses, olive oil,
olives, and other gourmet-quality regional provisions are
complemented by a wealth of Italian imports in an atmospheric
old building tucked behind citrus trees and a lush picnic area.

★   **Oakville Grocery Co.**   *(707)944-8802*   *(800)736-6602*
6 mi. SE at 7856 S. St. Helena Hwy. - Oakville

oakvillegrocery.com
The Wine Country's premier purveyor of international and regional gourmet groceries is still going strong in their original little roadside location. There are no tables or chairs, but this is a great place to assemble a picnic.

Lake Berryessa Recreation Area   *(707)966-2111*
18 mi. E via Hwy. 128
Swimming, boating, fishing, picnicking and camping are enjoyed on this fifteen-mile-long reservoir in grass-covered hills.

Lyman Park
downtown on Main St.
This photogenic little tree-shaded park by the heart of town is a pleasant spot for a picnic.

Silverado Museum   *(707)963-3757*
downtown at 1490 Library Lane
One of the world's largest collections of Robert Louis Stevenson memorabilia is displayed in a "jewel box" extension of the fine St. Helena Public Library Center with its picture-window view of adjoining vineyards. The **Napa Valley Wine Library** is next door. Closed Mon.

★ *Wineries*
St. Helena is the heart of the world famous Napa Valley viticultural district. It is now surrounded by thousands of acres of premium vineyards and more than two hundred wineries. Many require an appointment. Most now charge tasting fees. Most have tours available at scheduled times or by appointment. The Chamber of Commerce has detailed guides and maps. Following are the author's favorites among distinguished premium wineries that offer tastes, tours, attractive picnic facilities and gift shops.

Beaulieu Vineyard   *(707)967-5230   (800)264-6918*
4 mi. SE at 1960 St. Helena Hwy. - Rutherford
bvwine.com
Founded in 1900 by Georges de Latour, this became one of California's grand old family wineries. It is still a landmark. A handsome woodcrafted visitor center and gift store (featuring their gourmet Winemaker's Table products) at one side of the brick winery is the beginning point for worthwhile free tours, and where selected wines may be (fee) tasted. Open 10-5 daily.

Beringer Wine Estates   *(707)963-4812   (866)244-1581*
just N at 2000 Main St.
beringer.com
Beringer is Napa Valley's oldest winery, in continuous operation since it was founded in 1876. Seventeen-room Rhine House, amid manicured lawns, is a baronial tribute to the Beringer brothers' homeland. Approached via a memorable tunnel of ancient

overarching elms, the building (on the National Historic Register) is remarkably photogenic. Inside is a well-stocked wine-related store. The gracious (fee) tasting center completes various award-winning tours of nearby cellar caves and hand-carved wine casks. Open 10-5 daily.

Cakebread Cellars   *(707)963-5221   (800)588-0298*
5 mi. SE at 8300 St. Helena Hwy. - Rutherford
cakebread.com
Cakebread is consistently among the most sophisticated producers of world class premium wines, especially cabernet sauvignon, chardonnay and sauvignon blanc. Free tours (by reservation) are offered twice daily from the handsome contemporary visitor center. (Fee) tasting 10-4 daily.

Chappellet Vineyard   *(707)963-7136   (800)494-6379*
9 mi. E at 1581 Sage Canyon Rd.
chappellet.com
A narrow paved road winds steeply through orchards and a luxuriant stand of oak to a dramatic hilltop winery. A pyramid-form building with a (fee) tasting bar overlooks stacks of French oak barrels where after a notable tour, visitors can enjoy premium cabernets and chardonnays, and oft-neglected dry chenin blanc. Open 10:30-2 Mon.-Fri. by appointment only.

Flora Springs   *(707)967-8032   (800)913-1118*
1 mi. SE at 677 S. St. Helena Hwy.
florasprings.com
This highway-front visitor center offers (fee) tastes of their regular and premium red and white wines in a pleasant tasting room and gift shop. Picnic tables on a patio and upstairs on a deck provide a view of vineyard surroundings. Open 10-5 daily.

Franciscan Oakville Estate   *(707)963-7111   (800)529-9463*
3 mi. SE (by St. Helena Hwy.) at 1178 Galleron Rd.
franciscan.com
Since 2001, Franciscan wines have been showcased in a monumental new facility that includes an island (fee) wine-tasting bar backed by a fireplace, dramatic wine-related displays, a gift shop, and a lovely sheltered courtyard. The special feature of Franciscan is (fee) "taste explorations" where (by appointment) visitors can enjoy exploring subtleties of combining different wine varieties in a hands-on demonstration hosted in intimate tasting rooms off the great hall. The garden vineyard out front showcases premium grape varietals. Open 10-5 daily.

Grgich Hills Cellars   *(707)963-2784   (800)532-3057*
4 mi. SE at 1829 St. Helena Hwy. - Rutherford
grgich.com
One of Wine Country's least affected, and best, wineries is Grgich

Hills. After more than a quarter century, legendary winemaker "Mike" Grgich's chardonnay and cabernet are still consistent benchmarks. The (fee) tasting room/gift shop provides a simply friendly counterpoint to the sophisticated wines. Open 9:30-4:30 daily.

Joseph Phelps Vineyards   *(707)963-2745   (800)707-5789*
2 mi. SE (via Silverado Trail) at 200 Taplin Rd.
jpvwines.com
Phelps is one of the longest-established (circa 1972) sources of benchmark premium wines in California. Cabernet sauvignon, chardonnay and related blends are all classics, and late harvest wines are American icons. Visitors can enjoy (fee) tasting next to a post-modern wooden building on trellis-covered redwood decks offering panoramic views of lush vineyards in the rolling hill country. Open 9-5 daily by appointment only.

Louis M. Martini Winery   *(707)963-2736   (800)321-9463*
just SE at 254 S. St. Helena Hwy.
louismartini.com
Founded in 1933, this remains a family operation all the way. The winery has a generous attitude about tasting the extensive roster of Martini wines available for free sampling (fee tasting for reserve wines). Open 10-4:30 daily.

Mumm Napa Valley   *(707)967-7730   (800)686-6272*
5 mi. SE at 8445 Silverado Trail - Rutherford
mummnapavalley.com
This French outpost of a famed champagne winery has, in a stylish contemporary complex that opened in 1990, established a major presence among America's sparkling wine producers. Premium and reserve benchmark sparklers are available for (fee) tastes in a handsome visitor center/gift shop and on a lovely deck overlooking gardens and vineyards. Their accompanying cheese crackers are also outstanding. Worthwhile tours are regularly scheduled. A gallery of Ansel Adams' photographs and a revolving collection of related art is next door. Open 10-5 daily.

Niebaum-Coppola Estate Winery *(707)968-1100 (800)575-9927*
4 mi. SE at 1991 St. Helena Hwy. - Rutherford
www.niebaum-coppola.com
The massive greystone Inglenook chateau (circa 1887) renamed by famed film director Francis Ford Coppola has been restored to its former grandeur and surrounded by colorful gardens and a fountain court. Capacious rooms house (fee) tasting of cabernet sauvignon, chardonnay and other varietals, plus a wealth of wine-related gifts. Upstairs are museum displays of Inglenook's glory days and Coppola's cinematic achievements, and there is a cozy wine bar beyond barrel storage areas. (Fee) combination tours with tasting are offered. Open 10-5 daily.

Opus One   *(707)944-9442*
5 mi. SE at 7900 St. Helena Hwy. - Oakville
opusonewinery.com
Opus One is the home of the most famous American top-premium cabernet sauvignon. Appropriately, it is showcased in a post-modern structure that has the right look and "feel" for Wine Country in the new millennium. The use of a sloping grass lawn over part of a complex finished in tasteful stone is a fine contemporary reflection of both grace and function. There is no charge for the one daily tour (by appointment). In the Opus One Partner's Room you can buy and (fee) taste. Open 9-4 daily.

Quintessa   *(707)252-1280*
5 mi. SE at 1601 Silverado Trail - Rutherford
quintessa.com
A graceful half-moon of limestone covers the facade of a dramatic winery storage complex that was dug (in 2003) into a hillside of the last large vineyard estate in the valley. A great Bordeaux-style blend of cabernet sauvignon, merlot, and cabernet franc is the goal. Combination (fee) tour and sit-down tasting by appointment only from 10-5 daily.

Robert Mondavi Winery   *(707)226-1395   (888)766-6328*
5 mi. SE at 7801 S. St. Helena Hwy. - Oakville
robertmondavi.com
Many of California's state-of-the-art advances in premium wine-making originated in this mission-style complex founded in 1966. The spacious lawn between wings of the winery is the site of acclaimed summer concerts, plus art shows and special tastings. (Fee) tasting of limited production and library wines, tours of vineyards and the winery and specialized (fee) tours, plus extensive wine/gift shop sales, are available 9-5 daily.

St. Clement Vineyards   *(707)967-3033   (800)331-8266*
1 mi. N at 2867 St. Helena Hwy. North
stclement.com
The more graceful prototype for the mansion used in the Falcon Crest television series crowns a hills in the heart of Napa Valley. The meticulously restored three-story Victorian (first used as a winery in 1878) is now a gracious hospitality center with a (fee) tasting area where estate-grown premium red and white varietals are offered. A splendid valley-view deck with picnic tables and stylish tables-for-two is surrounded by tree-shaded gardens and vineyards. Tours by appointment. Open 10-4 daily.

Sawyer Cellars   *(707)963-1980   (800)818-2252*
5 mi. SE at 8350 St. Helena Hwy. - Rutherford
sawyercellars.com
One of the valley's hidden gems is Sawyer Cellars, noted for cabernet sauvignon, merlot, and Bordeaux-style blends. The (fee)

tasting room is in a meticulously transformed 1930s barn distinguished by polished knotty-pine cedar interiors. Guided (fee) vineyard tram rides with a winery tour are an unusual, fun treat in summer and fall, and patrons can also enjoy the picturesque picnic patio. Open 10-5 daily by appointment.

Silver Oak Cellars *(707)944-8808 (800)273-8809*
7 mi. SE at 915 Oakville Crossroad - Oakville
silveroak.com

One of Wine Country's winery icons has, since 1972, been a quintessential source of cabernet sauvignon wine. In an urbane stone building surrounded by gardens and renowned vineyards, visitors can enjoy the latest world class vintage. The polished wood and stone (fee) tasting room is backed by picture-window views of barrel aging areas and a temperature-controlled bottle storage area. Tours by reservation. Open 9-4 daily except closed Sun.

Sutter Home Winery *(707)963-3104*
just SE at 277 S. St. Helena Hwy.
sutterhome.com

White zinfandel was created here during the 1970s. It remains the hallmark on a greatly expanded selection of value-oriented wines available for complimentary and reserve tastings in an expansive visitor center that also includes a large, well-stocked wine/gift store. A lovely flower and herb garden adjoins, and there is an appealing bed-and-breakfast inn next door. Open 10-5 daily.

V. Sattui Winery *(707)963-7774 (800)799-2337*
1 mi. SE (by St. Helena Hwy.) at 1111 White Lane
vsattui.com

One of the most picturesque winery complexes in California includes romantic stone buildings amid luxuriant gardens surrounded by vineyards. A wide range of premium wine (sold exclusively here) is generously offered in one of Napa Valley's very scarce free tasting rooms. The visitor center also houses the valley's best deli and gift shop. Shady picnic areas with winery/gardens/vineyards views adjoin. Open 9-5 daily.

RESTAURANTS

★ **Auberge du Soleil** *(707)963-1211*
5 mi. SE at 180 Rutherford Hill Rd. - Rutherford
aubergedusoleil.com
L-D.   *Very Expensive*

Fresh, flavorful Wine Country cuisine is given skilled attention in the resort's new-in-2003 state-of-the-art kitchen. The informally elegant dining room occupies a spectacular chateau high on a hill with panoramic views of the vineyards. Cocktails or wine are unforgettable when savored on the deck by the plush lounge.

Gillwoods Cafe   *(707)963-1788*
downtown at 1313 Main St.
B-L.   *Expensive*
Contemporary American dishes include build-your-own omelets
with biscuit or muffin, buttermilk pancakes, and skillet egg dishes
in a popular little dining room enhanced by wall art for sale.

★ **La Toque**   *(707)963-9770*
4 mi. SE at 1140 Rutherford Cross Rd. - Rutherford
latoque.com
D only. Closed Mon.-Tues.   *Very Expensive*
La Toque is the quintessential example of creative California
cuisine presented in a Wine Country setting. One of America's
best chefs, Ken Frank, dazzles gourmets and oenophiles with
dishes that maximize seasonally fresh ingredients from the best
farms and foraged sources of the region. Peerless presentations
on a prix fixe menu might feature green and white asparagus
soup, medallion of venison with spring vegetables/red wine, and
a luscious unique housemade dessert–perhaps chocolate-hazelnut
cake with crème brûlée ice cream. Fresh flowers, candles, crystal
and china grace fourteen well-separated tables in a firelit room
with an easygoing sophistication that reinforces La Toque's
growing stature as *the* Wine Country restaurant.

★ **Martini House**   *(707)963-2233*
downtown at 1245 Spring St.
martinihouse.com
L-D.   *Very Expensive*
Martini House is one of California's best restaurants. The
gourmet haven opened in 2001 under the talented guidance of
local legend Todd Humphries. The changing menu is based on
locally-sourced farm-raised meats and wild game and the freshest
seasonal fruits, vegetables and herbs, plus exotic mushrooms from
area foragers. Dishes like chanterelle soup with smoked bacon;
grilled loin of venison with braised dandelion greens; and Meyer
lemon torte with huckleberry compote are true celebrations of
Wine Country cuisine. A 1920s California Craftsman-style bungalow has casually elegant firelit dining areas overlooking an expo
kitchen, a polished staircase to the ever-popular Wine Cellar bar,
and a vine-covered fountain court.

★ **Meadowood Napa Valley**   *(707)963-3646*
2 mi. E at 900 Meadowood Lane
meadowood.com
B-L-D.   *Very Expensive*
In the resort's **Restaurant at Meadowood** (D only), dinners are
masterfully transformed from fresh and unusual seasonal
ingredients into artistic and flavorful Wine Country cuisine.

Consider watercress salad with apples, gouda, walnuts and dijon vinaigrette; seared scallops with black truffle risotto; and luscious apple cobbler with housemade ice cream for dessert. Quiet country grace distinguishes a beautiful octagonal dining room complemented by picture-window views to manicured fairways and forested hills. Downstairs, the **Meadowood Grill** serves all meals in a more casual setting, and on a tranquil terrace overlooking croquet lawns and fairways.

Miramonte Restaurant & Cafe   *(707)963-1200*
downtown at 1327 Railroad Av.
L-D. Sat. & Sun. brunch.   *Expensive*
A historic restaurant site has been reborn as an upscale Latin American dining venue. Traditional dishes and creative updates including desserts made here (like a signature tres leche cake) are served in colorful dining rooms, a cantina and a little patio.

★ **The Model Bakery**   *(707)963-9731*
downtown at 1357 Main St.
B-L. Closed Mon.   *Expensive*
A long-established St. Helena institution is still a deservedly popular source for all sorts of first-rate pastries, muffins, desserts and brick-oven breads and pizzas from organic flours. Several tables overlook the displays, and assorted drinks and light fare for lunch can also be enjoyed here or to go.

★ **Roux**   *(707)963-5330*
downtown at 1234 Main St.
restaurantroux.com
D only. Closed Sun.-Mon.   *Very Expensive*
A major newer source of Wine Country cuisine is Roux. Top-quality fresh ingredients of the season are featured in bold "adventure cuisine" like chanterelle and lobster risotto with mascarpone and tarragon, or strawberry shortbread with house-made black pepper ice cream. The dinner-dish decor somehow contributes to urbane ambiance in an intimate burgundy-colored dining room where each table is set with full linen, candle and fresh flowers.

Rutherford Grill   *(707)963-1792*
4 mi. SE (by St. Helena Hwy.) at 1180 Rutherford Rd. - Rutherford
houstons.com
L-D.   *Expensive*
Rustic and robust California Wine Country cuisine has made this roadside restaurant (part of a diverse collection) a popular stop. Hardwood-fired rotisserie chicken is a specialty among eclectic choices like bangers and mash or barbecued ribs. The casual comfortable split-level dining room affords a view of the kitchen, rotisserie and nearby winery.

★ **Taylor's Refresher**   *(707)963-3486*
   just S at 933 Main St.
   taylorsrefresher.com
   L-D.   *Moderate*
Taylor's Refresher, for over half a century, has been *the* drive-in
for Napa Valley. Third-pound burgers (try one with mushrooms,
bacon, cheddar cheese, mayo and barbecue sauce on grilled
sourdough); chicken, fish or vegie tacos and treats like chili
cheese dog, onion rings, or chicken fingers are served with a
cherry coke, designer milkshake (with white pistachio ice cream)
or assorted draft beers and wines. Picnic tables surround the
drive-in and spill onto an oak-shaded lawn.

★ **Terra**   *(707)963-8931*
   downtown at 1345 Railroad Av.
   D only. Closed Tues.   *Very Expensive*
For many years, Chef Hiro Sone has harvested accolades for his
finesse at blending Asian, Continental and American influences
into superb dishes that bring together textures and tastes that
contrast and surprise. Housemade desserts like chocolate truffle
cake with espresso ice cream are similarly appealing. Crisp white
linens and padded blondewood chairs contribute to the upscale
ambiance of two large dining rooms in a historic stone building.

★ **Tra Vigne**   *(707)963-4444*
   just S (on St. Helena Hwy.) at 1050 Charter Oak Av.
   travignerestaurant.com
   L-D.   *Expensive*
Ever-popular seasonally fresh Italian classics and gutsy California
updates are made here from scratch, including luscious desserts.
A landmark stone building houses a posh, monumental dining
room backed by striking Italian poster art, a Tuscan-inspired expo
kitchen, and a grandiose polished mahogany bar. The garden
courtyard, especially appealing on a warm day, adjoins. An
inviting **Cantinetta** (Italian wine bar/market/deli/cafe) with
more than 100 wines by the glass, plus excellent light fare and
gourmet items for a picnic, also fronts on the courtyard.

★ **Wine Spectator Greystone Restaurant**   *(707)967-1010*
   1 mi. N at 2555 Main St. (St. Helena Hwy.)
   ciachef.edu
   L-D.   *Very Expensive*
One of the world's largest stone wineries (circa 1889) now houses
the Culinary Institute of America's unique West Coast facility and
this restaurant. Organic herb, vegetable, fruit and flower gardens
surround the building. Expo kitchens are showcased in a big
romantic dining room where local seasonal ingredients become
Wine Country cuisine. Luscious breads and desserts are also

made here. Nearby, **The Spice Islands Marketplace** offers fine culinary equipment, books and gifts. **DeBaun Cafe** features breads, pastries and sweets made by students in the CIA program. Exhibits of giant antique barrels are showcased in heraldic rooms with a Medieval-castle ambiance.

LODGINGS

St. Helena has become one of the country-inn capitals of the West. The town carefully protects its distinction of having no large-scale or chain accommodations. High season rates (March through November and all weekends) are often reduced by 20% or more in winter.

★ **Adagio Inn**   *(707)963-2238*
   downtown at 1417 Kearney St. - 94574
   adagioinn.com
   3 units   *(888)823-2446*   *Very Expensive*
In a quiet neighborhood a block from the heart of town, a lovely new (in 2003) bed-and-breakfast inn occupies a historic home in a garden with a mature orange tree. A full breakfast and afternoon wine and appetizers are complimentary. Each room is beautifully, individually furnished with antiques and quality reproductions and has all contemporary amenities including a refrigerator, private bath and king bed.
   "Prelude"–private balcony with two-person whirlpool
      tub overlooking trees and hills.
   "Sonata Suite"–in-bath two-person whirlpool.

★ **Auberge du Soleil**   *(707)963-1211*
   5 mi. SE at 180 Rutherford Hill Rd. (Drawer B) - Rutherford 94573
   aubergedusoleil.com
   50 units   *(800)348-5406*   *Very Expensive*
One of the nation's most lavish adult hideaways is nestled in an olive grove on a hillside overlooking Napa Valley's lush vineyards. Scenic trails wind among the estate's olive groves and large-scale sculptures. Two tennis courts; a large pool; whirlpool; a refined (fee) fitness and beauty center offering a wealth of facial and body treatments for individuals and couples, plus a sauna and infinity view-pool; a renowned restaurant (see listing); resort shop; and low-rise villas are features. Each spacious, luxuriously furnished room and suite has a wet bar/refrigerator, complimentary wine and cheese and basket of snacks, skylit tub (many with whirlpool jets), a fireplace with pressed-wood logs, private patio or balcony (many with valley views), and a king bed.
   "Auberge King" (11 of these)–pressed-wood fireplace,
      big in-bath whirlpool, private view terrace.

217

St. Helena

El Bonita Motel *(707)963-3216*
1 mi. SE at 195 Main St. (St. Helena Hwy.) - 94574
elbonita.com
43 units *(800)541-3284* *Expensive-Very Expensive*
A landscaped pool, whirlpool, and sauna are attractions of this
contemporary single-level motel surrounded by gardens. All
attractively furnished rooms have a refrigerator and microwave
and two doubles, a queen or king bed.
"Spa Room" (5 of these)–large in-bath whirlpool, king bed.
★ **Forest Manor Bed & Breakfast** *(707)965-3538*
8 mi. N at 415 Cold Springs Rd. - Angwin 94508
forestmanor.com
6 units *(800)788-0364* *Very Expensive*
A Tudor-style home in a forest above Napa Valley serves as a bed-
and-breakfast with a large pool and whirlpool. Full gourmet
breakfast, afternoon refreshments, and Friday and Saturday
cheese and wine tasting are complimentary. Each well-furnished
room has some antiques and a refrigerator (stocked with complimentary sodas and water), private bath, and queen or king bed.
"William Shakespeare"–very spacious, big
    woodburning fireplace, two-person whirlpool
    on private deck with forest view, king bed.
"Ernest Hemingway"–large, romantic forest-view
    nook, woodburning iron stove, in-bath two-person
    whirlpool and double-head shower, king bed.
★ **Harvest Inn** *(707)963-9463*
1 mi. S at 1 Main St. (St. Helena Hwy.) - 94574
harvestinn.com
54 units *(800)950-8466* *Very Expensive*
Situated in a working vineyard is a fantasy motor inn for adults.
Amid carefully tended gardens with two large pools and
whirlpools are imposing, brick Tudor-style buildings. Expanded
Continental breakfast (delivered to the room by request), use of
mountain bikes, and Fri.-Sat. wine tastings are complimentary.
In-room (fee) spa treatments and massage are available. Each
spacious room is beautifully appointed with antiques and quality
reproductions, contemporary and extra amenities, and two
doubles, a queen or king bed.
#30 "Knight of Nights"–grandiose suite, grand
    curved staircase, wet bar, in-room two-person
    whirlpool, two woodburning fireplaces, private
    balcony with vineyard view, king bed.
#32 "Lord of the Manor"–grandiose suite, wet bar,
    in-room whirlpool, two woodburning fireplaces,
    private balcony, vineyard views, king bed.

Hotel St. Helena   *(707)963-4388*
downtown at 1309 Main St. - 94574
hotelsthelena.com
18 units   *(888)478-4355*   *Expensive*
This historic 1881 hotel has been completely refurbished. A
European light breakfast is complimentary. Each lushly carpeted,
comfortably furnished room has Victorian accents, most contemporary conveniences, and a queen or king bed. Four rooms have
a shared bath.

The Ink House   *(707)963-3890*
4 mi. SE at 1575 St. Helena Hwy. (at Whitehall Lane) - 94574
inkhouse.com
7 units   *Expensive-Very Expensive*
Ink House is one of the most prominent historic landmarks along
the St. Helena Highway. The Italianate mansion (circa 1884) is
surrounded by mature gardens with a fountain backed by
vineyards. Full gourmet breakfast, afternoon appetizers and wine
and evening brandy, and mineral water are complimentary. The
cupola on top of the building provides unforgettable views of Wine
Country. A game room including a full-sized pool table, and use
of bicycles are also complimentary. All but two of the cozy rooms
have a private bath and are well furnished with quality antiques
and reproductions that convey the feeling of a Victorian home;
live greenery; and a double or queen bed.
"Turino," "French Room"–fine vineyard views, queen bed.

The Inn at Southbridge   *(707)967-9400*
just SE at 1020 Main St. (St. Helena Hwy.) - 94574
innatsouthbridge.com
21 units   *(800)520-6800*   *Very Expensive*
This conference-oriented small hotel opened in 1997 a short stroll
from downtown. A pleasant restaurant with a Mediterranean
menu and ambiance is on the ground floor. Use of the on-site day
spa's pool, whirlpool, steam room and fitness center, plus a
Continental breakfast buffet, are complimentary. Each spacious,
attractively furnished room has a woodburning fireplace, a tiny
private balcony and a king bed.

★ **Meadowood Napa Valley**   *(707)963-3646*
2 mi. E at 900 Meadowood Lane - 94574
meadowood.com
85 units   *(800)458-8080*   *Very Expensive*
In this magnificent adult retreat, two large pools, a whirlpool, and
hiking trails throughout the resort and into the surrounding
wooded hillsides are available to guests. In addition, there are (for
a fee) seven championship tennis courts; a scenic 9-hole executive
golf course; two professional croquet courts; a complete health

and fitness spa with a wide range of treatments and refined facilities; bicycle rentals; a world class wine center; plus a gift boutique. A renowned classic Wine Country restaurant (see listing) overlooks the golf course and majestic oaks in a secluded canyon. Each unit (up to four bedrooms) is spacious and elegant with every contemporary convenience including an (honor) wet bar/refrigerator, and either a queen or king bed. Most have a woodburning fireplace, and/or a private deck with a peaceful view.

"Hillside Terrace" (16 of these)–extra-large,
romantic, soaking tub, forest-view private deck,
woodburning fireplace in view of king bed.

★ **Rancho Caymus Inn**   *(707)963-1777*
4 mi. SE at 1140 Rutherford Rd. (Box 78) - Rutherford 94573
ranchocaymus.com
26 units   *(800)845-1777*   *Very Expensive*
Rancho Caymus is one of Wine Country's most picturesque fantasy lodgings for adults. The romantic Colonial-California-style hacienda encircles a private garden court. Acclaimed chef Ken Frank's La Toque (see listing) is on site. Expanded Continental breakfast is complimentary. Each artistically decorated unit has an (honor) wet bar/refrigerator and all contemporary amenities, plus an outside sitting area and queen or king bed.

"Master Suites" (4 of these)–spacious, split-level,
in-bath two-person whirlpool with stained-glass
window, kiva woodburning fireplace, private patio
or balcony, microwave, king bed.

Sunny Acres Bed & Breakfast   *(707)963-5105*
1 mi. SE at 397 Main St. - 94574
sunnyacresbandb.com
3 units   *Expensive*
An 1879 Victorian farmhouse is now an appealing bed-and-breakfast surrounded by colorful gardens and lush vineyards. The property also includes **Salvestrin Estate Vineyard and Winery** (tours and tasting by appointment). A full country breakfast is complimentary. Each attractively furnished room has a fine vineyard view, a private bath, some antiques, and a queen bed.

Vineyard Country Inn   *(707)963-1000*
just SE at 201 Main St. (St. Helena Hwy.) - 94574
www.vineyardcountryinn.com
21 units   *Expansive-Very Expensive*
French country decor, plus a pool and whirlpool, enhance this all-suites bed-and-breakfast inn. Continental buffet breakfast is complimentary. Each spacious, beautifully furnished suite has a wet bar/refrigerator and sitting area by a woodburning fireplace, and two queens or a king bed. Most have a private deck.

St. Helena

White Sulphur Springs Inn & Spa   *(707)963-8588*
2 mi. W at 3100 White Sulphur Springs Rd. - 94574
24 units   (800)593-8873   Moderate-Very Expensive
A natural hot springs and clear creek are the centerpieces of this
historic inn (circa 1852) in a luxuriant forest. A mineral water
soaking pool by a gentle waterfall, a pool, and a spa with various
(fee) treatments are amenities. Cottages and inn rooms each have
a private bath and two twins, queen or king bed. In addition,
"The Carriage House" has fourteen small plain rooms with a
shared bath.

★ **The Wine Country Inn**   *(707)963-7077*
2 mi. N (off St. Helena Hwy.) at 1152 Lodi Lane - 94574
winecountryinn.com
26 units   (888)465-4608   Very Expensive
Hidden away on a knoll above vineyards is a charming bed-and-
breakfast motor inn with a pool and whirlpool. Full buffet
breakfast and afternoon wine and appetizers are complimentary.
Individually decorated rooms have good vineyard views, a blend
of antique furnishings and contemporary amenities, a private
bath and a queen or king bed. Many of the spacious, attractively
decorated units have a woodburning fireplace and/or a private
deck, and/or a whirlpool tub.

    #24–large, sitting area, woodburning fireplace, private
    balcony with panoramic vineyard view, in-bath large
    whirlpool with a view, canopy queen bed.
    #28–large, sitting area, woodburning fireplace, private
    mountain-view deck, in-bath two-person whirlpool, king bed.

★ **Zinfandel Inn**   *(707)963-3512*
3 mi. SE at 800 Zinfandel Lane - 94574
zinfandelinn.com
3 units   Expensive-Very Expensive
A large contemporary English Tudor home now serves as a
delightfully plush bed-and-breakfast. A pool, fish pond, fountains,
waterfall and gazebo enhance two acres of colorful gardens. Full
breakfast is complimentary. So are champagne or wine and
truffles upon arrival. Each spacious room is beautifully individually furnished, and has all contemporary conveniences, extra
amenities, and a queen or king bed.

    "Zinfandel Suite"–extra-large, romantic, private balcony
    over garden, octagon window, two-person whirlpool with
    stained glass, big dual-head shower, (glass-fronted)
    woodburning stove, four-poster king bed.
    "Chardonnay Room"–private garden-view patio, massive
    stone fireplace, in-bath two-person whirlpool, king bed.

Sonoma

Sonoma is the treasury of Northern California history. For more than 170 years, the heart of town has been a large plaza surrounded by distinctive 19th century buildings. Beyond, the "Valley of the Moon" extends to gentle grass-and-oak-covered hills north of San Francisco Bay. All around are luxuriant vineyards and some of America's most famous wineries.

Sonoma was founded in 1823 by Spanish Franciscan fathers as the twenty-first of their El Camino Real chain of California missions. It became "the birthplace of California viticulture" a decade later with General Vallejo, the first major non-missionary grower. During the Civil War, Sonoma again made history when America's first big experimental vineyard was established by Count Haraszthy, a Hungarian nobleman at Buena Vista.

The wine industry remains the key to Sonoma's prosperity. Vineyards dating from momentous early times endure as charming reminders of a rich heritage that now include more than thirty premium wineries in the valley. Downtown, the spacious plaza still delights strollers and picnickers, and continues as the site of California's oldest wine celebration. Treasured buildings on all sides house uncommon specialty shops, gourmet food stores and restaurants, and atmospheric bars and lounges. Beyond, the normally sunny temperate climate beckons visitors into the "Valley of the Moon" for winery touring, bicycling, picnics and hiking in the hills. Most of the area's best lodgings are romantic small hotels and inns in skillfully transformed historic structures on or near the plaza.

WEATHER PROFILE

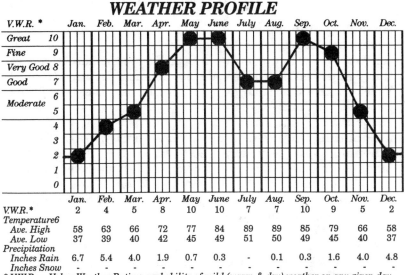

V.W.R. *		Jan.	Feb.	Mar.	Apr.	May	June	July	Aug.	Sep.	Oct.	Nov.	Dec.
Great	10												
Fine	9												
Very Good	8												
Good	7												
Moderate	6												
	5												
	4												
	3												
	2												
	1												
	0												

	Jan.	Feb.	Mar.	Apr.	May	June	July	Aug.	Sep.	Oct.	Nov.	Dec.
V.W.R.*	2	4	5	8	10	10	7	7	10	9	5	2
Temperature6												
Ave. High	58	63	66	72	77	84	89	89	85	79	66	58
Ave. Low	37	39	40	42	45	49	51	50	49	45	40	37
Precipitation												
Inches Rain	6.7	5.4	4.0	1.9	0.7	0.3	-	0.1	0.3	1.6	4.0	4.8
Inches Snow	-	-	-	-	-	-	-	-	-	-	-	-

* V.W.R. = Vokac Weather Rating: probability of mild (warm & dry) weather on any given day

BASIC INFORMATION

Population: *9,128*
Elevation: *81 feet*
Location: *50 miles Northeast of San Francisco*
Airport (regularly scheduled flights): *San Francisco - 60 miles*

Sonoma Valley Visitors Bureau (707)996-1090   (800)576-6662
   on the plaza at 453 First St. East - 95476
   www.sonomavalley.com
Second Visitor Center   7 mi. SW on Hwy. 121

ATTRACTIONS

Bear Flag Monument
downtown at NE corner of plaza
A heroic bronze figure holding a Bear Flag marks the site where thirty American horsemen rode into Sonoma, captured General Vallejo without a struggle, and proclaimed the "California Republic" on June 14, 1846.

★ *Bicycling*
Goodtime Bicycle Co. *18503 Sonoma Hwy. (707)938-0453*
Sonoma Valley Cyclery *20093 Broadway (707)935-3377*
Miles of separated bikeways supplement well-marked highways and byways in the gentle Valley of the Moon. Mountain bikes, tandems, even electric bikes may be rented by the hour or day to tour the pastoral countryside.

Blue Wing Inn
downtown just off NE corner of plaza at 131 Spain St. East
Built in 1840 by General Vallejo for travelers, this structure is probably Sonoma's oldest original building. Its ancient register includes famous names like John C. Fremont, U.S. Grant, and Kit Carson. The whole building is in a state of atmospheric disrepair.

Food Specialties
Gourmet and specialty foods are produced in abundance in Sonoma. Several places offer samples. The best are:

★ **Sonoma Cheese Factory** *(707) 996-1931 (800)535-2855*
downtown at 2 W. Spain St.
sonomajack.com
Sonoma Cheese Factory (established in 1931) is a nationally famous maker of Sonoma jack brand cheeses. At their large store on the plaza, view cheese-making, enjoy samples of their assorted cheese styles, and browse a large selection of cheese and related specialties. There is also a full deli/barbecue and picnic area. Open 8:30 to 5:30 Mon.-Fri.; 8:30 to 6 Sat.- Sun.

★ **Sonoma Market** *(707)996-3411*
just W at 500 W. Napa St.
sonoma-glenellenmkt.com
Sonoma Market is Wine Country's fair-price supersource for the full range of gourmet food and wine products produced in the region. Here is a cornucopia of cheese varieties, premium meats, exotic condiments; artisan breads; an enormous salad bar and deli case selections; a gourmet four-style chowder bar; and a fine array of world class olives. The store also features remarkably diverse assortments of coffees, teas, wines (of course), and other beverages. In addition, there are many regional health-related products like lavender aromatherapy body lotion, a cutting-edge treat from a locally abundant herb.

★ **Sonoma Sausage**   *(707)938-1215*
downtown on E side of plaza at 414 First St. East
sonomasausage.com
After a seven-year hiatus, the Sonoma Sausage Company is back
in a tucked-away courtyard by the plaza. Nearly a dozen delicious
kinds of housemade sausage are on display to go, or to be grilled
up and served on a stick or in a fresh bun with appropriate
condiments to go. Their weisswurst is especially delicious, an
unusual treat worth going out of the way for. Open 11-5 daily.

★ **Vella Cheese Company**   *(707)938-3232*   *(800)848-0505*
just E at 315 Second St. East
vellacheese.com
For more than seventy years, Vella has been acclaimed for their
aged dry Monterey jack cheese, plus flavored jack cheeses.
Samples are available in the small retail shop on request, as are
tours. Open 9-6. Closed Sun.

★ **The Wine Exchange of Sonoma** *(707)938-0969 (800)938-1794*
downtown on E side of plaza at 452 First St. East
wineexsonoma.com
Here is Sonoma County's largest selection of Wine Country's
premium red and white wines. More than 250 brands of bottled
beers also share well-organized display cases. A backroom (fee)
bar features tastes of a top-notch assortment of premium wines,
draft and bottled beers. Open 10-6 Mon.-Sat., 11-6 Sun.

Golf
Sonoma Mission Inn Golf & Country Club   *(707)996-4852*
3 mi. NW at 17700 Arnold Dr.
This attractive 18-hole championship course in the Valley of the
Moon is open to the public year-round. Facilities include club and
cart rentals, plus a clubhouse, driving range, and restaurant.

Horseback Riding
Sonoma Cattle Co.   *(707)996-8566*
Guided trail rides in Jack London State Park and Sugarloaf Ridge
State Park can be arranged.

★ **Jack London State Historic Park**   *(707)938-5216*
9 mi. NW (via Hwy. 12) at 2400 London Ranch Rd. - Glen Ellen
parks.sonoma.net/jlpark
The park is part of the famed author's "Beauty Ranch" where he
resided from 1905 until his death in 1916. The "House of Happy
Walls," a large fieldstone structure built in 1919 by his widow, has
an excellent collection of his memorabilia, and is the park
interpretive center. There is also a well-stocked park store. A
short walk leads to the grave site of Charmain and Jack London.
A half-mile trail through a dense mixed forest ends at stone walls
that are the grim ruins of "Wolf House," destroyed by fire shortly

before the Londons could move in. Trails beyond the "Beauty Ranch" extend to London's lake and bathhouse, and beyond to the top of Sonoma Mountain.

★ **Sonoma State Historic Park**   *(707)938-1519*
downtown on N side of plaza
A number of major historic structures have been restored downtown. The Mission San Francisco Solano de Sonoma, the last (1823) of twenty-one started by Father Junipero Serra, is a long adobe structure housing many historic relics. The restored Sonoma Barracks (1836) housed General Vallejo's troops when he was California's last Mexican governor.

Spring Lake Regional Park   *(707)539-8092*
17 mi. NW (via Hwy. 12) at 5390 Montgomery Dr.
A small reservoir in a lovely rural setting has become a popular water (fee) recreation facility. Tree-shaded grounds include a warm spring-fed swimming lagoon (open in summer) with a sandy beach, concession stand and lifeguards. The adjoining lake has boating (electric only), canoe and paddleboat rentals, fishing, hiking, bicycle paths, and a campground.

★ **Vallejo Home ("Lachryma Montis")**   *(707)938-1578*
1 mi. NW on 3rd St. West
This stately Carpenter Gothic home of General Mariano Vallejo was built in 1852. "Lachryma Montis," as it was called; the adjoining Swiss chalet; and several outbuildings are now state-owned museums housing his mementos. Carefully maintained grounds reflect Vallejo's fascination with horticulture. A giant old pomelo tree in front of the chalet is especially spectacular early in the year when the huge grapefruit-like fruit is ripe. Open 10-5 daily.

Warm Water Features
Morton's Sonoma Springs Resort   *(707)833-5511*
11 mi. NW at 1651 Warm Springs Rd. - Kenwood
Two mineral springs pools are the centerpieces of a historic facility that includes picnic tables under shade trees along a gently winding creek; recreation fields; a cafe; and a shop.

★ *Wineries*
Sonoma is the birthplace of America's premium wine industry. Grapes for sacramental purposes were first grown here in 1823. Soon, secular wines were also being produced. After the Civil War, Sonoma became the state's largest wine producer. It is still one of America's most illustrious producers of world class wine. Most of the delightfully individualized facilities have gift shops and attractive picnic areas. Many offer tours (often by appointment only). Best of all (unlike Napa Valley), many still feature free tasting! For detailed information and a map of all wineries, contact the Visitors Bureau on the plaza.

Arrowood Vineyards & Winery   *(707)938-5170 (800)938-5170*
6 mi. NW at 14347 Sonoma Hwy. (Hwy. 12) - Glen Ellen
arrowoodvineyards.com
One of Wine Country's legendary producers presides over a
handsome complex on a hill surrounded by vineyards. The tasting
room/gift shop offers (fee) tastes of super-premium varietals and
a grand view of surrounding vineyards. Open 10-4:30 daily.

Bartholomew Park   *(707)935-9511*
1 mi. E at 1000 Vineyard Lane
bartholomewparkwinery.com
Historic winery buildings surrounded by vineyards crown a hill
adjacent to secluded oak-shaded picnic tables. The complex
includes a warm and friendly (fee) tasting room and gift shop and
a well-done small wine-related museum. Open 10-4:30 daily.

Benziger Family Winery   *(707)935-4046   (800)989-8890*
9 mi. NW at 1883 London Ranch Rd. - Glen Ellen
benziger.com
Two redwood fairy rings encircling picnic tables tower over this
outstanding family-owned winery estate. All premium whites and
reds are generously poured in a large tasting room and gift shop.
Educational/entertaining 45-minute tractor tram tours are also
well worthwhile, as are self-guided hikes to descriptive displays in
gardens and surrounding vineyards. Open 10-4:30 daily.

Buena Vista Winery   *(707)938-1266   (800)325-2764*
1 mi. E at 18000 Old Winery Rd.
buenavistawinery.com
Founded in 1857 by Count Agoston Haraszthy, this was once the
largest winery in the world. The oldest winery in the valley is a
state historic landmark. An expansive stone-walled chamber
includes a (fee) tasting bar, wine and gift shop, and upstairs art
gallery. The 1857 cellar dug into the hillside once served as California's first champagne cave. Sadly, it can now only be viewed
from outside. Picnic grounds in front of the ivy-covered old stone
building are set amidst ancient eucalyptus by a creek. Open 10-5
daily. There is also a (fee) tasting room on the plaza downtown.

Chateau St. Jean   *(707)833-4134   (800)543-7572*
11 mi. NW at 8555 Sonoma Hwy. (Hwy. 12) - Kenwood
chateaustjean.com
Visitors are free to enjoy informative self-guided tours of the
impressive wine production and storage complex in this long-
established major premier producer. Nearby, a splendid old
Mediterranean-style chateau includes a gracious visitor center
with a retail shop, charcuterie, and wood-paneled room where
selected tastes are offered. Attractively landscaped grounds also
feature romantic, shady picnic areas. Open 10-5 daily.

Gloria Ferrer Champagne Caves   *(707)996-7256*
5 mi. SW at 23555 Carneros Hwy.
www.gloriaferrer.com
High on a hill near the southern end of the Valley of the Moon is one of America's great sparkling wine producers. Several (fee) kinds of methode champenoise sparklers are served with a palate pleaser at tables in a handsome tasting area indoors and on a deck with tables and chairs overlooking the valley. Tours 11-4 daily. Open 10:30 to 5:30 daily.

Gundlach-Bundschu Winery   *(707)939-3015*
3 mi. E at 2000 Denmark St. - Vineburg
www.gunbun.com
"Gunbun" is managed by the sixth generation in this family estate dating from 1862. The tasting room/gift shop/bottling plant is in a building surrounded by picturesque vineyards with well-located picnic areas and a Shakespearean festival amphitheater. Nearby, an impressive cave is used for aging premium wines including a notable gewürztraminer. Open 11-4:30 daily.

Imagery Estate Winery   *(707)935-4515*   *(877)550-4278*
6 mi. NW at 14335 Hwy. 12 - Glen Ellen
imagerywinery.com
An "Appellation Trail" provides a whimsically appealing introduction to this young winery. The complex includes a big modish (fee) tasting room for sampling diverse premium varietals. Numerous surrounding alcoves feature regional artwork and the world's largest wine label art collection. The large shop is a good source for wine, art, and regional gifts. Umbrella-shaded picnic tables overlook colorful gardens. Open 10-4:30 daily.

Keller Estate   *(707)765-2117*
10 mi. SE at 5875 Lakeville Hwy.
kellerestate.com
Excellent chardonnay and pinot noir distinguish this winery. Both are served in Riedel goblets in a sophisticated stone-and-wood-trimmed tasting room adjoining extensive hand-wrought storage caves. A new state-of-the-art winery will open in late 2003. Open 10-4:30 daily by appointment only.

Kenwood Vineyards   *(707)833-5891*
10 mi. NW at 9592 Sonoma Hwy. (Hwy. 12) - Kenwood
kenwoodvineyards.com
A rustic redwood building with stained-glass windows and a ceiling of grape stakes is used to house a congenial tasting room and gift shop. Up to four tastes of all varietals are generously offered. This outstanding winery has been notably successful in developing benchmarks of reasonably priced, premium quality wines. Open 10-4:30 daily.

Kunde Estate Winery & Vineyards   *(707)833-5501*
10 mi. NW at 10155 Sonoma Hwy. (Hwy. 12) - Kenwood
www.kunde.com
In a dramatic contemporary building surrounded by young vineyards and a water garden, generous tastings of premium wines and quality gift displays are coupled with picture-window vineyard and garden views. Notable tours feature a photogenic demonstration vineyard and wine cave labyrinth including a subterranean dining/party area. Open 10:30-4:30 daily.

Landmark Vineyards   *(707)833-0053   (800)452-6365*
12 mi. N at 101 Adobe Canyon - Kenwood
landmarkwine.com
This young premium winery is surrounded by lush vineyards near the base of forested mountains. An imposing mission-style facility includes a pleasant tasting room/gift shop with a fireplace and vineyard views where featured premium chardonnay and pinot noirs are generously offered. Scenic picnic sites are available. Open 10-4:30 daily.

Ledson Winery & Vineyards   *(707)537-3810*
13 mi. NW at 7335 Sonoma Hwy. (Hwy. 12) - Kenwood
ledson.com
One of the valley's newer premium wineries is at the north end of the storied producing district. For a superb introduction to Sonoma Valley wines, make time for a (fee) tasting of premium varietals in "the castle," the spectacular manor house (complete with the *Gone With the Wind* staircase) ensconced among vineyards. In the adjoining large world market/gift shop you can enjoy free samples of gourmet treats. Picnic areas under noble oaks; by vineyards; or alongside a fountain also convey the essence a California answer to Provence. Open 10-5 daily.

Matanzas Creek Winery   *(707)590-6464   (800)590-6464*
15 mi. NW at 6097 Bennett Valley Rd. - Santa Rosa
matanzascreek.com
One of Wine Country's most delightful destinations is Matanzas Creek Winery. Sequestered amid vineyards at the base of a mountain is a graceful contemporary complex with an expansive deck overlooking colorful gardens and noble oaks. Thousands of lavender plants imported from Provence and other prime growing areas of Europe fill terraces below the visitor center. Premium estate-grown merlot, cabernet sauvignon, sauvignon blanc and chardonnay are poured at the (fee) tasting bar. The adjoining meticulously well-organized store is a lavender lover's delight filled with all kinds of fresh dried lavender flower and seed products and oils and related lavender and wine gift items. Beyond are museum-quality displays related to first-rate tours of the winery. Open 10-4:30 daily.

Ravenswood   *(707)938-1960*
1 mi. E at 18701 Gehricke Rd.
ravenswood-wine.com
Notable zinfandel, merlot and cabernet sauvignon are available for (fee) tastes in a handsome stone tasting center and gift shop with picture-window views of vineyards. Open 10-4:30 daily.

St. Francis Winery & Vineyards *(707)833-466 (800)543-7713*
13 mi. NW (just off Hwy. 12) at 100 Pythian Rd. - Santa Rosa
stfranciswine.com
St. Francis is earning a reputation for reasonably priced premium wines, as well as a source for reserve varietals. An evocative Spanish-Colonial-style visitor center houses the (fee) tasting room and gift shop with a fireplace and vineyard views. Picnic tables are on an adjoining scenic patio. Open 10-5 daily.

Schug Carneros Estate Winery *(707)939-9363 (800)966-9365*
5 mi. S (just off Hwy. 121) at 602 Bonneau Rd.
schugwinery.com
Schug is a premium family-owned winery that features premium pinot noirs and chardonnays. In the pleasant tasting room/shop, regular wines are generously poured. (Fee) reserves can also be enjoyed. Picnic tables adjoin. Open 10-5 daily.

Sebastiani Vineyards & Winery *(707)938-5532 (800)888-5532*
just E at 389 4th St. East
sebastiani.com
Sebastiani is the largest winery in Sonoma Valley. Dating from 1904, this historic landmark is still a family operation. Numerous varietals with an increasing focus on quality are produced. In addition to a couple of free tastes, there are several levels of (fee) tasting flights. The expansive complex also includes a museum. A fascinating collection of carved casks is a highlight of historical tours. Open 10-5 daily. There is also an attractive (fee) tasting room/gift shop on the plaza at 40 W. Spain St.

Valley of the Moon   *(707)996-6941*
5 mi. NW (just off Hwy. 12) at 777 Madrone Rd. - Glen Ellen
vomwinery.com
One of the Wine Country's most appealing wine tasting/gift shops is a delightful destination for sampling premium red and white wines and a fine sparkler made here. Vines and flowers in abundance surround buildings that contribute to the charm of the Valley of the Moon. Open 10-4:30 daily.

Viansa Winery & Italian Marketplace *(707)935-4700 (800)995-4740*
7 mi. SW (on Hwy. 121) at 25200 Arnold Dr.
viansa.com
Viansa provides a superb introduction to Sonoma Valley Wine Country. The hike to the visitor center atop a knoll is well worth

it. Free premium-quality wine tastes are generously offered (fee for reserves) and there is an elaborate adjoining gourmet food market (with free samples) and a gift shop. Panoramic views of a waterfowl preserve and the Valley of the Moon, Tuscan-style architecture, fresco-style hand-painted murals and related objects of art, and scenic picnic grounds also appeal. Open 10-5 daily.

RESTAURANTS

Artisan Bakers   *(707)939-1765*
1 mi. W at 750 W. Napa St.
B-L.   *Moderate*
This casual storefront bakery, winner of a prestigious international artisan baking competition, appeals to locals and visitors with assorted breakfast pastries and distinctive breads to go.

★ **Basque Boulangerie Cafe**   *(707)935-7687*
downtown on E side of plaza at 460 First St. East
B-L.   *Moderate*
All sorts of baked breakfast treats can be enjoyed with a cup of coffee or a wealth of other beverages in the cozy, ever-popular cafe or to go. Breads, especially the classic Sonoma sourdough, are some of the best anywhere. Soups, sandwiches and salads are fine accompaniments. Don't miss the wealth of desserts like an ambrosial "beehive cake" (sponge cake, custard, caramel, and honey-almond praline in a five-inch-high confection) or mini-chocolate truffle gateau, or pecan sandies.

Breakaway Cafe   *(707)996-5949*
1 mi. NW at 19101 Sonoma Hwy.
breakawaycafe.com
B-L-D.   *Expensive*
Contemporary California cafe fare stars in updated comfort foods like homemade corned beef hash, or Joe's special for breakfast. Hearty lunches can be topped off with a milkshake with seasonal fresh fruit. There is also a bar by the big cheerful room with padded booths, live greenery and flowers, and colorful murals.

★ **Cafe La Haye**   *(707)935-5994*
downtown just E of plaza at 140 E. Napa St.
cafelahaye.com
D only. Sun. brunch. Closed Mon.   *Expensive*
In one of Sonoma Valley's best gourmet havens, each dish reflects fresh seasonal ingredients given expert attention. Results are always creative and boldly flavorful. Consider seared black-pepper-lavender fillet of beef with gorgonzola-potato gratin. The cozy split-level dining room surrounded by flamboyant wall hangings has an intimate view of the expo kitchen.

The Coffee Garden   *(707)996-6645*
downtown on W side of plaza at 421 First St. West
B-L-D.   *Moderate*
Assorted beverages with light fare are available to go, at tables
overlooking the plaza, or in a lush historic garden out back.

★ **Cucina Viansa**   *(707)935-5656*
downtown on NE corner of plaza at 400 First St. East
cucinaviansa.com
L-D.   *Moderate*
Cucina Viansa is a Wine Country showcase for Italian-inspired
California cuisine like braised artichoke hearts, designer panini
sandwiches, rotisserie chicken, calzones, and desserts like tiramisu
and luscious gelatos. There is also an appealing wine bar with
Viansa premium wines by the taste or glass backed by cheerful,
wood-trimmed dining areas. Or, put together a memorable picnic
from the market's gourmet products.

★ **Della Santina's**   *(707)935-0576*
downtown just E of plaza at 133 E. Napa St.
L-D.   *Expensive*
Traditional and contemporary Italian cuisine includes first-rate
handmade pasta dishes and sauces, and rotisserie meats like spit-
roasted Petaluma duck or rabbit. A well-thought-out menu also
features desserts like tiramisu made here. The spiffy little firelit
trattoria adjoins an umbrella-shaded garden court.

★ **Depot Hotel Restaurant & Garden**   *(707)938-2980*
downtown just N of plaza at 241 First St. West
depothotel.com
L-D. No L Sat. & Sun. Closed Mon.-Tues.   *Expensive*
Northern Italian cuisine is prepared from scratch with fresh
regional ingredients for dishes like center-cut medallions of filet
mignon sautéed with fresh mushrooms in a red wine reduction.
So are the luscious desserts. A historic (1870) stone building
provides intimate dining rooms. Better yet, get a romantic
candlelit table by the pool in a garden court.

★ **The Fairmont Sonoma Mission Inn & Spa**   *(707)939-2410*
3 mi. NW at 18140 Sonoma Hwy. (Hwy. 12)
fairmont.com
B-L-D.   *Expensive-Very Expensive*
The resort's main dining room is **Santé Restaurant** (B-D–Very
Expensive) where the region's quality seasonal ingredients
become flavorful New California cuisine served amid informal
elegance and on a poolside terrace. **The Big 3 Diner** (B-L-
D–Expensive) offers country breakfasts and, later, designer pizzas
and smoked meats in a cheerful bistro setting next to the resort's
specialty boutique.

Garden Court Cafe & Bakery   *(707)935-1565*
6 mi. NW at 13875 Sonoma Hwy. (Hwy. 12) - Glen Ellen
gardencourtcafe.com
B-L.   *Expensive*
Omelets, scrambles, benedicts, and more are prepared from
scratch in the cheerful little roadside cafe/bakery. Coffee cake and
scones are among homemade specialties.

★ **The General's Daughter**   *(707)938-4004*
just W at 400 W. Spain St.
thegeneralsdaughter.com
L-D.   *Expensive*
Seasonally fresh local produce is featured in gourmet
Mediterranean and Southwestern cuisine like crisp buttermilk
and cornmeal onion rings with pepper-blue cheese aioli, or grilled
double-cut pork chops with apple-mango chutney and Madeira
glaze. Casually elegant dining rooms fill a large, meticulously
restored Victorian home. A garden-view dining porch adjoins.

★ **The Girl & the Fig**   *(707)938-3634*
downtown on NW corner of plaza at 110 W. Spain St.
thegirlandthefig.com
L-D.   *Expensive*
The Girl & the Fig is one of Sonoma's most delightful dining
experiences. The cuisine is an appealing adaptation of French
country dishes with robust flavors and hearty portions that reflect
the freshest seasonal produce from the region. Superb local duck,
wild salmon, or halibut cheeks pan-seared with lemon and herb
(when available) are especially notable. Comfortable colorful
dining rooms by the historic Sonoma Hotel's ever-popular bar
room, and the luxuriant patio with a fountain and sculpture out
back, provide a fine backdrop.

★ **The Girl & the Gaucho**   *(707)938-2130*
8 mi. NW at 13690 Arnold Dr. - Glen Ellen
thegirlandthegaucho.com
D only.   *Expensive*
A classic paella with clams, mussels, shrimp, braised rabbit, and
roasted chicken chorizo stars along with traditional and creative
Latin American and Spanish style dishes in a dining room
enhanced by candles and full linens and an expo kitchen.

★ **Glen Ellen Inn Restaurant**   *(707)996-6409*
8 mi. NW at 13670 Arnold Dr. - Glen Ellen
glenelleninn.com
L-D. No L Wed.-Thurs.   *Expensive*
Innovative California cuisine is presented in delightfully
adventurous dishes like a wild mushroom and sausage pastry
purse with a brandy mushroom cream sauce, and decadent

housemade desserts like frozen lemon bavarian in a cage of chocolate. The cottage's romantic little dining rooms and covered patio near a pond in an organic herb garden nicely balance the sophisticated cuisine. Romantic creekside cabins, some with a fireplace and whirlpool tub for two, were recently added nearby.

La Casa Restaurant & Bar   *(707)996-3406*
downtown just E of plaza at 121 E. Spain St.
lacasarestaurant.com
L-D. Closed Tues.   *Moderate*
La Casa has been a popular destination for Mexican food since 1967. Seafood dishes are a highlight, along with traditional and updated Mexican/California specialties. Several colorful dining rooms and a fountain court adjoin a popular cantina.

★ **La Salette Restaurant**   *(707)938-1927*
2 mi. NW at 18625 Sonoma Hwy.
lasalette-restaurant.com
D only. Closed Mon.-Tues.   *Expensive*
Authentic Portuguese cuisine stars in this appealing young restaurant. Consider dishes like roast duck with honey glaze and pistachios, or Portuguese stew of marinated pork tenderloin, tomatoes, onions and clams. From the breads to luscious desserts made here, the roadside dinner house outfitted with tasteful decor is worth trying for a genuine culinary adventure.

★ **The Lodge at Sonoma**   *(707)935-6600*
1 mi. S at 1325 Broadway
B-L-D.   *Very Expensive*
At **Carneros**, "Wine Country cuisine" is given serious attention involving regional artisan ingredients of the season for bold, unusual dishes. The casually elegant dining room includes views of an expo kitchen with a wood-fired oven.

Marioni's   *(707)996-6866*
downtown at N side of plaza at 8 W. Spain St.
L-D. Closed Mon.   *Moderate*
Steak and seafood are served amidst colorful Western decor in multilevel dining areas. A tiled courtyard with an adobe fireplace that fronts on the plaza is especially charming.

★ **Maya**   *(707)935-3500*
downtown at SE corner of the plaza at 101 E. Napa St.
mayarestaurant.com
L-D.   *Expensive*
Seasonal fresh regional ingredients are expertly prepared in creative Mexican-inspired dishes like lime/tortilla/roasted chicken soup or oak-grilled ribeye steak with papaya salsa and spicy onion rings. For dessert, don't miss "pastel de tres leches." A stone wall; freeform hand-carved wooden chairs and tables; a nifty bar and cantina; and colorful art objects contribute to fine, fun dining.

★ **Meritâge** *(707)938-9430*
  downtown just S of plaza at 522 Broadway
  sonomameritage.com
  B-L-D. Sat. & Sun. brunch. Closed Mon.-Tues.   *Expensive*
Meritâge is one of Wine Country's best newer restaurants. From designer scrambles and pecan waffles among morning treats to creative dishes that capture the best of top-quality fresh seasonal ingredients and regional artisan produce, here is an adventure in fine dining. An oyster/raw bar features live Dungeness crab and Maine lobsters. Guests can choose comfortable dining areas enhanced by regional art (for sale), or go out back to a shaded fountain court. Luscious desserts include the chef/owner's outstanding seasonal gelatos and a grand rose-petal sorbet.

Murphy's Irish Pub   *(707)935-0660*
  downtown on E side of plaza at 464 First St. East
  sonomapub.com
  L-D.   *Moderate*
Irish pub grub features fish and chips, shepherd's pie, beef pasty, lamb stew and desserts like sourdough pudding with Jameson whiskey sauce. Two pub rooms showcase a wealth of Celtic artifacts and live music several nights weekly, and there is partially covered courtyard dining.

★ **Pearl's**   *(707)996-1783*
  just W at Fifth St. W in West Plaza Shopping Center
  B-L-D. No D Sun.-Tues.   *Moderate*
Pearl's is where locals (and smart visitors) go for homestyle American breakfasts in Wine Country. Bright, cheerful rooms in the retro-diner cafe are often full of happy customers enjoying delicious homemade biscuits and gravy, assorted designer omelets and scrambles, or gourmet pancakes. Out front are a couple of tables for people waiting for a seat inside, or who are dining with their dogs.

★ **The Red Grape**   *(707)996-4103*
  downtown just S of plaza at 529 First St. West
  theredgrape.com
  L-D.   *Moderate*
"Red" (plum tomato sauce) or "white" (extra virgin olive oil or pesto) designer and traditional pizzas and calzones prepared in a stone-lined oven are featured. All are well crafted and generous of quality ingredients. Creative soups, salads and assorted pastas and gelatos further enhance the cheerful, capacious parlor with a mod look. Umbrellas shade a landscaped adjoining dining patio.

Rob's Rib Shack   *(707)938-8520*
  4 mi. NW at 18709 Arnold Dr.
  robsribshack.com
  L-D.   *Moderate*

Barbecued baby back ribs, beef ribs, spare ribs and half chickens are hardwood-smoked in their brick oven and come with appropriate fixin's, or special extras like beer-batter onion rings or beer-boiled shrimp. Soups, salads, and sandwiches are also served to go, or at picnic tables in the low-slung rustic roadhouse, or in a shady patio out back.

Swiss Hotel and Restaurant   *(707)938-2884*
downtown on N side of plaza at 18 W. Spain St.
   L-D.   *Expensive*
The little landmark hotel's restaurant has been serving hearty helpings of richly flavored rustic Italian country fare for many years. The relaxed and comfortable whitewashed dining room overlooks a shaded garden patio that is especially popular on warm days. Out front is a nostalgic little worn-wood room full of memorabilia.

LODGINGS

Accommodations in and around Sonoma now include several distinctive upscale properties ranging from a famed resort to outstanding romantic inns. April through October is high season. Rates are often reduced by at least 20% during the winter, except on weekends.

★ **Above the Clouds**   *(707)996-7371*
11 mi. N at 3250 Trinity Rd. - Glen Ellen 95442
sonomabb.com
   3 units   *(800)736-7894*   *Expensive*
At the top of three miles of winding climbing road, this bed-and-breakfast lives up to its name 2,000 feet above the Valley of the Moon. A historic dwelling on a tranquil forested slope has been lovingly transformed into a charming bed-and-breakfast with a panoramic-view pool and a whirlpool in a rock grotto. Full breakfast is complimentary as is wine in the afternoon. Each cozy well-furnished room has a private bath, access to a mountain-view veranda, and a queen bed.

Beltane Ranch   *(707)996-6501*
8 mi. NW at 11775 Sonoma Hwy. (Hwy 12) (Box 395) - Glen Ellen 95442
beltaneranch.com
   6 rooms   *Expensive*
An authentic Victorian-era ranch (circa 1892) now serves as a bed-and-breakfast country inn with fine pastoral views of the Valley of the Moon from porches that surround rooms. Miles of hiking trails and a tennis court are amenities. Full breakfast (often including home-grown products) is complimentary. Each well-furnished room has period antiques, a ceiling fan, private bath, and a queen bed.
   Room #1–gas fireplace in sitting room.

★ **The Cottage Inn & Spa**   *(707)996-0719*
downtown just N of plaza at 302 First St. East - 95476
cottageinnandspa.com
7 units   (800)944-1490   Expensive-Very Expensive
The Cottage Inn and Spa with the adjoining Mission Bed &
Breakfast is one of America's most romantic lodgings. Only a
block from Sonoma's historic plaza, it is cloistered on a quiet side
street. A complex of seven units, each with private access, has
been built around two lovely fountain courts. Relaxing in-room
(fee) massage or facials contribute to the dreamy ambiance of this
peaceful place. Complimentary gourmet breakfast is served to the
room. Each room reflects the spirit of Early California and the
Southwest while providing all of the conveniences of the best
contemporary lodgings, along with extras like fresh-cut roses in
vases, candles in wrought-iron objects of art by whirlpool tubs,
dimmer switches to control mood lights, and private patios with
soothing garden decor. All of the spacious rooms are luxuriously
individually furnished and include a refrigerator, microwave, wet
bar, high-tech DVD/CD players (some with home-theater
surround sound) and a queen or king bed. All but one have a
private whirlpool tub.
  "Vineyard View Suite"–extra-large upstairs, windows
    on four sides, big wooden doors open to flower-view
    balcony above courtyard, raised gas fireplace in view
    of two-person whirlpool and adjoining open shower,
    CD/DVD stereo with surround sound, king bed.
  "Mission Suite"–extra-large, private terrace with bamboo
    garden visible from raised two-person whirlpool,
    sitting area by woodburning fireplace, king bed.
  "The East Suite"–spacious, private garden patio,
    two-person whirlpool in view of raised woodburning
    fireplace, king bed.
El Dorado Hotel   *(707)996-3030*
downtown on NW corner of plaza at 405 First St. West - 95476
hoteleldorado.com
26 units   (800)289-3031   Expensive
A pre-Civil War landmark overlooking the plaza has been
artistically reconstructed into a small hotel with a lovely garden
court, pool, upscale Italian chain restaurant, saloon, and two
shops. A Continental breakfast and bottle of wine are complimentary. Upstairs, each room has been attractively furnished
including all contemporary amenities, and features a small
balcony with a view of the plaza or lush courtyard, plus a queen
or king bed.
  #2–corner of top floor, plaza/hills view, queen bed.

★ **The Fairmont Sonoma Mission Inn & Spa**   *(707)938-9000*
3 mi. NW at 18140 Sonoma Hwy. (Box 1447) - 95476
fairmont.com
228 units   *(800)862-4945*   *Very Expensive*
A large 1927 Spanish-Colonial style landmark is the valley's premier resort hotel. Guests can enjoy (for a fee) two hot mineral water pools, sauna, steam room and whirlpools as part of a complete European-style health and beauty spa (how about a couples' fragrant lavender soak followed by soothing massage with lavender oil?) Notable restaurants (see listing), a lounge, and a resort shop are also housed on expansive tree-shaded grounds with colorful gardens and fountains. All rooms ranging from cozy to spacious fireplace suites are beautifully furnished including extra amenities, a mini-bar/refrigerator, and a queen or king bed.
"Mission Suite" (31 of these)–romantic, spacious, sitting
    area, private patio, woodburning fireplace and
    two-person whirlpool in view of four-poster king bed.
"Wine Country One Bedroom Suite" (6 of these)–big,
    living room with woodburning fireplace, in-bath
    two-person whirlpool, private deck, king bed.
"Wine Country Junior Suite" (23 of these)–spacious, sitting
    area, (some with woodburning fireplace), (some with
    private deck), in-bath two-person whirlpool, king bed.
★ **Gaige House Inn**   *(707)935-0237*
8 mi. NW at 13540 Arnold Dr. - Glen Ellen 95442
gaige.com
15 units   *(800)935-0237*   *Very Expensive*
The Gaige House, centered around a Victorian mansion next to tiny downtown Glen Ellen, is one of Wine Country's finest bed-and-breakfasts. Amenities include a large pool and a whirlpool in a semi-tropical garden. An expansive wooden deck is built into oak trees by a year-round stream. A sybaritic (fee) massage facility adjoins with a variety of treatments. Full gourmet breakfast and afternoon wine and refreshments are complimentary. Each spacious room is beautifully furnished with a blend of period pieces and all contemporary amenities, a private bath and queen or king bed. Some have both a fireplace and large whirlpool bath.
"Creekside"–spacious suite, gas fireplace, window wall
    to private deck by creek, large whirlpool tub and
    dual-head shower, king bed.
"Woodside"–floor-to-ceiling window view of zen garden
    and big private patio, two-person Japanese soaking tub
    and large dual-head shower, gas fireplace, king bed.
"Gaige Suite"–spacious, in main house, private porch,
    large whirlpool tub and shower, gas fireplace, king bed.

Jack London Lodge   *(707)938-8510*
8 mi. NW at 13740 Arnold Dr. (Box 300) - Glen Ellen 95442
jacklondonlodge.com
     22 units   *Moderate*
An outdoor pool and a quiet, scenic location next to Sonoma
Creek are features of this motel complex by a historic bar and a
restaurant. Each comfortably furnished room has all contemporary amenities, a refrigerator and two queens or a king bed.

★ **Kenwood Inn & Spa**   *(707)833-1293*
10 mi. NW at 10400 Sonoma Hwy. - Kenwood 95452
kenwoodinn.com
     12 units   *(800)353-6966*   *Very Expensive*
Kenwood Inn & Spa is a truly romantic bed-and-breakfast.
Reminiscent of an Italian country villa, the inn has a courtyard
pool, whirlpool and (fee) full service health and beauty spa.
Gourmet breakfast is complimentary as is a bottle of wine upon
arrival. Each beautifully furnished room has a queen or king
featherbed, pressed-wood fireplace, and sitting area. Some also
have a large in-room whirlpool and/or a private deck.

★ **Ledson Hotel**   *(707)996-9779*
downtown on E side of plaza at 480 First St. East - 95476
ledson.com
     6 units
The newest hotel on the plaza opened in 2003 above the Harmony
Club Wine Bar. Each beautifully furnished room has all
contemporary and extra amenities like surround sound, and in-
bath two-person whirlpool, gas fireplace, private balcony, and a
king bed.

★ **The Lodge at Sonoma - Renaissance Resort & Spa** *(707)935-6600*
1 mi. S at 1325 Broadway - 95476
marriott.com
     182 units   *(888)710-8008*   *Very Expensive*
One of the area's newest large lodgings is a low-profile hotel with
a pool, whirlpool, sauna and exercise room on attractively
landscaped grounds. A restaurant (see listing), lounge, gift shop,
and related (fee) spa services are also available. Each well-
furnished guest room has contemporary and extra amenities and
two queens or a king bed. Some rooms also have a gas fireplace.

★ **MacArthur Place**   *(707)938-2929*
just S at 29 E. MacArthur St. (at Broadway) - 95476
macarthurplace.com
     64 units   *(800)722-1866*   *Very Expensive*
MacArthur Place is one of California's finest country inns. Low-
rise whitewashed buildings surrounded by beautiful gardens and
sculptures suggest a Victorian village. A large pool, whirlpool, and

bicycles are available to guests, along with a fitness room and posh (fee) spa with a wide variety of body treatments. At **Saddles Restaurant** (L-D. Sat. & Sun. brunch–Very Expensive), prime beef and Western rusticity are featured. An expanded Continental breakfast buffet and afternoon wine and appetizers are complimentary. Each spacious, individually decorated room is beautifully furnished and has all contemporary amenities plus extras like their own line of grapeseed bath products, and a queen or king bed. Extras include an outstanding built-in surround sound system for DVD players in some units.

"Premium Suites & Cottages" (6 of these)–spacious, romantic, flat-screen TV with DVD/CD player & six-speaker surround sound, wet bar/refr., pvt. deck by garden, in-bath two-person whirlpool and woodburning fireplace in view of king bed.

★ **Ramekins Bed & Breakfast**   *(707)933-0452*
just W at 450 W. Spain St. - 95476
ramekins.com
6 units   *Expensive-Very Expensive*
Wine Country's finest culinary school available to the general public opened in 1998 in a tranquil setting near the appealing General's Daughter restaurant (see listing). Lodgings are upstairs. Decor throughout emphasizes food as art. Complimentary light breakfast is included. Each spacious, beautifully furnished room has all contemporary amenities, a town or mountain view, and queen or king bed. Some have a large private balcony.

#1–extra-large, raised gas fireplace, king bed.
Sonoma Chalet   *(707)938-3129*
1 mi. NW at 18935 Fifth St. West (Box 595) - 95476
sonomachalet.com
7 units   *(800)938-3129*   *Expensive*
Cows graze on the hillside next to a quaint old chalet that has been made into a quirky bed-and-breakfast country inn chock full of knickknacks. Features include use of bicycles, an outdoor hot tub with a tranquil pastoral view, an upstairs sitting room warmed by a pot-belly stove, and fowl strolling among citrus trees on luxuriant grounds. Expanded Continental breakfast is complimentary. All but two of the individualized, comfortably furnished rooms have a private bath and queen bed.

"Sara's Cottage"–spacious, private bath with clawfoot tub, woodburning pot-belly stove, refr., view on three sides.
Sonoma Hotel   *(707)996-2996*
downtown on NW corner of plaza at 110 W. Spain St. - 95476
www.sonomahotel.com
16 units   *(800)468-6016*   *Expensive-Very Expensive*
The valley's oldest lodging is a three-story Victorian landmark

(circa 1880) that was remodeled for the millennium. The popular
Girl and the Fig (see listing) restaurant and saloon are
downstairs. Continental breakfast and afternoon wine are complimentary. Each small room has rustic-nouveau decor and is well
furnished with all contemporary and some extra amenities, a
private bathroom, and a double or queen bed.
#30–corner overlooking plaza from top (3rd) floor, queen bed.
★ **Sonoma Valley Inn - Best Western**　*(707)938-9200*
downtown by the plaza at 550 Second St. West - 95476
sonomavalleyinn.com
83 units　*(800)334-5784*　*Expensive-Very Expensive*
The Valley's best motel has a garden-court pool, whirlpool and
fitness center. Light breakfast delivered to the room and a bottle
of wine are complimentary. Each well-furnished room has a
private deck, refrigerator and two queens or king bed. Most have
a pressed-wood fireplace, large in-bath whirlpool, and private deck.
"Mission Suites" (7 of these)–second floor, private
  balcony, wet bar/refrigerator, raised pressed-wood
  fireplace, two-person whirlpool in view of king bed.
Thistle Dew Inn　*(707)938-2909*
downtown near NW corner of plaza at 171 W. Spain St. - 95476
thistledew.com
6 units　*(800)382-7895*　*Expensive-Very Expensive*
This bed-and-breakfast inn offers turn-of-the-century ambiance
in two converted historic buildings close to the heart of town. Full
gourmet breakfast, appetizers and refreshments each evening,
and bicycles are complimentary, as is an outdoor hot tub. Each
well-furnished room has a private bath and a queen bed. Most
have a large whirlpool tub, gas fireplace, and/or private deck.
"Mimosa"–large, in-bath two-person whirlpool, private
  deck with swing, gas fireplace in view of queen bed.
"Wisteria"–small sitting room with gas fireplace, private
  grape-arbor deck, in-bath two-person whirlpool.
Victorian Garden Inn　*(707)996-5339*
downtown just SE of plaza at 316 E. Napa St. - 95476
victoriangardeninn.com
4 units　*(800)543-5339*　*Expensive-Very Expensive*
A secluded bed-and-breakfast inn occupies an 1870 farmhouse
and water tower surrounded by lush Victorian-style gardens, a
small stream, and an outdoor pool and whirlpool. Expanded
Continental breakfast and evening refreshments are complimentary. Each room is beautifully furnished including country-
style antiques, a private bath, and a double or queen bed.
"Woodcutter's Cottage"–spacious, vaulted ceiling,
  large clawfoot tub, gas fireplace, by stream, queen bed.
"Garden"–private bath, gas fireplace in view of queen bed.

Sonora

Sonora is the robust "Queen of the Mother Lode." A choice collection of notable Victorian homes and businesses still lends a Gold Camp flavor to this thriving hub in the Sierra foothills.

Gold was discovered here in 1849. When California became a state in 1850, Sonora was already a boom town. After a disastrous fire in 1852, the town was rebuilt more substantially with stone, brick, adobe and iron. The big Bonanza Mine, located just north of downtown, was perhaps the richest pocket mine in the Mother Lode. Mines played out decades ago, but gold is still being found nearby, including the recent discovery of the world's largest pure nugget.

Today, the rich heritage is showcased in a very real Old West downtown, where workers and travelers still gather for uncomplicated American fare; and logging trucks rumble down the main drag as they have for more than a century. Many notable Victorian buildings serve their original purposes as saloons, stores or churches including an Episcopal church that was built in 1859 and may be California's oldest. Many consider it the most beautiful frame building in the Mother Lode. Lodgings, while not abundant, include historic hotels downtown and in the vicinity. Several Victorian homes featuring atmospheric Gold Camp furnishings now serve as bed-and-breakfast inns within walking distance of the heart of town. All around, a remarkable assortment of lakes and rivers in the oak-and-grass-covered foothills and pine-forested mountains provide a bonanza of water-oriented recreation opportunities–including gold panning.

WEATHER PROFILE

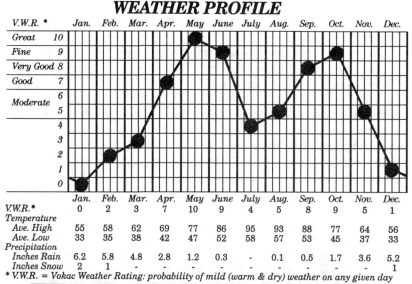

V.W.R. *		Jan.	Feb.	Mar.	Apr.	May	June	July	Aug.	Sep.	Oct.	Nov.	Dec.
Great	10												
Fine	9												
Very Good	8												
Good	7												
Moderate	6												
	5												
	4												
	3												
	2												
	1												
	0												

	Jan.	Feb.	Mar.	Apr.	May	June	July	Aug.	Sep.	Oct.	Nov.	Dec.
V.W.R.*	0	2	3	7	10	9	4	5	8	9	5	1
Temperature												
Ave. High	55	58	62	69	77	86	95	93	88	77	64	56
Ave. Low	33	35	38	42	47	52	58	57	53	45	37	33
Precipitation												
Inches Rain	6.2	5.8	4.8	2.8	1.2	0.3	-	0.1	0.5	1.7	3.6	5.2
Inches Snow	2	1	-	-	-	-	-	-	-	-	-	1

* V.W.R. = Vokac Weather Rating: probability of mild (warm & dry) weather on any given day

BASIC INFORMATION

Population: 4,537
Elevation: 1,825 feet
Location: 132 miles East of San Francisco
Airport (regularly scheduled flights): Modesto - 50 miles

Tuolumne County Visitors Bureau (209)533-4420 (800)446-1333
   downtown at 542 W. Stockton Rd. (Box 4020) - 95370
   thegreatunfenced.com
Tuolumne County Chamber of Commerce   (209)532-4212
   downtown at 222 S. Shepherd St. - 95370
   tcchamber.com

ATTRACTIONS

Carriage Rides

Peppermint Creek Carriage Company   *(209)533-2599*
downtown on Washington St.   *(800)555-1147*
peppermintcreekcarriage.com
By reservation, half-hour narrated tours of Sonora can transport you back in time in authentic carriages pulled by Belgian draft horses.

★ **Columbia State Historic Park**   *(209)532-0150*
4 mi. N (off Hwy. 49) on Parrotts Ferry Rd. - Columbia
www.columbiacalifornia.com
For a few years during the 1850s, thousands of people lived here and worked fabulously rich placer mines. The State has restored part of the old business district that may be viewed on a self-guided walking tour. A tour of a gold mine; stagecoach or guided horseback rides; and gold panning are other options. Restaurants, saloons, lodgings and live entertainment (see listings), plus shops featuring regional souvenirs, arts and crafts also flourish downtown.

★ **Don Pedro Lake**   *(209)989-2383*
15 mi. S on Hwy. 49
The Mother Lode country's largest water body is a twenty-six-mile-long reservoir with a shoreline of 160 miles reaching deep into picturesque wooded foothills. Motorized and sail boating and fishing are especially popular on long warm summer days. Swimming coves are numerous and a large sandy beach area has been provided. Picnic and full-service camping areas are located at several scenic sites near the lake. Houseboats (for overnight and longer cruises) and fishing boats can be rented at either of two full service marinas.

Lake Don Pedro Marina   *(209)852-2369*
24 mi. S at 81 Bonds Flat Rd.
Moccasin Point Marina   *(209)989-2206*   *(800)255-5561*
16 mi. S at 11405 Jacksonville Rd.   *(foreverresorts.com)*

Flying

Fly Yosemite Air Tours   *(209)532-2345*
4 mi. N (via Hwy. 49) at 10767 Airport Rd. - Columbia
flyyosemite.com
Scenic flights of from one-half to two-and-one-half hours over the Mother Lode country, the Sierra and Yosemite Valley can be reserved any day at this aviation service with many years of experience flying from the Columbia Airport.

Food Specialties

★ **Cover's Apple Ranch**   *(209)928-4689*
8 mi. SE (via Tuolumne Rd.) at 19200 Cherokee Rd.

coversappleranch.com

"Mile-high" apple pie and other homemade apple pies, pastries and preserves, plus many varieties of apples (in season) are sold at this old-fashioned roadside farm. Extensive grounds include a people-carrying mini-railroad complete with tunnels (runs on Saturdays); a picnic area; and a petting zoo. Closed Sun.

★ **Oakdale Cheese & Specialties**   *(209)848-3139*
34 mi. SW at 10040 Hwy. 120 - Oakdale
oakdalecheese.com

Gouda cheese (made and aged in the Holland tradition) stars, and is made here in many flavors. There is a complimentary tasting bar for cheeses and related gourmet items sold in an expansive store that also displays their baked goods, deli items, and souvenirs. Quark (another Dutch treat) lends distinction to several kinds of spreads and German cheesecakes (sold by the slice or pie). A small museum and windows overlook the production and storage area in a handsome complex that opened in 1995. Tree-shaded lawns and picnic tables surround tranquil ponds and a waterfall. There is also a small petting zoo and a local seasonal fresh fruit, nuts and vegies stand. Open 9-6 daily.

★ **Jamestown**
3 mi. SW via Hwy. 49 - Jamestown

A narrow main street lined with two-story balconied buildings is the highlight of this Mother Lode relic. Don't be surprised if the picturesque heart of town looks familiar. It has been used as the setting for many classic Hollywood westerns. Numerous specialty shops and several restaurants, plus historic bars and hotels, are well worth visiting.

★ *Live Theaters*
Fallon House Theatre   *(209)532-3120*
4 mi. N (off Hwy. 49) at Broadway/Washington Sts. - Columbia
sierrarep.com

A 114-year-old theater with 274 seats and a balcony has been fully restored. Musicals, comedies, and dramas are staged through most of the year by Sierra Repertory Theatre, an established professional company with a second location (a contemporary theater) in east Sonora. The complex also houses an inn with period rooms and an ice cream parlor. Closed Mon.-Tues.

Stage 3 Theatre Company   *(209)536-1778*
downtown at 208 S. Green St.
stage3.org

Since 1993, Stage 3 Theatre Company has produced new and contemporary works including some world premieres. The Arts Center, an intimate "black box" comfortably seating 80 patrons, is a proper showcase for adventurous theater.

★ **New Melones Lake Marina**   *(209)785-3300*
12 mi. NW on Hwy. 49
newmelones.com
The newest big lake in the Gold Country was filled in 1983. More than one hundred miles of scenic shoreline extend into oak-studded foothills. Houseboats (some featuring a hot tub on the upper deck) and fishing boats can be rented at this full-service marina with a snack bar and store. Boating, fishing, water-skiing, and swimming are all popular. Picnic and full-service camping areas are also available.

★ **Railtown 1897 State Historic Park**   *(209)984-3953*
3 mi. SW (off Hwy. 49) on 5th Av. - Jamestown
csrmf.org/railtown
Since 1982, the State has operated steam-powered passenger trains over a historic six-mile route through oak-studded Sierra foothills each weekend from April through October. Railtown's locomotives and cars have appeared on these tracks in more than 200 movie and TV productions. The forty-minute trip is narrated by well-informed tour guides. The complex includes the only surviving original operating roundhouse west of the Mississippi, trains and railyard facilities, and a depot museum store. Guided walking trips are available daily year-round.

★ *River Running*
Sonora is between two of the most famous whitewater streams in America–the Stanislaus and Tuolumne Rivers. Some rapids are now submerged beneath waters of huge downstream reservoirs. However, exciting raft trips (everything from Class I-Class V rapids tailored to every paddler's skill level) can still be enjoyed upstream on the remaining portions of the rivers where natural grandeur and whitewater remain unspoiled. For example, expert paddlers will thrill to the Cherry Creek/Upper Tuolumne (a designated "Wild and Scenic River") as the standard by which all Class V (the most difficult runnable rapids) are measured. Nearby downstream, anyone can enjoy easy riffles and clear swimming holes (especially on hot summer days) on long gentle Class I stretches. Several established, professional guide services operate between March and October. Following are the most complete and best.

Ahwahnee Whitewater   *(800)359-9790   ahwahnee.com*
Beyond Limits Adventures *(800)234-7238   rivertrip.com*
O.A.R.S.   *(800)346-6277   oars.com*
River Journey   *(800)292-2938   riverjourney.com*
Sierra Mac River Trips   *(800)457-2580   sierramac.com*
Whitewater Voyages *(800)400-7238   whitewatervoyages.com*
Zephyr River Expeditions *(800)431-3636   zrafting.com*

St. James Episcopal Church   *(209)532-7644*
downtown at Washington & Snell Sts.
The photogenic Episcopal church, built in 1859 on a rise at the
north end of downtown, may be California's oldest. Many consider
it to be the most beautiful frame building in the Mother Lode. A
Victorian mansion across the street is also notable.
★ **Stanislaus National Forest**
Forest Supervisor's Office: 1 mi E at 19777 Greenley Rd.
www.r5.fs.fed.us/stanislaus
All of the Sierra Nevada mountains between Sonora and Yosemite
National Park are included in this extraordinary forest. Features
(beginning five miles east of town) include dozens of campgrounds
ranging from primitive to full service, and more than 1,000 miles
of hiking, backpacking, and horseback riding trails along the
splendid canyons of the Tuolumne and Stanislaus river drainages.
Upper reaches of these rivers include some of America's great
whitewater rafting opportunities (see listing). In calmer stretches,
swimmers are attracted to crystal-clear natural rock-and-boulder
pools with sandy beaches. A magnificent stand of primeval
sequoia gigantea, the Calaveras Big Trees (see listing in
Murphys), has been famous since its discovery in 1852. It is less
than an hour by car north of town. A similar distance to the east
are trailheads for the Emigrant Wilderness bordered by Yosemite
National Park to the south and the crest of the Sierra to the east.
This forest of pine and aspen, interspersed with broad meadows
and numerous small lakes and streams, is a favorite with
fishermen, hunters, and backpackers. In winter, Sonora is an easy
drive from Dodge Ridge Ski Area (see listing), which has expanded
into a major winter sports center. Mt. Reba and Bear Valley Ski
Areas are farther to the northeast. Information, maps and
permits are available at the Forest Supervisor's Office in town.
★ **Tuolumne County Museum & History Center** *(209)532-1317*
downtown at 158 W. Bradford Av.
www.tchistory.com
Here is the largest museum in the Mother Lode. Gold Camp
photographs and memorabilia are displayed in and out of
authentic jail cells in a building that housed the local Hoosegaw
well over a century ago.
★ *Water Features*   *(209)533-4420   (800)446-1333*
A remarkable number of lakes, streams, and reservoirs are within
an hour's drive around town. During uniformly hot summers,
Sierra waters are a compelling attraction for swimmers, as well
as fishermen, water-skiers, sailors, river runners, and all others
who enjoy cool, clear water recreation. Public parks with sandy
beaches and private coves abound on Don Pedro, New Melones,

McClure, Woodward, Modesto, Turlock and other nearby manmade lakes. There are also excellent swimming holes and sandy beaches on the Stanislaus, Tuolumne and other surrounding rivers.

Winter Sports

★ **Dodge Ridge Ski Area**   *(209)965-3474*
32 mi. NE (off Hwy. 108) on Dodge Ridge Rd. - Pinecrest
dodgeridge.com
With a vertical drop of 1,600 feet from a top elevation of 8,200 feet, the longest run is two miles. Eight chairlifts serve the expanded area that now includes three terrain parks and a halfpipe. Concessions at the base include ski and snowboard rentals, instruction, and related facilities, plus food and drinks. The skiing season is December through April.

Leland High Sierra Snow Play   *(209)965-4719*
35 mi. NE (off Hwy. 108) on Leland Meadows Rd. - Strawberry
snowplay.com
This may be the biggest snow play facility in the Sierra. Features include a broad hill where saucers, sleds, or inner tubes can be rented–or bring your own tubes or sleds (nonmetal or wooden). There is also a day use lodge and snack bar with a warm fire and sundeck overlooking the area. Open daily from (usually) December to April.

★ **Yosemite National Park**   *(209)372-0200*
52 mi. SE via Hwy. 49 & Hwy. 120
nps.gov/yose   yosemite.com
Yosemite's magnificent waterfalls (including the highest on the continent) and sheer granite domes are unsurpassed. Primeval groves of giant sequoia, vast high country wilderness areas, snowfields, and crystal-clear lakes and streams with sandy beaches are other attractions that have won the acclaim of increasing hordes of recreation enthusiasts since 1890. Today, about four million people visit this world famous national park each year. Tourist facilities in Yosemite Valley and nearby are often full in summer, the busiest season. Crowds are smaller and the weather can be mild in spring and fall. For camping reservations, call (800)436-7275.

RESTAURANTS

Alfredo's   *(209)532-8332*
downtown at 123 S. Washington St.
L-D.   *Moderate*
Traditional and California-style Mexican dishes include some unusual specialties like shrimp prepared several ways and desserts like apple chimichangas. The dining room shares an attractive rock-walled skylit space with a cozy cantina.

★ **City Hotel Restaurant** *(209)532-1479 (800)532-1479*
4 mi. N (off Hwy. 49) at 22768 Main St. - Columbia
cityhotel.com
   D only. Sun. brunch. Closed Mon.   *Expensive*
The City Hotel Restaurant is *the* bonanza of gourmet discoveries
in California's Mother Lode. A short tempting selection of
contemporary California cuisine showcases top-quality seasonal
ingredients in presentations that are as artistic as they are
delectable. Dinner might include baked oyster casserole with
champagne spinach sauce; pan-seared steelhead fillet with lemon,
crème fraîche and asparagus sauce, and lemon soufflé with Grand
Marnier sauce for dessert. Costumed staff serve amid authentically restored Gold Rush elegance. Epicurean food, the nostalgic
setting, and reasonable prices combine to make this one of the
best bets in California for any traveling gourmand. A classic old-
time saloon adjoins. Upstairs are nostalgic little bedrooms (see
listing) that realistically evoke the Victorian era.

Diamondback Grill   *(209)532-6661*
downtown at 110 S. Washington St.
   L-D. No D Sun.   *Moderate*
All sorts of half-pound burgers star. For the really hungry, there
is the double Diamondback cheeseburger weighing in at one full
pound. A good selection of soups, salads and sandwiches and
distinctive blackboard entrees-of-the-day are also served in the
spiffy little cafe/grill.

★ **The Eproson House**   *(209)586-3700*
12 mi. E at 22930 Twain Harte Dr. - Twain Harte
   L-D. Sun. brunch.   *Moderate*
Delicious housemade breads accompany mesquite-grilled
specialties like veal chop stuffed with pancetta and sautéed
spinach, or filet mignon with truffle oil essence, and other
skillfully prepared traditional and creative California and Italian
dishes. A long-established restaurant recently was remodeled, and
reopened with an orientation once again toward serving fine food
in a handsome country setting that includes a full bar and dance
floor.

Jamestown Hotel   *(209)984-3902 (800)205-4901*
3 mi. SW (off Hwy. 49) at 18153 Main St. - Jamestown
jamestownhotel.com
   L-D. Closed Tues.-Wed. Sun. brunch.   *Expensive*
Updated Continental dishes like steak Diane or roast duckling are
served in a handsome firelit dining room where tables set with
full linen overlook an elegant polished-wood bar. A seasonal
outdoor patio adjoins.

John's 49er Bakery   *(209)532-4253*
3 mi. SE (on Hwy. 108) at 14505 Mono Way
B-L. Closed Sun.   Low
This unassuming little shop in a strip mall is special for delicious
designer bagels, traditional and innovative pastries, and luscious
desserts. The tucked-away bakery is worth finding.

★ **Josephine's Europa Cafe**   *(209)532-2111*
downtown at 275 S. Washington St.
B-L-D.   *Moderate*
In 2003, a long-standing restaurant site became the new home of
a remodeled, upgraded dining room and lounge overseen by one
of Gold Country's best chefs. Contemporary California and Italian
dishes are enhanced by housemade focaccia. Don't miss the chef's
signature dessert–chocolate strata–while enjoying this special
addition to fine dining in downtown Sonora.

★ **Michelangelo**   *(209)984-4830*
3 mi. SW (off Hwy. 49) at 18228 Main St. - Jamestown
L-D. Closed Mon. & Tues.   *Moderate*
All sorts of traditional and innovative Italian dishes are served,
like artichoke dip, designer pizzas, and grilled filet mignon with
port wine and mushroom sauce. Generous portions start with
tasty housemade focaccia. Save room for their signature
dessert–mascarpone-in-a-glass. It is both luscious and pretty. The
room overlooking main street is enhanced by Michelango-inspired
wall hangings. A dining patio with a town park view opened in
2003. A comfortable bar adjoins.

The Miner's Shack Cafe   *(209)532-5252*
downtown at 157 S. Washington St.
B-L.   *Low*
The Miner's Shack has, for many years, been a low-cost landmark
for hungry natives and visitors. A wealth of omelet varieties and
other traditional American favorites like biscuits and gravy and
specialties like buffalo in chili, burger, and stew are served all day
at casual, comfortable booths in the cafe.

Morelia   *(209)984-1432*
3 mi. SW (off Hwy. 49) at 18148 Main St. - Jamestown
L-D.   *Moderate*
Specialties like Morelia special enchiladas (corn tortilla filled with
shrimp topped with green tomatillo sauce, Monterey jack and sour
cream) star. Traditional Mexican dishes are also served in several
congested dining areas and on an alfresco patio fronting on
Jamestown's picturesque main street.

★ **Nanna's Brick Oven Deli Cafe**   *(209)533-3289*
downtown at 362 S. Stewart St.
B-L-D. Only brunch on Sun.   *Moderate*

Sonora

In 2002, Nanna's Brick Oven Deli Cafe opened as serious competition for the best deli in the Mother Lode. Superb sticky buns, muffins, cinnamon rolls and other pastries are displayed near the entrance. Other cases hold decadent desserts and arrays of cheeses and meats, all in view of a raised comfortable dining area amidst live greenery. A heated shaded patio adjoins. Wood-fired pizza, house calzone, hot and cold sandwiches made with their fine breads, pastas, salads, soups, and light entrees also reflect San Francisco sophistication.

National Hotel Restaurant   *(209)984-3446   (800)894-3446*
3 mi. SW (off Hwy. 49) at 18183 Main St. - Jamestown
national-hotel.com
L-D.   *Moderate*
Traditional American dishes are served at tables set with full linen amid mining camp decor in a nostalgic dining room of a restored pre-Civil War hotel, or (in summer) on a vine-covered courtyard. A delightfully authentic little Gold Camp saloon is next door.

★ **One-twenty-four Restaurant & Suites**   *(209)533-2145*
downtown at 124 N. Washington St.
onetwentyfour.com
D only. Sun. brunch.   *Expensive*
"Inspired cuisine for gourmet dining" is the intent of this young dinner house in the heart of town. Consider crabcakes with tropical fruit salsa, and wild salmon with chardonnay buerre blanc or seared oversized veal chop with roasted local grapes, followed by a luscious housemade dessert. A historic house has been tastefully transformed into dining rooms with full linen and flowers at tables and stylish wall hangings and lamps. Out back, a peaceful garden court is built around an entrance to a (sealed) historic gold mine shaft. Upstairs are two spacious well-furnished guest rooms.

Peppery Gar & Brill   *(209)533-9033*
2 mi. SE at 13299 Mono Way
L-D.   *Moderate*
A wide assortment of contemporary California dishes includes specialties like a tri-tip red chile wrap or beer-battered peppery onion strings for an appetizer. Several casual dining areas surround a central sports bar with one dozen-plus beers on tap.

Pie Tin   *(209)536-1216*
downtown at 51 S. Washington St.
B-L.   *Moderate*
Cinnamon rolls and assorted muffins, scones, bagels and pies made here can be enjoyed with light fare and a wealth of beverages in a pleasant old-fashioned coffee shop.

Sonora Days Inn   *(209)586-0600*
downtown at 160 S. Washington St.
sonoradaysinn.com
D only.   *Moderate*
In the **Victoria Room**, assorted steaks, prime rib and seafood
dishes are served amid casual decor in the landmark hotel. There
is also an entertainment lounge.
Willows Steak House   *(209)984-3998*
3 mi. SW off Hwy. 49 at 18723 Main St. - Jamestown
L-D. No L Sat. & Sun.   *Moderate*
Fondue precedes contemporary Italian and American dishes
including a variety of steaks from the char-broiler in this casual
dining room. For a genuine glimpse of yesteryear, check out the
adjoining saloon's polished brass-foot railing, pot-belly stove,
ornate backbar and several trophy elk.
Woods Creek Inn   *(209)984-4001*
3 mi. SW (off Hwy. 49) at 18256 Hwy. 108 - Jamestown
B-L.   *Moderate*
Sausage scrambled with eggs inside a bread bowl covered with
country gravy and cheddar cheese has pleased natives and visitors
for years, along with skillet dishes, omelets and treats like
banana-nut bread, or buckwheat with applesauce hot cakes. The
casual coffee shop has a wealth of moo-ving spotted cow art.

LODGINGS

Visitors can choose between numerous authentically furnished
historic hotels and inns or several modern motels with contemporary amenities. High season is summer. Non-weekend rates at
other times are usually reduced 15% or more.
Aladdin Motor Inn Motel   *(209)533-4971*
2 mi. E (on Hwy. 108) at 14260 Mono Way - 95370
aladdininn.com
61 units   *(800)696-3969*   *Moderate*
A small pool, whirlpool and cafe are features of this modern motel
on a hill. Each nicely furnished room includes a refrigerator and
a queen or king bed.
★ **Barretta Gardens Bed & Breakfast**   *(209)532-6039*
just S at 700 S. Barretta St. - 95370
barrettagardens.com
5 units   *(800)206-3333*   *Expensive*
A century-old home on a hillside overlooking Sonora is now a
stylish bed-and-breakfast amid lovely terraced gardens. Full
breakfast including their own fresh-baked pastries, afternoon
refreshments, and a stocked refrigerator are complimentary. Each
well-furnished room combines period decor and contemporary

amenities including a private bath, and queen or king bed.

"The Odette Suite"–garden-view solarium, gas
fire stove, in-bath two-person whirlpool, king bed.
"The Isabelle"–spacious, downstairs, two-person
whirlpool with a view, queen bed.

★ **Blue Nile Inn Bed & Breakfast**   *(209)532-8041*
4 mi. N (off Hwy. 49) at 11250 Pacific St. - Columbia 95310
blue-nile-inn.com
4 units   *Expensive*

The main street of Columbia State Historic Park is only a block from this peaceful bed-and-breakfast inn, a contemporary replica of a Victorian farmhouse with covered porches. Full gourmet breakfast and fresh-baked treats and beverages in the afternoon are complimentary. Each beautifully furnished room has most contemporary amenities, a private bath and a queen bed.

"Angel Room," "Victorian Garden Room"–spacious,
gas fireplace/stove, in-bath two-person whirlpool.

★ **Bradford Place Inn & Gardens**   *(209)536-6075*
downtown at 56 W. Bradford St. - 95370
bradfordplaceinn.com
4 units   *(800)209-2315*   *Expensive*

Bradford Place is one of the Gold Country's most appealing bed-and-breakfasts. A handsome Victorian house (circa 1889) in the heart of town has been skillfully transformed to retain the spirit of yesteryear in architectural and decor details, while meeting up-to-date needs of today's guests. A gourmet breakfast (like the Miner's Omelet) is served in the parlor, to your room, or in the colorful gardens surrounding the house. Afternoon treats and refreshments are also complimentary. Each room is individually beautifully furnished and has a private bath, all contemporary plus extra amenities, and a queen bed.

"Bradford Suite"–spacious, sun porch, window loveseat,
original woodburning fireplace, refrigerator/microwave,
in-room long clawfoot tub-for-two (separate shower).
"Yosemite Room"–gas Franklin fire stove, refrigerator/
microwave, long clawfoot tub/shower, private garden patio.
"Tuolumne Room"–two-person whirlpool
with shower in view of queen bed.

★ **City Hotel**   *(209)532-1479*
4 mi. N at 22768 Main St. (Box 1870) - Columbia 95310
cityhotel.com
10 units   *(800)532-1479*   *Expensive*

Built in the midst of the Gold Rush before the Civil War, this small two-story brick hotel remains a landmark of that era. The fully restored building exudes authentic Old Western Victorian charm, especially in the gourmet dining room (see listing) and saloon. Expanded Continental buffet breakfast is complimentary as is evening sherry served in the parlor. Each compact room is comfortably furnished including period antiques and a double or queen bed, but has a toilet and marble sink as concessions to modern times. A shower room is down the hall.

#1,#2 ("Balcony Suite")–corners, (#1 above bar, #2 quieter), elaborately woodcrafted antiques, semi-private deck above main street, double bed.

#9–end, quiet, 2 large windows, private hill view, double bed.

The Gunn House Hotel   *(209)532-3421*
downtown at 286 S. Washington St. - 95370
19 units   *Low-Moderate*
Many changes since 1851 have occurred to Sonora's oldest downtown hotel. There is now a pool and distinctive stonework out back. Housemade pastries distinguish a complimentary Continental breakfast. Each of the recently refurbished, nicely furnished room has some period pieces, a private bath, and a queen bed.

Inns of California   *(209)532-3633*
downtown at 350 S. Washington St. - 95370
innsofcal.com
112 units   *(800)251-1538*   *Moderate-Expensive*
The area's largest lodging is a modern motel a stroll from the heart of town with an outdoor pool and whirlpool. Each room is comfortably furnished and has two doubles, a queen or king bed.

"Spa Suite" (3 of these)–refrigerator/microwave, in-room two-person whirlpool, king bed.

Jamestown Hotel   *(209)984-3902*
3 mi. SW (off Hwy. 49) at 18153 Main St. - Jamestown 95327
jamestownhotel.com
11 units   *(800)205-4901*   *Moderate-Expensive*
The photogenic little brick hotel is a Gold Camp landmark in the heart of Jamestown. Downstairs is a nostalgic firelit dining room (see listing) with an elegant backbar. Breakfast is complimentary. All compact rooms are individually nicely furnished, including some antiques, a private bath with whirlpool or clawfoot tub, and a queen or king bed.

Jamestown Railtown Motel   *(209)984-3332*
3 mi. SW at 10301 Willow St. (Box 1039) - Jamestown 95327
20 units   *(800)252-8299*   *Moderate-Expensive*
The village center is right around the corner, and a pool and whirlpool are available in Jamestown's alternative to period lodging. Each motel room is simply furnished and has a queen or king bed. Eight units have an in-room large whirlpool tub.

Knowles Hill House   *(209)536-1146*
just SW (via W. Church St.) at 253 Knowles Hill Dr. - 95370
knowleshillhouse.com
    4 units   *(866)536-1146*   *Expensive*
Knowles Hill House (circa 1927) is in one of the Gold Country's
most dramatic manor houses. A historic mansion in a lush garden
on a hilltop overlooking downtown Sonora now serves as a
romantic getaway bed-and-breakfast. Full breakfast is complimentary, as is a stocked guest refrigerator. Each nicely furnished
room has some antiques and contemporary amenities, a private
(some detached) bathroom, and a queen or king bed.

Lavender Hill Bed & Breakfast   *(209)532-9024*
just S at 683 S. Barretta St. - 95070
lavenderhill.com
    4 units   *(800)446-1333x290*   *Moderate-Expensive*
Atop a rise within walking distance of downtown is this bed-and-
breakfast in a historic home. Full homestyle breakfast and
afternoon refreshments are complimentary. Each cozy, well-
furnished room has some antiques, a private bath, and queen or
king bed.
    "Lavender Room"–spacious, sitting area, clawfoot tub, king bed.

★ **McCaffrey House**   *(209)586-0757*
12 mi. E at 23251 Hwy. 108 - Twain Harte 95383
mccaffreyhouse.com
    8 units   *(888)586-0757*   *Expensive*
McCaffrey House is one of the most gracious bed-and-breakfasts
in the Sierra. The large contemporary country inn is in a quiet
hollow surrounded by luxuriant cedar, oak and pines at the edge
of Stanislaus National Forest. Full breakfast and afternoon wine
or sparkling cider and cheese are complimentary, as is use of an
outdoor spa in a garden. Each room is beautifully individually
furnished, and has a private bath, a black iron gas fire stove, all
contemporary amenities (and then some), and a queen or king
bed. Some have a private patio or balcony overlooking the serene
forest and gardens.
    "Evergreen Room"–spacious, iron gas fire stove, window
        alcove and private balcony forest views, sleigh queen bed.
    "True Blue"–iron gas fire stove, forest views from bay
        window and private balcony, four-poster queen bed.
    "Burgundy"–iron gas fire stove, bay window overlooking
        the creek and forest, sleigh queen bed.

National Hotel   *(209)984-3446*
3 mi. SW at 18183 Main St. (Box 502) - Jamestown 95327
national-hotel.com
    9 units   *(800)894-3446*   *Moderate-Expensive*

One of the Mother Lode's oldest continuously operated hotels (1859) has been fully restored. Downstairs is a popular restaurant (see listing) and classic Gold Rush saloon. An expanded Continental breakfast is complimentary. Each compact room is individually comfortably furnished with antiques, all contemporary amenities, private (some detached) bathroom, and twins or a queen bed.

Sonora Days Inn   *(209)532-2400*
   downtown at 160 S. Washington St. - 95370
   sonoradaysinn.com
   64 units   *(800)580-4667*   *Moderate-Expensive*
Sonora's historic three-story landmark (circa 1896) has been refurbished to continue to serve as the county's only full-service hotel. Amenities include a small rooftop pool, restaurant (see listing) and entertainment lounge. Recently remodeled nicely furnished hotel rooms have all contemporary conveniences. Many have a microwave and refrigerator. Comfortably furnished motel units out back by a creek also have a choice of a double, queen or king bed.
   #31,#32–in motel section, microwave/refrigerator,
      only rooms with creek view/sound, king bed.
   #201–in hotel, corner, spacious, microwave/refrigerator,
      overlooking main street, king bed.

★ **Sonora Oaks Hotel - Best Western**   *(209)533-4400*
   4 mi. E (on Hwy. 108) at 19551 Hess Av. - 95370
   rimcorp.com
   101 units   *(800)532-1944*   *Moderate-Expensive*
Noble Oaks by a seasonal creek provide cooling shade to Sonora's best country motel. The well-maintained contemporary complex includes a large landscaped pool and whirlpool. A restaurant adjoins. Each attractively furnished room has a wealth of business amenities and two queens or a king bed.
   "King Fireplace" (4 of these)–private deck, gas fireplace
      and two-person whirlpool overlook king bed.

Sterling Gardens   *(209)533-9300*
   2 mi. S at 18047 Lime Kiln Rd. - 95370
   sterlinggardens.com
   4 units   *(800)510-2225*   *Expensive*
An English country-style manor amid expansive gardens and woodlands serves as a serene, secluded bed-and-breakfast. A gourmet breakfast and evening snacks and Sterling Vineyards wine are complimentary. Each room is individually, beautifully furnished and has a private bath and queen bed.

South Lake Tahoe

South Lake Tahoe is a matchless recreation wonderland. It is ideally situated in a dense pine forest along the southern shore of one of nature's most sublime high mountain lakes. Today, South Lake Tahoe has an amazing concentration of outdoor and indoor recreation and leisure pursuits. To the delight of some and the dismay of others, the urbane enclave is so complete that fun-lovers can keep busy twenty-four hours a day, year-round—indoors. Fortunately, even more attention has been given to providing recreation facilities and access to magnificent surroundings which are perfectly complemented by the right weather during winter and summer.

Growth was slow until the 1950s, when construction of major casinos just across the Nevada state line and an enormous skiing complex established the town as both a year-round action center and a winter sports capital.

Today, a tight cluster of high-rise casinos offers gambling and big-name entertainment. Adjoining visitor-related facilities in pine-shaded South Lake Tahoe are finally coalescing around a defined town center complete with a gondola connecting down-town with nearby mountaintops. Lodgings are super-abundant and range from small motels to large lakefront resorts. So are restaurants, including some offering gourmet cuisine or spectacular views. Shops are surprisingly ordinary and scattered along a busy linear strip. But, good sources of outdoor recreation equipment are plentiful, in keeping with unlimited opportunities to enjoy the area's natural grandeur.

WEATHER PROFILE

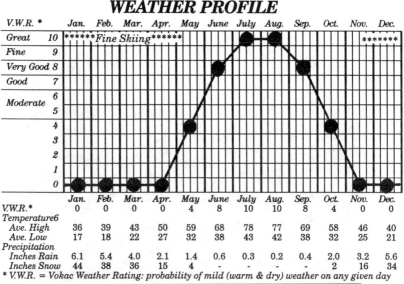

V.W.R. *		Jan.	Feb.	Mar.	Apr.	May	June	July	Aug.	Sep.	Oct.	Nov.	Dec.
Great	10												
Fine	9												
Very Good	8												
Good	7												
Moderate	6												
	5												
	4												
	3												
	2												
	1												
	0												

******Fine Skiing****** (Jan–Apr) ******* (Dec)

	Jan.	Feb.	Mar.	Apr.	May	June	July	Aug.	Sep.	Oct.	Nov.	Dec.
V.W.R.*	0	0	0	0	4	8	10	10	8	4	0	0
Temperature6												
Ave. High	36	39	43	50	59	68	78	77	69	58	46	40
Ave. Low	17	18	22	27	32	38	43	42	38	32	25	21
Precipitation												
Inches Rain	6.1	5.4	4.0	2.1	1.4	0.6	0.3	0.2	0.4	2.0	3.2	5.6
Inches Snow	44	38	36	15	4	-	-	-	-	2	16	34

* V.W.R. = Vokac Weather Rating: probability of mild (warm & dry) weather on any given day

BASIC INFORMATION

Population: 23,609
Elevation: 6,260 feet
Location: 190 miles Northeast of San Francisco
Airport (regularly scheduled flights): Reno - 53 miles

Lake Tahoe Visitors Authority   (530)544-5050 (800)288-2463
 1 mi. SW at 1156 Ski Run Blvd. - 96150
 virtualtahoe.com
South Lake Tahoe Chamber of Commerce   (530)541-5255
 2 mi. SW on Hwy. 50 at 3066 Lake Tahoe Blvd. - 96150
 tahoeinfo.com unofficial website for Lake Tahoe: tahoesbest.com

ATTRACTIONS

Aerial Tramway
★ **Heavenly Scenic Gondola Rides** *(775)586-7000 (800)243-2836*
downtown near Hwy. 50 & Park Av.
skiheavenly.com
Since the millennium, South Lake Tahoe has experienced the opening of one of the West's great attractions. A gondola is now the centerpiece of a billion-dollar renaissance in the heart of town. Eight-person enclosed cars take passengers swiftly and silently up a mountain slope adjacent to downtown to a mid-station observation deck where passengers can disembark. Walk around a rocky peak for 360° panoramic views that are genuinely breathtaking of Lake Tahoe, surrounding mountains, and deserts of Nevada to the east. Take a picnic or buy one at the gift shop to enjoy at some tables on the view deck. Passengers then continue to the top (9,136 feet) which is the base of a high mountain ski area that connects to all the runs of Heavenly Ski Resort (see listing). In addition to its obvious appeal to skiers and sightseers, the gondola also provides easy access to scenic high station trailheads designated according to level of difficulty for summer hikers.

★ *Ballooning*
During the summer months, passengers on sunrise balloon flights experience the natural grandeur of Lake Tahoe and the Sierra from a tranquil–and unique–vantage. **Lake Tahoe Balloons** offers the world's only launch and recovery from the deck of a boat. Two long-standing balloon companies offer flights over the lake daily.
Balloons Over Lake Tahoe *(530)544-7008*
balloonsoverlaketahoe.com
Lake Tahoe Balloons *(530)544-1221 (800)872-9294*
laketahoeballoons.com

★ *Bicycling* *(530)544-1221*
Many miles of exclusive bike paths are on relatively flat, scenic terrain through forests near south shore beaches, and throughout town. Beyond are a wealth of alpine backcountry trails and roads. Shops offer hourly and longer rentals of touring and mountain bikes, all related equipment and maps. Some also rent mopeds.
Anderson's Bike & Skate Rental *(530)541-0500*
Lakeview Sports *(530)544-0183*
tahoesports.com
Richardson's Resort *(530)542-6570 (800)544-1801*
camprich.com
Ski Run Boat Company *(530)544-0200 (888)542-2111*
tahoesports.com

★ *Boat Rentals*
Every kind of boating imaginable can be enjoyed on nearly two hundred square miles of deep, clear water. Visitors can rent an extraordinary assortment of craft–fishing boats, ski or cruising boats, jet skis, sailboats, catamarans, canoes, kayaks, windsurf boards or inner tubes–by the hour or longer at several marina facilities in town including:

Camp Richardson Marina   *(530)542-6570 (800)544-1801*
camprich.com
Lakeview Sports   *(530)544-0183*
tahoesports.com
Ski Run Boat Company   *(530)544-0200*
tahoesports.com
Zephyr Cove Resort Marina   *(775)589-4908*
tahoedixie2.com

★ *Boat Rides*
Large modern sightseeing boats cruise several times daily, including a sunset dinner-dance cruise to picturesque Emerald Bay. Most include glass-bottom windows to give passengers another perspective on the crystal-clear depths. Some vessels (ranging from speedboats to a large trimaran or multi-deck paddlewheelers) operate year-round.

Action Watersports   *(speedboats plus)*   *(530)544-2942*
action-watersports.com
M.S. Dixie II   *(paddlewheeler)*   *(775)589-4906*
zephyrcove.com
Tahoe Queen   *(paddlewheeler)*   *(530)541-3364*
laketahoecruises.com   *(800)238-2463*
Woodwind Sailing Cruises *(sailboats)*   *(888)867-6394*
sailwoodwind.com

★ *Casinos*
casinos adjoin downtown along Hwy. 50 by Nevada stateline
Lake Tahoe's casino resorts occupy the most spectacular gambling location in America. Six properties (including three world class resorts) are clustered in a compact district within an easy stroll of Lake Tahoe. Downtown South Lake Tahoe adjoins on the California side of the state line, where a billion dollar improvement has already provided easy access via gondola to California's largest ski resort in the mountains above downtown.

★ **D.L. Bliss and Emerald Bay State Parks**   *(530)525-7277*
11 mi. NW on Hwy. 89
parks.ca.gov
The most famous landmark of Lake Tahoe is Emerald Bay, which includes the lake's only island–Fannette. Cut into solid-rock mountain slopes high above the water, the highway around the

two-mile-long bay provides panoramic views that are unforgettable. At the head of the bay is a half-mile trail up to scenic Eagle Falls. A mile-long footpath from Inspiration Point leads steeply down to the shore, where Vikingsholm, a thirty-eight-room rock-clad mansion, can be toured during the summer. It was built in 1929 as a summer residence patterned after a Viking's castle. On the bay's east side is a large sylvan campground, with fishing, boating, and a swimming beach nearby. Just north, D.L. Bliss offers excellent hiking trails in the forests, swimming off one of the lake's most picturesque sandy beaches (especially on the south shoreline where the sand gives way to dramatic boulders), and a large full-service campground with well-spaced sites in the pines, some with lake views.

★ **Desolation Wilderness**   *(530)573-2600*
   12 mi. W off Hwy. 89
One of America's most exceptional wilderness areas covers nearly 100 square miles of pristine high country above Lake Tahoe's southwestern shoreline highway. More than one hundred named lakes lie amid a "desolation" of huge boulders and glacier-polished granite slopes nearly devoid of trees in mountains that reach almost 10,000 feet above sea level. Clear streams and waterfalls, vast pine forests, and fields of wildflowers can also be accessed by more than fifty miles of trails (some accessible by day hikes from the highway). Backpacking and camping are so popular that a campsite reservation quota system is in effect in summer. Horses and guides are available nearby for overnight and longer pack trips. Information and permits are available at Lake Tahoe Visitor Center (see listing).

★ *Fishing Charters*
Several sportfishing boats are available daily (year-round) for guided excursions in search of Mackinaw and other big trout and kokanee salmon. These long-time operators offer all necessary services and equipment for trips of various lengths:
   Dennis' Eagle Point Fishing Charters   *(530)577-6834*
   Don Sheetz Fishing Service   *(530)541-5566*   *(877)270-0742*
   Tahoe Sport Fishing   *(800)696-7797*   *(530)541-5448*

★ *Horseback Riding*
Quiet, wooded trails are found throughout the Tahoe basin. Several riding stables are located near town. The long-established stables listed offer (with reservation) guided horse rentals by the hour, half day, or day. They also can provide guides for riders on breakfast, dinner, or moonlight rides, for fishing or pack trips, plus hayrides or (in winter) sleigh rides.
   Camp Richardson Corral   *8 mi. W on Hwy. 89*   *(530)541-3113*
   Zephyr Cove Stables   *4 mi. N on Hwy. 50*   *(775)588-5664*

261

★ **Lake Tahoe**
the northern border of town
Straddling the California/Nevada state line in a luxuriant pine
forest 6,229 feet above sea level is a mountain-rimmed lake that
is one of nature's grandest achievements. The water is so clear
that a white dinner plate can be seen at a depth of nearly eighty
feet. Lake Tahoe is the largest deep alpine lake on the continent.
In fact, with its twenty-two-mile length, twelve-mile width, and
maximum depth of 1,645 feet, the lake's volume would cover the
entire State of California with more than a foot of pure water. But
statistics can't do justice to this serious contender for the world's
most beautiful water body. It's also one of the most usable, with
a remarkable assortment of watercraft available for rent, charter,
or tours. The water is cool, but swimmable in summer. Onshore
recreation facilities are plentiful, yet concentrated to better enjoy
the forest, sandy beaches, dramatic bouldered coves, streams and
mountains that surround the lake. A seventy-two-mile highway
loop around the lake is immodestly described by the South Lake
Tahoe Visitor's Bureau as "The Most Beautiful Drive in America"
on their map and guide describing points of interest.

★ **Lake Tahoe State Park (Nevada)**   *(775)831-0494*
starts 13 mi. NE via Hwy. 50 on Hwy. 28
Several miles of the lake's northeastern shoreline are included in
this large Nevada park. Pine-shaded picnic grounds near
picturesque granite boulders and sandy beaches are especially
appealing. The most popular is Sand Harbor, where lifeguards
oversee a lovely stretch of soft sand backed by picnic areas, a
visitor center, and boat launch.

★ **Lake Tahoe Visitor Center**   *(530)573-2674*
8 mi. W on Hwy. 89
The U.S. Forest Service provides an ingeniously-designed
underground stream profile chamber where you look through
glass windows into a large pool on Taylor Creek to watch trout
pass and (in fall) kokanee salmon turn bright red and spawn.
Interpretive programs, self-guided trails and guided nature walks
into the surrounding forest also originate from here. This is the
best place to get information and maps about the surrounding
Eldorado National Forest, and permits for the Desolation
Wilderness Area (see listing).

South Lake Tahoe Recreation Area   *(530)542-6056*
2 mi. SW at Hwy. 50 & Rufus Allen Blvd.
An impressive contemporary recreation center, small museum,
and campground are in a pine forest by the lake. A long sandy
beach is the local favorite for swimming and sunbathing with
splendid views of the mountain-rimmed lake.

★ **Tahoe Rim Trail**   *(775)588-0686*
 S of town and around lake
 tahoerimtrail.org
The 165-mile loop along the rim of the entire Tahoe Basin is open
to hikers, bikers, horseback riders and cross-country skiers.
Elevations range from 6,300 to 10,330 feet and the trail averages
a ten percent grade. Fourteen accesses connect the trail to
highway trailheads. Energetic adventurers are rewarded with
unforgettable natural grandeur and Lake Tahoe panoramas.

★ **Tallac Historic Site**   *(530)541-5227*
 8 mi. W on Hwy. 89
Several estates from the era when Lake Tahoe was a popular
retreat for the wealthy can now be visited. These museum
monuments to that flamboyant time are connected by forest-and-
beach trails. The Baldwin Estate is a choice example of a
lakeshore getaway as are the Pope and Valhalla Estates nearby.
Among them, visitors can get some feeling for what cabins,
gardens, boat houses were like in that "era of opulence."

Winter Sports
Lake Tahoe has the largest concentration of skiing facilities in the
world. There are three downhill ski areas surrounding town, and
seventeen near the lake. Several cross-country skiing centers are
located near the south shore. Ski rental equipment and lessons
for both downhill and cross-country skiing are available at most
major ski areas, and in town. Non-skiers can rent a snowmobile
by the hour or tour with a guide; go for a sleigh ride; or take a
tube or saucer down a hill in town at Hansen's Resort. The
biggest and best Lake Tahoe-view ski area is:

★ **Heavenly Ski Resort**   *(775)586-7000*   *(800)243-2836*
 downtown on Hwy. 50 near state line
 skiheavenly.com
One of America's largest ski areas sprawls into two states with
spellbinding views of both Lake Tahoe and the Carson Valley. The
vertical rise (the West Coast's longest) is 3,500 feet with runs up
to 5.5 miles long. The summit is 10,040 feet. There are twenty-
nine lifts (including an aerial tram and a high-speed twenty-first-
century gondola). Both day and night skiing are available on well-
groomed slopes designed for every ability. All facilities and rentals
are at the base for downhill and cross-country skiing and
snowboarding, including a snowboard park, snowboard-cross
course, and a halfpipe. An "Adventure Park" at the top of the
gondola features sledding and a lift-accessed snow tubing hill.
World class resorts, casinos, and nightclubs, plus an abundance
of restaurants and lodgings, surround the burgeoning development at the base of the gondola in the heart of town. The season
is mid-November into May.

RESTAURANTS

Beacon Bar & Grill   *(530)541-0630*   *(800)544-1801*
8 mi. W at 1900 Jameson Rd.
camprichardson.com
L-D. Sat. & Sun. brunch.   *Expensive*
Updated California standards are served in a casual dining room, bar and large pine-shaded deck by a beach and marina. The real draw is the lakefront location and lake/mountains backdrop.

Bert's Cafe   *(530)544-3434*
5 mi. SW at 1207 Emerald Bay Rd.
B-L.   *Moderate*
American breakfast standards are served in a shaped-up little wood-trim cafe with a choice of counter or padded booth seating.

★ **The Brewery at Lake Tahoe**   *(530)544-2739*
1 mi. SW at 3542 Lake Tahoe Blvd.
L-D.   *Moderate*
The Brewery is the place to check out premium beers and ales made here. You can enjoy a sampler lineup of several with one of their many pizza varieties made special by use of both beer and basil (!) in the dough.

Caesars Tahoe   *(775)588-3515*   *(800)648-3353*
downtown at 55 Hwy. 50 (Box 5800) - Stateline, NV
caesars.com/tahoe
B-L-D. Sun. brunch.   *Moderate-Very Expensive*
Caesars Resort at Lake Tahoe has a full range of dining rooms including **The Broiler Room** (D only–Very Expensive) for premium steak and seafood; **Cuvee** (D only–Very Expensive) for California cuisine; **Primavera** (D only–Expensive) for Italian dining; **The Roman Feast** (L-D–Moderate) for buffet; and **Aroma Cafe** (B-L-D–Expensive) for snacks.

★ **Cafe Fiore**   *(530)541-2908*
1 mi. SW at 1169 Ski Run Blvd.
cafefiore.com
D only.   *Expensive*
Classic and creative Italian cuisine, like boneless breast of chicken rolled with prosciutto and mango and mozzarella sautéed and finished with Madeira and wild mushroom, is carefully prepared, and served in generous portions in an intimate urbane dining room and on a patio when weather permits.

Cafe Lorraine   *(530)544-4685*
5 mi. SW at 2179 S. Lake Tahoe Blvd.
B-L-D.   *Expensive*
Many tempting desserts and breakfast pastries are displayed and served in the cheerful highway-front coffee shop, opened in 2002, or to go.

★ **The Cantina Bar & Grill**   *(530)544-1233*
5 mi. SW at 765 Emerald Bay Rd.
cantinatahoe.com
L-D.   *Moderate*
Some of California's best New Southwestern cuisine reflects the
creative genius of the owners and their skilled staff in dishes like
house-smoked chicken breast in a chili tortilla with caramelized
onions, mushrooms and cheeses served with sour cream and
guacamole; crabcakes with jalapeño cream sauce; and desserts
like tangy lime pie in coconut cookie crust. The colorful
comfortable dining rooms and cantina enhance the exciting
cuisine.

Chart House   *(775)588-6276*
2 mi. NE at 392 Kingsbury Grade - Stateline, NV
chart-house.com
D only.   *Expensive*
Contemporary American fare (prime rib, steaks, seafood) is
offered with a salad bar at this prime representative of an upscale
restaurant chain. The main attraction is an awe-inspiring
panorama of Lake Tahoe from picture windows in the big stylish
dining room and lounge high on a mountain slope east of town.

Christiania Inn   *(530)544-7337*
2 mi. S via Ski Run Blvd. at 3819 Saddle Rd.
christianiainn.com
D only. Closed Mon. except in winter.   *Very Expensive*
Continental classics are complemented by warm contemporary
furnishings including a window view of a wine cellar and a great
stone fireplace. There is also a handcrafted lounge.

★ **Dixon's**   *(530)542-3389*
5 mi. SW at 675 Emerald Bay Rd.
L-D.   *Moderate*
Dixon's is really serious about freshness, from hand-cut french
fries through homemade sauces to several luscious desserts.
Specialties like tri-fries (sweet yam and russet potato fries) or a
flaky-crust chicken pot pie can be enjoyed with any of fifteen
premium tap beers. The beer-bottle-and-taps decor is a must-see
for brew-lovers enjoying the cheerful dining room, pub with a
fireplace, and roadside garden patio.

The Driftwood Cafe   *(530)544-6545*
downtown at 4119 Laurel Av.
B-L.   *Moderate*
Unusual omelets and big buttermilk pancakes highlight light fare
in a pleasant little cafe where breakfast is featured all day.

Edgewood Restaurant   *(775)588-2787   (888)881-8659*
just N at 100 Lake Parkway - Stateline, NV

edgewood-tahoe.com
D only. Closed Mon.-Tues. Plus L in summer. *Very Expensive*
Contemporary California cuisine is served in distinctive dishes
like roast elk loin with sun-dried cherry relish. Housemade
desserts are also notable. The capacious tri-level dining room
amidst wood-trim decor offers a superb Lake Tahoe panorama.

Ernie's Coffee Shop   *(530)541-2161*
5 mi. SW at 1146 Emerald Bay Rd.
B-L.   *Moderate*
Assorted hearty omelets and scrams are featured, along with
build-your-own breakfast burritos, or biscuits and country gravy.
Hearty helpings and a full range of traditional American
breakfasts have attracted crowds to this roadside coffee shop with
padded booths since 1968.

★ **Evans American Gourmet Cafe**   *(530)542-1990*
6 mi. SW at 536 Emerald Bay Rd.
evanstahoe.com
D only.   *Very Expensive*
Evans is the best restaurant on the south shore of Lake Tahoe.
New American cuisine reflects the chef/owner's classic training,
creative confidence, and dedication to the use of choice seasonal
ingredients. Almost everything from the biscotti for cappuccino to
sensational desserts is made here from scratch. Gourmet appetizers, pasta, pizza, salads and entrees can be topped off with
lavish and luscious housemade desserts. The romantic contemporary decor of a vintage Tahoe cottage is the right setting for one
of the most enchanting dining experiences in California.

★ **The Fresh Ketch**   *(530)541-5683*
6 mi. SW (via Tahoe Keys Blvd.) at 2435 Venice Dr.
thefreshketch.com
L-D.   *Expensive*
The Fresh Ketch is the South Shore's best specialty seafood
restaurant. Expert attention is given to all dishes. Desserts can
also be fine (don't miss the delicious key lime pie). The split-level
upstairs dining room is a relaxed setting with a view of a marina,
the lake, and mountains. Downstairs is a popular lounge and
heated umbrella-shaded dining deck by the water.

★ **Freshies**   *(530)542-3630*
1 mi. SW at 3330 Lake Tahoe Blvd. #3
L-D.   *Expensive*
Fresh and flavorful are the hallmarks of Freshies. Consider
hearts of palm salad with baby field greens, gorgonzola and
hazelnuts tossed with a creamy basil dressing; or grilled salmon
with a mango-pineapple chili sauce. Luscious desserts are made
here. The snug bar and dining room have a warm "island" look,
and there is a lake-view deck upstairs.

★ **Harrah's Lake Tahoe**   *(775)588-6611   (800)553-1022*
downtown on Hwy. 50 at Stateline, NV
www.harrahs.com
B-L-D. Sun. brunch.   *Moderate-Very Expensive*
In Lake Tahoe's premier upscale hotel/casino, the **Summit** (D only–
Very Expensive) presents gourmet Continental cuisine in an
opulent setting with a grand 16th floor view of Lake Tahoe.
Forest Buffet (B-L-D–Moderate) features the region's finest
buffet amidst whimsical forest decor in an 18th floor setting with
panoramic mountain and lake views. **American River Cafe** (B-L-D–
Moderate) has casual American fare served in a delightful dining
room with a faux forest and cascading stream. **Friday's Station**
(D only–Expensive) offers steaks, chops, and seafoods with a
spectacular lake view.

★ **Harvey's Resort Hotel**   *(775)588-2411   (800)553-1022*
downtown on Hwy. 50 at Stateline, NV
www.harrahs.com
B-L-D. Brunch.   *Expensive-Very Expensive*
The area's original major hotel/casino houses three notable
restaurants. **Llewellyn's** (L-D–Very Expensive) presents Continental cuisine in an elegant setting with a panoramic lake view
from the 19th floor. The **Sage Room Steak House** (D only–
Expensive) has featured outstanding steaks amid plush Western
elegance for more than half a century. In **El Vaquero** (L-D–
Moderate), Mexican specialties are served in a colorful setting.

★ **Lake Tahoe Pizza Company**   *(530)544-1919*
5 mi. SW at 1168 Emerald Bay Rd.
D only.   *Moderate*
One of the most popular pizza parlors around the lake (since
1973) features a wide range of traditional, designer, and create-
your-own pizzas using fresh-made house or whole wheat dough
and homemade sauces. "Lake Tahoe style" rustic decor defines
dining areas outfitted with highback wooden booths.

Mirabelle French Cuisine   *(775)586-1007*
1 mi. NE at 290 Kingsbury Grade - Stateline, NV
D only. Closed Mon.   *Very Expensive*
Traditional French dishes like lobster bisque through bouilla-
baisse and on to crème brûlée are served in a casual little dining
room tucked into a shopping center near the casino district.

Nephele's   *(530)544-8130*
1 mi. SW at 1169 Ski Run Blvd.
nepheles.com
D only.   *Expensive*
Fresh seasonal California cuisine has been the highlight here
since 1977. Dishes like elk or sautéed venison are presented in an

intimate setting blending wood tones and beveled glass with garden and forest views. Private hot tub spas can also be reserved next door.

The Red Hut Cafe   *(530)541-9024*
3 mi. SW at 2149 Lake Tahoe Blvd.
B-L.   *Moderate*
A variety of well-constructed waffles and pancakes, plus fresh omelets, tops the selection in one of the area's longest established breakfast houses. Not much has changed over the years in the casual roadside cafe. A newer Red Hut is up the hill a mile east of stateline.

Riva Grill   *(530)542-2600   (888)734-2882*
1 mi. SW at 900 Ski Run Blvd., Suite 3
rivagrill.com
B-L-D.   *Very Expensive*
A diverse selection of contemporary American fare is served, but the view from a dining room with polished mahogany accents across a heated shaded deck to a marina and the lake is the primary draw. Better yet is the lounge where elevated chairs showcase the same great view.

Rockwater Bar & Grill   *(530)544-8004   (866)544-8004*
5 mi. SW at 787 Emerald Bay Rd.
rockwaterbarandgrill.com
L-D.   *Expensive*
A wide selection of California comfort foods is featured in a shaped-up historic building with a nifty pub patio open to the sky.

★ **Rude Brothers Bagel & Coffee Haus**   *(530)541-8195*
2 mi. SW at 3117 Harrison Av. - B
B-L.   *Moderate*
In a little strip shopping center near a popular beach park is the best bagelry/coffee house on the south shore. In the contemporary shop, all kinds of bagels, including a fine pizza bagel, are displayed along with assorted varieties of cinnamon rolls and a bodacious bear claw. These can be enjoyed with a wealth of hot and cold premium coffee drinks and refreshing designer smoothies in the spiffy shop, or to go.

Scusa! On Ski Run   *(530)542-0100*
1 mi. SW at 1142 Ski Run Blvd.
D only. Closed Mon. off-season.   *Expensive*
Classic Southern Italian dishes with a garlic accent are supported by enticing starters like Italian salad with gorgonzola, mixed greens and bay shrimp, or purée of roasted red pepper soup with crab and toasted crouton. Housemade desserts are also popular in this tucked-away trattoria with its light snazzy dining areas enhanced by avant-garde art.

Swiss Chalet Restaurant   *(530)544-3304*
4 mi. SW (on Hwy. 50) at 2544 Lake Tahoe Blvd.
tahoeswisschalet.com
D only. Closed Mon.   *Expensive*
Old-fashioned European and American dishes including house-
baked pastries and cheese or beef fondues accompany Swiss-
themed decor in a large, comfortable dinner house that has been
a local landmark since 1957.
★ **Tahoe Donut**   *(530)544-0615*
5 mi. SW (at the Y) at 1036 Emerald Bay Rd.
Open 24 hours.   *Moderate*
Dozens of different delectable donut varieties distinguish this
little takeout in a shopping center. Specialties like their luscious
bear claws and apple fritters and giant walnut muffins are worth
going out of the way for.

LODGINGS

One of the West's biggest concentrations of lodgings extends from
the hotel/casinos at stateline for four miles along or near the
south shore. Many year-round bargain-rate motels line Lake
Tahoe Boulevard (Highway 50). High season is mid-June to mid-
September. At other times apart from weekends, rates may be
reduced 30% or more.
★ **Black Bear Inn Bed & Breakfast**   *(530)544-4451*
1 mi. SW at 1202 Ski Run Blvd. - 96150
tahoeblackbear.com
9 units   *(877)232-7466*   *Very Expensive*
Black Bear Inn Bed & Breakfast is one of the finest adult
hideaways in the Sierra. The dramatic log complex (circa 1999)
has a gazebo whirlpool on beautifully landscaped pine-shaded
grounds with a lodge and cabins that epitomize elegant rusticity.
Full gourmet breakfast and afternoon wine and appetizers served
in a great room with a monumental river-rock fireplace and
serene pines/garden views are complimentary. Each beautifully,
individually decorated room captures the romantic spirit of the
Tahoe area and has a gas river-rock fireplace, all contemporary
amenities plus extras like a DVD player, and a king bed.
   "Snowshoe Thompson Cabin"–extra-large, kitchenette,
      romantic, in-bath two-person whirlpool, big
      walk-in shower, three-sided river-rock fireplace.
   "Fallen Leaf Room"–vaulted open-log-beam ceiling, corner
      riverstone fireplace, large private garden-view balcony.
Blue Jay Lodge   *(530)544-5232*
downtown at 4133 Cedar Av. - 96150

bluejaylodge.com
65 units   *(800)258-3529*   *Moderate-Expensive*
This modern motel is a stroll from the beach, casinos and gondola and has a small pool and whirlpool. Each room is nicely furnished and has two doubles or a king bed.
  #150–woodburning fireplace and two-person
    whirlpool in view of king bed.
  #253,#254–large in-bath whirlpool, gas fireplace
    in view of king bed.

★ **Caesars Tahoe**   *(775)588-3515*
downtown at 55 Hwy. 50 (Box 5800) - Stateline, NV 89449
caesers.com/tahoe
440 units   *(800)648-3353*   *Expensive*
Caesars' contemporary fourteen-story resort has a lagoon-style indoor pool, whirlpool, saunas, plus (fee) tennis courts, beauty salon and full-featured spa. There are also several restaurants (see listing); a top-name showroom and nightclub; a vast 24-hour casino; and resort boutiques and gift shops. Most of the well-furnished rooms have a Roman tub, a distant lake or mountain view, and doubles, queen or king bed.

Cedar Lodge   *(530)544-6453*
downtown at 4069 Cedar Av. - 96150
cedarlodgetahoe.com
54 units   *(800)222-1177*   *Moderate*
This contemporary motel amid pines a stroll from the beach, casinos and gondola has a small pool and two whirlpools. Each room is comfortably furnished and has a queen or king bed. Rooms with a gas fireplace and refrigerator are available.

Christiania Inn   *(530)544-7337*
2 mi. S at 3819 Saddle Rd. (Box 18298) - 96151
christianiainn.com
6 units   *Moderate-Expensive*
This small inn overlooks a base of Heavenly Ski Resort across a parking lot, and has a restaurant and bar (see listing). A Continental breakfast brought to your room and decanter of brandy are complimentary. Each spacious, well-furnished unit has dramatic ski slope views and a queen or king bed. Suites also have a fireplace.
  "suite #4"–split level, wet bar, woodburning fireplace,
    high window wall with ski slope view, in-loft queen bed.
  "suite #5"–wet bar, woodburning fireplace, sauna, king bed.

★ **Embassy Suites Hotel Lake Tahoe Resort**   *(530)544-5400*
downtown at 4130 Lake Tahoe Blvd. - 96150
embassytahoe.com
400 units   *(877)497-8483*   *Expensive-Very Expensive*

The casinos and gondola are only steps from this nine-story all-suites resort, and Lake Tahoe is within walking distance. Amenities of the contemporary chalet-style complex include an indoor pool, whirlpool, sauna, fitness center, stylish restaurant, lounge, and gift shop. Complimentary full breakfast and manager's afternoon reception with beverages take place in a tranquil garden atrium with a historic flume and waterwheel. Each spacious, beautifully furnished suite has a living room, microwave, stocked mini-bar, and two doubles or a king bed.
"Balcony King" (4 of these)–spacious, private
lake/town-view deck, king bed.
★ **Embassy Vacation Resort Lake Tahoe**   *(530)541-6122*
1 mi. SW at 901 Ski Run. Blvd. - 96150
embassyvacationresorts.com
280 units   (800)362-2779   Expensive-Very Expensive
The Ski Run Marina adjoins this contemporary six-story timeshare/resort hotel. Amenities include a large indoor/outdoor pool with a lake view, whirlpool, sauna, exercise room, ping pong table, coffee shop, lounge and gift shop. Overnight guests have a choice of studios, one- or two-bedroom units. Some have partial lake views. Each well-furnished suite has a kitchenette or kitchen, a gas fireplace, and two doubles and/or a king bed.
one-bedroom suite (142 of these)–kitchen, private deck,
gas fireplace, in bath large whirlpool, king bed.
★ **Fantasy Inn**   *(530)541-6666*
1 mi. SW at 3696 Lake Tahoe Blvd. - 96150
fantasy-inn.com
53 units   (800)367-7736   Very Expensive
One of America's most sophisticated paeans to passion opened in 1994. Behind a contemporary motel facade are a tantalizing variety of playful adult "theme rooms." Each spacious, beautifully furnished unit has a large in-room whirlpool (some are heart-shaped), a European shower for two with "his" and "hers" shower-head, mood lighting and mirrors, extra amenities and a king bed.
"Rain Forest," "Romeo and Juliet," "Romans"–extra-large
in-room sunken whirlpool, gas fireplace, refrigerator,
mirrored alcove with round king bed.
★ **Harrah's Lake Tahoe**   *(775)588-6606*
downtown (on Hwy. 50) at state line (Box 8) - Stateline, NV 89449
harrahs.com
525 units   (800)427-7247   Expensive-Very Expensive
The Lake Tahoe area's preeminent hotel/casino is Harrah's. Both the lake and gondola to the mountain top are nearby. The contemporary eighteen-story resort has an indoor/outdoor pool and whirlpools, (fee) full-service salon and spa with gym, sauna,

steam, and whirlpool; (fee) tanning beds, plus a game room and shopping arcade. There are also (fee) yacht cruises aboard Harrah's Tahoe Star, four major restaurants (see listing), a top-name showroom, nightclub, Improv Cabaret, free entertainment bar with dueling pianos, and an expansive 24-hour casino. All of the extra-spacious, beautifully furnished rooms have two complete bathrooms, extra amenities, and two doubles or a king bed. Many also have a grand lake/mountains view.

★ **Harvey's Resort Hotel/Casino**   *(775)588-2411*
   downtown (on Hwy. 50) at state line (Box 128) - Stateline, NV 89449
   harrahs.com
   740 units   *(800)427-8397*   *Expensive-Very Expensive*
Tahoe's first gaming establishment is now the largest hotel/casino overlooking the lake. It is also near the gondola to the mountain top. The post-modern nineteen-story complex has a large pool, whirlpool, full-service (fee) health club, game rooms, and a shopping arcade. There are three notable restaurants (see listing), cabaret theater, entertainment lounges, and a large 24-hour casino. Beautifully furnished spacious rooms have two doubles or a king bed. Many have a superb lake-and-mountains view. A few suites also have an in-bath large whirlpool.

Horizon Casino Resort   *(775)588-6211*
   downtown at 50 Hwy. 50 (Box C) - Stateline, NV 89449
   horizoncasino.com
   539 units   *(800)648-3322*   *Expensive-Very Expensive*
Many rooms in a contemporary fourteen-story tower have some view of Lake Tahoe beyond a pine forest. In addition to a casino, there is the area's largest outdoor pool, big whirlpools, exercise room, shopping arcade, three restaurants, multiplex cinema, and a cabaret show lounge. Each well-furnished room has two doubles or a king bed. Some have a private balcony with a lake view. A few large elaborate suites have a gas fireplace and/or two-person whirlpool.

Inn at Heavenly   *(530)544-4244*
   1 mi. SW at 1261 Ski Run Blvd. - 96150
   innatheavenly.com
   14 units   *(800)692-2246*   *Expensive-Very Expensive*
For years, this little motel-in-the-pines with log-cabin-style rooms has provided a quiet getaway. A large spa room with whirlpool, steambath, and sauna is complimentary for one hour per day of private use, as are an expanded Continental breakfast, and evening wine and appetizers. Each compact, well-furnished room has a gas fireplace, private bath, refrigerator, microwave, all contemporary amenities, and a queen or king bed. There are also three 3+ bedroom cabins on-site.

★ **Inn by the Lake**   *(530)542-0330*
2 mi. SW (on Hwy. 50) at 3300 Lake Tahoe Blvd. - 96150
innbythelake.com
100 units   *(800)877-1466*   *Expensive-Very Expensive*
The lake and a fine public beach are across the highway from this contemporary motel in the pines with a large pool, whirlpool, and sauna. Bicycles, and (in winter) snowshoes are complimentary, as is Continental breakfast. Many of the well-furnished rooms have, in addition to queens or a king bed, a small private balcony with a lake view.
"one-bedroom suite" (4 of these)–spacious, kitchen, in-bath two-person whirlpool, king bed.

Lakeland Village Beach & Mountain Resort   *(530)544-1685*
1 mi. SW at 3535 Lake Tahoe Blvd. - 96150
lakeland-village.com
212 units   *(800)822-5969*   *Expensive-Very Expensive*
Nestled among pines by Lake Tahoe is a large condo complex with a quarter mile of private sandy beach that is ideal for swimming and sunning. A boat pier, rental boats, two landscaped pools, two whirlpools, sauna, and (fee) two tennis courts are also available to guests. Each lodge room or studio to four-bedroom townhouse is well furnished and has a kitchen, fireplace, and a private balcony or deck. Unfortunately for couples, only units with three or more bedrooms have lakefront views.

Motel 6   *(530)542-1400*
4 mi. SW at 2375 Lake Tahoe Blvd. - 96150
motel6.com
143 units   *(800)466-8356*   *Moderate*
"They'll leave the light on for you" at the chain's modern motel with a pool. Each room is compact and simply furnished with two doubles or a queen bed.

Royal Valhalla Motor Lodge   *(530)544-2233*
just W at 4104 Lakeshore Blvd. - 96150
tahoeroyalvalhalla.com
80 units   *(800)999-4104*   *Expensive*
This contemporary motel offers guest privileges at a splendid private beach across the street. A large outdoor pool, whirlpool, and expanded Continental breakfast are also complimentary. Most spacious, well-furnished rooms have a queen bed and a private balcony. Some have a lake view and/or kitchenette.

Stardust Tahoe   *(530)544-5211*
downtown at 4061 Lake Tahoe Blvd. - 96150
stardust-tahoe.com
86 units   *(800)262-5077*   *Moderate-Expensive*
The Stardust timeshare/motel is at the heart of South Lake Tahoe

across the street from the new super gondola and a stroll from the casino district and the beach. The complex includes two pools, two whirlpools, ping pong, and a gym. Use of bicycles and golf and fishing gear are complimentary during summer. Each well-furnished unit (studio to two-bedroom) has a microwave, refrigerator, wet bar, a large tiled dual-head shower, extra amenities, and a queen or king bed.

Station House Inn - Best Western   *(530)542-1101*
   downtown at 901 Park Av. - 96150
   stationhouseinn.com
   100 units   *(800)822-5953*   *Moderate-Expensive*
A sandy lakefront beach and casino district are a short stroll from this contemporary complex amidst a garden in the pines. A pool, whirlpool, and full breakfast are complimentary to guests. A restaurant (B-L-D. Closed Wed.–Moderate) and lounge are on site. Each attractively furnished room has doubles, queens, or a king bed.
   "California," "Nevada"–two-person whirlpool by raised king bed.

Tahoe Chalet Inn   *(530)544-3311*
   just SW at 3860 Lake Tahoe Blvd. -96150
   www.tahoechaletinn.com
   66 units   *(800)821-2656*   *Moderate-Very Expensive*
The Tahoe Chalet Inn has a pool and whirlpool. Each compact motel room is simply furnished and has a queen bed. The eight themed rooms have many extra touches.
   "Queen's Parlor"–refrigerator, microwave, two-
      person in-room heart-shaped bubble tub, wood-
      burning fireplace in view of queen bed.

★ **Tahoe Lakeshore Lodge & Spa**   *(530)541-2180*
   2 mi. SW at 930 Bal Bijou Rd. - 96150
   tahoelakeshorelodge.com
   71 units   *(800)448-4577*   *Expensive-Very Expensive*
One of the best locations on the lake is the site for this contemporary motel/condo complex. In addition to 500 feet of scenic sandy beach, the recently remodeled and upgraded four-story complex also houses a lake-view pool, whirlpool, sauna, and (fee) full-service spa. Each of the spacious, beautifully furnished lodge or condo units has a fireplace (gas in lodge, woodburning in condos), balcony or patio with lake view, and one or two queen beds. Most also have a kitchen.

★ **Tahoe Seasons Resort**   *(530)541-6700*
   2 mi. SW at 3901 Saddle Rd. (Box 16300) - 96151
   tahoeseasons.com
   160 units   *(800)540-4874*   *Expensive-Very Expensive*
A short walk from the slopes of Heavenly Ski Resort, this large modern resort in the pines has a pool, whirlpool, two tennis

courts, game room, restaurant, lounge, gift shop, and seasonal ski shop. Each spacious, nicely decorated unit has a living area, bedroom, a kitchenette, and a queen bed. Most also have a gas fireplace and a large whirlpool in view of the fireplace and bed. Some have a slope view.

Tahoe Valley Lodge   *(530)541-0353*
3 mi. SW at 2241 Lake Tahoe Blvd. - 96150
tahoevalleylodge.com
19 units   *(800)669-7544*   *Moderate-Expensive*
This motel has a pool and whirlpool. Each comfortably furnished room has a gas fireplace and queen or king bed.
    "King Suite"–microwave/refrigerator, gas fireplace,
        in-room two-person whirlpool, king bed.

★ **Timber Cove Lodge Marina Resort-Best Western** *(530)541-6722*
1 mi. SW (on Hwy. 50) at 3411 Lake Tahoe Blvd. - 96150
timbercovetahoe.com
262 units   *(800)972-8558*   *Expensive*
This large contemporary motor hotel is on attractively landscaped lakefront grounds including six hundred feet of sandy beach next to one of the best public beaches on the lake. In addition to fine lake swimming, there is a fishing pier, full marina with boat rentals and cruises, large pool and whirlpool, fitness center and (fee) massage studio, plus a fireplace lobby/lounge and dining room. Full breakfast is complimentary. Each spacious room is well furnished, and has two doubles or a king bed.
    "Honeymoon Suite" (2 of these)–full lake view,
        gas fireplace, private deck, in-room two-person
        whirlpool with view, round king bed.
    #512,#508,#504,#269,#245,#221–end rooms, fine
        lakefront view, semi-private balcony, king bed.

★ **Zephyr Cove Resort**   *(775)589-4907*
4 mi. NE at 760 Hwy. 50 (Box 830) - Zephyr Cove, NV 89448
zephyrcove.com
28 units   *Moderate-Expensive*
Zephyr Cove has evolved since 1862 into Tahoe's most fun-filled lakefront resort. The choice location on a sandy cove in the pines has a nearly mile-long beach with a sunny southwest exposure. There is a full-service marina, gift shop, restaurant, and various fees for boat rentals, cruises, horseback rides, and (in winter) snowmobiles. Plain lodge rooms have a private bathroom and twins or double bed. Rustic cabins in the pines near the beach range from simply furnished studios to four bedrooms with twins, doubles or queen beds. Most have lake views and full kitchens with a refrigerator, oven, and microwave. Some have a gas fireplace and a private wood deck.

275

Tahoe City

Tahoe City is the outdoor recreation hub of the Sierra high country. It is situated in a dense pine forest along the northern shore of one of the world's most beautiful high mountain lakes. Two seasons perfectly complement this splendid natural environment. Summer days are ideal for enjoying both Lake Tahoe and the Truckee River which flows out of the lake through town. In winter, the other peak season, enormous snowfalls entice throngs to a remarkable number of major facilities for snow sports in the mountains around town.

Summer resorts began to develop along the north shore during the 1870s. In part because of its unique location at the only river outlet of the lake, Tahoe City became the terminus for a small railroad a century ago. In the late 1950s development of the first ski areas and casinos began to turn the Tahoe basin into a year-round attraction.

Today, this is the best-defined business district on the lake. Recent improvements have enhanced walkways, landscapes and the main street connecting shopping complexes sporting wood-toned "Tahoe style" architecture that blends nicely with the luxuriant pine forest. Downtown also has a concentration of good restaurants. Other in-town attractions include a scenic lakeshore park, idyllic sites for starting a river trip, and the aptly named "Fanny Bridge." Not surprisingly, the main road around the lake in both directions provides a linear route to a wealth of water-oriented recreation sites, gourmet restaurants and romantic lodgings with spellbinding views.

WEATHER PROFILE

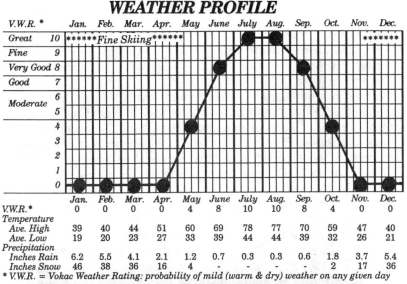

V.W.R. *		Jan.	Feb.	Mar.	Apr.	May	June	July	Aug.	Sep.	Oct.	Nov.	Dec.
Great	10	******Fine Skiing******											*******
Fine	9												
Very Good	8												
Good	7												
Moderate	6												
	5												
	4												
	3												
	2												
	1												
	0												

	Jan.	Feb.	Mar.	Apr.	May	June	July	Aug.	Sep.	Oct.	Nov.	Dec.
V.W.R.*	0	0	0	0	4	8	10	10	8	4	0	0
Temperature												
Ave. High	39	40	44	51	60	69	78	77	70	59	47	40
Ave. Low	19	20	23	27	33	39	44	44	39	32	26	21
Precipitation												
Inches Rain	6.2	5.5	4.1	2.1	1.2	0.7	0.3	0.3	0.6	1.8	3.7	5.4
Inches Snow	46	38	36	16	4	-	-	-	-	2	17	36

* V.W.R. = Vokac Weather Rating: probability of mild (warm & dry) weather on any given day

BASIC INFORMATION

Population: 1,600
Elevation: 6,252 feet
Location: 205 miles Northeast of San Francisco
Airport (regularly scheduled flights): Reno - 44 miles

North Lake Tahoe Chamber of Commerce (530)581-6900
  downtown near jct. of hwys. 89 & 28
  at 245 N. Lake Blvd. (Box 884) - 96145
North Lake Tahoe Resort Association (888)434-1262
Visitors & Convention Bureau (Box 1757) - 96145
  mytahoevacation.com

ATTRACTIONS

Aerial Tramway
★ **Squaw Valley Cable Car**   *(530)583-6985*
8 mi. NW via Hwy. 89 & Squaw Valley Rd. - Olympic Valley
squaw.com

Visitors in a big heated enclosure with panoramic windows are whisked 2,000 feet up from the valley floor to High Camp atop a nearby ridge. The lake and mountains provide a magnificent backdrop for facilities including an ice skating rink, an enormous swimming pool and spa, tennis courts, two restaurants and lounges, and a 1960 Olympics museum. Scenic hiking and biking trails are plentiful. Down in the village, the cable car building includes a thirty-foot simulated rock climbing wall and a cafe.

★ Bicycling
Miles of separated bike paths extending through town from Sugar Pine to Squaw Valley are relatively flat, safe, and memorably scenic. In the surrounding mountains are hundreds of miles of maintained trails for mountain bikes. Both regular and mountain bicycles can be rented by the hour or longer with all necessary equipment, plus trail maps and information, at:

The Back Country *downtown at 255 N. Lake Blvd. 581-5861*
thebackcountry.net
Cyclepaths *2 mi. S at 1785 W. Lake Blvd. (800)780-2453*
cyclepaths.com
Olympic Bike Shop *downtown at 620 N. Lake Blvd. 581-2500*
tahoebikerentals.com
Porter's Ski & Sport *downtown at 501 N. Lake Blvd. 583-2314*

★ Boat Rentals
Every kind of boating imaginable is enjoyed on Lake Tahoe. Several marinas and stores along the north shore rent watercraft, including fishing, pleasure, ski and sail boats, canoes, kayaks, or jet skis. Following are the most convenient.

Homewood Marina	*Homewood*	*(530)525-5966*
Meeks Bay Marina	*Meeks Bay*	*(530)525-5588*
North Tahoe Marina	*Tahoe Vista*	*(530)546-8248*
Sunnyside Marina	*Sunnyside*	*(530)583-7201*
Tahoe City Marina	*Tahoe City*	*(530)583-1039*

Boat Rides
★ **North Tahoe Cruises**   *(530)583-0141   (800)218-2464*
downtown at 850 N. Lake Blvd.
tahoegal.com

Sightseeing, happy hour, and sunset dinner cruises along the north shore of Lake Tahoe and lunch cruises to Emerald Bay aboard the "Tahoe Gal," a paddlewheel boat with a glass-bottom window, are offered daily from mid-April through October.

278

Boating

★ **Kayak Cafe & Rentals** *(530)546-9337*
5 mi. NE at 5166 N. Lake Tahoe Blvd. - Carnelian Bay
tahoepaddle.com
A nifty pine-trimmed freestanding building by Lake Tahoe is the place to rent kayaks and canoes–ideal for leisurely adventures along the picturesque shoreline. All related equipment is available in the full-service shop. Guided tours and lessons can be arranged. There is also a pleasant lakeside patio and grill with assorted beverages plus bagels and other light breakfasts, lunches and snacks to enjoy at tables inside and on a waterside garden deck.

Fanny Bridge
downtown on Hwy. 89 just S of Hwy. 28
Everyone should take the time to walk out on this bridge and look over the railing into the crystal-clear Truckee River to see big rainbow trout waiting below to snap up food that's tossed down to them. Nearby, Lake Tahoe outlet gates are used to control the flow of water into the Truckee River–the lake's only outlet.

★ *Fishing Charters*
Trout and kokanee salmon fishing can be excellent on Lake Tahoe and the Truckee River. Professional guides have charter sportfishing boats and the latest in fishing equipment to improve visitors' luck year-round. In town and nearby are:

Kingfish Guide Service *(530)525-5360* *(800)622-5462*
Mickey's Big Mac Charters *(530)546-4444* *(800)877-1462*
Reel Deal Sport Fishing *(530)581-0924*

★ **Gatekeeper's Cabin Museum** *(530)583-1762*
downtown at 130 W. Lake Blvd. (Truckee River outlet)
The North Lake Tahoe Historical Society has restored the cabin once used by the person who controlled the flow of water out of Lake Tahoe. It now contains historic Tahoe photos and relics. Adjacent pine-shaded picnic tables are beautifully located overlooking the Truckee River outlet. Closed in winter.

Golf

★ **The Golf Courses at Incline Village** *(702)832-1144 (888)236-8725*
15 mi. NE at 955 Fairway Dr. - Incline Village, NV
golfincline.com
A beautifully landscaped 18-hole (par-72) "Championship Course" and an 18-hole (par-58) "Mountain Course" were designed by Robert Trent Jones. Views of the lake through the pines are outstanding. Both are open to the public (May-October), and offer all facilities and services.

Tahoe City Golf Course *(530)583-1516*
downtown at 251 N. Lake Blvd.
www.tcgc.com
Conveniently located downtown, this genteel pine-studded 9-hole

golf course with some lake views is open to the public. There is also a putting green, bar, and restaurant.

★ *Hiking*

The U.S. Forest Service and the California State Parks Department maintain many miles of scenic hiking trails near town and around the lake. The "Tahoe Rim Trail" (see South Lake Tahoe chapter) can be accessed nearby and rewards energetic hikers with natural grandeur and lake panoramas.

★ *Horseback Riding*

Several area stables rent horses by the hour or longer for guided trail rides into pristine high country from May through September. Trips doing portions of the inspiring Tahoe Rim Trail and longer pack trips can also be arranged at:

Alpine Meadows Stables   *(530)583-3905*
5 mi. NW at 2600 Alpine Meadows Rd.
Ponderosa Ranch Stables   *(775)831-2154*
21 mi. NE at 100 Ponderosa Ranch Rd. - Incline Village, NV
Squaw Valley Stables   *(530)583-7433*
8 mi. NW at 1525 Squaw Valley Rd. - Olympic Valley

★ **Lake Tahoe**

the eastern border of town

One of the world's most beautiful lakes straddles the California/Nevada border in the Sierra Nevada mountains 6,229 feet above sea level. This water wonderland is 22 miles long and 12 miles wide. With an average depth of almost 1,000 feet, and at 1,645 feet at the deepest point, it is the second deepest lake in America. In spite of major developments along the shoreline, the lake is still so clear that it is said a white dinner plate can be seen at a depth of nearly eighty feet! A splendid assortment of recreation facilities contributes to the appeal of forests, streams, river, sandy beaches and dramatic boulder-studded coves that surround the mountain-rimmed lake. Even though the maximum water temperature is never warm, swimming in crystal-clear water is popular on sunny summer days. The entire shoreline is backed by a 72-mile highway loop immodestly described as "The Most Beautiful Drive in America." Visitors can judge for themselves using a map and brochure describing points of interest along the route–available at the Chamber of Commerce.

★ **Ponderosa Ranch**   *(775)831-0691*

21 mi. NE at 100 Ponderosa Ranch Rd. - Incline Village, NV
ponderosaranch.com

The ranch house of Ben Cartwright and his sons (of TV's *Bonanza* fame) is the centerpiece for a complex that includes dozens of Old West-style buildings filled with memorabilia from that era (everything from horse-drawn hearses to sleighs). There are ranch house tours, mining exhibits, and movie props. From Memorial Day through Labor Day, take a hay wagon breakfast ride or a guided horseback trail ride, interact with Western stunt shows or gun fights, and prospect for nuggets. Almost all of the buildings and displays are delightfully as they were pre-electricity. Family fast-food places are themed to the cast (like "Hoss burgers"), and you may see authentic crafts and craftsmen doing horse shoeing, glass blowing, etc. Open mid-April to October.

★ *River Running*
Truckee River Rafting with Mountain Air Sports
(530)583-7238   (888)584-7238
downtown at jct. of Hwys. 89 & 28 by Fanny Bridge
Do-it-yourself rafting (family-operated since 1974) from Fanny Bridge is a world class attraction thanks to skilled friendly operators making sure that everyone is properly outfitted, has a delightful safe trip, and is picked up and shuttled back to their cars. The four-mile float on some of the clearest water anywhere is enhanced by a mixed-pine backdrop, the adjacent bike path, occasional ducks and geese along the route, deep clear pools, plus enough riffles for easy exhilaration. Related equipment is sold in the shop by the river.

★ **Royal Gorge Cross Country Ski Resort**   *(800)500-3871*
25 mi. NW (via I-80) at 9411 Hillside Dr. - Soda Springs
royalgorge.com
High in the Sierra, with more than 9,000 acres of skiing terrain and hundreds of miles of groomed trails, this is the largest cross-country ski resort in North America. Facilities include four user-friendly surface lifts, two trailside lodges and a day lodge, ten warming huts, and four trailside cafes. All appropriate rentals and a ski school are available.

★ **Sugar Pine Point State Park**   *(530)525-7982*
10 mi. S on Hwy. 89
parks.ca.gov
In a dense forest of sugar pines, this very popular park offers more than one mile of beaches along Lake Tahoe for swimming and sunbathing, plus picnic sites, hiking trails, and camping in summer. The imposing turn-of-the-(19th)-century Hellman-Ehrman Mansion (former vacation residence of a wealthy San Francisco family) is now an interpretive center with several daily tours and museum with Tahoe memorabilia. In winter, cross-country skiing, snowshoeing, and winter camping attract visitors.

★ **Tahoe City Commons Beach**
downtown
Downtown has a recently enhanced, pine-shaded lawn with picnic tables, play equipment, restrooms, and a photogenic sandy beach for swimming and sunbathing.

Tahoe State Recreation Area   *(530)583-3074*
just N on N. Lake Blvd.
parks.ca.gov
The short beach is nearly always crowded in summer, as is the small neighboring campground, because of the pine-forested lakefront location at the north end of the business district.

★ **Truckee**   *(530)587-2757*
15 mi. N on Hwy. 89 - Truckee
truckee.com
Truckee sprawls along a narrow valley well over a mile high in the Sierra Nevada Mountains. The town prospered with completion of the first transcontinental railroad in 1869 as a main line stop on the Union Pacific Railroad, and from completion of a transcontinental interstate freeway more than a century later. The railroad and highway dominate the confined valley, but the historic downtown is notable. "Commercial Row" is a long block of antique buildings opposite the depot that has been enhanced by wooden sidewalks, shade trees, flowers and benches. It's an inviting place to browse for regional arts, crafts, and gourmet treats. The area's best restaurants are here, too. **Pacific Crest** (10042 Donner Pass Rd., (530)587-2626)(L-D–Expensive) offers first-rate contemporary California cuisine ranging from designer wood-fired pizzas to poached wild salmon and housemade seasonal fresh fruit cobblers in a stylish dining room. A historic saloon adjoins. **Pianeta** (10068 Donner Pass Rd., (530)587-4694) (D only–Expensive) is a sophisticated landmark for Northern Italian cuisine like grilled double-cut lamb chops, fresh homemade pastas, and tiramisu and other luscious housemade desserts in a classy trattoria with stone walls and worldly art objects. Truckee's most appealing lodging is **Richardson House** (10154 High St.-96161, (530)587-5388). A transformed Victorian home is now a bed-and-breakfast on a hill overlooking downtown. Most well-furnished rooms include some antiques, a private bath, queen bed and a valley view.

Winter Sports
  Skiing
With eight downhill ski areas within a dozen miles of town and many more around the lake, this is one of the most thoroughly developed alpine skiing regions in the world. In addition, cross-country ski touring centers are numerous. The attraction is the awesome snowpack each winter and breathtakingly beautiful mountain and lake scenery. Ski and snowboard equipment rentals, sales, maps, and information can be obtained at any of the ski areas or from several sporting goods stores downtown. Ski season usually begins in mid-November and ends in May in most areas.

★ **Homewood Mountain Resort** *(530)525-2992 (888)434-1262*
6 mi. S at 5145 W. Lake Blvd.
skihomewood.com
The key feature of this ski area is that ski slopes are closest to the
shoreline, and virtually all runs have fine views of Lake Tahoe
and surrounding peaks. With a vertical rise of 1,650 feet, there
are four chairlifts, half the terrain is intermediate, and 15% is for
beginners, ski patrol and ski school, plus rental and repair shop.
A dining room, cafe, and bar are also at the site.

★ **Squaw Valley U.S.A.** *(530)483-6955 (800)545-4350*
8 mi. NW (off Hwy. 89) on Squaw Valley Rd. - Olympic Valley
www.squaw.com
The site of the 1960 Winter Olympics is the largest downhill ski
area in North Tahoe. With more than 4,000 acres of skiable
terrain, the world class complex has an outstanding variety of
slopes for skiers; and snowboarders have three complete areas
with terrain, parks, and half-pipes. A vertical drop of 2,850 feet
from a 9,050-foot summit is served by twenty-seven lifts,
including a cable car and a super gondola. The longest run is
three miles. A major cross-country ski center, night skiing, and
snow-tubing arena with its own lift are other features. All rentals
and services are provided along with many restaurants, bars, and
lodgings at the base. The first phases of a new quarter-billion-
dollar alpine village are now open at the base of the gondola.

★ **Tahoe Nordic Ski Area** *(530)583-5475*
3 mi. NE (via Hwy. 28) at 925 Country Club Dr.
More than thirty miles of groomed trails provide spectacular
views of Lake Tahoe from pine-forested slopes and brilliant
meadows. Rentals, lessons, guided tours (both day and moonlight), and a day lodge are at the area.

Sleigh Rides
Squaw Valley Riding Stables *(530)583-0419*
8 mi. NW (via Hwy. 89) at 1525 Squaw Valley Rd. - Olympic Valley
Sleigh rides can be arranged here any day in winter.

Snow Play Area
Granlibakken *(530)583-4242*
1 mi. SW (via Hwy. 89) on Tonopah Dr.
A rope tow takes beginner skiers up gentle-to-intermediate slopes
at the oldest established ski resort in the Tahoe basin. Plastic
saucers, plus downhill and cross-country rentals, are provided.
The lodge has a restaurant and lounge.

Snowmobiling
Tahoe City Recreation Area *(530)583-1516*
downtown at 251 N. Lake Blvd.
In winter, the downtown golf course becomes part of a recreation
area where snowmobiles can be rented by the hour or half hour.

RESTAURANTS

The Big Water Grille   *(775)833-0606*
20 mi. NE at 341 Ski Way - Incline Village, NV
bigwatergrille.com
D only.   *Very Expensive*
Innovative Pacific Rim cuisine is showcased in dishes like grilled
venison flank with wild rice, and creative flavorful housemade
desserts. Big tri-level dining areas and a snazzy firelit bar offer
window-wall views through the pines to the lake far below.

★ **Boulevard Cafe & Trattoria**   *(530)546-7213*
8 mi. NE at 6731 N. Lake Blvd. - Tahoe Vista
D only.   *Very Expensive*
Northern Italian cuisine accompanied by housemade breads and
pastas is given expert attention in traditional and innovative
dishes. Consider a double-cut rack of venison with a cabernet sun-
dried cherry sauce, or sweet-and-sour roast half duck with sun-
dried fruit and almonds. Crisp white linens enhance a simply
elegant intimate dining room.

★ **Bridgetender Tavern & Grill**   *(530)583-3342*
downtown at 65 W. Lake Blvd.
L-D.   *Moderate*
Contemporary California comfort food and nearly two dozen tap
beers complement quintessential Tahoe City decor with its rough
beams, two handcrafted bars, and whimsical wood carvings. A
heated garden patio is shaded by pine trees and umbrellas and
has a delightful view along the Truckee River across from the
river raft rental's launching dock.

Brockway Bakery   *(530)546-2431*
9 mi. NE at 8710 N. Lake Blvd. - Kings Beach
B-L.   *Expensive*
Bear claws and other breakfast pastries including assorted
croissants are supported later by treats like designer sandwiches
and desserts. All are well made and available with coffee at a few
tables inside and by the highway, or to go.

Cafe Cobblestone   *(530)583-2111*
downtown at 475 N. Lake Blvd.
B-L.   *Moderate*
An American cafe menu is offered in a casual contemporary
restaurant where both the dining room and an inviting outdoor
patio have lake views across the highway.

Cafe 333   *(775)832-7333*
15 mi. NE at 333 Village Blvd. - Incline Village, NV
B-L-D. Closed for D some nights off season.   *Expensive*
Fresh and flavorful creative California cuisine with an

adventurous flair is served in a roadside cottage transformed into a cozy casual dining room and bar with a garden dining deck.

★ **Christy Hill** *(530)583-8551*
downtown at 115 Grove St.
christyhill.com
D only. Closed Mon. Very Expensive
Innovative American cuisine includes expert presentations of bold dishes using fresh quality ingredients from nationwide sources. Luscious desserts like seasonal fruit cobblers, or homemade pecan ice cream with warm bourbon caramel sauce, are uniformly appealing. The intimate, elegant dining room and dining terrace share a window-wall panoramic view of Lake Tahoe.

Coyote's Mexican Grill *(530)583-6653*
downtown at 521 N. Lake Blvd.
D only. Closed Mon. Expensive
Traditional Mexican cuisine has a California accent in dishes like chiles rellanos with roasted chiles stuffed with bay scallops. Imaginative fare topped off with housemade desserts like creamy lime pie served with orange lime custard is served in a cheerful little dining room or a flower-decked courtyard.

Fiamma Cucina Rustica *(530)581-1416*
downtown at 521 N. Lake Blvd.
D only. Expensive
Build-your-own pizzas from all sorts of toppings, or enjoy specialty pizzas and calzones, as well as updates of classic Italian dishes. Housemade desserts contribute to the appeal of this trattoria with a central island bar and a picture-window view of their planter garden and the lake through pines across the street.

★ **Fire Sign Cafe** *(530)583-0871*
2 mi. S at 1785 W. Lake Blvd.
B-L. Moderate
The Fire Sign has the best breakfasts on the lake. Delicious fresh-baked muffins, coffee cakes and desserts complement light, luscious homestyle meals prepared with a creative flair. Nostalgic furnishings distinguish several wood-trimmed dining areas, and a dining deck is shaded by aspens and pines. This little landmark has been deservedly popular for decades.

Gar Woods Grill & Pier Restaurant *(530)546-3366 (800)298-2463*
5 mi. NE at 5000 N. Lake Blvd. - Carnelian Bay
garwoods.com
L-D. Sun. brunch. No L off-season. Very Expensive
Contemporary American fare is served in an upscale split-level dining room with a fine lakefront view. A sophisticated lounge with a massive fireplace and entertainment on weekends shares the view, as does a big tree-shaded heated deck.

★ **Graham's**   *(530)581-0454*
8 mi. NW (via Hwy. 89) at 1650 Squaw Valley Rd. - Olympic Valley
dinewine.com
D only. Closed Mon.-Tues. except winter.   *Very Expensive*
Skillfully prepared fusion cuisine is attractively ensconced in a
historic cottage. The casually elegant dining room sports a peaked
pine ceiling and a massive river-rock fireplace. A covered redwood
dining deck in a garden among the pines adjoins.

Hacienda del Lago   *(530)583-0358*
downtown at 760 North Lake Blvd.
L-D. No L Labor Day-Memorial Day.   *Moderate*
For many years this Cal-Mex restaurant has served south-of-the-
border dishes with assorted margaritas in large dining rooms and
on an aspen-shaded deck above a lakefront marina.

★ **Hyatt Regency Lake Tahoe Resort & Casino**   *(775)832-1234*
20 mi. NE at 111 Country Club Dr. - Incline Village, NV
laketahoehyatt.com
B-L-D. Sun. brunch.   *Expensive-Very Expensive*
In the **Lone Eagle Grille** (L-D. Sun. brunch–Very Expensive),
mesquite-grilled Angus beef steaks and slow-roasted prime rib
compete with a wealth of seafoods and other dishes that reflect
first-rate creative American cuisine. Capacious well-appointed
dining areas and a plush lounge are accented by massive see-
through stone fireplaces and a window-wall view of the nearby
lake. A heated shaded dining deck adjoins by a sandy beach. At
Ciao Mein Trattoria (D only. Closed Mon.-Wed.–Expensive) an
odd mixture of Italian and Oriental specialties is offered amid
plush surroundings. **Sierra Cafe** (B-L-D–Expensive) offers
homestyle fare and expansive buffets in a casual setting.

Jake's on the Lake   *(530)583-0188*
downtown at 780 N. Lake Blvd.
hulapie.com
L-D. No L Mon.-Fri. No L off-season.   *Expensive*
A wide selection of contemporary American dishes is served on
two levels of a very large wood-trimmed dining room with a
picture-window view of a heated umbrella-shaded dining deck and
the adjacent marina and lake.

Lakehouse Pizza   *(530)583-2222*
downtown at 120 Grove Ct.
B-L-D.   *Moderate*
Tasty traditional or designer pizzas in various sizes star, along
with a dozen tap beers, and a nifty lakefront view from the wood-
trimmed pub and heated deck. The restaurant changes
complexion for breakfast each morning and becomes the
Eggschange with (guess what?) featured.

★ **Le Petit Pier** *(530)546-4464*
8 mi. NE (on Hwy. 28) at 7238 N. Lake Blvd. - Tahoe Vista
lepetitpier.com
D only. Closed Tues. *Very Expensive*
Le Petit Pier is one of the most delightful restaurants in America. The classically trained chef has a remarkable ability to create extraordinary dishes that reflect both French traditions and cutting-edge American innovation. Imported venison medallions with shitake and portabello mushrooms or lavender-honey-glazed duck breast with huckleberry and orange confit are superb reflections of his skill, as are desserts like the towering Grand Marnier soufflé, a house specialty. The lakefront dinner house has several intimate dining areas that share a splendid window-wall view of the mountain-rimmed lake. Peerless cuisine, romantic decor, and grand view blend perfectly for an unforgettable dining experience.

★ **Log Cabin Caffe** *(530)546-7109*
9 mi. NE at 8692 N. Lake Blvd. - Kings Beach
B-L. *Expensive*
The Log Cabin Caffe has earned a reputation as one of the best breakfast spots on the lake. Classic and creative fresh egg scrambles are a highlight along with cranberry-orange and other designer waffles, vanilla custard pancakes, Arizona (crunchy) French toast, and homemade breakfast rolls. The cozy casual roadside coffee shop is deservedly popular.

Naughty Dawg *(530)581-3294*
downtown at 255 N. Lake Blvd.
L-D. *Moderate*
All kinds of tap and bottled beers and designer drinks enhance a good selection of pub grub in a rowdy colorful little dive that has cheerfully gone to the dawgs.

The Old Post Office *(530)546-3205*
6 mi. NE at 5245 N. Lake Blvd. - Carnelian Bay
B-L. *Moderate*
Create-your-own omelets and other American breakfast fare, plus homemade sweet rolls, have made this casual roadside cafe a popular stop for early meals for many years.

The Pfeifer House *(530)583-3102*
1 mi. W (on Hwy. 89) at 760 River Rd.
D only. *Expensive*
Traditional Middle European dishes, steaks, and a Bavarian apple strudel are served in this long-established dinner house with warm firelit dining areas that reflect the Continental theme.

PlumpJack Squaw Valley Inn *(530)583-1576*
8 mi. NW at 1920 Squaw Valley Rd. - Olympic Valley

plumpjack.com
B-L-D.   *Very Expensive*
"Adventure cuisine" comes to the Sierra. Surprisingly elaborate
entrees and support dishes plus complex abundant sauces reflect
the determinedly innovative inclinations of the chef. Desserts are
similarly ambitious and unusual. Avant-garde grey-tone decor
gives the hotel's edgy, elegant dining room a big-city feel.
★ **Resort at Squaw Creek**   *(530)583-6300   (800)403-4434*
   8 mi. NW at 400 Squaw Creek Rd. - Olympic Valley
   squawcreek.com
   B-L-D. Sun. brunch.   *Expensive-Very Expensive*
In **Glissandi** (D only–Very Expensive), creative fusion cuisine
includes unusual provisions from around the world. The stylish
contemporary dining room has a window-wall view of fairways,
ski slopes and mountains. In **Cascades Restaurant** (B only–
Expensive), breakfast and periodic buffets are featured in wood-
trim dining areas backed by a grand view of the resort's waterfall
and the mountains. In **Ristorante Montagna** (L-D–Very
Expensive) classic and creative Italian cuisine is served in an
elegant trattoria with an expo kitchen and mountain view. In
Bullwhackers Pub (L-D–Expensive) upscale pub grub and
designer pizzas are served in a handsome sports bar.
River Grill   *(530)581-2644*
   downtown at 55 W. Lake Blvd. (at the Y)
   L-D. No L Mon.-Fri.   *Expensive*
Contemporary California fare is featured in this restaurant that
opened in 2001. Comfortable dining areas are enhanced by good
displays of local art for sale, and a fine view of the adjoining
Truckee River–especially from the heated riverside deck.
River Ranch Lodge   *(530)583-4264   (800)535-9900*
   4 mi. NW (on Hwy. 89) at Alpine Meadows Rd.
   riverranchlodge.com
   D only. L on Sat. & Sun. and daily in summer.   *Expensive*
A good selection of American entrees is served in well-furnished
dining rooms in a historic lodge. The firelit lounge and pine-
shaded terrace overlook Truckee River rapids.
Rosie's Cafe   *(530)583-8504*
   downtown at 571 N. Lake Blvd.
   B-L-D.   *Moderate*
Hearty breakfasts are served including innovative dishes like
cajun eggs or Swedish oatmeal pancakes. The dining room/bar is
a study in rustic "Old Tahoe" charm, with well-worn wooden
floorboards, a big stone fireplace, many plants, and local bric-a-
brac. Several tables are also used on the lakeview porch when
weather permits.

★ **The Soule Domain**   *(530)546-7529*
13 mi. NE at 9983 Cove St. (at Stateline Rd.) - Kings Beach
souledomain.com
D only.   *Expensive*
Soule Domain is the most romantic dinner house in the Sierra. A picturesque log cabin in the pines is a delightful location for intensely flavorful creative American cuisine that reflects the whims and classic skill of the talented chef/owner. Consider smoked pheasant sausage salad with mixed greens tossed with light dressing, gorgonzola, candied pecans and sliced pears; filet mignon pan-roasted with shitakes, gorgonzola, brandy and burgundy butter; or sea scallops poached in champagne with kiwi and papaya cream sauce. The firelit lower dining room with tables set with candles, fresh flowers, and linen napery amid rough-hewn log beams and pine walls is especially enchanting. Be sure to save room for the Queen of Sheba, one of the great chocolate desserts of all time.

Spindleshanks American Bistro   *(530)546-2191*
8 mi. NE at 6873 N. Lake Blvd. -Tahoe Vista
D only.   *Expensive*
American bistro fare and a wine bar with a dozen wines by the glass are features of this Tahoe roadhouse with knotty-pine decor and a dining porch by the highway.

Steamers   *(530)546-2218*
9 mi. NE at 8290 N. Lake Blvd. - Kings Beach
L-D.   *Moderate*
Designer or build-your-own pizzas star on a good selection of pub grub in a cozy firelit bar or umbrella deck that overlook the lake.

★ **Sunnyside Lodge**   *(530)583-7200*
2 mi. S at 1850 W. Lake Blvd.
sunnysideresort.com
L-D. Sun. brunch. No L in winter.   *Moderate-Expensive*
In the **Chris Craft Dining Room** (Expensive), contemporary California fare includes carefully prepared fresh fish, grill and pasta dishes, plus delicious housemade desserts. Simply stylish dining rooms overlook a pine-shaded deck/marina and the lake, and there is a view lounge. In the **Mountain Grill** (Moderate), American comfort dishes with a Tahoe topspin are served on a delightful deck amidst towering pines by a beach.

★ **Swiss Lakewood Lodge**   *(530)525-5211*
6 mi. S (on Hwy. 89) at 5055 W. Lake Blvd. - Homewood
D only. Closed Mon.   *Moderate*
Continental and Swiss specialties receive disciplined gourmet treatment. Full linen, fresh flowers, and Swiss background music also contribute to the long-established restaurant's allure.

★ **Tahoe House Bakery & Gourmet**   *(530)583-1377*
   1 mi. S at 625 W. Lake Blvd.
   tahoe-house.com
   B-L.   *Moderate*
The best gourmet bakery/deli cafe in the Sierra is Tahoe House. For more than twenty years, this has been a major destination for delicious Continental and American breads, pastries and desserts. Items like the ciabatta Italian sandwiches for two and black forest ham and gruyere cheese croissant are ideal for takeout or for enjoyment by their great stone fireplace or on a flower-lined patio by the pines. An entire room full of gourmet jams, sauces and condiments is another feature. Many tastes are available.

Wild Goose   *(877)367-8246*
   8 mi. NE at 7360 N. Lake Blvd. - Tahoe Vista
   wildgoosetahoe.com
   D only. Plus L in summer.   *Very Expensive*
The Wild Goose opened in early 2003 with a classically trained chef with an affinity for California cuisine with bold flavors prepared with fresh seasonal ingredients. The upscale dining room and lounge share a fine lakefront view and a dramatic fireplace. Tall pines shade an adjoining split-level dining deck near the water.

★ **Wolfdale's Cuisine Unique**   *(530)583-5700*
   downtown at 640 N. Lake Blvd.
   www.wolfdales.com
   D only. Closed Tues.   *Very Expensive*
In this long-popular dinner house destination, innovative fusion cuisine is skillfully prepared from scratch–seasonally fresh ingredients are emphasized, and all breads and pastries are homemade. Sophisticated casually elegant dining rooms complement the food. There is a lake view from some tables and from a heated terrace.

LODGINGS

Accommodations are sparce but distinctive in town. Numerous motels are concentrated near the lake along Highway 28 in Tahoe Vista and Kings Beach between seven and twelve miles northeast of town. A few hotel/casinos are on the Nevada side of the state line starting twelve miles northeast. Bargains and vacancies are scarce during summer, but rates are usually at least 20% less in spring and fall.

★ **The Cottage Inn**   *(530)581-4073*
   2 mi. S at 1690 W. Lake Blvd. (Box 66) - 96145
   thecottageinn.com
   17 units   *(800)581-4073*   *Expensive-Very Expensive*

The Cottage Inn is one of the most delightful bed-and-breakfasts in the Tahoe region. Enormous pines shade a complex of romantic duplex cottages a short stroll from a private beach and dock on Lake Tahoe. Full breakfast and afternoon refreshments are complimentary as is a sauna. Each of the rock-and-knotty-pine-trimmed rooms is beautifully furnished including all contemporary amenities, conveys the Tahoe style with elegant rusticity, and has a gas fireplace and queen or king bed.

"Romantic Hideaway"–gas fireplace & large rock
   whirlpool with waterfall in view of queen bed.
"Bit of Bavaria"–room-divider gas fireplace, private
   balcony with large whirlpool, kitchen, queen bed.
"Bird Nest"–room-divider gas fireplace,
   lake view, loft with queen bed.
"Evergreen Heaven"–natural bark gas fireplace,
   large thermal massage tub, queen bed.

Crown Motel   *(530)546-3388*
9 mi. NE at 8200 N. Lake Blvd. (Box 845) - Kings Beach 96143
tahoecrown.com
50 units   (800)645-2260   Moderate-Expensive
The Crown Motel is in the middle of one of the best swimming beaches on Lake Tahoe's north shore. There is also a large pool that shares the shoreline with an enclosed whirlpool. This long-established motel has a range of nicely furnished units from standard rooms to spacious two-bedroom units with kitchenettes and queen or king beds. Many units have a lake view.

Granlibakken Ski & Racquet Resort   *(530)583-4242*
1 mi. SW at 725 Granlibakken Rd. (Box 6329) - 96145
granlibakken.com
160 units   (800)543-3221   Expensive-Very Expensive
An updated conference and family oriented historic lodging complex sprawls across pine-covered hills with three-story condo buildings. Breakfast buffet is complimentary. In summer, grounds include hiking and biking trails, four (fee) tennis courts, plus a large pool and whirlpool. In winter, surface lifts serve gentle slopes for easy-going skiing and snowboarding; and snowshoeing, cross-country and saucer/snow play areas are on site. Comfortably furnished lodge units have all contemporary amenities and twins, doubles, queen or a king bed.

"studio" (several)–gas fireplace, private
   deck, kitchen, queen or king bed.

★ **Hyatt Regency Lake Tahoe Resort & Casino** *(775)832-1234*
20 mi. NE at 111 Country Club Dr. - Incline Village, NV 89450
laketahoehyatt.com
450 units   (800)553-3288   Very Expensive

The North Shore's most complete casino resort is undergoing a major upscale renovation and expansion. When completed in late 2003, there will be a large state-of-the-art spa, and an "Aquatic Oasis" with three tiered swimming pools. The twelve-story complex has, in addition to a massive casino and showroom, a nearby private beach, plus three restaurants (see listing) and a resort shop. The well-furnished rooms have views of surrounding pines and either two doubles or a king bed.

"Lakeside Cottage" (24 of these)–one- or
two-bedrooms, parlor with woodburning
fireplace, (some) kitchen, lakeview
balcony, king bed.

Lake of the Sky Motor Inn   *(530)583-3305*
downtown at 955 N. Lake Blvd. (Box 227) - 96145
23 units   *Expensive*
A pool is a feature of this modern motel across a highway from the lake and a state park. Some of the nicely furnished rooms have a lake view. All have two queens or a king bed.

Mayfield House   *(530)583-1001*
downtown at 236 Grove St. (Box 8529) - 96145
mayfieldhouse.com
6 units   *(888)518-8898*   *Expensive-Very Expensive*
A charming older home has been attractively converted into a bed-and-breakfast inn a block from the downtown beach. Full breakfast and afternoon wine, other beverages, and snacks are included. Each room is individually well furnished including a private bath and queen or king bed.

"Mayfield Suite"–spacious, two-person
whirlpool bath, king bed.

"The Cottage"–romantic private cottage,
gas fireplace, skylights, queen bed.

"Julia's Room"–spacious, king bed.

Meeks Bay Resort & Marina   *(530)525-6946*
10 mi. S at 7941 Emerald Bay Rd. - Meeks Bay 96145
meeksbayresort.com
50 units   *(877)326-3357*   *Moderate-Expensive*
Meeks Bay Resort offers lodgings in motel units, log cabins and a historic mansion sequestered in a towering pine forest next to a white sand beach on Lake Tahoe. Open from May through November, it is an idyllic getaway for rest and relaxation or recreation–swim, fish, boat, sail, water-ski, or hike along the shore, or into a nearby mountain wilderness. Facilities include a marina with all sorts of water sports, snack bar, convenience and gift stores; and full-service campground. All lodgings are comfortably furnished, including a private bath and double or

queen bed. Log cabins are equipped with kitchens. Many rooms have fine lake views.

★ **Mourelatos' Lakeshore Resort**   *(530)546-9500*
   7 mi. NE at 6834 N. Lake Blvd. (Box 77) - Tahoe Vista 96148
   www.mourelatosresort.com
   32 units   *(800)824-6381*   *Expensive-Very Expensive*
The best contemporary motel complex on the North Shore has a private white-sand beach as its centerpiece, and there are two lakeview whirlpools. All of the recently upgraded, well-furnished units have some lake view, a refrigerator, wet bar and microwave, and either two queens or a king bed. Some also have a gas fireplace or an in-bath whirlpool.
   #141–upstairs, kitchen, in-bath whirlpool, fine
      lakefront views on two sides, gas fireplace, king bed.
   #131–spacious studio, full kitchen, lakefront
      view on two sides, in-bath whirlpool, king bed.

Pepper Tree Inn   *(530)583-3711*
   downtown at 645 N. Lake Blvd. (Box 29) - 96145
   51 units   *(800)624-8590*   *Moderate-Expensive*
This modern seven-floor motel near the heart of town offers good lake views from upper floors. A recently improved public beach and park are across the highway. Amenities include an outdoor pool (covered in winter) and a whirlpool, plus covered parking. Each of the spacious rooms is comfortably furnished and has doubles, a queen or king bed.

★ **PlumpJack Squaw Valley Inn**   *(530)583-1576*
   8 mi. NW at 1920 Squaw Valley Rd. (Box 2407)-Olympic Valley 96146
   plumpjack.com
   62 units   *(800)323-7666*   *Very Expensive*
The cable car and slopes adjoin this elegant small hotel. In addition to ski-in/ski-out convenience, there is upscale dining (see listing) and a lounge, a landscaped swimming pool, and two whirlpools, resort shops, and a conference center. An expanded Continental breakfast buffet is complimentary. Each beautifully appointed, spacious unit has an honor bar, some mountain view and a queen or king bed.
   "penthouse" (2 of these)–living room,
      in-bath two-person whirlpool, king bed.

★ **Red Wolf Lodge at Squaw Valley**   *(530)583-7226*
   8 mi. NW at 2000 Squaw Loop Rd. (Box 2612) - Olympic Valley 96146
   www.redwolflodge.com
   32 units   *(800)791-0081*   *Very Expensive*
Slopes that extend down to the heart of the village provide ski-in/ski-out convenience for this modern three-story condo complex. Two whirlpools, an exercise room, and a large sauna are on-site

amenities. As an added convenience, the complex is a few steps from the quarter-billion-dollar village under construction at the heart of the valley. Each well-furnished studio-to-two-bedroom condo has a gas-log fireplace, kitchen, washer/dryer, ski storage, an in-bath whirlpool tub, and a queen bed. Many have a semi-private balcony with slope views.

★ **Resort at Squaw Creek**   *(530)583-6300*
   8 mi. NW at 400 Squaw Creek Rd. (Box 3333) - Olympic Valley 96146
   squawcreek.com
   403 units   *(800)403-4434*   *Very Expensive*
The Resort at Squaw Creek is the finest alpine ski resort in the Sierra. Opened in 1990, the luxurious nine-story complex has a picturesque site that features the resort's own (fee) adjacent ski lift for ski-in/ski-out access to all of Squaw Valley's slopes, plus a cross-country ski center with miles of well-maintained scenic trails on the gentle valley floor. Summer facilities include a championship 18-hole golf course, two tennis courts, bicycle trails and rentals, elaborate health and beauty facilities, and a retail promenade. The "Water Garden" features a giant freeform pool, whirlpools, a waterslide, and a smaller pool perfectly sited to maximize mountain views. Nearby, a multi-story waterfall/cascade is the centerpiece of elaborate waterscaping and colorful gardens and grounds. There are also several distinguished dining and drinking venues (see listing) and a grandiose lobby with a massive fireplace and multi-story window view of the valley and mountains. Each room is beautifully furnished, including a stocked (honor) refrigerator/mini-bar, and a queen or king bed. Many have a gas fireplace and an outstanding alpine view.
   "Fireplace Suite Floor Plan 1 & 2" (12 of these)–
       spacious one-bedroom, ask for valley-view
       windows, gas fireplace, king bed.

River Ranch Lodge   *(530)583-4264*
   4 mi. NW (on Hwy. 89) at Alpine Meadows Rd. (Box 197) - 96145
   riverranchlodge.com
   19 units   *(800)535-9900*   *Expensive*
A scenic restaurant (see listing), lounge, and dining terrace all fronting on the Truckee River are features of this long-established lodge. Complimentary Continental breakfast is served each morning. Each room is beautifully, individually furnished with cedar log and Western wrought-iron accents, all contemporary conveniences and doubles, queens, or a king bed.
   #26,#23–spacious, corner, fine
       river view, two balconies, king bed.
   #25,#22–balcony, intimate
       river view, king bed.

★ **The Shore House**   *(530)546-7270*
8 mi. NE at 7170 N. Lake Blvd. (Box 499) - Tahoe Vista 96148
shorehouselaketahoe.com
9 units   (800)207-5160   Expensive-Very Expensive
The Shore House is the best waterfront bed-and-breakfast on
Lake Tahoe. In this romantic escape for adults, a lovely garden
and lawns extend to a pier on the lake and a large whirlpool tub
with a lake view. The adjoining sandy beach connects to a pine-
shaded public park with picnic tables. Full gourmet breakfast (the
award-winning Monte Cristo is scrumptious!) and afternoon wine
with appetizers and evening treats in your room are complimentary. (Fee) massage and lakeview public areas lend further
distinction. Each room is beautifully, individually furnished and
is themed to capture the Tahoe spirit (especially those with full
knotty-pine decor and furniture) including a refrigerator and
extra touches like plush robes and a queen or king bed.
"The Honeymoon Cottage"–separate waterfront cabin,
    gas-log fireplace, in-room two-person whirlpool,
    fine lake/mountain view, queen bed.
"The Pine Room"–spacious, gas fireplace, two-person
    whirlpool tub overlooking king bed.
"The Forest Room"–sitting area with gas-log fireplace,
    in-room two-person whirlpool, queen bed.
"The Moon Room"–large, gas-log fireplace, unique
    "evening sky" ceiling, in-bath two-person whirlpool, king bed.

★ **Squaw Valley Lodge**   *(530)583-5500*
8 mi. NW at 201 Squaw Peak Rd. (Box 2364) - Olympic Valley 96146
squawvalleylodge.com
125 units   (800)549-6742   Very Expensive
Ski-in/ski-out convenience is only part of the appeal of Squaw
Valley Lodge, a California-contemporary low-rise resort sequestered
at the base of the mountains adjoining the massive Village Center
Cable Car. On-site amenities include two tennis courts; a large
pool and three whirlpools in a garden courtyard; three indoor
whirlpools with a fireplace, sauna, steam room and exercise room;
plus on-call (fee) massage. Each spacious, attractively furnished
(studio to two-bedroom) condo suite has a fully equipped mini-
kitchen, a private deck or balcony (some with fine slope views),
and a soaking tub in the bathroom, plus a queen or king bed. One-
or two-bedroom suites also have a living room with a gas fireplace.

Sunnyside Lodge   *(530)583-7200*
2 mi. S at 1850 W. Lake Blvd. (Box 5969) - 96145
sunnysideresort.com
23 units   (800)822-2754   Expensive-Very Expensive
A historic wood lodge in towering pines by the lake has been

restored and enhanced. In addition to a beach and marina with rental boats, there is a lakeview restaurant (see listing) and lounge. Complimentary Continental breakfast including baked goods made here, and afternoon tea and cookies, are offered. Each room is well furnished and has a queen or king bed. Many have a private balcony with a lake view.

#39–lakefront view, woodburning fireplace, king bed.

Tahoe City Travelodge   *(530)583-3766*
downtown at 455 N. Lake Blvd. (Box 84) - 96145
travelodge.com
47 units   (800)578-7878   Moderate-Expensive
Only steps away from the beach and golf course in the center of town is a recently refurbished modern motel with a heated pool and sauna. A whirlpool is on a deck overlooking the lake. Each spacious room is well furnished and has doubles or a king bed. Some have a refrigerator and microwave.

★ **Tahoe Marina Lodge**   *(530)583-2365*
downtown at 270 N. Lake Blvd. (Box 92) - 96145
24 units   (800)748-5650   Expensive-Very Expensive
This older Western-style condominium complex is perfectly sited along the shore of Lake Tahoe near the Truckee River outlet. Well-landscaped grounds include a peaceful sandy beach, two tennis courts, and a large scenic outdoor pool. Each one- or two-bedroom unit (ranging from simply to well furnished) has a kitchen, private deck and/or patio, a native-stone woodburning fireplace, and a queen or king bed.

#38 thru #40–2 BR, private beachfront view, queen or king bed.

Tamarack Lodge   *(530)583-3350*
1 mi. NE on Hwy. 28 at 2311 N. Lake Blvd. (Box 859) - 96145
tamarackattahoe.com
21 units   (888)824-6323   Moderate
Off the highway in tall pines a stroll from the beach is an older wood-trimmed motel. Each nicely furnished unit has a knotty-pine interior, and a queen or king bed. Some are spacious, and have a kitchen and partial lake view.

The Village at Squaw Valley   *(530)584-1000*
8 mi. NW at 1985 Squaw Valley Rd. - Olympic Valley 96146
thevillageatsquaw.com
100 units   (866)818-6963   Very Expensive
In 2002, this condo complex opened in the heart of the "new" village by the cable car and other lifts. Amenities include ski-in/ski-out convenience, four outdoor whirlpools, an exercise room, and an adjoining restaurant. Each well-furnished one- to three-bedroom unit has a gas fireplace in the living room, a private deck, and queens or a king bed. A few have good slope views.

Quality of Life in the Great Towns

The preceding pages have all of the information you need to transform your ideas and dreams into fun-filled travel adventures and vacations. But, suppose you fall in love with one of the great towns of Northern California after a memorable visit. What if you decide that you might want to live there?

The following pages will help you consider relocation to a great town. To support easy consistent comparisons, numbers shown in most categories are a percentage of the national norm. Data sources included: U. S. Bureau of the Census; U. S. Department of Commerce, Comparative Climatic Data for California; County and City Data Books; local police and sheriff departments and Federal Bureau of Investigation Uniform Crime Reports; local publications in each town featuring real estate information; each great town's chamber of commerce and/or convention and visitors bureau, plus extensive field research.

Seven indicators summarize key aspects about quality of life. A final chart addresses demographics through selected basic characteristics of the population of each town.

(1) Most would agree that a great town should have certain amenities and services that we take for granted in big cities. Towns are checked for each of ten "Basic Facilities" (airport, hospital, library, etc.) and given a percentage score for overall availability.

(2) Downtown Vitality reflects the way a town charms us with places to go and things to do day and night in a compact, engaging heart of town.

(3) Crime concerns everyone. While recent data suggest that major cities are becoming safer, most great towns continue to be substantially safer than cities.

(4) Weather in Northern California's great towns ranges from mild (supporting semi-tropical palms and flowers) year-round, to classic four seasons (including heavy winter snow).

(5) The Overall Livability Rating is a composite of the above factors plus extent of: independence from other places; a notable geographic setting; and cultural amenities.

(6) Housing Affordability compares housing cost in each town to the national median.

(7) In the final table, the Vokac Index of Livability and Affordability (VILA)© is used to quantify the relationship between Quality of Life and Housing Cost. An ideal town with a "perfect" Quality of Life and the nation's median housing cost would score "100." How well do you suppose Northern California's great towns did? Their rank and score compared to each other are presented in the Livability/Affordability Table.

Basic Facilities

	% of All Facilities	Airport	Hospital	Library	High School	Lodging Landmark	Theater	Park	Swimming Pool	Newspaper	Radio Station
Calistoga	70		✓	✓	✓	✓		✓	✓	✓	
Carmel	90	✓	✓	✓	✓	✓	✓	✓		✓	✓
Eureka	100	✓	✓	✓	✓	✓	✓	✓	✓	✓	✓
Ferndale	80		✓	✓	✓	✓	✓	✓		✓	✓
Fort Bragg	90		✓	✓	✓	✓	✓	✓	✓	✓	✓
Gualala	50			✓	✓			✓		✓	✓
Healdsburg	90		✓	✓	✓	✓	✓	✓	✓	✓	✓
Mendocino	80		✓	✓	✓	✓	✓	✓	✓	✓	
Monterey	100	✓	✓	✓	✓	✓	✓	✓	✓	✓	✓
Murphys	50		✓			✓	✓	✓	✓		
Napa	90	✓	✓	✓	✓	✓	✓	✓		✓	✓
Nevada City	90	✓	✓	✓	✓	✓	✓	✓		✓	✓
Pacific Grove	90	✓	✓	✓	✓	✓	✓	✓		✓	✓
St. Helena	80		✓	✓	✓	✓	✓	✓	✓	✓	
Sonoma	80		✓	✓	✓	✓	✓	✓	✓	✓	
Sonora	90	✓	✓	✓	✓	✓	✓	✓		✓	✓
So. Lake Tahoe	90	✓	✓	✓	✓	✓	✓	✓	✓	✓	✓
Tahoe City	70	✓	✓	✓	✓	✓	✓		✓		

To be viewed as "complete and convenient," a community needs easy access to important amenities and services. Easy access to an airport (within a half-hour drive) and a hospital (within fifteen minutes) are conveniences that people do not want to give up when they leave the big city. Other facilities are important to have right in town in order to foster community identity and spirit. Those include a library (preferably located downtown), high school (within town limits), landmark lodging (preferably downtown), movie or live theater, public park, and swimming pool. Local media (newspaper and radio station) provide a fundamental communication link among residents, and an important local perspective. When these facilities are located in adjoining towns or cities, there is a price to pay in loss of town character and fellowship. The table displays a check mark for available facilities, and rates each town based on the total percentage of facilities that exist within the town limits or (for airport and hospital) nearby.

Downtown Vitality

Rank		Total Score*
1	Monterey	92
2	Napa	91
3	Carmel	90
4	Mendocino	87
5	Pacific Grove	86
6	Sonoma	86
7	Eureka	86
8	Healdsburg	82
9	Nevada City	82
10	South Lake Tahoe	81
11	Calistoga	77
12	Sonora	76
13	Tahoe City	74
14	Murphys	73
15	St. Helena	68
16	Ferndale	65
17	Fort Bragg	55
18	Gualala	51
---		
(3)	San Francisco	90

Total Score=% of a "perfect" downtown (expressed as 100).

Vitality of the heart of town is a keystone of any community. In order to qualify as a "great town," each downtown was evaluated in terms of many characteristics regarded as important to a flourishing central business district. More than two dozen attributes were grouped into ten factors rated for each downtown on a scale of 1 to 10. The size, compactness, and completeness of the "heart" of town was carefully assessed. Library architecture, book collection and special facilities were considered. Since a lodging landmark often provides a central place for meetings, dining and drinking as well as overnight lodgings, the facilities of the principal hotel were reviewed. Quality and quantity of restaurants were rated since dining is both a necessity and a pleasure. Another favorite pastime, shopping, was rated for distinctiveness and breadth. The placement and scope of movie and live theater venues were reviewed, along with choices of both day and nighttime leisure pursuits. Availability of free (non-metered) parking both on the street and in lots; quality of parks; and scenic, usable water features were also given careful attention. The composite score represents the extent to which a downtown succeeds as an exciting, pedestrian-friendly center appealing to both residents and visitors for business and leisure-time fun.

Crime

Rank		Risk of Violent Crime*
1	Sonoma	20
2	St. Helena	23
3	Carmel	29
4	Pacific Grove	34
5	Murphys	57
6	Napa	62
7	Healdsburg	68
8	Ferndale	72
9	Calistoga	76
10	Gualala	79
11	Mendocino	83
12	Tahoe City	87
13	Nevada City	92
14	Fort Bragg	93
15	Sonora	121
16	South Lake Tahoe	142
17	Monterey	164
18	Eureka	180
------------------------------------		
(15)	San Francisco	117
(15)	United States	100

Violent Crime Risk=violent crime (homicide, rape, robbery, aggravated assault) rate of each town compared to the norm (expressed as 100) for the United States as a whole.

One of the top reasons people give for leaving the big cities is the search for kinder, gentler places where people can still leave their doors unlocked, and where anyone can fearlessly stroll downtown in the evening. While there are no guarantees of complete safety anywhere, there are fortunately many places where law and order uniformly prevail. The above chart ranks the great towns based on relative safety. There are, of course, limitations to the validity of any data on crime due to unknowns about the extent to which crime is actually reported. Comparable information about criminal activity is based on reports prepared for the Federal Bureau of Investigation by city police and county sheriff departments, who graciously provided data for the above table. To make great towns and cities comparable, raw data were converted into a percentage of the crime rate for the nation as a whole. For example, Sonoma's violent crime rate is remarkably low—merely one-fifth that of the nation. At the other extreme, the data suggest that only four great towns in Northern California are more dangerous than the United States average.

Weather

Rank		VWR	Quality	Seasons
	Vokac Weather Rating*		**Weather Norms**	
1	Carmel	7.3	Good	mild year-round
2	Napa	7.1	Good	mild winter, warm summer
3	Monterey	7.0	Good	mild year-round
3	Pacific Grove	7.0	Good	mild year-round
5	Sonoma	6.6	Good	mild winter, hot summer
5	Healdsburg	6.6	Good	mild winter, hot summer
7	St. Helena	6.4	Good	mild winter, hot summer
8	Calistoga	6.2	Good	mild winter, hot summer
9	Murphys	5.4	Moderate	cool wet winter, hot summer
10	Sonora	5.3	Moderate	cool wet winter, hot summer
11	Gualala	5.0	Moderate	cool wet winter, warm summer
12	Nevada City	4.9	Moderate	cool wet winter, hot summer
13	Mendocino	4.5	Bracing	wet winter, cool year-round
14	Fort Bragg	4.4	Bracing	wet winter, cool year-round
15	Ferndale	4.1	Bracing	cool wet winter, warm summer
16	So. Lake Tahoe	3.7	Bracing	four full seasons
16	Tahoe City	3.7	Bracing	four full seasons
18	Eureka	3.4	Brisk	wet winter, cool year-round

| (7) | San Francisco | 6.4 | Moderate | mild year-round |

*Vokac Weather Rating© (VWR) =The average of monthly ratings for the year where #10 is "perfect weather"–mild, warm and dry.

Residents and visitors alike talk about the weather–a lot. It is one of the most distinguishing elements of any place. Northern California has an advantage over most of the rest of America in weather. Thanks to the "California climate," most of the great towns in the region have uniformly warm, dry, and sunny summers, while winters are typically mild with substantial rainfall but little frost or snow. Since 1985, the Vokac Weather Rating © has served as one of the most popular features of the "great towns" guidebook series, using historical weather data to predict the probability of pleasant (warm and dry) weather during each month of the year. The table above averages the Vokac Weather Rating © for each town in all twelve months, yielding a score on a basis of 0 to 10, where 10 is "perfect" weather. The highest scoring locales in Northern California are the three Monterey Peninsula towns on the Pacific Coast, plus the surprising addition of Napa–on the mild side of the Wine Country. Low scoring towns around Lake Tahoe constitute Northern California's most acclaimed ski areas, while towns along the Northern California coast have brisk weather year-round and wet winters.

301

Livability

Rank		Overall Livability Rating*
1	Carmel	90
2	Pacific Grove	88
3	Napa	88
4	Healdsburg	86
5	Sonoma	85
6	Monterey	83
7	Nevada City	82
8	Mendocino	81
9	Calistoga	80
10	St. Helena	80
11	Sonora	78
12	Ferndale	75
13	Tahoe City	74
14	Murphys	73
15	South Lake Tahoe	73
16	Fort Bragg	73
17	Eureka	72
18	Gualala	65
-------	-------------------	-------
(11)	San Francisco	80

Overall Livability Rating=Average score of all elements of livability (where 100 would be perfect).

This is the list everyone has been waiting for–which town has the "best" quality of life! Keep in mind that the competition is intense–these eighteen towns are the author's perception of Northern California's best blends of small town independence; scenic, recreation-oriented locales, and notable cultural amenities. The overall rating is based on the following elements: independent site and identity far enough from large cities to escape their congestion; proximity to significant natural attractions like an ocean, lake, river, or mountains offering recreation opportunities and scenic grandeur; easy access to basic facilities like hospitals, libraries, and newspapers for both convenience and town identity; safety; weather; and downtown vitality. The top-rated great town, Carmel, scored a "90" out of a possible "100"–a nearly perfect place! Next door, Pacific Grove, and Napa in Wine Country, follow closely behind as idyllic locales with delightful settings and plenty to do. As a tribute to San Francisco, while it was penalized in points for its size (and does not qualify as a "town"), it scored better than several great towns. In fact, San Francisco would have ranked among the dozen most livable great towns in the region.

Housing Cost

Rank		Housing Cost*
1	Eureka	$250,000
2	Sonora	$340,000
3	South Lake Tahoe	$360,000
4	Ferndale	$360,000
5	Napa	$380,000
6	Fort Bragg	$400,000
7	Nevada City	$400,000
8	Murphys	$430,000
9	Gualala	$550,000
10	Healdsburg	$650,000
11	Pacific Grove	$660,000
12	Tahoe City	$700,000
13	Sonoma	$730,000
14	Calistoga	$750,000
15	Monterey	$760,000
16	Mendocino	$870,000
17	St. Helena	$1,290,000
18	Carmel	$1,500,000
(10)	San Francisco	$630,000
(1)	United States	$170,000

* *Housing Cost=Median price (in thousands of dollars) of all houses and condos for sale (Spring, 2003)*

The evidence shows that Northern California has a lot of desirable towns, but who can afford to move there? While the region is renowned for its wealth of cultural attractions, great natural beauty, and relatively desirable weather, it is also nationally known to be a high cost-of-living area. Compared to the average cost of housing in the rest of the nation, housing in every one of the region's great towns is more expensive.

This is not surprising. Great towns are compact. The limited supply of residential land and ever-growing demand for these popular locales explain the cost of housing in great towns. Eureka, once the largest city north of San Francisco in California, has by far the lowest housing costs because it has a large stock of long-lasting redwood homes and relatively low demand as the local economy switches from lumbering to tourism. All of the eight least expensive great towns are on the Redwood Coast or in the Sierra, except Napa, the newly discovered gateway to America's famed Wine Country. At the other extreme are Carmel (the renowned seaside art colony) and St. Helena (the heart of Napa Valley) averaging well over $1 million.

Livability/Affordability

Rank		VILA*
1	Napa	375
2	Nevada City	290
3	Sonora	280
4	Eureka	275
5	Ferndale	235
6	Pacific Grove	220
7	South Lake Tahoe	210
8	Healdsburg	205
9	Fort Bragg	185
10	Sonoma	180
11	Murphys	175
12	Monterey	160
13	Calistoga	145
14	Mendocino	125
15	Tahoe City	115
16	Carmel	105
17	St. Helena	85
18	Gualala	75
--		
(13)	San Francisco	155
(17)	United States	100

* VILA© (Vokac Index of Livability and Affordability)= the ratio of quality of life to housing affordability compared to the national average (expressed as 100)

In preceding tables, livability and housing costs are noted for each great town in Northern California. Combined, they can serve as a powerful tool for summarizing the overall allure of each locale as an investment compared to the others.

While other towns have more affordable housing, the biggest "bang for the bucks," or quality of life value for the money, is in Napa, the gateway to America's most renowned Wine Country. Nevada City and Sonora, the mainsprings of the Mother Lode Country, are also major bargains. Eureka, the keystone of the Redwood Coast, is surprisingly affordable during its transition from a hard-working lumbering past to a playful, visitor-pleasing future. The two most winsome havens of tranquility in Northern California–Ferndale and Pacific Grove–offer more quality-of-life-for-the-money than all but a few places. Expect to see these towns flourish among the hottest real estate markets in California during the next few years. Only Gualala and St. Helena have scores below the national average, because housing costs in these much-sought enclaves are even greater than their impressive quality of life attributes.

Demographics

	2000 Population	% White	% Black	% Asian	% Hispanic
Calistoga	5,190	77	-	1	38
Carmel	4,081	95	-	2	3
Eureka	26,128	83	2	4	8
Ferndale	1,382	93	-	1	4
Fort Bragg	7,026	80	1	1	23
Gualala	1,200	88	-	1	10
Healdsburg	10,722	80	-	1	29
Mendocino	824	95	-	1	3
Monterey	29,674	81	2	7	11
Murphys	2,061	94	-	1	6
Napa	72,585	80	-	2	27
Nevada City	3,001	94	-	1	4
Pacific Grove	15,522	88	1	5	7
St. Helena	5,950	82	-	1	28
Sonoma	9,128	94	-	2	7
Sonora	4,423	91	1	1	8
So. Lake Tahoe	23,609	76	1	6	27
Tahoe City	1,600	87	-	1	18
San Francisco	776,733	50	8	31	14
California	33,871,648	60	7	11	32
United States	281,421,906	75	12	4	13

* Percentages will not add up to 100 because "% Hispanic" can also be in other categories, and there are other minor categories.

Demographics

	Age % under 21	Age % over 65	Housing % owner-occupied	Vote for President % for Bush
Calistoga	27	20	60	35
Carmel	11	31	57	44
Eureka	27	14	47	42
Ferndale	25	17	63	56
Fort Bragg	29	14	43	30
Gualala*	29	14	61	36
Healdsburg	30	14	60	33
Mendocino*	17	22	63	36
Monterey	23	15	39	35
Murphys*	22	29	63	55
Napa	29	14	61	38
Nevada City	23	15	61	38
Pacific Grove	20	20	49	31
St. Helena	28	17	56	38
Sonoma	21	24	62	32
Sonora	24	20	40	47
So. Lake Tahoe	30	9	43	39
Tahoe City*	26	6	60	60
San Francisco	17	14	35	16
California	32	11	57	42
United States	30	12	66	48

* In these unincorporated towns, "% for Bush" is % of total vote in
county unincorporated area

Index

Index

Index

Index

Index

About the Author

David Vokac was born in Chicago and grew up on a ranch near Cody, Wyoming. During summers while an undergraduate, he served as the first airborne fire-spotter for the Shoshone National Forest next to Yellowstone National Park. Later, he taught courses in land economics while completing a Master's degree in geography at the University of Arizona. In Denver, Colorado, Vokac was in charge of economic base analysis for the city's original community renewal program, and later became Chief of Neighborhood Planning. He moved to Southern California in 1974 to initiate a local parks plan for San Diego County, and stayed to act as Park Development Director.

Mr. Vokac is now a full-time travel writer living in Southern California. He is the author of nine guidebooks, including the acclaimed *Great Town of America* series. During the past year, he logged more than twenty thousand miles while field-checking Northern California's eighteen great towns and more than 1,000 of their notable features that are described and rated in this book. When he's not researching, writing, speaking, or producing updated material and photographs for West Press' website (www.greattowns.com), you might pass him on a road he's traveling for the sheer joy of it somewhere in America.

The "Great Towns" Series

Over the years since 1985, David Vokac's guidebooks have delighted travelers nationwide and earned critical acclaim.

The "Great Towns" series of travel guides offers accurate, comprehensive information about the most scenic and civilized communities throughout America. All noteworthy attractions, lodgings, restaurants, and more (like the weather) are described and rated by the author for each exciting locale.

The Great Towns of America (released in 1998) featured for the first time the 100 most delightful towns from coast to coast and added a chapter about livability for anyone considering relocation to one of these welcome havens.

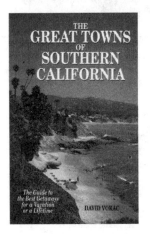

The Great Towns of Southern California, the first subregional book, made its debut in 2002. Features include updated and expanded descriptions and ratings for restaurants, attractions and lodgings in five towns that were in the 1998 book plus thirteen additional places that qualified as great towns in Southern California. The livability chapter was expanded and refined to identify and rank each locale's quality of life based on weather and safety, plus natural and cultural amenities.

The Great Towns of Northern California, released in 2003, is the companion book which provides the same timely information for the northern half of the Golden State.

Information will stay current through websites included for all listings in both books, and with updates presented in our website:

greattowns.com

This vital internet portal to great towns throughout America is West Press' ongoing tribute to the best getaways for a vacation or a lifetime. With it, you can link directly to each town; enjoy detailed updates and color pictures of restaurants, attractions and lodgings in featured great towns; and discover new ways to enjoy these special getaways.